GIFTED & TORTURED

Gifted & Tortured

Mastering the Poet-Brain Phenotypes of ADHD, Anxiety, and Autism

by Andrew Hill, PhD

Peak Brain Press LLC
Los Angeles, California

2026

ISBN: 978-1-971402-00-0 Published by Peak Brain Press LLC, Los Angeles, California

---

Dedication

To every poet-brain who's been told they're "too much" or "not enough"—you were never broken. Your intensity is your instrument. Your sensitivity is your signal. Your tortured patterns are balanced by your gifts.

This is the manual you should have received at birth.

Good job, be weird.

Acknowledgements

This book exists because 25,000 brains taught me more than any textbook could.

To every client who trusted me with their brain maps, their stories, and their breakthroughs—you're in these pages. Your patterns became the framework. Your wins proved the protocols work.

To the Peak Brain Institute team and my colleagues in the neurofeedback and QEEG community—your research, your clinical infrastructure, your debates, and your innovations shaped everything in these pages.

To the actors, entrepreneurs, artists, and creatives who proved that gifted and tortured aren't opposites. To the researchers whose work grounds this book—any errors in interpretation are mine.

To my family, for allowing me to be myself.

Contents

How to Use This Book

Welcome! This book introduces **The Poet-Brain Model**: a framework for understanding *and regulating* twelve distinct brain circuits that make you who you are. Whether you prefer the path of deep understanding, immediate tools, or complex transformation, here are some tools to explore.

By the time you finish this book, you will:

- **Have identified your 3-5 dominant phenotypes** and understand how they interact (your unique constellation)
- **Know your "core support stack"**: sleep foundation + 1-2 targeted interventions prioritized for your brain
- **Be running the Mastery Loop** on real situations (Notice → Normalize → Regulate → Reassign → Reflect)
- **Have an action plan**: whether that's implementing the MVP sleep protocol, exploring neurofeedback, or redesigning your life around supporting your phenotypes

No matter which path you choose, read the Introduction. It teaches The Poet-Brain Mastery Loop: a 5-step practice *(Notice → Normalize → Regulate → Reassign → Reflect)* used throughout. This is your core method. Everything else serves it.

Understanding the Framework: Three Lenses on Your Brain (For Nerds)

If you're overwhelmed, skip this section. Just stay with the phenotypes (the 12 characters). The systems and networks are for zooming out later.

For those who like big picture: Phenotypes (12 characters), systems (5 functional groupings), networks (large-scale wiring). Different zoom levels. Part I overview expands the architecture. Chapter 22 shows how it integrates.

Most readers: Find your phenotypes, use the tools. That's enough.

Path 1: "I Want to Understand Myself" (Identity Path)

Start here if: You want to know "why am I like this?" and want to read deeply.

Your journey:

1. Read Introduction (30 min)
2. Part I: Phenotypes (Chapters 1-12, 6-8 hours)
3. Part II: Interventions (Chapters 13-18, 8-10 hours)
4. Part III: Living Gifted (Chapters 19-22, 4-5 hours)

You'll gain deep self-understanding, your phenotype profile, and a comprehensive toolkit. (Those time estimates are loose, skimming counts, jumping ahead counts, reading one chapter and implementing for a week counts.)

Path 2: "I Need Tools Now" (Action Path) — Most readers start here

Start here if: You're struggling and need help immediately.

Your journey: Read Introduction first (30 min, you need the Mastery Loop), then jump to the chapter that matches your primary issue:

- Can't sleep → Ch 13 (Sleep)
- Using substances to cope → Ch 14 (Self-Medication & Substance Patterns)
- Anxiety, overwhelm, shutdown → Ch 15 (Stress Response Regulation)
- Procrastination, can't start → Ch 16 (Productivity)
- Racing thoughts, can't slow down → Ch 17 (Meditation)
- Want precision brain training → Ch 18 (Neurofeedback)
- Want complete action plan → Ch 22 (Self-Mastery)

Read that chapter (1-2 hours), implement immediately, come back later for Parts I and III. You'll get immediate protocols, quick wins, and foundation for deeper work.

Path 3: "I'm All In" (Complete Journey)

Start here if: You're ready for full transformation.

Your journey: Read straight through (Introduction → Parts I, II, III), do reflection questions at end of each chapter, implement as you go, consider QEEG brain mapping (optional but valuable). You can achieve deep transformation, comprehensive understanding, and lasting changes.

What Each Part Does

Cadence = the pattern and tempo with which your circuits fire, rest, and hand off control. Your brain's rhythms across a day, a week, a project, a conversation.

Introduction: Validates your experience, introduces The Poet-Brain Phenotype Model, teaches The Mastery Loop (your 5-step practice method)

Part I: Phenotypes (Chapters 1-12): Meet your brain's 12 "characters." Which circuits, which patterns, why you struggle

Part II: Interventions (Chapters 13-18): Precision tools for sleep, substances, resilience, productivity, meditation, neurofeedback

Part III: Living Gifted (Chapters 19-22): Integration. Life design, social navigation, creative flow, self-mastery

Think of Part I as mapping your internal cadences, Part II as training new cadences, and Part III as designing a life that matches them.

Quickstart for the Maxed-Out Reader

If you're maxed out and need the fastest path:

Step 1: Do the Phenotype Self-Assessment (page after this section), then circle your top phenotypes in the Part I Cast List

Step 2: Jump straight to tool chapters:

- Everyone → Ch 13 (Sleep), Ch 14 (Substances if using)
- Anxious/catastrophizing → Ch 15
- Can't start tasks → Ch 16
- Racing thoughts → Ch 17
- Want precision training → Ch 18

Step 3 (Optional): Flip to Ch 22 for the complete "This Week / This Month / This Year" master plan

How Chapters Are Organized

Each phenotype chapter (Part I) follows this structure:

- **Opening vignette**: Lived experience you'll recognize instantly
- **The Torture**: When this circuit creates suffering
- **The Gift**: When this circuit creates genius
- **The Neuroscience**: What's actually happening in your circuits, with **Under the Hood** boxes for deeper technical detail
- **Toolkit Preview**: One immediately actionable step and chapter pointers to detailed protocols in Part II
- **Key Takeaways**: Core insights in one place
- **Reader Reflections**: Self-exploration prompts

Intervention chapters (Part II) follow a similar pattern: mechanism, phenotype-specific tools, case examples, and key takeaways.

Your Next Step

If you're not sure where to start, most readers choose Path 2 (tools first) or the Maxed-Out Quickstart.

The minimum path to real results: Introduction → Your top 3-5 phenotype chapters → One or two tool chapters that match your biggest issue → Chapter 22 (master plan). That's it. You don't need to read everything to transform.

Right now, pick one of these four on-ramps:

- Introduction (get the model and method)
- Tool chapter you need (immediate help)
- Part I (discover your constellation)
- Chapter 22 (complete master plan)

All paths are valid. Choose what serves you.

You're not malfunctioning. You're mis-briefed on your own hardware. This book is the manual you should have received at birth.

Let's learn the controls.

Introduction: The Trouble with Poets

"The trouble with poets is they talk too much.
They tell us how it hurts them, and it hurts them just a little more."

, Peter Mulvey, "The Trouble with Poets"

(Two musicians thread through this book: Peter Mulvey, whose "Trouble with Poets" gave us our title and our thesis, and Paul Simon, whose twin songs "Think Too Much" (a) and (b) map the left-brain/right-brain, activation/inhibition dynamics you'll learn about in these pages. Both are worth seeking out.)

Prologue: We've Never Stood in Their Shoes

We've never inhabited anyone else's nervous system. Nobody truly knows how we feel, how we experience pain or fear, joy or excitement. But what if poet-brains feel differently? Feel more?

What if poet-brains aren't exaggerating? What if they're accurately reporting the experience of circuits tuned for:

- Faster processing
- Deeper feeling
- Pattern-detection on overdrive
- Social-sensory hypervigilance
- Associative creativity that never shuts off

Not defective. Your emotional and cognitive cadences just run faster, deeper, or more irregular than the world expects.

My thesis:
You're not "too much." You're running different hardware.

Section 1: "They Think Too Much"

The Overactive Cortex Problem

You know you should be sleeping. You're exhausted. Tomorrow's going to be long. But your brain has other plans.

Maybe it's running disaster scenarios about tomorrow's meeting. Maybe it's replaying that conversation from three weeks ago, analyzing every word, every tone, every microexpression. Maybe it just generated seventeen new business ideas and now you're too wired to sleep.

It's 3am. You're still awake. And you can't turn it off.

"They think too much."

Yeah, no shit.

Here's what I see when I look at 25,000 brain maps: your "thinking too much" isn't a character flaw. It's circuits. Measurable, reproducible circuits that light up on QEEG like a Christmas tree.

The Happy Little Kid (left frontal / approach system): Your brain's approach system in the left DLPFC. When it's engaged, you feel joy, motivation, genuine interest in life. When it goes offline, everything feels gray, effortful, pointless. I see left frontal activation (or lack of it). Richard Davidson's frontal asymmetry research. This is about engagement and positive emotion, not impulsivity.

The Grumpy Old Man (right frontal / avoidance system): Your brain's effort accountant and avoidance system in the right DLPFC. Generating reasons why things are too much work, too annoying, too irritating to bother with. I see right frontal hyperactivation. Your brain stuck in avoidance mode, not because things are threatening, but because they feel like too much effort. "Why bother?" is his favorite phrase.

The CEO (front midline, anterior cingulate): Your brain's project manager, trying to choose between approach (left) and avoidance (right). When it fails to select, you get procrastination: stuck between wanting to engage and finding reasons not to. When it selects too firmly, you get perseveration: locked onto one thing, can't let go. Interruptions feel like violence. You can't release slights.

The Timekeeper (processing speed): Your brain running at 2x speed, which *feels* like 10x. I see excess beta, fast processing markers. Racing thoughts. Can't slow down. Anxiety as speed dysregulation.

The torture? You can't turn it off. Rumination. Anxiety. Racing thoughts. ADHD mental restlessness. The world tells you to "just relax" and you want to punch them because if you could just relax, you would have done it already.

The gift? This is where innovation lives. Every paradigm shift, every creative breakthrough, every "what if we tried..." that changed the world came from a brain that couldn't stop thinking.

You think too much because your brain is built to synthesize patterns others miss. The same circuits that create your torture are the source of your genius.

Here's what I see on QEEG: Excess beta (racing thoughts). Theta-beta ratios (ADHD). Cingulate hyperactivation (stuck on wrong thing). It's not "in your head," it's *on* your head. Measurable. Objective. Real.

The Post-Genius Drag: Fast Brain, Slow Life

Some of you reading this are brilliant. High IQ. Fast processing. Connect dots others miss. **Ferrari brain.**

But you're exhausted. Foggy. Can't focus. Can't start tasks. Can't finish projects. Productivity feels impossible. The problem isn't just speed, your acceleration, braking, and recovery all run on non-standard cadences.

This is the paradox I see constantly: High intelligence, low output. Fast brain, slow life. Gifted and tortured.

Here's what's happening: Your processing speed is at the genius threshold, or above it, but you're dragging through fatigue. Poor sleep, chronic stress, resource depletion. And you're grinding to use all that processing power.

I don't know where your processing speed is going to be once you're rested. Because it's already at the top of the bell curve. But you're dragging down hard. Your Ferrari brain is running with the parking brake on, wheels grinding against resistance.

You're not broken. You're untapped.

The frustration you feel, the gap between what you know you're capable of and what you're actually achieving: that's not evidence of failure. That's evidence of potential above what's currently measurable.

This book is about closing that gap. Not by working harder. By removing the drag. By training the circuits that bottleneck you. By restoring the resources you're burning through.

Your brain is fast. Let's get it running smooth.

When I say **poet-brain**, I mean anyone whose brain runs hot on pattern-detection, emotion, and intensity: founders, engineers, artists, therapists, actors, not just literal poets. If you see connections others miss and feel things others don't, you probably have what I call a poet-brain, whether or not you've ever written a line of verse.

Section 2: "It Hurts Them a Little More"

Emotional Amplification & Rejection Sensitivity

Your partner says "I'm fine" with a slightly tight smile. Your brain immediately generates seventeen possible subtexts:

- They're mad at me
- They're disappointed
- They're about to leave
- I did something wrong
- They're lying to protect me
- They're...

And you can't tell which one is true. So you catastrophize all seventeen simultaneously.

Welcome to the Princess & the Pea: your right temporoparietal junction, the circuit behind your right ear that processes social and sensory information and decides what's yours, what's about you, and what you caused.

Here's what's actually happening in your brain: Right TPJ hyperactivation. Your brain is processing social cues with higher gain than average.

The same circuit that gives you:

- Exquisite empathy (you feel what others feel)
- Social nuance detection (you catch microexpressions others miss)
- Tone-reading superpowers (you hear what's unspoken)

Also creates:

- Rejection sensitivity dysphoria (criticism feels like annihilation)
- Emotional amplification (everything feels more intense)
- Sensory overwhelm (the world is too loud, too bright, too much)

"Maybe they make that part up." The gaslighting poet-brains endure.

But here's what I see in 25,000 brain maps: You're not imagining it. Your circuits are processing with higher gain. What others experience at volume 5, you experience at volume 11. It's not exaggeration. It's accurate reporting.

The torture? It hurts you a little more. Rejection that others shrug off feels like annihilation. Sensory input that others don't notice makes you want to crawl out of your skin.

The gift? You feel what others are blind to. You sense what's unspoken. You create art from depth that shallow processors can't access.

But damn, it's exhausting.

In this book, when I say **gifted and tortured**, I mean exactly this: You're not gifted *despite* being tortured, or tortured *because* you're gifted. The gift and the torture are the same circuit, firing in different contexts. That's the whole book in one sentence.

Section 3: "I Can't Tell What's Behind Your Smile"

The Social Sensing Dilemma

Social sensing splits into two camps. Some of you are reading everyone's microexpressions like you have a PhD in facial analysis. You catch the slight tension in someone's jaw, the way their smile doesn't quite reach their eyes. You're basically a human lie detector, and it's exhausting.

Others? You miss the obvious stuff. Your boss is furious and you think they're just "being quiet today."

Both are torture.

The over-sensors (right TPJ hyperactive, high alpha): You're processing social information with the gain turned way up. Every interaction is a data tsunami. The problem? You can't tell which signals are real and which are noise. Is your friend actually mad, or just tired? You generate a dozen possible interpretations and catastrophize all of them.

The flooded sensors (right TPJ cramped in high beta, or low alpha filtering): Here's the paradox. You're not missing cues because you're not picking them up. You're missing them because you're picking up *too many* and flooding. The signal-to-noise ratio is so bad that everything becomes noise. You feel it all (the tension, the microexpressions, the unspoken discomfort), but it floods your system so intensely you can't parse or integrate it. So you miss the sarcasm, don't notice someone's discomfort, and later hear you "came on too strong" while you're genuinely confused. **This is poet-brains and autistic brains: feeling everything so much it overflows and cannot be organized.**

Here's what I see in brain maps: When these circuits are well-regulated, you infer accurately. When they're hyperactive with good filtering (high alpha), you over-infer but catch it. When they're dysregulated with poor filtering (high beta, low alpha), you flood. Too much signal, can't parse. Neither is wrong, just different wiring that needs different regulation.

The torture? The social world expects you to operate at "normal" sensitivity. Too much and you're "oversensitive." Flooded and you're "oblivious" (even though you're actually drowning in signal).

The gift? Over-sensors become therapists, writers, artists who capture human nuance. Flooded sensors who learn to parse become engineers, scientists, system-thinkers who can focus on patterns without getting overwhelmed by social noise.

Is This Book For You?

You don't need a formal diagnosis to benefit from this book. But if you mentally tick 6 or more of these, you're in the right place:

- ☐ People say I "think too much" or "feel too much"
- ☐ I feel things more intensely than people around me seem to
- ☐ I'm either hyper-engaged or completely flat (there's not much in between)
- ☐ Stimulants, alcohol, or cannabis have felt like "finally, quiet" or "finally, focus"
- ☐ I can hyperfocus for 12 hours on the "wrong" thing but can't start the "right" thing
- ☐ Social situations exhaust me even when I enjoy them
- ☐ I've been called "gifted," "sensitive," "intense," or "too much"
- ☐ I struggle with sleep, substances, or anxiety more than seems normal
- ☐ I feel like I have a Ferrari brain with bicycle brakes
- ☐ I've tried a dozen productivity systems and they all work… for a week
- ☐ I suspect my brain works differently, but no one's ever explained *how*
- ☐ I'm smart, but I feel like I'm underperforming my potential

If you recognize yourself here, you don't just have different traits. You run on different cadences.

> **What "cadence" means in this book:** The word appears throughout, *activation cadence* (how quickly your circuits fire up when you want to engage), *sustain cadence* (how long you can hold focus before slipping out of gear), *recovery cadence* (how quickly your circuits downregulate after activation), and *switching cadence* (how cleanly you shift between tasks and states). When a cadence is stuck (locked too fast, too slow, or unable to shift) that is dysfunction. When a cadence is flexible and context-appropriate, that is mastery. The interventions in Part II train cadence flexibility, not cadence elimination.

If you ticked 6+, this book is probably speaking your language. You likely have what I call a poet-brain.

Section 4: "They See Poetry Everywhere"

The Pattern-Hungry, Meaning-Making Mind

Poet-brains don't experience life directly. You experience life, then immediately narrativize it, find the metaphor, extract the meaning, connect it to seventeen other things. You can't turn it off.

Your kid says something funny and you're already thinking "This would make a great story." You're having an argument and part of your brain is observing the argument, analyzing the dynamics.

It's exhausting. It's also where everything interesting comes from.

Here's what I see in brain maps: **high associative connectivity**. Your brain's networks are talking to each other more than average. Default mode network is hyperconnected to executive networks. Sensory networks cross-talk with emotional networks.

This creates pattern detection on overdrive (you see connections others miss), associative creativity (one idea triggers a cascade of others), and narrative drive. You story-ify everything. Your life isn't just events, it's a narrative arc with themes and callbacks.

The torture? You can't experience anything simply. A sunset isn't just beautiful. It's a metaphor for impermanence, which reminds you of that thing your dad said when you were twelve, which connects to that article you read about entropy, which makes you think about your own mortality, and now you're having an existential crisis while everyone else is just enjoying the sunset.

The gift? Every paradigm shift came from a brain that couldn't stop seeing patterns. Newton watching an apple fall and seeing *universal gravitation*. Darwin seeing finches and seeing *evolution*. Einstein imagining riding a beam of light and seeing *relativity*.

You see poetry everywhere because your brain is built to extract signal from noise, find order in chaos, synthesize meaning from raw experience. This is where innovation lives. Where art emerges. Where "what if we tried..." becomes "holy shit, it worked."

You're not overthinking. You're doing exactly what your brain was built to do. The world just hasn't caught up to the value of pattern-hungry, meaning-making minds.

Section 5: "They Talk Too Much"

The Verbal Phenotype

You know you should stop talking. But you can't stop because you're not done processing the thought yet, and if you stop you'll lose the thread, and besides there are a dozen related points that all connect...

"Wow, you really talk a lot."

Yeah. I know.

Here's what's actually happening: you're using language as an external working memory system.

The Interpreter (left posterior temporal): Your brain's language decoder and generator, taking raw experience and converting it to words. For some of you, this circuit is hyperactive. You think *in* language. You process *through* language. You don't know what you're thinking until you hear yourself say it out loud.

The Speaker (left frontal, Broca's area): The motor output system that executes speech. It's driven by the Interpreter. Wernicke's (posterior) generates the language, Broca's (frontal) produces it. Posterior drives frontal. When it's damaged (stroke, trauma), you get expressive aphasia: you know what you want to say but can't get it out. That's different from word-finding issues, which come from slowing alpha in language areas (words are there, just can't access them quickly).

Why verbal processing feels uncontrollable: Your Interpreter is generating faster than your Speaker can filter. The thoughts → words pipeline is wide open, running hot. You talk to think because verbalizing *is* processing; you need to explain because insights lead to more insights, and over-share because you're downloading to make room for the next thought.

In brain maps: **left temporal hyperactivation** (Interpreter), often with **high left hemisphere beta**. Your language networks are running hot, generating words faster than you can filter them.

The torture? Others experience your verbal processing as "too much." They want the summary. You need the full download. They tell you to "get to the point." You're trying, but the point has twelve sub-points.

The gift? This is where teaching happens. Where therapy works. Where podcasts thrive. Where "let me think out loud for a second" becomes a breakthrough. You're externalizing cognition, which means others can follow your thinking, learn from your process, catch errors in real-time.

Some of the best therapists, teachers, and communicators I know are verbal processors. They think out loud, which makes their thinking transparent.

You can see how they got from A to B to Z. It's not polished. It's real-time cognition.

In the right context, "talking too much" becomes "incredibly articulate." Put a verbal processor in front of a microphone, give them a topic they care about, and suddenly "too much" becomes "I could listen to this for hours."

The world needs summarizers. It also needs people who can articulate the nuance, unpack the complexity, make the implicit explicit.

Keep talking. Just maybe learn when to hit pause.

Section 6: "Nobody Knows How We Feel"

The Loneliness of Intensity & Interoceptive Differences

Here's the loneliest part: even when you're incredibly articulate, self-aware, and introspective, even when you can describe your experience in exquisite detail, you often don't fully understand what you're feeling.

You know something is wrong. You can feel it in your body. But you can't locate it. Can't name it. Can't explain it in a way that makes sense to others, or even to yourself.

The poet's paradox: You feel *more* than others. But you understand your feelings *less*.

Your interoception (sensing your body's internal state) is often offline. You might not notice you're hungry until you're shaking. You might feel "bad" but can't tell if it's anxiety, anger, sadness, or low blood sugar. Add fast processing and you get feelings that hit before you can identify them.

And here's the kicker: you have multiple phenotypes running simultaneously. The Happy Little Kid wants to start a new project. The Grumpy Old Man is catastrophizing about wasted effort. The CEO can't decide which to listen to. It's not one feeling. It's a committee of feelings, all shouting at once.

You try to explain this and people say "Have you tried just calming down?" or "Maybe you're overthinking it."

And you wonder: Am I making this up?

No. **Your brain has stable, interpretable patterns (phenotypes) that explain why you feel what you feel and why you struggle with what you struggle.** These are measurable, reproducible brain patterns with genetic influences, high reliability, treatment prediction, and stability over time. Your phenotype profile is relatively consistent. This is who you are, not a phase.

When you see your broken shoulder on the X-ray, you're not mad at it. You're not guilty about it. You see the break, you understand why it hurts, you know what needs healing. Objective, not shameful.

Your brain map works the same way. When I show you your QEEG and you see that right frontal hot spot (Grumpy Old Man generating dread) or that high theta/beta ratio (Stabilizer offline), you're seeing the circuits that explain your experience. Not "what's wrong with you" but "here's what's happening."

This is where QEEG becomes the external mirror for internal traits you can't directly perceive. Your brain map shows what you can't sense yourself: which circuits are driving your current state, why substances seemed to help, what actually works to regulate it.

The self-assessment in Part I gives you a starting mirror. You don't need a brain map to begin, you need pattern recognition, and you're about to build it.

Section 7: The Promise - "Let Us Go Then, You and I"

"Let us go then, you and I,
when the evening is spread out against the sky
like a patient etherized upon a table."

, T.S. Eliot, "The Love Song of J. Alfred Prufrock"

Prufrock is paralyzed by overthinking, asking "Do I dare disturb the universe?" about eating a peach. When your brain runs hot, when every decision triggers a dozen disaster scenarios, yeah, a peach feels like disturbing the universe.

But here's what Prufrock didn't have: **a map**.

These aren't character flaws. They're resources, circuits, parts. Measurable, reproducible, and trainable.

For technical readers: For QEEG methodology, genetics, medication patterns, and technical depth, see **The QEEG Field Guide** (Hill & Lomeli, forthcoming).

What We Know, What We Don't, What's Extrapolation

I'm a scientist and a clinician. That means I'm standing with one foot in peer-reviewed research and one foot in 25 years of clinical observation. Here's where the line is:

What's solid: EEG phenotypes correlate with symptoms. Neurofeedback works for ADHD and anxiety. Sleep, HRV, and meditation affect brain states. This is well-replicated.

The lineage: The idea of EEG phenotypes isn't mine. It comes from Jay Gunkelman and colleagues. Gunkelman developed his initial phenotype concepts by reviewing tens of thousands of EEGs coming in from hospitals all over the country. He kept seeing the same features in the signals: patterns that repeated across people, across diagnoses, across contexts. In 2005, Johnstone, Gunkelman, and Lunt published the foundational paper describing reproducible EEG phenotypes (Johnstone, Gunkelman, & Lunt, 2005). Several phenotypes have clear genetic correlates, and all have been linked to specific physiological or clinical patterns (Arns et al., 2008; Menon, 2011).

What's my clinical framework: The 12-phenotype system is an evolution of that work. Many of the features Gunkelman and Johnstone described show up across diagnostic criteria, but they also cluster toward areas of human performance and suffering most relevant to poet-brains (gifted, tortured, neurodivergent minds). I didn't invent the underlying circuits or EEG signatures. Those are well-established. But organizing them into these 12 "characters," naming them with personality, and linking them to lived experience is my interpretation, built from 25,000+ brain maps over 25 years.

Is this exhaustive? No. There are other stable EEG patterns, phenotype clusters, and variants we often see in clinical practice. My model isn't meant to capture everything, it's meant to emphasize what matters most for the gifted and tortured. These are the 12 phenotypes that show up most consistently in intelligent, sensitive, intense, neurodivergent minds. If your brain is doing something else interesting, there's room for that too.

Bottom line: The brain patterns are real. The interventions are evidence-based. The foundational phenotype science is peer-reviewed (Johnstone, Gunkelman, and colleagues). The specific phenotype names, constellation approach, and "gifted and tortured" framing are my way of making it usable for this population. These are levers, not labels. If that works for you, use it.

How This Relates to ADHD, Autism, HSP, Trauma

If you already have a diagnosis (ADHD, autism, Highly Sensitive Person (HSP), CPTSD, anxiety, depression), you might be wondering: "How does this phenotype model fit with what I've already been told about my brain?"

Short answer: This model adds resolution, not replacement. It's complementary, not competing.

Think of DSM diagnoses like saying "your computer is slow." That's true and useful for insurance billing, but it doesn't tell you *which processes are hogging resources*. The phenotype model is like opening Task Manager and seeing: "Oh, your Stabilizer is offline (ADHD motor component), your Grumpy Old Man is running 47 futility simulations (effort-avoidance), and your CEO is stuck on a single tab with 300 open threads (OCD-like loops)."

Here's how common diagnoses typically map to phenotype constellations:

If you have ADHD:
You likely have 3-5 of these phenotypes especially loud: Stabilizer offline (can't initiate tasks), CEO stuck (hyperfocus on wrong thing), Timekeeper (racing thoughts, time blindness), Happy Little Kid offline (need intensity to feel engaged), Supervisor (impulsivity OR perfectionism). The phenotype model shows you *which ADHD circuits* are loudest for you, so you can target interventions precisely.

If you identify as Highly Sensitive (HSP):
You likely have Princess & the Pea (high-gain sensory/social processing, RSD), Lifeguard (environmental scanning, picking up threats), Bard (reading emotional prosody), and possibly Grumpy Old Man (protective effort-conservation, everything feels like too much). This model shows you *which circuits* create that experience and how to regulate them.

If you're autistic or identify with Asperger's traits (an older term, now included under ASD):
You likely have Bard dysregulated (flooding on prosody, can't parse tone/sarcasm), Interpreter dominant (verbal, literal), CEO or Supervisor patterns (routine, precision, quality control), and possibly Princess & Pea flooded (exquisite sensitivity that paradoxically looks like "missing" cues). This model shows which circuits are calibrated differently, so you can work *with* your wiring, not against it.

If you have trauma or CPTSD:
You likely have Lifeguard hyperactive (threat hypervigilance, environmental scanning), Grumpy Old Man loud (everything feels like too much effort to handle), Problem Child (reactive opposition when feeling unsafe), and Princess & Pea (amplified pain from rejection). This model shows you *which circuits* were affected, so you can train them back to baseline.

If you use substances to cope:
Chapter 14 maps how each phenotype self-medicates. The model explains *why* your substance of choice works (which circuit it's regulating) so you can find precision tools that do the same job without the side effects.

The key insight: You're not choosing between models. You're layering them. Use what works. Keep what helps. This is another lens, another map, another way to understand your hardware. If the phenotypes resonate more than your diagnosis, use them. If your diagnosis feels more accurate, keep it. If both help, use both. This is pragmatism, not dogma.

The peace you've been stealing? It's already in your circuits. We just need to teach them a new rhythm.

The calm you borrowed from alcohol? We can train your brain to generate it. The focus you stole from stimulants? We can build it without the crash. And the tools that build it? Most of them are free. Morning light. Breathing. Movement. Sleep. The expensive tools accelerate, they don't replace. Over time, running the loop trains new cadences: how often you spike, how long you stay stuck, how quickly you come back. It takes longer than popping a pill. Neurofeedback is 40 sessions, not 40 minutes. But the calm you build? Yours to keep.

Let's go then, you and I.

Not like a patient etherized upon a table, passive, waiting for someone else to fix you. But like a pilot learning the controls.

This book is your map. Your phenotype profile. Your user manual.

By the end, you'll understand your brain better than most people understand their smartphones. You'll have tools matched to your circuits. You'll know how to work with your intensity instead of fighting it.

You'll still be a poet. You'll still think too much, feel too much, see poetry everywhere.

But you'll be a poet who knows how to conduct the orchestra. Same gifts. Less torture.

Good job. Be weird. Let's go.

A Note on Neurodiversity, Identity, and Training

Before we dive in, let me be clear: **this book is not trying to make you neurotypical.**

The nuance: You can be neurodivergent AND want better sleep. You can embrace your intensity AND not want to wake up catastrophizing at 3am. You can be proud of your sensitivity AND want tools for when crowds feel overwhelming.

Identity vs. suffering: Your phenotypes describe how your circuits tend to run. The torture components (insomnia, anxiety, RSD, paralysis) are what happens when those circuits cramp up. We're not trying to erase your wiring. We're trying to reduce unnecessary suffering.

When I say "train your circuits," I don't mean "become normal." I mean: teach your Grumpy Old Man when effort is genuinely wasted vs. worthwhile. Teach your Stabilizer to engage without needing crisis. Teach your Princess & Pea to process at appropriate gain. You'll still be sensitive, intense, pattern-hungry, creative. You'll just suffer less while being those things.

Traits, Regulation, and States: Your **traits** are your resources, measurable circuit patterns visible on QEEG regardless of how you're feeling in the moment. Sensitivity, processing speed, focus capacity, empathy depth. These are stable but not frozen: with sustained training (neurofeedback, meditation, sleep optimization), traits shift slowly at a deep level. That's the real change, your resources themselves getting stronger, more resilient, more flexible. **Regulation** is how those traits tend to operate, stuck at one setting (cramped, dysregulated) or flexible across a range (mastery). Training targets regulation first, and over time, the traits themselves shift. **States** are how you feel and perform right now, anxious or calm, focused or foggy, activated or flat. States ride on top of trait strength and regulation. Better traits + better regulation = more flexible states. You'll still be sensitive, but it won't flood you. You'll still hyperfocus, but you won't HAVE to when it's not useful. (You'll learn this distinction fully in Chapter 22.)

This book's position: Your neurodivergent wiring is valuable, real, and not going anywhere (nor should it). Some patterns cause genuine suffering not because of the trait itself, but because the trait is STUCK, cramped up, dysregulated, no range of motion. You deserve tools to train regulation without losing your gifts. Training ≠ conforming. Regulation ≠ suppression. Mastery ≠ becoming someone else.

We're not trying to make you neurotypical. We're trying to give you the controls so you can conduct your own orchestra. You get to decide which instruments play loud, which play soft, which lead, which rest. That's mastery. That's agency. That's the opposite of pathology.

Either way, you're in charge. What you do with this is entirely up to you.

A Word About Grief, Anger, and Dread

As you read this book (especially the phenotype chapters in Part I) you might feel something unexpected: grief, anger, or dread.

Grief for the years you spent struggling without this map. For the relationships that ended because no one understood your circuits. For the opportunities you missed because you were fighting your own wiring instead of working with it.

Anger that no one taught you this. That you were pathologized instead of instructed. That the world told you to "just focus" or "just relax" or "just be normal" when what you needed was a user manual for circuits nobody explained.

Dread about how much of your life was shaped by circuits you didn't understand. About how many years you might have lost to misregulation. About whether it's too late to change.

If you're feeling any of this: good. That means you're seeing clearly. That means this model is landing. That means you're recognizing yourself, maybe for the first time, and seeing how different things could have been.

Don't rush past these feelings. They're not pathology. They're data. They tell you this is real, that your struggles weren't character flaws.

Feel the grief. Name the anger. Sit with the dread. They're appropriate responses to recognizing how hard you've been working with the wrong instructions.

And then, when you're ready, use that energy as fuel.

Grief becomes motivation. Anger becomes agency. Dread becomes determination.

You weren't broken. You were under-instructed, under-regulated. And now you're learning the controls.

Let's build what you've been searching for all along.

The Method: Working with Your Phenotypes

Twelve distinct phenotypes (Part I). Targeted tools for regulating them (Part II). Strategies for designing your life around them (Part III).

But all of that serves one core practice: **The Poet-Brain Mastery Loop**. A five-step method you'll learn by using it:

Notice → Normalize → Regulate → Reassign → Reflect

Here's what it looks like in practice. It's Tuesday morning. Your Grumpy Old Man is running hot, every task looks impossible, the effort assessment is catastrophizing, you're dreading starting anything. Instead of calling yourself lazy and powering through on willpower (borrowed peace) or giving up (avoidance), you run the loop. *Notice:* "My right frontal is stuck in avoidance mode. I know this pattern." *Normalize:* "Of course this is happening. I slept badly and I have three competing deadlines. My avoidance circuit is doing exactly what it's built to do." *Regulate:* You use the physiological sigh, take a 10-minute walk to wake the Stabilizer, break one task into a 10-minute start.

Reassign: You let the Grumpy Old Man be a consultant, not CEO, he gets to flag concerns but not veto action. *Reflect:* At the end of the day, you note what worked.

That's built capacity. You didn't need alcohol, a crisis, or a Herculean act of will. You ran the loop. Over hundreds of repetitions across Part II's protocols, these circuits train, and what took 20 minutes of deliberate effort begins to happen automatically, the regulation wired in.

The Mastery Loop is a secondary framework, not the spine of this book. The twelve phenotypes are the spine. But the Loop gives you a repeatable method for working with any phenotype in real time. You'll see it throughout Part I and Part II, with full integration in Chapter 22.

Now you have the promise. Let's meet your twelve phenotypes.

Phenotype Self-Assessment

Discovering Your Constellation

Before you read Part I, take a few minutes to identify which phenotypes resonate most. This isn't a diagnosis, it's a mirror. You're likely a combination of 3-5 dominant phenotypes, with others playing supporting roles.

How to use this: First pass = gut response. Don't overthink it, you can revise later.

This takes 8–10 minutes. First-pass gut responses only. You can retake it anytime, your answers will sharpen as you read Part I.

- Read each statement
- Rate yourself: **0** (not me) → **1** (sometimes) → **2** (often) → **3** (very much me)
- Tally your score for each phenotype
- Your top 3-5 scores are likely your dominant constellation
- Whichever 3-5 scores cluster highest are your starting constellation, start with those chapters in Part I

Your constellation today is a snapshot, not a sentence. Phenotype scores change as you train the underlying circuits.

Example: If your top three are Grumpy Old Man, Princess & the Pea, and CEO, the rest of this book will suddenly make your entire life make sense. That's the "Tortured Poet" core: catastrophizing (Grumpy), rejection sensitivity (Princess), stuck in loops (CEO). Welcome home.

THE EMOTIONAL CORE (Front = Self-Focused)

What lives here: Your internal world, mood, motivation, conflict monitoring, impulse control.

Happy Little Kid (Left Frontal / Approach System)

- ☐ I struggle with depression, not sadness, but flatness, amotivation, "why bother"
- ☐ Nothing feels rewarding or interesting unless it's intense, novel, or dramatic
- ☐ I need crisis, deadlines, or high stakes just to feel engaged with life

- ☐ I start projects with enthusiasm, then lose interest when they become routine
- ☐ Exercise and morning sunlight reliably lift my mood

Total: ___ / 15

Grumpy Old Man (Right Frontal / Avoidance System)

- ☐ I wake up with dread or anxiety before I'm fully conscious
- ☐ I catastrophize, every scenario plays out as worst-case disaster in my mind
- ☐ Criticism or rejection feels like annihilation, not just disappointment
- ☐ I avoid situations because my brain generates seventeen reasons they'll go wrong
- ☐ Alcohol, benzos, or cannabis made me feel "finally, I can relax"

Total: ___ / 15

CEO (Anterior Cingulate / Conflict Monitor)

- ☐ I get stuck on internal conflicts and can't let go (perseveration, rumination)
- ☐ I replay slights, arguments, or decisions endlessly in my mind
- ☐ I have OCD-like loops (checking, nail-biting, mental rituals, intrusive thoughts)
- ☐ Interruptions feel like violence. I can't easily shift between tasks
- ☐ I procrastinate because I can't resolve the conflict between "I should" and "I don't want to"

Total: ___ / 15

Problem Child (Right Inferior Frontal / Brake System)

- ☐ I'm oppositional, automatic "you can't make me" even when it hurts me
- ☐ I have anger without brakes, zero to explosion, saying things I regret
- ☐ I burn bridges, self-sabotage, or defy authority even when I know the consequences
- ☐ I'd rather lose on my own terms than win on someone else's
- ☐ Sleep deprivation makes me much more angry and oppositional

Total: ___ / 15

THE SENSING NETWORK (Back = World-Focused)

What lives here: Sensing the world, social nuance, language, context.

Lifeguard (Posterior Cingulate / Environmental Scanner)

- ☐ I'm hypervigilant, constantly scanning environments for threats or changes
- ☐ I ruminate, can't stop replaying conversations, past events, interactions endlessly
- ☐ Social situations exhaust me because I'm monitoring everyone constantly
- ☐ I have PTSD or trauma history, and I can't turn off the threat-scanning
- ☐ I notice exits, changes in room energy, or "something off" before anyone else does

Total: ___ / 15

Princess & Pea (Right TPJ / High-Gain Processor)

- ☐ Rejection sensitivity, criticism feels like annihilation, neutral cues feel like rejection
- ☐ Sensory overwhelm, sounds, lights, textures, crowds, or specific sounds (chewing, tapping) are too much
- ☐ I feel what others feel (exquisite empathy, but also absorbing everyone's emotions)
- ☐ I catch micro-expressions and social nuances others completely miss
- ☐ Uncertain sense of control, hard to tell what outcomes I caused versus just happened

Total: ___ / 15

THE ACTION ENGINE (Axis = Doing & Rhythm)

What lives here: Execution, pacing, timing, energy management.

Stabilizer (Left Sensorimotor / Motor Engagement)

- ☐ I can't start tasks even when I want to, decision is made, but body won't move
- ☐ I struggle with sustained attention on boring tasks (every distraction hijacks me)
- ☐ I'm fidgety, restless, can't sit still (or can't fall asleep because body won't idle)
- ☐ Stimulants made me feel "finally I can focus and get things done"

☐ I have high theta/beta ratio, ADHD diagnosis, or "Frontal Slow" pattern

Total: ___ / 15

Supervisor (Right Sensorimotor / Impulse Control)

☐ I'm impulsive, act without thinking, interrupt, buy things without considering
☐ OR I'm over-inhibited, perfectionism paralysis, can't act because nothing's good enough
☐ I swing between golden retriever (chasing shiny objects) and frozen cat (can't move)
☐ I struggle with quality control, either no filter or infinite filter
☐ Stimulants either help me brake (if weak) or make me more frozen (if strong)

Total: ___ / 15

Interpreter (Left Temporal / Language Comprehension)

☐ I have to read things multiple times for words to land (processing delays)
☐ I have constant internal narration, my brain narrates everything I experience
☐ I talk to think, don't know what I'm thinking until I hear myself say it
☐ I have dyslexia, word-finding difficulties, or verbal processing challenges
☐ I'm incredibly articulate when I have time to process, but slow in fast conversations

Total: ___ / 15

Bard (Right Temporal / Prosody Processor)

☐ I miss sarcasm and take things literally (or people say "I was kidding!")
☐ I sound flat or monotone, my voice doesn't match my emotions
☐ OR I over-read tone, hear criticism or hostility in neutral speech
☐ I struggle to tell if someone's joking, teasing, or serious
☐ Text communication is easier for me than voice (removes prosodic layer)

Total: ___ / 15

Timekeeper (Alpha Frequency / Processing Speed)

- ☐ Racing thoughts, my brain won't stop, can't slow down to rest
- ☐ OR sluggish processing, everything takes longer, falling behind, word-finding issues
- ☐ I can't downshift, high gear at night, can't access deep sleep
- ☐ Anxiety feels like speed dysregulation (brain running too fast)
- ☐ People say I'm either "too fast" (can't keep up) or "too slow" (need more time)

Total: ___ **/ 15**

The Fog (Low Energy State / Cognitive Slowing)

- ☐ Chronic brain fog, everything feels slow, effortful, like thinking through molasses
- ☐ I wake unrefreshed no matter how long I sleep
- ☐ Words don't come, memory is poor, processing is laggy
- ☐ I have history of viral illness, sleep disorders, or chronic health issues
- ☐ OR: Fog appears after intense periods (protective rest, not dysfunction)

Total: ___ **/ 15**

Worked Example: Alex's Results

Alex's Scores: Grumpy Old Man (12/15) | Fog (11/15) | Princess & Pea (10/15) | Lifeguard (7/15) | CEO (6/15) | Stabilizer (4/15) | All others (0-3)

Alex's constellation: Sensitive Empath with Fog

Now it's your turn:

Your Phenotype Constellation

Tally your scores and identify your top 3-5:

Dominant phenotypes (scores 9-15):
These describe you most accurately. Start with these chapters in Part I.

Supporting phenotypes (scores 5-8):
Partially resonate. Read these chapters after your dominant ones.

Quiet phenotypes (scores 0-4):
Don't match your experience. Skim or skip these chapters.

Pattern to notice: Most people are heavy in 1-2 neighborhoods and 2-3 systems, not just isolated phenotypes. If your top scores cluster in the

Front neighborhood (Happy Little Kid, Grumpy, CEO, Problem Child), your struggles and gifts are primarily emotional and executive. If they cluster in the Back (Lifeguard, Princess & Pea, Interpreter, Bard), you're processing the world and social information intensely. If they cluster in the Axis (Stabilizer, Supervisor, Timekeeper, Fog), your challenges are about execution, pacing, and energy.

Note on Stabilizer + Supervisor: These two phenotypes bridge neighborhoods, they're part of Motivation (can't engage with tasks) and Executive Control (can't execute behavior). If you score high on both, you're likely struggling with both "wanting to" and "being able to."

Phenotype Quick Reference Card

Your At-A-Glance Guide to the 12 Brain Circuits

Phenotype	One-Line ID	Ch	Torture	Gift
Happy Little Kid	Approach & joy system (left frontal)	1	Flatness, anhedonia, can't engage	Motivation, resilience, optimism
Grumpy Old Man	Avoidance & negativity	2	Catastrophizing, anxiety, withdrawal	Risk assessment, wisdom
Stabilizer	Task initiation engine	3	Can't start, heavy body	Sustained attention, execution
Supervisor	Impulse control	4	Impulsive, scattered	Quality control, patience
CEO	Task-switcher	5	Stuck on wrong thing, loops	Executive attention, focus
Lifeguard	Environmental scanner	6	Hypervigilance, rumination	Contextual awareness, safety
Problem Child	Defiant brake	7	Oppositional, self-sabotage	Boundary-setting, rebellion
Princess & Pea	Empathy & sensitivity	8	RSD, sensory overwhelm	Deep empathy, social nuance
Interpreter	Meaning decoder	9	Can't track speech/text	Language comprehension
Bard	Emotional prosody	10	Miss sarcasm/tone	Humor, social warmth
Timekeeper	Processing speed	11	Racing mind, can't slow	Quick thinking, synthesis
Fog	Energy & clarity	12	Brain fog, exhaustion	(Gift is clarity when regulated)

How to use this card:

- Circle your top 3-5 after taking the assessment
- These are your dominant circuits: read those chapters first
- Keep this page bookmarked for quick reference throughout the book

---

Example Constellations

The Tortured Poet: Stabilizer + Grumpy Old Man + CEO + Lifeguard + Princess & Pea → Can't start, catastrophizing, stuck in loops, hypervigilant, RSD

The Anxious Achiever: Grumpy Old Man + CEO + Timekeeper + Supervisor (strong) → Catastrophizing, perfectionism, racing thoughts, can't slow down

The Scattered Creative: Stabilizer + Supervisor (weak) + Happy Little Kid + Timekeeper → Can't start boring tasks, impulsive, needs intensity, racing mind

The Sensitive Empath: Princess & Pea + Lifeguard + Grumpy Old Man + Fog → RSD, sensory overwhelm, hypervigilance, exhaustion from processing

The Frozen Engine: Stabilizer + Fog + CEO + Grumpy Old Man → Paralyzed, foggy, looping, heavy, knows what to do but can't move

The Lightning Rod: Timekeeper + Princess & Pea + Lifeguard + Happy Little Kid → Fast, sensitive, scanning, intensity-seeking, everything comes in loud and fast

The Quiet Rebel: Problem Child + Grumpy Old Man + Stabilizer + CEO → Oppositional, avoidant, stuck in loops, resisting the world while battling your own inertia

The Exhausted Empath: Fog + Princess & Pea + Lifeguard + Interpreter → Drained, sensitive, scanning, processing delays, absorbing the world at full gain with no energy to show for it

---

How to Use Your Results

Your top 3-5 phenotypes are your "dominant constellation."

In Part I:

- Read your dominant phenotype chapters first
- Note which Torture sections feel personal

- Pay attention to Gift sections (these are your superpowers)
- Skim or skip chapters that don't resonate

In Part II (Your Core Stack):

Use this quick-nav guide based on your TOP phenotype. **Everyone should read Ch 13 (Sleep) and Ch 14 (Substances) regardless of phenotype.**

- **Happy Little Kid** → Chapters 13, 14, 17 (loving-kindness meditation), 18 (left frontal NF)
- **Grumpy Old Man** → Chapters 13, 14, 15 (anxiety/HRV), 17 (loving-kindness), 18 (right frontal NF)
- **CEO** → Chapters 14, 16 (productivity), 17 (noting meditation), 18 (midline frontal NF)
- **Problem Child** → Chapters 13 (sleep is critical), 14, 15 (anxiety), 18 (right IFG NF)
- **Lifeguard** → Chapters 14, 15 (anxiety/HRV), 17 (body scan), 18 (PCC NF), 20 (social)
- **Princess & Pea** → Chapters 13 (sleep is critical), 14, 15, 17 (gentle practices), 18 (alpha NF), 20 (social)
- **Stabilizer** → Chapters 13, 14, 16 (productivity), 18 (left sensorimotor training)
- **Supervisor** → Chapters 14, 16 (productivity), 17 (focused attention), 18 (right sensorimotor training)
- **Interpreter** → Chapters 16 (productivity), 17 (mantra meditation)
- **Bard** → Chapters 17 (sound awareness), 20 (social navigation)
- **Timekeeper** → Chapters 13 (sleep), 14, 17 (slowing practices), 18 (SMR/alpha NF)
- **Fog** → Chapters 13 (sleep is diagnostic), 14, 18 (posterior NF), 19 (life design)

If multiple phenotypes: Read the overlapping chapters first. If 3 of your top phenotypes say "Ch 13," that's your starting point.

In Part III:

- Integration strategies work for all constellations
- Use The Poet-Brain Mastery Loop (introduced in the Introduction) with your specific phenotypes

---

Ready? Let's meet your brain's characters.

Part I
Phenotypes & Features

Overview: Your Internal Orchestra

Mastery Loop Steps: NOTICE + NORMALIZE

Your brain isn't one thing. It's a cast of characters, circuits with distinct personalities, each contributing to your experience of being neurodivergent.

You're about to meet **The Poet-Brain Phenotype Model**, the 12 phenotypes that shape how you think, feel, process, and navigate the world.

What you're learning: Steps 1 and 2 of the Poet-Brain Mastery Loop, how to **NOTICE** which circuits are active ("My Stabilizer is offline" vs. "I'm broken") and **NORMALIZE** why they do what they do ("Of course this is happening. Here's the neuroscience.").

Think of it this way: You're learning to identify which instruments in your orchestra are playing too loud, too soft, or out of tune, and understanding why.

Navigate Part I by what's loudest:

- **Can't feel motivated, everything's gray?** Start with Chapter 1 (Happy Little Kid).
- **Catastrophizing, everything feels like too much effort?** Chapter 2 (Grumpy Old Man).
- **Can't start tasks despite wanting to?** Chapter 3 (Stabilizer).
- **Impulsive or frozen by perfectionism?** Chapter 4 (Supervisor).
- **Stuck in loops, can't let go?** Chapter 5 (CEO).
- **Hypervigilant, constantly scanning for threats?** Chapter 6 (Lifeguard).
- **Anger without brakes, oppositional?** Chapter 7 (Problem Child).
- **Rejection feels like annihilation, sensory overwhelm?** Chapter 8 (Princess & the Pea).
- **Word-finding trouble, verbal flooding?** Chapter 9 (Interpreter).
- **Missing tone, sarcasm, social music?** Chapter 10 (Bard).
- **Racing thoughts, time blindness?** Chapter 11 (Timekeeper).
- **Brain fog, fatigue, can't think clearly?** Chapter 12 (The Fog).

Or start with the **Phenotype Self-Assessment** (just before this section) to discover your top 3-5.

Skip to the chapters that scored highest on your self-assessment. You can always come back to the others.

The Architecture: 3 Regions, 6 Systems, 12 Phenotypes

Before you meet the individual characters, here's how they're organized:

Three Regions (Anatomical Geography)

FRONT / EMOTIONAL CORE / INSIDE WORLD
Focus: Mood, motivation, internal narrative, conflict monitoring, impulse control
Phenotypes: Happy Little Kid, Grumpy Old Man, CEO, Problem Child

BACK / SENSING & SOCIAL / OUTSIDE WORLD
Focus: Environmental scanning, social nuance, language, context
Phenotypes: Lifeguard, Princess & the Pea, Interpreter, Bard

AXIS / ACTION ENGINE / DOING & RHYTHM
Focus: Execution, pacing, timing, energy management, your action cadence
Phenotypes: Stabilizer, Supervisor, Timekeeper, Fog

If the front and back neighborhoods are your content, the Axis is your cadence: how quickly you initiate, how long you stay engaged, how you cycle between effort and recovery.

Six Functional Systems (How Phenotypes Work Together)

1. **Motivation System** (Front + Axis), Happy Little Kid + Grumpy Old Man + Stabilizer + Supervisor Approach vs. withdrawal (frontal), initiating action (Stabilizer), monitoring task relevance (Supervisor). When you can't get started, it's often Motivation (not just Executive), your brain hasn't decided the task is worth engaging with.
2. **Executive Control & Behavioral Execution System** (Front + Axis), CEO + Problem Child + Stabilizer + Supervisor Attention direction (CEO), reactive braking (Problem Child), motor engagement (Stabilizer), impulse gating (Supervisor). Executive control IS motor control, deciding what to do and doing it are the same system.
3. **Emotional Regulation System** (Front + Back), Grumpy Old Man + Problem Child + Princess & the Pea + CEO Emotional dysregulation is not a side effect of ADHD. It is a core dimension with its own circuitry: DLPFC, OFC, amygdala, ventral striatum, and medial prefrontal cortex form a

distinct regulatory network (Shaw et al., 2014). Recent biotyping confirms a severe ADHD subgroup defined primarily by emotional dysregulation (Pan et al., 2026). The phenotypes in this system overlap with Motivation and Executive Control because emotional regulation is woven through both.

4. **Orienting & Sensing System** (Back), Lifeguard + Princess & the Pea Environmental scanning + high-gain sensory/social processing. Your receptive system for context and nuance.
5. **Language & Social Communication System** (Back + Front), Interpreter + Bard (with Speaker as motor output) Meaning decoder (Interpreter/left temporal), prosody processor (Bard/right posterior), verbal expression (Speaker/Broca's area, motor node not phenotype). What you hear, how you hear it, what you say.
6. **Processing & Recovery System** (Axis, global), Timekeeper + Fog & the Tide Clock speed + energy cycling, pacing + rest. The infrastructure underneath everything, affects all other systems.

The 12 Phenotypes (Your Orchestra's Instruments)

- **The Happy Little Kid** (Left DLPFC): Curiosity engine and dopamine chaser
- **The Grumpy Old Man** (Right DLPFC): Catastrophe generator and protective guardian
- **The Problem Child** (Right VLPFC/IFG): Defiant brake failure and oppositional energy
- **The CEO** (Anterior Cingulate): Task-switcher who gets stuck on the wrong thing
- **The Lifeguard** (Posterior Cingulate): Hypervigilant scanner watching for danger
- **The Princess & the Pea** (Right TPJ): Exquisitely sensitive empath
- **The Stabilizer** (Left Motor): Engine that won't start
- **The Supervisor** (Right Motor): Brake that won't release
- **The Interpreter** (Left Language): Narrator who translates everything into words
- **The Bard** (Right Posterior): Receiving and tuning expression through nonverbal music
- **The Timekeeper** (Processing Speed): Racing thoughts and temporal dysregulation
- **The Fog & the Tide** (Processing & Recovery): Natural energy cycles and what happens when they get stuck

Note on the Speaker (Broca's area, left frontal): The Speaker is motor production of speech, moving your mouth to form words. It's driven by the Interpreter (Wernicke's generates language, Broca's produces it). When damaged (stroke, trauma), you get expressive aphasia (can't produce speech). That's different from stuttering (coordination issue) or word-finding (Timekeeper/slowed alpha). Speaker is a "bonus phenotype", covered in Chapter 9 as part of the Language System, but driven by the Interpreter rather than being a standalone circuit.

Common Confusions: Key Differentiators

Some phenotypes look similar but operate on different circuits. Here are the crisp distinctions:

Happy Little Kid vs. Grumpy Old Man:
Approach vs. withdrawal. Left frontal (engagement, joy, curiosity) vs. right frontal (avoidance, threat assessment, protection). Same neuroanatomical axis, opposite directions.

Grumpy Old Man vs. Problem Child:
Anxious compliance vs. defiant brake failure. Both are threat-based, but Grumpy generates catastrophe narratives and withdraws, while Problem Child reactively opposes and pushes back. Grumpy says "it's too dangerous," Problem Child says "you can't make me."

CEO vs. Lifeguard (the evaluation pair):
Inside vs. outside anchoring. CEO (anterior cingulate, front midline) evaluates *internally,* what should I do? what's the priority? is this conflict resolved? Lifeguard (posterior cingulate, back midline) evaluates *externally,* what's happening out there? is the environment safe? Together they form the Orienting System: CEO directs attention inward, Lifeguard monitors outward. When CEO is stuck, you perseverate. When Lifeguard is stuck, you hypervigilate. When both are stuck, you ruminate about threats while scanning for new ones.

Stabilizer vs. Supervisor (the motor pair):
Go vs. stop. Stabilizer (left motor cortex) *initiates and sustains* action, the engine. Supervisor (right motor cortex) *inhibits and monitors,* the brake. They cross-talk through the corpus callosum: Supervisor brakes the Stabilizer when you need to slow down, releases it when you need to go. When Stabilizer is weak, you can't start. When Supervisor is weak, you can't stop (impulsivity). When Supervisor is overactive, you can't start either (perfectionism paralysis). Both work with CEO and Lifeguard through the Executive System, CEO decides the priority, Stabilizer executes, Supervisor monitors quality.

When procrastination hits, ask which one: Can't *decide* what to do? (CEO stuck.) Can't *start* even though you've decided? (Stabilizer stalled.) Can't *sustain* and keep drifting to shiny objects? (Supervisor weak.) Can't start because it has to be perfect? (Supervisor overactive.) Each needs different tools.

Lifeguard vs. Princess & the Pea:
Threat scanning vs. pain amplification. Lifeguard (posterior cingulate) monitors environment for danger, hypervigilance, rumination, context-tracking. Princess & Pea (right TPJ) amplifies sensory/social input, RSD, overwhelm, exquisite empathy. Lifeguard watches *outward* for threats; Princess feels *inward* amplification of pain.

Supervisor vs. Problem Child:
Overactive brake vs. broken brake. Supervisor (right motor cortex) is quality control, perfectionistic, can't release inhibition, second-guesses everything. Problem Child (right frontal) is reactive opposition, impulsive, oppositional, brake fails under threat. Supervisor won't *let* you act; Problem Child can't *stop* acting.

Interpreter vs. Bard:
Words as meaning vs. words as music. Interpreter (left language) decodes *what* is said, literal meaning, semantics, verbal comprehension. Bard (right posterior) decodes *how* it's said, tone, prosody, irony, emotional subtext. Interpreter reads the lyrics; Bard hears the melody.

Timekeeper vs. Fog:
Too fast vs. too slow. Timekeeper is racing thoughts, fast processing, can't slow down, often feels like anxiety. Fog is cognitive fatigue, slow processing, can't speed up, often feels like depression or brain fog. Same axis (processing speed), opposite extremes.

Why these distinctions matter: Precision in identification = precision in intervention. If you think you're CEO-stuck when you're actually Stabilizer-offline, you'll choose the wrong tool. If you confuse Grumpy Old Man catastrophizing with Problem Child opposition, your regulation strategy won't land. Know which circuit is leading, choose the right intervention.

How This Maps to Large-Scale Brain Networks

The phenotypes and systems plug into three major brain networks described by neuroscience (Menon's Triple Network Model):

Default Mode Network (DMN)

- Core hub: **Lifeguard** (posterior cingulate)
- Most visible in Back neighborhood phenotypes

- Function: Internal narrator, context, mind-wandering, autobiographical memory
- You'll see this explicitly in Chapter 6 (Lifeguard) and Chapter 21 (Creative Flow)

Central Executive Network (CEN)

- Key nodes: **Happy Little Kid, Grumpy Old Man** (frontal cortex), **Stabilizer, Supervisor** (sensorimotor)
- Most visible in Front and Axis phenotypes during task mode
- Function: Focused attention, working memory, cognitive control
- Active when you're "doing" rather than "being"

Salience Network (SN)

- Core: **CEO** (anterior cingulate), with contributions from **Princess & the Pea** (social salience) and **Problem Child** (reactive control)
- The switchboard between DMN and CEN
- Function: Detect what's important, decide what deserves attention, switch between internal and external focus
- You'll see this explicitly in Chapter 5 (CEO)

Why this matters: These aren't competing theories, they're different zoom levels on the same map. The 12 phenotypes are how you experience these circuits from the inside. The 6 systems explain how they work together. The 3 regions show where they live anatomically. The Triple Network Model describes the large-scale wiring they plug into.

By Chapter 22, you'll see how all these lenses describe the same orchestra.

Chapter Order (Thematic Pairing Logic)

The chapters are organized by **neuroanatomical pairing,** circuits that work as opposing forces on the same axis. **Before each pair of phenotypes, you'll see a short Systems Interlude** that shows how those circuits work together. Read or skim as needed, they're optional help, not extra homework.

- **Chapters 1-2:** Motivation System (Front): Happy Little Kid + Grumpy Old Man *Approach vs. Avoid, the push and pull of engagement*
- **Chapters 3-4:** Attention System (Axis): Stabilizer + Supervisor *Left GO vs. Right STOP, motor execution axis, executive control through action*
- **Chapters 5-6:** Orienting System (Midline): CEO + Lifeguard *Internal Focus vs. External Scanning, anterior cingulate (conflict detection) vs. posterior cingulate (environmental monitoring)*

- **Chapters 7-8:** Nonverbal Sensing System (Right Hemisphere), Problem Child + Princess & the Pea *Oppositional vs. Sensitive, right frontal (reactive braking) vs. right back (high-gain processing)*
- **Chapters 9-10:** Language & Social Communication System (Back), Interpreter + Bard *Words vs. Prosody, left language (meaning) vs. right posterior (tone and nuance)*
- **Chapters 11-12:** Processing & Recovery System (Axis): Timekeeper + Fog & the Tide *Too Fast vs. Natural Cycling, racing thoughts vs. rhythmic energy oscillation*

Note on distributed systems: Executive control and motivation are **distributed across multiple systems**, they don't live in just one place. CEO (Ch 5), Problem Child (Ch 7), Stabilizer (Ch 3), Supervisor (Ch 4), and the motivation system (Ch 1-2) all participate in executive function. Each System Interlude focuses on one neuroanatomical pairing while acknowledging the broader networks.

What You'll Learn

Each chapter in this section follows the same structure:

1. **Opening vignette**: What this phenotype feels like in lived experience
2. **The Torture**: When this circuit creates suffering
3. **The Gift**: When this circuit creates genius
4. **The Neuroscience**: QEEG signatures, brain maps, mechanisms (with Under the Hood boxes for technical depth)
5. **Toolkit Preview**: One immediately actionable step and pointers to detailed protocols in Part II

The Promise

By the end of Part I, you'll:

- Recognize your own phenotype profile (you're not just one, you're a combination)
- Understand why you've struggled with what you've struggled with
- See your "torture" as the flip side of your "gift"
- Know which circuits you've been trying to regulate with substances
- Have a map of your brain's characters

Reader's Note

Don't expect to be just one phenotype. Most neurodivergent brains have 3-5 dominant characters, with others playing supporting roles. You might be:

- Happy Little Kid + Grumpy Old Man (the "push and pull")
- Princess + Timekeeper (sensitive and fast: overwhelm central)
- CEO + Lifeguard (stuck and hypervigilant)
- Stabilizer offline + Supervisor overactive (can't start, can't stop second-guessing)
- Grumpy Old Man + Problem Child (anxious compliance → defiant brake failure)

As you read, note which chapters resonate most. That's your phenotype profile.

Remember: These are levers, not labels. Phenotypes are tools for understanding your circuits and choosing which interventions will work. They're not diagnostic categories or identity markers. You're learning the controls, not defining who you are. And levers move. Every phenotype score you have today can shift with training.

A Note on the Names

The phenotype names are metaphors, not moral judgments.

"Problem Child," "Princess & the Pea," "Grumpy Old Man", these are shorthand for patterns, not verdicts about who you are as a person. If any name feels pathologizing, infantilizing, or just doesn't land for you, **rename it in your head.**

What matters is the pattern, not the label:

- Problem Child = brake system under threat
- Princess & the Pea = high-gain sensory processing
- Grumpy Old Man = avoidance system / threat assessment

Call them whatever works for you. The circuits are real. The names are just handles to grab them.

A Note on Self-Medication

Every chapter includes a section on substance use patterns. This isn't judgment. You've been trying to regulate circuits that neuroscience barely understands.

Part II (Interventions) gives you the right tools.

QEEG 101: Understanding Brain Maps

Optional. Skip this if you just want the phenotypes, the chapter descriptions give you everything you need. This section explains the "QEEG Signature" sections you'll see in each chapter.

What is QEEG? Quantitative EEG, your brain's electrical activity measured at the scalp and analyzed statistically against normative databases. It reveals reproducible patterns that help explain your experience, but it's not a diagnosis, it always needs clinical context.

Frequency bands: Theta (slow: drowsiness, mind-wandering; excess = fog). Alpha (medium: relaxed awareness; excess = disengagement). Beta (fast: active thinking; excess = anxiety). SMR (sensorimotor rhythm: calm focus, inhibition; helps sleep, reduces impulsivity).

Common terms: Frontal asymmetry (left approach vs. right withdrawal). LVF (beta-dominant, low-amplitude; linked to GABAA genetics and anxiety). Theta/beta ratio (high in ADHD; Stabilizer offline). For QEEG methodology and technical depth: *The QEEG Field Guide* (Hill & Lomeli, forthcoming).

Why These Phenotypes Are Not Just Metaphors

The twelve phenotypes in this book are not arbitrary labels. EEG studies identify at least three distinct subgroups of children with ADHD based on electrical signatures: an elevated-theta group (the Stabilizer pattern), a hyperarousal/excess-beta group (the Supervisor/Problem Child pattern), and a mixed slow-fast group associated with emotional dysregulation (Clarke et al., 2001, 2011). A 2022 systematic review confirmed that EEG measures capture real heterogeneity in ADHD, though clinical diagnostic use of EEG biomarkers is not yet established (Slater et al., 2022). Imaging work converges on the same direction. A 2026 JAMA Psychiatry study mapped three ADHD biotypes using structural brain-network analysis, each with distinct frontal-striatal signatures and clinical profiles: predominantly inattentive, predominantly hyperactive/impulsive, and a severe combined type defined by emotional dysregulation (Pan et al., 2026). Those biotypes map directly onto the phenotype axes in these chapters.

Phenotype Quick Reference

For your full quick-reference card (Torture, Gift, and chapter numbers for each phenotype), see the **Phenotype Quick Reference Card** in the Self-

Assessment section. Circle your top 3-5 phenotypes there and use the Part II overview table to route into interventions.

"The trouble with poets is they talk too much. They tell us how it hurts them, and it hurts them just a little more."

Now you know why it hurts you just a little more. Twelve circuits, tuned high, running deep. Not pathology, configuration.

Let's meet your orchestra's twelve instruments.

Systems Interlude: Motivation System

Front + Axis Neighborhoods: Approach, Withdrawal, Initiation, Relevance

Location: Front of brain (left and right dorsolateral prefrontal cortex) + Axis (left and right sensorimotor cortex)
Phenotypes: Happy Little Kid (Chapter 1) + Grumpy Old Man (Chapter 2) + Stabilizer (Chapter 3) + Supervisor (Chapter 4)
System function: Decides whether to engage with or avoid the world, initiates action, monitors task relevance

This is your motivational cadence: when you lean in, when you lean away, how quickly enthusiasm spikes and how long dread lingers.

What This System Does When Balanced

This system is built around the push-pull between the Happy Little Kid (your approach system) and the Grumpy Old Man (your avoidance system), plus the Stabilizer and Supervisor that translate those decisions into movement. When it's balanced:

- You can engage with rewarding activities (Happy Little Kid active)
- You can assess risk and pull back when needed (Grumpy Old Man protective)
- You can initiate action when you decide to (Stabilizer engaged)
- You can monitor whether tasks are worth your effort (Supervisor assessing relevance)
- You toggle between optimism and caution appropriately
- You feel motivated without being reckless, cautious without being paralyzed

This is **frontal asymmetry** (left approach, right withdrawal) PLUS **motor initiation** (Stabilizer) and **task relevance monitoring** (Supervisor). When you can't start a task, it's often Motivation, your brain hasn't decided it's worth engaging with.

What Dysregulation Looks Like

Happy Little Kid offline (left frontal underactive):
Depression, anhedonia, flatness, "why bother," nothing feels rewarding, can't engage with life

Grumpy Old Man hyperactive (right frontal overactive):
Catastrophizing, chronic anxiety, withdrawal, avoidance, "everything will go wrong," predicting future disasters, **effort evaluation dysregulated** ("everything feels like too much work," "not worth it," sense of burden)

Stabilizer offline (left sensorimotor underactive):
Can't start tasks even when you've decided to, motor paralysis, procrastination, "my body won't cooperate"

Supervisor weak or overactive (right sensorimotor dysregulated):
Weak: can't assess if tasks are worth effort, everything feels equally irrelevant
Overactive: nothing feels worth the effort, perfectionism paralysis, "why bother if it won't be perfect"

Multiple dysregulated:
The classic "can't start" pattern, want to engage (Happy Little Kid trying) but predict disaster (Grumpy blocking) AND evaluate everything as "too much effort" (Grumpy's cost-benefit analysis stuck on "not worth it") AND body won't move (Stabilizer offline) AND nothing feels relevant (Supervisor saying "why bother"). This is Motivation System collapse, not just "laziness."

Network Connection

The Motivation System is part of the **Central Executive Network (CEN)**, task-positive circuits that determine whether you approach or avoid.

In your life, this is the cadence of wanting: how quickly you light up about something new, how long before dread creeps in, how often your body says "not today" even when your mind says "let's go." When you learn to read this rhythm, you stop calling it laziness and start calling it what it is, a negotiation between four circuits with different risk tolerances.

First up: The Happy Little Kid and The Grumpy Old Man, your brain's approach-avoidance engine. These two chapters are the motivational foundation. Everything else builds from how these two relate to each other.

Ch 1: The Happy Little Kid (Left DLPFC)

The Engine of Joy and Engagement

Your alarm goes off. You're not awake yet, but already your brain is making a decision: *Is today worth engaging with?*

1.1 "The Engine of Joy and Engagement"

Some mornings, the answer is yes. You wake up excited. Not because anything special is happening, just because you're alive and there are things to do, people to see, ideas to explore. Your brain says: "Hello world, wanna play?" You feel motivated. Energized. Ready to engage.

Other mornings? You wake up heavy. Flat. Nothing sounds interesting. You know you should get up, but you can't find the energy. Not tired, just unmotivated. Like someone turned down the volume on your capacity to care.

Same brain. Same life. Different mornings. What changed?

This is the Happy Little Kid, your brain's approach system (left frontal cortex, left DLPFC). Left = approach, engagement, "let's go." Its mirror (right frontal, the Grumpy Old Man) is withdrawal, "don't bother." When the Happy Little Kid is engaged, you feel joy, motivation, positivity. Life feels worth living. When it's offline, everything feels gray, effortful, pointless.

Here's what I see when I map brains: **left frontal activation**, specifically, the balance between left and right frontal cortex. This is **Richard Davidson's frontal asymmetry research**, decades of work showing that left frontal activation predicts positive affect, approach motivation, engagement with life (Davidson, 1992, 1998). (The effect sizes in frontal asymmetry research are debated, some meta-analyses find moderate rather than large effects, and individual variability is substantial (Thibodeau et al., 2006). What's consistent: the direction of the relationship holds, and the pattern is clinically useful even when the magnitude varies across studies.)

The Happy Little Kid isn't about chasing shiny objects (that's the Supervisor when underengaged, Chapter 4). It's about **cognitive appraisal of interest**. It's the circuit that says "this matters, this is worth doing, I want to engage with this."

When your Happy Little Kid is strong, you have:

- **Joy**: Capacity for genuine positive emotion
- **Motivation**: Drive to engage with life
- **Positivity**: Seeing opportunities, not just threats
- **Approach motivation**: Moving toward goals, people, experiences

When your Happy Little Kid is weak (excess theta or alpha in left frontal), you get:

- **Depression**: Not sadness, but flatness, amotivation
- **Anhedonia**: Nothing feels rewarding
- **Need for intensity**: Only extreme stimulation gets you engaged
- **Can't get off your ass**: Not laziness, but a lack of approach drive

The torture? When your Happy Little Kid goes offline, life loses color. You're going through the motions without feeling alive.

The gift? When your Happy Little Kid is engaged, you bring energy, enthusiasm, and genuine joy to everything you do.

The challenge isn't to chase more novelty. It's to keep your approach system engaged with life.

1.2 The Torture: When the Happy Little Kid Goes Offline

Let's talk about what it's actually like when your approach system shuts down, or when you need extreme intensity just to feel engaged.

1.2.1 Depression: When Nothing Feels Worth Doing

You wake up and nothing sounds interesting. Not depressed in the crying-on-the-floor way. Depressed in the flat, gray, "why bother" way.

You know you should get up. You know you have things to do. But you can't find the motivation. It's not that you're tired, you're unmotivated. Like someone turned off the circuit that makes things feel worth doing.

This is **left frontal hypoactivation**, when your Happy Little Kid goes offline. In brain maps, I see low left frontal beta, or excess theta/alpha in the left frontal region. Your approach system isn't generating the drive to engage with life.

Anhedonia: Nothing feels rewarding. **Amotivation**: Not laziness, just no approach drive. **Flat affect**: You're not sad. You're not happy. You're... nothing. Emotionally flat. Life in grayscale.

This is the Happy Little Kid's signature torture: life loses color. You're alive but not engaged.

1.2.2 Needing Intensity to Engage

Here's the paradox: when your Happy Little Kid is weak, you need EXTREME stimulation just to feel engaged.

Normal activities feel boring. Routine feels unbearable. You need novelty, intensity, drama, crisis, something to kick your approach system into gear.

This is why you:

- **Start projects with enthusiasm, then lose interest**: The initial excitement activates your Happy Little Kid. But when it becomes routine, your approach system goes offline. Now it feels like a chore.
- **Need deadlines and crises**: Last-minute panic activates your left frontal cortex. Suddenly you can engage. But you can't sustain it without the intensity.
- **Self-create drama**: Conflict, chaos, intensity. These activate your approach system when normal life doesn't.
- **Chase novelty**: New relationships, new jobs, new hobbies, the newness activates your Happy Little Kid. Until it doesn't.

This isn't ADHD impulsivity (that's the Supervisor, Chapter 4). This is **needing intensity to activate a weak approach system**.

In brain maps, I see this as low left frontal beta or excess theta/alpha. Your baseline approach motivation is low. You need external stimulation to kick it into gear.

The pattern: excitement (Happy Little Kid engaged!) → routine (Happy Little Kid offline) → abandon → seek new intensity → repeat.

Your approach system needs more activation energy than average to engage.

1.2.3 Positivity Bias Gone Wrong: Toxic Optimism

When your Happy Little Kid is TOO engaged (or when you're forcing positivity to compensate for underlying depression) you get toxic optimism.

"Everything will work out!" (Even when it clearly won't.)

"Just stay positive!" (While ignoring real problems.)

"Good vibes only!" (Suppressing legitimate concerns.)

This isn't genuine joy. This is **defensive positivity**, using forced enthusiasm to avoid dealing with the Grumpy Old Man's legitimate concerns.

The problem: you ignore red flags. You don't prepare for realistic challenges. You exhaust people with relentless cheerfulness that feels fake. And when reality hits, the crash is brutal.

True Happy Little Kid engagement is joyful but grounded. **Toxic positivity** is manic avoidance.

1.2.4 The Crash: When Stimulation Stops

Here's what happens when you've been running on intensity to keep your Happy Little Kid engaged, and then the intensity stops:

Crash. Hard.

The project ends. The relationship stabilizes. The crisis resolves. And suddenly, you're flat again. Nothing feels interesting. You're back to gray, unmotivated, "why bother."

This is **state-dependent engagement**. You were engaged because of external intensity, not because your baseline approach system is strong. When the intensity stops, your Happy Little Kid goes offline.

And now you're seeking the next hit of intensity to feel alive again. The cycle continues.

1.3 The Gift: When the Happy Little Kid Is Your Superpower

Now let's talk about why you wouldn't want to eliminate your Happy Little Kid even if you could.

1.3.1 Genuine Joy: The Capacity to Feel Alive

When your Happy Little Kid is engaged, you have access to something many people lose after childhood: **genuine joy**.

Not forced positivity. Not "good vibes only." Not toxic optimism. But real, authentic enthusiasm for being alive.

When your Happy Little Kid is engaged, it sounds like this: "Hi! Yay! Can I do the thing? That looks so cool! I don't care if it's hard or messy. I want to try it!" Pure enthusiasm. Genuine engagement. Not calculated, not forced, not chasing intensity for the sake of intensity. Just: authentic interest in being alive. This is what engagement circuitry sounds like when it's working, your left frontal cortex generating joy not because something amazing happened, but because being alive is interesting enough.

You wake up excited about the day. You find things interesting. You engage with people, ideas, experiences with genuine curiosity and energy. You bring enthusiasm that's infectious.

This is **positive affect**, the capacity for genuine positive emotion. It's not about being happy all the time (that's not realistic). It's about having access to joy, interest, engagement when life offers something worth engaging with.

People with strong Happy Little Kids are energizing to be around. They make things feel possible. They find the interesting angle in boring topics. They bring enthusiasm that makes others want to engage too.

1.3.2 Motivation: The Drive to Engage

When your Happy Little Kid is strong, you don't need external pressure to engage. You're intrinsically motivated. Things feel worth doing because they're interesting, meaningful, engaging, not because someone's making you do them.

This is **approach motivation**, the drive to move toward goals, people, experiences. You're not avoiding pain (that's the Grumpy Old Man's job). You're pursuing what feels alive, interesting, worth your energy.

This makes you:

- Self-directed (you don't need someone pushing you)
- Engaged (you're present, not just going through motions)
- Energized (motivation creates energy, not drains it)
- Resilient (setbacks don't kill your drive)

People with strong approach motivation are the ones who build things, create things, pursue goals not because they "should" but because they genuinely want to.

1.3.3 Positivity: Seeing Opportunities

When your Happy Little Kid is engaged, you see opportunities where others see obstacles. Not because you're naive, because your cognitive appraisal system is biased toward "this could work" instead of "this will fail."

This is the opposite of the Grumpy Old Man's threat-focused assessment. The Happy Little Kid says "what if this goes right?" while the Grumpy Old Man says "what if this goes wrong?"

Both are useful. But when your Happy Little Kid is strong, you:

- See possibilities others miss
- Find the interesting angle in boring situations
- Maintain hope when others give up
- Bring energy that makes others believe things are possible

This isn't toxic positivity (ignoring real problems). This is **realistic optimism**, seeing both challenges and opportunities, but being drawn toward the opportunities.

1.3.4 Energy & Enthusiasm: The Infectious Quality

When your Happy Little Kid is engaged, you bring energy to everything you do. Not manic energy (that's different). But genuine enthusiasm that's infectious.

You make boring meetings more interesting. You find the fun in tedious tasks. You bring curiosity to conversations. You make people feel like what they're doing matters.

This is a gift, not just for you, but for everyone around you. The world has plenty of cynics, plenty of people going through the motions. It needs people who still find life interesting.

1.3.5 Resilience: Bouncing Back

When your Happy Little Kid is strong, setbacks don't destroy you. You're disappointed, sure. But you bounce back. Because your approach system is still generating the signal: "there are other things worth trying, other goals worth pursuing, life is still interesting."

This is **psychological resilience**, not because you're tough or disciplined, but because your brain's approach system keeps you engaged with life even when things go wrong.

People with weak Happy Little Kids (right > left asymmetry) struggle more with depression after setbacks. Their approach system goes offline and they can't find their way back to engagement. People with strong Happy Little Kids recover faster, not because they're stronger, but because their circuits are configured for approach.

The same circuits that bring you joy and engagement make you resilient, motivated, and energizing to be around.

The challenge isn't to eliminate your Happy Little Kid, it's to keep him engaged. To build a life that activates your approach system naturally, without needing constant intensity. To train your circuits to find engagement in sustainable ways, not just crisis and drama.

Pay attention to this circuit's cadence: short bursts of intense engagement work better than expecting a steady, eight-hour slog.

1.4 The Neuroscience: Left DLPFC & Approach Motivation

Let me show you where joy actually lives in your brain.

The Happy Little Kid lives in your **left dorsolateral prefrontal cortex (DLPFC)**, outer left frontal lobe, above your left eyebrow. This is the **Behavioral Activation System (BAS)**, your brain's gas pedal driving movement toward rewards, goals, engagement.

The opposite is **Behavioral Inhibition System (BIS)**, your brake pedal in right DLPFC (Grumpy Old Man, Chapter 2). When balanced: pursue opportunities, avoid real threats. When Happy Little Kid dominates (left

> right asymmetry): optimism, resilience, but may ignore warnings. When Grumpy Old Man dominates (right > left): caution, but also anxiety, avoidance, depression.

1.4.1 QEEG Signature

Strong (engaged, motivated): Increased left frontal activation, shows as a "hot spot" on brain maps. Left > right frontal asymmetry (see QEEG 101 and Introduction for frontal asymmetry details). Your approach system is lit up, engaged, ready.

Weak (depressed, amotivated): Low left frontal activation. Excess slow or idling rhythms (resting when should be engaging). Right > left asymmetry, predicts depression, anhedonia, withdrawal motivation. This pattern tends to be consistent within individuals, your baseline configuration. These asymmetry patterns emerge remarkably early: even infants with more right-leaning frontal activity are more likely to cry when separated from a caregiver, while left-leaning babies stay calmer (Davidson & Fox, 1989). But importantly, these patterns can shift with training, meditation, neurofeedback, and behavioral activation can all move frontal asymmetry leftward.

Dopamine: Engagement dopamine (not impulsive seeking). When strong: sustained interest, intrinsic motivation, positive affect, resilience. When weak: anhedonia, amotivation, depression, need for intensity to activate approach system.

Depression as approach offline: Right > left asymmetry + low left frontal beta = measurable pattern (not "chemical imbalance" myth). Trainable with neurofeedback, behavioral activation, sustained practice.

The Happy Little Kid: Left DLPFC

Gifts	Torture
• Genuine joy and enthusiasm • Intrinsic motivation (self-directed drive) • Seeing opportunities ("this could work") • Infectious energy that others feel • Resilience (bouncing back from setbacks) • Making life feel worth living	• Depression (flat, gray, "why bother") • Anhedonia (nothing feels rewarding) • Need intensity to engage (crisis, novelty, drama) • Intensity-seeking cycles (start $\rightarrow$ abandon $\rightarrow$ repeat) • Toxic optimism when overactive (forced positivity) • State-dependent engagement (crash when intensity stops)

1.5 Toolkit Preview

Your Happy Little Kid is trainable. If you've been using intensity, stimulants, or caffeine to force engagement, build the approach system instead.

Movement first: vigorous exercise (running, lifting, cycling hard) is the most reliable way to activate left frontal approach motivation, more reliable than motivation itself.

- **Sleep** (Ch 13): consistent morning light exposure within 30-60 minutes of waking is one of the strongest natural activators of the approach system.
- **Meditation** (Ch 17): loving-kindness practice is one of the few practices that measurably shifts frontal asymmetry toward approach.
- **Neurofeedback** (Ch 18): left frontal training builds baseline engagement so you don't need intensity to feel alive.

Detailed protocols are in Part II. These circuits respond to training.

The left frontal circuits that create flatness and amotivation are the same circuits that, once trained, produce baseline engagement and sustained curiosity. Part II shows you how to build that.

1.6 Key Takeaways

The Happy Little Kid (Left DLPFC) is your brain's approach system, the circuit that generates joy, motivation, and engagement with life.

- **Not about chasing novelty:** This is cognitive appraisal of interest (approach motivation), not impulsivity, the Supervisor (Chapter 4) handles impulse control
- **Depression as approach system offline:** When weak, you get flatness and anhedonia, not sadness, but absence of motivation and color in life
- **Intensity-seeking as intelligent regulation:** If you need crisis, drama, or stimulants to engage, you're targeting the right system (left frontal approach), you just need better tools than borrowed activation
- **BAS vs. BIS balance:** Your Happy Little Kid (Behavioral Activation System) opposes your Grumpy Old Man (Behavioral Inhibition System), when CEO can't reconcile them, you get procrastination
- **Training builds baseline engagement:** Morning light, exercise, behavioral activation, loving-kindness meditation, and frontal asymmetry neurofeedback can strengthen approach motivation so you don't need intensity to feel alive

1.7 Reader Reflections

1. **When was the last time you felt engaged with life, not because of intensity or crisis, but because something felt interesting?** What were you doing?
2. **What does your "gray" feel like?** When your Happy Little Kid goes offline, how do you experience it?
3. **Are there current situations where you might invite the Happy Little Kid to take the lead?** What would it look like to let curiosity guide instead of obligation? If they need encouragement to find their voice, keep reading, the tools in Part II will help.
4. **What's one small step you could take this week to strengthen your approach system?** Morning light walk? Exercise? One interesting activity?
5. **When during the day does your Happy Little Kid naturally come online? What cadence of sprints and breaks actually works for it?**

Ch 2: The Grumpy Old Man (Right DLPFC)

The Voice That Says "Don't"

You wake up with an idea. A project. A possibility. Something you're excited about. Then the voice speaks: "Don't. It won't work. Too much effort. Not worth it. You'll put in all that work and it'll fail anyway. Why bother? Stay home. Don't try."

2.1 "The Avoidance System"

Or maybe you're lying in bed at 3am, and tomorrow's meeting fills you with dread.

It's 3:17am. Your eyes are open. Tomorrow's presentation loops in your head: *It's going to be so much work. Preparing will take hours. The whole thing will probably be pointless anyway. They won't care. It won't matter. Why am I putting myself through this?*

Everything feels heavy, oppressive. That familiar dread settles in, not fear of danger, but the cognitive overwhelm of "this is too much, I can't handle this effort."

The rational part of your brain knows the presentation isn't actually that hard. But the voice doesn't do rational effort-benefit analysis. It generates seventeen futility scenarios, all the ways the effort won't be worth it, all the reasons the work will be wasted, all the evidence that trying is pointless. One conclusion: *don't bother. Call in sick. Stay home. Why waste the energy?*

Or maybe you're just driving, stuck behind someone going slow, and fury rises: "Get OUT of my way!" Everything feels effortful. Everyone's annoying. Your tank's on empty and the world won't cooperate. Nothing ever works anyway.

This is the Grumpy Old Man, your brain's **avoidance system**. The right frontal circuit that says "withdraw, don't engage, it's not worth the effort." The opposite of the Happy Little Kid's approach drive.

Here's what I see when I map brains like yours: **right frontal hyperactivation**. Your brain's withdrawal system (BIS, Behavioral Inhibition System) is stuck in overdrive. While the Happy Little Kid (Chapter 1) says "go explore!", your Grumpy Old Man says "don't, it's too much work, too effortful, won't work anyway."

The torture? You can't turn it off. **Avoidance** dominates. Dread. Resistance. Catastrophizing futility. Everything feels like too much work. The voice that says "don't try, don't engage, don't waste the effort, just stay home where it's easy."

The gift? This is your effort accountant. The circuit that keeps you from wasting energy on pointless endeavors. The critical thinker who spots when effort won't pay off. The voice that says "I've seen this before, and it wasn't worth the work."

The challenge isn't to silence your Grumpy Old Man. It's to teach him the difference between genuine waste of effort and opportunities worth pursuing.

2.2 The Torture: When Avoidance Dominates Your Life

Let's talk about what it's actually like when your avoidance system won't shut off.

The Happy Little Kid (Chapter 1) wants to approach life, explore, engage, try new things. The Grumpy Old Man wants to withdraw, avoid, resist, stay safe. When Grumpy Old Man dominates, **avoidance becomes your default**. Don't try. Don't risk. Don't engage. Stay home. Stay safe.

2.2.1 Avoidance Motivation: The "Don't" Circuit

Your brain has two core motivational systems:

- **Happy Little Kid (left frontal)**: BAS: Behavioral Activation System. "Go toward this. Explore. Engage."
- **Grumpy Old Man (right frontal)**: BIS: Behavioral Inhibition System. "Stay away. Withdraw. Don't try."

When your Grumpy Old Man is loud, it sounds like this: "This all sucks. Leave me alone. It's too hard. **Go away.**" Not reasoned risk assessment, automatic avoidance. Active rejection, protective withdrawal. While the Happy Little Kid wants to engage ("Let's try this!"), your Grumpy Old Man is already generating a dozen reasons why it won't work, why it's too much effort, why you should just stay home where it's safe.

When your Grumpy Old Man is loud, **withdrawal dominates**. Everything gets appraised as "not worth it." This isn't laziness or low motivation (that's Happy Little Kid offline). Your avoidance system is saying "danger, withdraw."

2.2.2 Dread & Overwhelm: Avoidance Through Futility Prediction

CLINICAL NOTE:

Dread isn't a character flaw. It's your right frontal cortex running futility simulations to protect your energy. Thank it for trying. Then teach it a new rhythm.

There's a feeling you wake up with. Before you're fully conscious, there it is. Heaviness. A sense that everything is too much.

This is **anticipatory dread**, your avoidance system generating reasons to withdraw. Your brain treats the future like an exhausting grind: "Don't go to the meeting. Don't start the project. Don't reach out. It will be too much work and won't pay off. Save your energy. Stay home."

The physical symptoms are real: heaviness, mental fog, muscle tension, lethargy. Your body is in withdrawal mode even though the effort isn't actually that extreme. Your Grumpy Old Man has activated your nervous system's brake pedal.

Grumpy Old Man often runs on a slow, sticky cadence: it spins up dread early, and lets go late, unless you deliberately shift the tempo with tools from Part II.

The function: Dread is your avoidance system's tool. Generate overwhelm → you withdraw → you conserve energy. It worked for your ancestors (wasting energy on futile efforts was dangerous when resources were scarce). But now it fires at everything.

2.2.3 Catastrophizing: How Avoidance Justifies Itself

Your friend doesn't text back for three hours. Your Grumpy Old Man immediately generates the worst possible explanation:

This friendship takes too much work. You're always the one reaching out. It's exhausting. They don't care as much as you do. Why bother maintaining this? You'll just end up disappointed anyway.

The rational part of your brain knows they're probably just busy. But the Grumpy Old Man doesn't do "probably just busy." He generates worst-case effort scenarios **to justify withdrawal**. If the relationship requires too much work with too little payoff, then disengaging makes sense.

This is **catastrophizing futility**, your avoidance system's reasoning engine. Every situation plays out as wasted effort, which gives you permission to not try. You're not worried about the presentation being dangerous. You're convinced it'll take hours to prepare, nobody will care anyway, nothing will come of it, and you'll have wasted all that energy. **Therefore: don't do**

the presentation. Your Grumpy Old Man generates futility predictions that justify avoidance.

The "what if" loops spiral: What if I put in all that work and it doesn't matter? What if I try hard and it still fails? What if I'm wasting my time? **Therefore: don't try.** Catastrophizing isn't about danger, it's your avoidance system providing reasons why effort won't pay off.

You can't enjoy anything because your brain is too busy generating reasons not to engage. Good news feels temporary (so don't invest energy). Bad news feels inevitable (so don't bother trying). The future is exhausting, which means: **stay home, save energy, don't bother.**

2.2.4 Overwhelm & Depression: When Avoidance Becomes Shutdown

Here's what happens when the Grumpy Old Man runs too hot for too long: everything becomes too much effort. Not just the big things, everything.

Getting out of bed? Too much work. Checking email? Exhausting. Making a phone call? Too many steps. Leaving the house? Why bother.

Your effort-assessment system has labeled so many things as not worth it that you're paralyzed. This is **overwhelm**, when your cognitive appraisal of effort exceeds your sense of capacity to handle it.

And when overwhelm persists, it becomes **depression**. Not sadness, shutdown. Your brain's withdrawal system has decided that the world requires too much effort, so the easiest thing to do is... nothing. Stay in bed. Avoid people. Don't try. Don't engage. Don't waste the energy.

This isn't laziness. This isn't "just feeling down." This is your right frontal cortex running an effort-benefit analysis and concluding that withdrawal conserves resources. Every potential action gets appraised as "too much work, too effortful, won't pay off."

The physical experience: heavy. Exhausted. Moving through molasses. Not because you lack energy (though you might), but because your effort-assessment system is applying the brakes to everything.

Quick distinction: Rumination (replaying past events endlessly) is the Lifeguard's territory (Chapter 6). The Lifeguard evaluates the *outside world*: Is the environment safe? What happened out there? The Grumpy Old Man evaluates *internal effort*: Is this worth doing? Can I handle it? Different circuits, different questions. When cramped, the Lifeguard produces trauma patterns and hypervigilance. The Grumpy Old Man produces dread and depression.

2.2.5 Rejection Sensitivity: When Criticism Overwhelms

Someone gives you mild, constructive feedback. You hear: "This relationship takes too much work and isn't worth the effort."

Your partner says "I'm fine" with a slightly flat tone. You immediately think: maintaining this is exhausting.

Your friend cancels plans. Obviously: this friendship requires too much energy for too little payoff.

This is part of **Rejection Sensitivity Dysphoria (RSD)**, emotional pain that's disproportionate to the trigger, combined with overwhelming sense of "this is too much to deal with."

How this works neurologically: RSD involves the right TPJ (the Princess & the Pea (Chapter 8)) detecting social pain, which then feeds into your Grumpy Old Man's avoidance system. Princess & Pea detects rejection and amplifies the pain; Grumpy Old Man evaluates it as "too much effort to handle, not worth engaging" and generates withdrawal.

Your Princess & Pea is detecting signs of disapproval. Every facial expression. Every tone shift. Every pause in conversation. She's reading social cues with high gain, catching micro-expressions of potential rejection. When she detects (or thinks she detects) disapproval, the signal goes to your Grumpy Old Man: "This interaction = high effort cost, painful to navigate." His response: "Withdraw. Don't engage. Too much work to fix. Not worth the energy."

And when rejection is detected? The pain is real. Physical. Overwhelming. Not "oh that's disappointing", more like "I need to crawl out of my skin and disappear forever." That's the social pain network (dACC, right insula, right TPJ) activating, same circuits as physical pain (Eisenberger et al., 2003; DeWall et al., 2010). Your Grumpy Old Man then generates avoidance motivation: dealing with this pain takes too much effort, easier to withdraw.

2.2.6 Avoidance Paralysis: The Ease of Not Trying

You have an idea for a project. It's exciting. You start planning. Then the Grumpy Old Man chimes in:

"That's going to take so much work. You'll spend hours on it and it probably won't pan out. You don't have the energy for this. Why waste the effort?"

So you don't start. Because if you don't try, you don't waste the energy.

This is avoidance paralysis, procrastination driven by dread of effort, not laziness. You're not avoiding the work because it's scary. You're avoiding it because your brain has decided the effort won't be worth the payoff (Steel, 2007; Botvinick et al., 2009).

Social situations become exhausting calculations. People = effort required. So you stay home. You cancel plans. You ghost friends. Not because you don't want connection, because your Grumpy Old Man has convinced you that maintaining relationships takes too much work for too little return.

The opportunity cost is devastating. You miss out on relationships, experiences, growth, not because you don't want them, but because your effort-assessment system has decided they require too much energy.

"If I don't try, I don't waste energy" feels like conservation. But it's a prison.

2.2.7 Pessimism & Complaining: The Downside Detector

Someone shares exciting news. Your first thought: "Here's how much work that's going to be."

Someone proposes a plan. Your first response: "I've seen this before, and it was a huge amount of effort for nothing."

You're not trying to be a downer. Your Grumpy Old Man is genuinely trying to protect you (and others) from wasting energy by pointing out the effort-to-payoff ratio. But it's exhausting, for you and everyone around you.

You see the downside of everything. Not because you're negative, because your effort-assessment system is always on. Every opportunity requires work. Every plan has costs. Every good thing comes with hidden effort requirements.

This is protective. Your ancestors who worried about wasting energy on futile efforts survived longer than the ones who didn't. But in modern life, where most activities aren't zero-sum survival games, it just makes you the person who dampens everyone's enthusiasm.

And here's the cruel irony: you know you're doing it. You can hear yourself complaining. You can see people's faces when you point out how much work their plans will be. But you can't stop. Because your Grumpy Old Man is convinced that if you don't point out the effort cost, everyone will waste their energy.

2.3 The Gift: When the Grumpy Old Man Is Your Guardian

Now let's talk about why you wouldn't want to eliminate your Grumpy Old Man even if you could.

2.3.1 Effort Assessment: The Red Flag Detector

While everyone else is excited about the new opportunity, you're the one who spots the problems. The hidden time commitment. The person who's going to create drama and require managing. The business plan that looks great on paper but will require twice the work for half the return.

You're not being negative. You're seeing what others miss.

This is your **effort-cost detector**, the ability to spot bad ROI before others waste their energy. Your Grumpy Old Man has kept you (and others) out of time-sink relationships, energy-drain business deals, exhausting commitments. While the Happy Little Kid (Chapter 1) wants to explore everything, your Grumpy Old Man says "wait, let's think about the actual cost here."

This is a survival advantage. Your ancestors who worried about wasting energy on futile efforts lived longer than the ones who didn't. The ones who conserved resources survived to pass on their genes. You inherited an effort-assessment system that's been refined over millions of years.

In modern life, this makes you the person who:

- Reads the fine print (and spots the hidden costs)
- Asks the hard questions (about time/energy required)
- Sees the effort-to-payoff ratio before committing
- Prevents exhausting commitments

You balance the Happy Little Kid's enthusiasm with realistic assessment of costs. This is valuable. Not fun at parties, maybe. But valuable.

2.3.2 Critical Thinking: The Bullshit Detector

You don't accept things at face value. When someone makes a claim, you immediately think: "Is that actually true? What's the evidence? What are they not telling me?"

This is critical thinking, questioning assumptions, seeing flaws in arguments, not being swayed by charisma or confidence. Your Grumpy Old Man is a natural skeptic.

This makes you:

- Hard to manipulate
- Good at quality control
- Able to see through marketing hype
- Valuable in decision-making roles

While others are nodding along, you're the one saying "wait, that doesn't make sense." Sometimes this makes you unpopular. But it also makes you right.

2.3.3 Strategic Planning: The Contingency Planner

"What could go wrong?" is an annoying question when you're excited about something. But it's also a useful question.

Your Grumpy Old Man thinks through consequences. Not just "what if this works?" but "what if it doesn't? What's Plan B? What are the risks? How do we mitigate them?"

This is strategic planning, preparing for challenges before they arise. You're the person who:

- Has backup plans
- Thinks through contingencies
- Prepares for worst-case scenarios
- Isn't blindsided when things go wrong

Yes, you sometimes overprepare. But you're also rarely caught completely off-guard. When disaster strikes, you're the one who already thought through what to do.

2.3.4 Protective Wisdom: Pattern Recognition

"I've seen this before, and it wasn't worth the effort."

This isn't just pessimism. It's pattern recognition. Your Grumpy Old Man learns from past wasted efforts, yours and others'. You remember what consumed energy without payoff last time. You notice when current situations resemble past time-sinks.

This is protective wisdom, the ability to learn from experience and apply those lessons to new situations. You're cautious with new people because maintaining shallow relationships takes energy you don't have. You're skeptical of promises because you've heard them before and the effort required never matched the claimed benefit.

This makes you:

- Less likely to repeat energy-wasting mistakes
- Good at spotting patterns of futility
- Able to learn from others' wasted efforts
- A guardian against naive optimism about effort-to-reward ratios

Yes, sometimes you're overly cautious. But you're also less likely to walk into obvious time-sinks.

2.3.5 Quality Control: The Perfectionist's Useful Side

Your standards are high. Maybe too high. But this also means you catch errors before they become problems. You notice details others miss. You're thorough.

This is quality control, attention to detail, high standards, catching mistakes before they ship. Your Grumpy Old Man won't let you submit work that's "good enough." It has to be right.

This makes you:

- Reliable
- Thorough
- Good at catching errors
- Valuable in roles requiring precision

Yes, perfectionism can be paralyzing. But it also means your work is usually excellent. You don't cut corners. You don't phone it in. Your Grumpy Old Man won't let you.

The bottom line: Your Grumpy Old Man is an effort accountant, not a villain. The challenge isn't to eliminate effort assessment, it's to calibrate it. To distinguish between genuine waste of energy and opportunities worth pursuing. To let him protect you from actual time-sinks without letting him paralyze you with catastrophizing futility about worthwhile efforts.

You need your Grumpy Old Man. You just need to teach him when to speak up and when to stand down.

2.4 The Neuroscience: Right DLPFC & Withdrawal Motivation

Let me show you where dread and effort-avoidance actually live.

The Grumpy Old Man lives in your **right DLPFC**, the Behavioral Inhibition System (BIS). While Happy Little Kid (left DLPFC, Chapter 1) drives approach, Grumpy Old Man drives withdrawal from effort and perceived futility.

When Grumpy Old Man dominates: Avoidance becomes default. **When both are loud:** "I want to but I'm scared", simultaneous approach and avoidance creating paralysis.

2.4.1 QEEG Signature

Right frontal hyperactivation: Excess fast-wave activity in right frontal regions, shows as a "hot spot" on brain maps. Right > left frontal asymmetry (see QEEG 101 and Introduction for frontal asymmetry details), predicts withdrawal motivation, negative affect, effort-avoidance, depression risk. Dread pattern: high right frontal theta (cognitive overwhelm). Depression pattern: high right frontal beta with low alpha (low mood, shutdown).

Special patterns:

- **Low Voltage Fast (LVF):** Beta-dominant, low-amplitude EEG linked to GABAA receptor genes and family history of alcoholism, genetically predisposed to find alcohol calming (see *The QEEG Field Guide* (Hill & Lomeli, forthcoming) for genetics and medication patterns)
- **Beta spindles:** Excessive beta bursts linked to GABAergic dysregulation, over-arousal, "can't turn brain off"

The Grumpy Old Man: Right DLPFC

Gifts	Torture
• Effort assessment (spotting bad ROI) • Quality control ("good enough" wisdom) • Strategic planning (effort costs) • Critical thinking (questioning assumptions) • Protective conservation (avoiding futile efforts) • Realistic assessment (not blindsided by optimism)	• Avoidance as default ("don't try" automatic) • Dread & overwhelm (future = exhausting grind) • Catastrophizing to justify withdrawal • Resistance & irritability (everything = too much work) • RSD component (social pain triggers withdrawal) • Overwhelm & shutdown (effort exceeds capacity) • Chronic pessimism & complaining

2.5 Toolkit Preview

Your Grumpy Old Man is trainable. You need his wisdom, just calibrated. If alcohol or benzos have been your off switch, you've been borrowing GABA regulation. Chapter 14 explains that pattern.

Try the physiological sigh when dread spikes: double inhale through the nose, long slow exhale through the mouth. It is the fastest nervous system downshift your body can generate without a substance.

- **Stress Response Regulation** (Ch 15): HRV biofeedback and vagal toning signal safety to the threat system and build durable calm.
- **Meditation** (Ch 17): loving-kindness practice specifically targets right frontal anxiety.
- **Neurofeedback** (Ch 18): right frontal calming protocols build the GABA regulation you have been borrowing.

Detailed protocols are in Part II. These circuits respond to training.

The right frontal circuits that generate 3am catastrophizing are the same circuits that, once trained, produce wise effort-evaluation. Part II shows you how to build that.

2.6 Key Takeaways

The Grumpy Old Man (Right DLPFC) is your brain's AVOIDANCE system (BIS), the circuit that says "don't try, withdraw, save energy" and generates reasons to justify not approaching life based on effort-cost assessment.

- **BAS vs. BIS:** Happy Little Kid = APPROACH. Grumpy Old Man = AVOIDANCE. When CEO can't reconcile them, you get procrastination.
- **Internal appraisal, not external threat:** Grumpy Old Man does INSIDE-self appraisal of effort and futility. Lifeguard (Ch 6) does OUTSIDE-world threat scanning. Front brain = internal; back brain = external.
- **Catastrophizing serves avoidance:** Your effort-assessment system generates worst-case scenarios to justify withdrawal. "If the effort won't pay off, staying home makes sense." This isn't irrational, it's your avoidance system's reasoning engine.
- **Dread vs. depression:** High theta = dread ("this is too much"). High beta with low alpha = depression ("nothing matters, why bother"). Both are effort-based withdrawal patterns.
- **RSD as two-step process:** Princess & Pea detects social pain with high gain → Grumpy Old Man evaluates as "too much effort to handle" → generates avoidance and withdrawal.
- **GABAergic regulation:** If alcohol felt like "finally I can relax," you likely have LVF pattern + GABAA receptor genes (see Ch 14).
- **Training calibrates, doesn't eliminate:** Right frontal alpha neurofeedback, building approach motivation to balance withdrawal. The goal: wisdom without paralysis.
- **Map your dread cadence:** When does it predict failure the loudest? Mornings, before big tasks, late at night?

2.7 Reader Reflections

1. **What does your 3am catastrophizing sound like?** Can you distinguish INTERNAL effort/futility appraisal (Grumpy Old Man - "too much work, won't pay off") from EXTERNAL threat/rumination (Lifeguard - "what's the danger out there?")?
2. **Can you identify the difference between protective wisdom and paralyzing dread?** Think of a time when your Grumpy Old Man correctly

spotted wasted effort versus unnecessarily catastrophizing about work that was actually worthwhile.

Systems Interlude: The Attention System

Motor Execution Axis: Left GO, Right STOP

Paul Simon wrote two companion songs called "Think Too Much" ((a) and (b)) on his *Hearts and Bones* album. In (b), he described the left side of the brain dominating the right, while the right side has to labor through the long and speechless night. That's the Stabilizer and Supervisor in one sentence. Left initiates. Right inhibits. And when they can't negotiate, you lie awake thinking too much. (Both versions are worth a listen, they map onto this book's themes with eerie precision.)

Location: Left sensorimotor cortex + Right sensorimotor cortex
Phenotypes: Stabilizer (Chapter 3) + Supervisor (Chapter 4)
System function: Motor initiation (left) vs. motor inhibition (right)

Key insight: Executive control IS motor control, the decision to act and the action itself are the same system. Your left hemisphere says GO (initiate), your right hemisphere says STOP (gate/inhibit).

What This System Does When Balanced

Your Attention System translates intentions into actions, or deliberately holds them back. When it's balanced:

- You can engage motor action to execute decisions (Stabilizer working)
- You can initiate tasks without excessive deliberation (Stabilizer engaged)
- You can gate impulses and maintain quality control (Supervisor working)
- You can inhibit premature responses and wait for the right moment (Supervisor functional)

This is the **behavioral expression of executive control**, your Stabilizer and Supervisor translate decisions (from CEO, motivation, and other systems) into actual behavior. Left says "go," right says "stop," and the two negotiate every action.

What Dysregulation Looks Like

Stabilizer underactive (left sensorimotor underactive):
Can't initiate action, procrastination at the motor level, knowing what to do but can't start, frontal slow / motor slow phenotype, "stuck in molasses"

Stabilizer overactive (left sensorimotor hyperactive):
Excessive motor engagement, restlessness, can't sit still, driven quality without satisfaction

Supervisor weak (right sensorimotor underactive):
No motor inhibition, blurting out responses, acting before thinking, impulsive actions slip through without gating

Supervisor overactive (right sensorimotor hyperactive):
Over-gating, perfectionism at the execution level, can't release actions because nothing passes the quality filter, analysis paralysis

Both dysregulated:
Can't start AND can't stop checking, either stuck unable to initiate, or initiating then obsessively revising. This is the "perfectionist procrastinator" pattern.

How This Connects to Other Systems

The Attention System (motor axis) doesn't decide *what* to do, that's the job of:

- **Motivation System (Ch 1-2):** Provides the drive (approach vs. avoid)
- **Orienting System (Ch 5):** The CEO detects conflicts and directs attention

The Attention System implements those decisions through action (or strategic inaction). When CEO decides "do this," Stabilizer initiates. When CEO decides "not yet," Supervisor gates.

Here you're learning your attention cadence: how often you can switch, how long you can stay, and what kinds of tasks stretch or snap that rhythm.

Map so far: 2 of 12. You've met the approach-avoidance engine, the Happy Little Kid and the Grumpy Old Man. Up next: The Stabilizer and The Supervisor, how your brain translates those motivational signals into action (or doesn't). Left hemisphere GO vs. right hemisphere STOP.

Ch 3: The Stabilizer (Left Pre/Postcentral Gyri)

I Know What to Do, But I Can't Make Myself Do It

Your workout clothes are on the chair. Right there. You've been staring at them for twenty minutes.

3.1 "The Engine That Won't Start"

You want to work out. You know you'll feel better. You know it helps. You even have time. The decision is made: "I'm working out. Now."

But your body won't move.

Not tired. Not lazy. Just: the gap between intention and action feels impossible to cross.

"Come on, just do it," you tell yourself. Nothing. Five more minutes pass. You give up, guilt crushing.

Or it's that email. Important. Been on your list for three days. Will take ten minutes. You know what to say. But you can't make yourself open your laptop. The decision is clear. The motor action won't engage.

Or you're lying in bed at night, exhausted. But your body won't power down. Restless. Fidgeting. Micro-movements. Can't lie still even though you desperately want to sleep.

This is the Stabilizer, your left sensorimotor cortex, the gearbox between decision and action. When it's working, it takes decisions from your frontal lobes ("go work out," "write the email," "lie still and sleep") and translates them into sustained, embodied action. It keeps you in gear.

When it's offline, **you pop back into neutral**, your brain disengages, attention drifts, the task slides away even though you decided to do it. The engine won't start. Or won't stop. This is less about character and more about boot-up cadence: how long it takes your motor system to come online.

This isn't a willpower problem. It's a circuit problem.

Here's what I see on brain maps: **excess theta at the left sensorimotor strip**. Your motor engagement system is idling. The Happy Little Kid can be fully engaged (you *want* to do this). The CEO can make the decision (you *decided* to do this). But the Stabilizer won't execute. The motor system won't shift into gear.

The torture? Paralysis. Staring at what you need to do, unable to start. Or restlessness, motor system won't settle, can't be still. Task initiation failure despite clear intention.

The gift? When it's engaged, the Stabilizer is sustained embodied action. You don't just decide, you *do*. Smoothly. Without constant re-deciding. Your motor system stays in gear until the task is complete.

The challenge isn't to want more or decide better. It's to wake up your motor engagement system so intention becomes action.

CLINICAL NOTE:

Procrastination isn't laziness. It's your Stabilizer offline. You made the decision. Your motor system won't execute. Not willpower, circuits.

Here's the crucial distinction: Your CEO (Chapter 5) makes the decision. Your Stabilizer executes it. When your CEO gets stuck arbitrating between approach (Happy Little Kid) and avoidance (Grumpy Old Man), you get procrastination. But even when your CEO decides to proceed, if your Stabilizer is offline, you still can't start. **This is the second failure mode of procrastination, not stuck deciding, but stuck executing.**

When your Stabilizer is offline (excess theta, low beta, cramping up in that "Frontal Slow" pattern), you get **activation energy deficit**. You know what to do. You've decided to do it. But you can't get your body into gear.

And at night, when your Stabilizer should idle so you can sleep, it won't power down. Restless. Moving. Can't sink into deep sleep.

This is the Stabilizer's double torture: **can't start when you need to, can't stop when you need to.**

3.2 The Torture: When the Engine Won't Start (or Won't Stop)

Let's talk about what it's actually like when your Stabilizer is dysregulated.

3.2.1 Task Initiation Paralysis: Stuck in Neutral

You're sitting there. You know what you need to do. You have the time. You even want to do it. Your CEO has made the decision. The conflict is resolved. But you can't make yourself start.

It's not that you're thinking about it and deciding not to, **the decision is made**. Your Happy Little Kid is interested. Your CEO said "do this." But the gap between "I've decided to do this" and "I'm doing this" feels impossible to cross.

This is the difference between CEO procrastination and Stabilizer procrastination:

- **CEO procrastination:** Stuck deciding, ping-ponging between "I should" and "I shouldn't," can't reconcile approach vs. avoidance
- **Stabilizer procrastination:** Decision is clear, but motor system won't execute, stuck between intention and action

Activation energy deficit, the energy required to start feels too high. Like trying to push a car uphill from a dead stop. You know once you're moving it will be easier. But you can't get moving.

This is the Stabilizer offline. Your motor cortex isn't generating the sustained activity needed to lock in the motor set. You're stuck in neutral. The CEO issued the command. The Stabilizer didn't execute.

3.2.2 Can't Maintain Boring Tasks

You start the task. For five minutes, you're doing it. Then… you're not. You didn't consciously decide to stop. You just… drifted off. Lost momentum. The motor set didn't hold.

Something more interesting caught your attention. A sound. A thought. A notification. Your vigilance for novelty pulled you away. Your Stabilizer couldn't inhibit the distraction or maintain the motor set.

This is the Stabilizer slipping out of gear. You can't maintain sustained attention on boring tasks because:

1. Your motor cortex isn't providing the embodied engagement that keeps you locked in
2. You can't turn off phasic alertness (vigilance for novelty)
3. Every interesting stimulus hijacks your attention away from the boring task

Interesting tasks? Fine. Your Happy Little Kid keeps you engaged. Novel tasks? No problem. Phasic alertness is helpful when things are dynamic. But boring, repetitive, maintenance tasks? Your Stabilizer can't hold the gear long enough, and can't inhibit the pull toward novelty.

This is what ADHD inattentiveness actually looks like: Not inability to focus, inability to sustain focus on boring things while inhibiting attention to interesting things.

3.2.3 Psychomotor Slowing: Your Body Feels Heavy

Everything feels effortful. Not tired, heavy. Like you're moving through molasses. Getting out of bed. Getting dressed. Starting tasks. Your body feels sluggish.

This is **psychomotor slowing**, your motor cortex is dominated by slow waves (theta/delta). The activation that should be there isn't. Your body is literally running slower than it should.

3.2.4 Restless Sleep: Can't Power Down

Night comes. You're exhausted. You lie down. But your body won't stop.

Restless legs. Fidgeting. Micro-movements. Tossing and turning. You can't lie still. Your Stabilizer won't shift into neutral.

This is **hyperarousal insomnia**. Your sensorimotor system won't idle. The SMR rhythm that should appear when you're still? It's not there. So you can't sink into deep sleep (Hoedlmoser et al., 2008).

You're exhausted but your body won't power down. The Stabilizer is stuck in a gear it can't release.

3.3 The Gift: When the Stabilizer Works Right

Now let's talk about why you need your Stabilizer, when it's working, not stuck.

3.3.1 Task Initiation: Getting Into Gear

When your Stabilizer works, you can start tasks without massive activation energy. You decide to do something, and your body just... does it. No paralysis. No stuck-in-neutral. Just: intention → action.

This is **behavioral activation**, the ability to get your body moving, engaged, doing the thing.

3.3.2 Sustained Engagement: Staying in Gear

When your Stabilizer works, you can maintain boring tasks. You keep typing even when it's tedious. You keep walking even when it's repetitive. You keep practicing even when it's not fun.

This is **sustained engagement**, the ability to hold a motor set over time, using continuous sensory feedback to stay on course.

This is how you:

- Finish projects (not just start them)
- Build skills (practice, repetition, maintenance)

- Complete boring tasks (paperwork, chores, admin)
- Exercise consistently (sustained physical engagement)

3.3.3 Motor Planning and Sequencing

When your Stabilizer works, you can sequence complex actions smoothly. Typing, playing instruments, sports, tool use, these require motor planning and execution.

Your Stabilizer coordinates: "First this movement, then that one, then that one." Smooth, automatic, embodied.

3.3.4 Sleep: Idling Smoothly

When your Stabilizer works, you can lie still at night. Your motor system shifts into neutral. SMR appears. Sleep spindles build. You sink into deep sleep.

Your body knows how to power down. The restlessness that plagued you when your Stabilizer was dysregulated. It's gone. You can rest.

The Stabilizer: Left Precentral Gyrus

Gifts	Torture
• Task execution (decision → action smoothly) • Sustained engagement (hours without crashing) • Inhibition of novelty-seeking (boring tasks stay on track) • ADHD gift: intensity + sustained attention • Embodied presence (grounded, physical) • Smooth state-shifting (rest ↔ action) • Deep sleep (restorative, wake refreshed) • Calm focus (still body, sustained attention)	• Task initiation paralysis (decision clear, body won't move) • Can't sustain engagement (brief effort then crash) • Vigilance for novelty won't turn off (every sound distracts) • ADHD paradox: hyperfocus on interesting, can't sustain on boring • Restlessness & fidgeting (can't sit still) • Poor sleep architecture (can't fall/stay asleep) • Stimulant dependence (borrowing engagement) • Stuck in gear or neutral (no smooth shifting)

3.4 The Neuroscience: The Gearbox of Your Dominant Body

Okay, let's get into the brain science. This is where we go from "I can't make myself do things" to "here's exactly which circuit is offline and why."

3.4.1 Where the Stabilizer Lives

The Stabilizer **anchors in your left sensorimotor strip** (the left precentral gyrus (primary motor cortex, M1) and left postcentral gyrus (somatosensory cortex, S1)) along with the supplementary motor area (SMA) just in front of M1. On a brain map this is the **left central region** over the top of your head, extending forward into medial frontal areas.

M1 initiates voluntary movement. S1 feeds it continuous sensory feedback. SMA is the motor preparation zone, it readies you to move before you move. Together they form the circuit that takes a decision from your frontal lobes and turns it into sustained physical action.

Under the Hood: Sensorimotor Architecture

M1 (primary motor cortex, Brodmann area 4): initiates and controls voluntary movements of the contralateral body. S1 (somatosensory cortex, Brodmann areas 3, 1, 2): first cortical stage for touch, proprioception, and body awareness, provides continuous feedback to M1. SMA (Brodmann area 6): motor planning, initiation, and bimanual coordination. When you can't start a task, SMA is typically part of the stuck system.

The integration loop: S1 feeds sensory data to M1; M1 executes movement; SMA prepares and sequences action. These three areas generate the sustained motor activity that keeps you doing a task even when it becomes boring or repetitive.

In your phenotype map:

- **Happy Little Kid** (left DLPFC): "This is interesting! Let's engage!" (approach motivation)
- **Grumpy Old Man** (right DLPFC): "Don't! Too much work!" (avoidance resistance)
- **CEO** (ACC): "Okay, reconciling… this is the priority. Decision made: Do this." (conflict resolution)
- **Stabilizer** (left sensorimotor): "Got it. Putting body into gear. Maintaining action. Turning off vigilance for novelty so we can focus on this boring thing." (motor execution + sustained engagement)

The procrastination cascade has two failure modes:

1. **CEO failure:** Can't reconcile approach vs. avoidance → stuck deciding → procrastination (see Chapter 5)
2. **Stabilizer failure:** CEO decides, but motor system won't execute → stuck initiating → procrastination (this chapter)

The Stabilizer is the one who actually keeps your body doing it, even when the task becomes boring, repetitive, or runs in the background. And the Stabilizer helps **turn off vigilance for novelty**, the distractibility that pulls you toward new, interesting things when you need to focus on the boring task in front of you.

3.4.2 "Frontal Slow" as the QEEG Signature

"Frontal Slow" is one of the most well-documented EEG phenotypes, excess slow-wave activity (theta/delta) in left motor and premotor cortex, with reduced fast-wave activity (beta). It is among the stronger physiological predictors of stimulant response in ADHD research (Arns et al., 2008; Chabot et al., 1999). And it is stable across time, not just a transient state.

One nuance worth flagging: "frontal theta" is not one thing. Midline frontal theta (generated by the anterior cingulate cortex, the CEO, Chapter 5) reflects error monitoring and conflict detection. Lateral and central theta is the Stabilizer's signature: under-activation of motor preparation. Both look like "too much slow activity" on a QEEG, but they arise from different generators. Midline theta that won't quiet down keeps you stuck re-checking decisions. Lateral theta that won't speed up keeps you stuck on the couch.

Under the Hood: Frontal Slow QEEG Metrics

On a brain map, Frontal Slow appears as: excess theta/delta in frontal regions (low-activation pattern); elevated theta/beta ratio (>4.0 is the typical clinical cutoff); left-sided dominance in motor/premotor areas. This is the most common QEEG signature in ADHD inattentive type. The midline frontal theta distinction (Cavanagh & Frank, 2014; Slater et al., 2022) matters clinically: lateral/central Frontal Slow responds to SMR/beta training; midline CEO theta responds to frontal midline regulation protocols. These are different circuits, different treatments.

Frontal Slow is the signature of "the engine that won't start."

When your left motor/premotor cortex is dominated by slow waves (theta/delta), you experience:

- Task initiation deficit ("I know what to do, can't make myself do it")
- Activation energy barrier (starting feels impossible)
- Motivation crashes (even when you want to do something)

- Sustained attention difficulty (can't maintain focus on boring tasks)
- Psychomotor slowing (your body feels heavy, sluggish)

This isn't laziness. It's a measurable brain pattern.

3.4.3 The Stabilizer as Gear Engagement + Cruise Control

Think of the Stabilizer as your body's gearbox and cruise control system.

Gear engagement (initiation):

Motor cortex takes "I should do X" from frontal decision systems and locks it into a motor set. You shift from "thinking about working out" to "actually working out." From intention to action.

Cruise control (maintenance):

Motor areas don't just fire once. They show sustained activity while a movement is being maintained. fMRI and ECoG work shows that precentral regions (and linked parietal areas) stay active while you're holding a posture, typing, walking, exercising.

This is the Stabilizer keeping you in gear: "I'll keep doing this because I said so."

Even when:

- The task is repetitive (typing, walking)
- The task is boring (paperwork, chores)
- The task is running in background (posture, breathing)

When the Stabilizer is offline (Frontal Slow):

You can't get into gear. The motor set won't lock in. You're stuck in neutral, revving the engine but not moving.

Or you get into gear briefly, then slip out. You start the task, then lose momentum. The sustained activity your motor cortex needs to maintain action. It's not there.

3.4.4 Visual vs Auditory Processing: Not All Attention Is Equal

Your Stabilizer's job is to activate and sustain attention. But attention isn't one thing, it has domains, modalities, subtypes. You might be strong in one and weak in another, and this matters for understanding your specific pattern.

Vigilance vs Focus:

- **Vigilance** is grabbing information when things *shift*: when the "1" pops up on the screen, when your name is called, when something changes
- **Focus** is grabbing information when it's *boring and repetitive*, when the "1" appears again and again, when you're reading dense text, when nothing changes for minutes

Auditory vs Visual: Some people lock in beautifully with auditory information (podcasts, conversations, lectures) but drift with visual information (reading, screens, watching). Others reverse.

What this means for you: If your vigilance is weak in the visual domain, you'll miss things as they fly by (exit signs on highways, quick changes on screens, facial expressions in conversation) then lock in a beat later. **Takes a moment. A little beat of time.** That's two standard deviations off the mean for vigilance, your brain's clearing a haze before it grabs the information.

Once you're locked in, you're fine. But shifting into gear is hard. The first moment of engagement has friction.

Real-world impact:

- Long road trips: You miss the exit, then realize it a moment later
- Reading: Information slides off the first pass, need to reread
- Conversations: Processing delay when topics shift quickly
- Screens: Visual information doesn't land immediately

Not "ADHD generally", specific, modality-dependent vigilance deficit.

Training: Neurofeedback can target this specifically. Left frontal beta increase, visual cortex regulation, theta suppression in sensorimotor areas. You're not training "attention generally", you're training vigilance in the visual domain.

Under the Hood: Why Stimulants Work (and Why They're Borrowed Activation)

The Frontal Slow phenotype is among the stronger physiological predictors of stimulant response in ADHD (Arns et al., 2008). Stimulants increase fast-wave activity (beta) in frontal regions, suppress slow-wave activity (theta), and normalize the theta/beta ratio, effectively "waking up" the Stabilizer. Effect size comparable to methylphenidate ($d \approx 0.5$). The catch: tolerance builds, sleep suffers, anxiety amplifies. You're borrowing tomorrow's activation today.

Genetic and neurochemical background: Reduced dopamine receptor availability affects achievement motivation and reward anticipation (Volkow et al., 2009). The activation sequence from decision centers to motor execution is disrupted, which explains the gap between "I decided to do this" and "I'm doing this" (Rubia et al., 2009). Sleep compounds the picture: children with ADHD show roughly 20% less slow-wave activity during sleep, a pattern present in both medicated and unmedicated children (Furrer et al., 2019). Stimulants address the waking theta problem without touching the sleep-side deficit.

3.4.5 SMR (Sensorimotor Rhythm): The Idle Gear

Sensorimotor rhythm (SMR) is the brain rhythm that appears over sensorimotor cortex when your body is still and your motor system is inhibited, the Stabilizer in "neutral gear." Not asleep. Not active. Idling, ready.

This matters for sleep: when the Stabilizer won't shift into neutral, you get hyperarousal insomnia. Can't downshift the body. Micro-movements, restlessness, light sleep, frequent arousals. The Stabilizer is stuck in gear when it should be idling.

SMR neurofeedback training teaches the Stabilizer to enter that still, gated state, which directly improves sleep onset, sleep spindle density, and slow-wave sleep quality. You're not just training attention; you're training the motor system to idle smoothly enough that sleep can emerge.

Under the Hood: SMR and Sleep Architecture

SMR training increases sleep spindle density (the brain rhythm of N2 sleep), N3 slow-wave sleep, subjective sleep quality, and reduces sleep onset latency (Lambert-Beaudet et al., 2021; Hoedlmoser et al., 2008). The mechanism: SMR reflects the same inhibitory gating pattern that underpins NREM sleep spindles. Training the sensorimotor cortex to generate this rhythm during wakefulness primes it to generate sleep spindles at night. Motor cortex activity drops during NREM (Wang et al., 2022); motor memory consolidation occurs during NREM replay (Ramanathan et al., 2015). The Stabilizer needs to fully power down for this process to run.

3.4.6 Sustained Attention and Tonic Alertness

The Stabilizer isn't the attention system (that's more CEO and Supervisor territory). But it's the **embodied half of sustained attention**, and it helps regulate what you pay attention to.

Tonic alertness (sustained over time) vs. **phasic alertness** (responding to specific stimuli). The Stabilizer provides the tonic component, the sustained embodied engagement that lets you maintain boring tasks.

Here's the critical piece most people miss: The Stabilizer also helps **turn OFF phasic alertness**, the vigilance for novelty and dynamic stimuli that constantly pulls your attention away from boring tasks.

When your Stabilizer is working:

- You can stay focused on repetitive tasks (typing, data entry, paperwork)
- Novel stimuli don't hijack your attention as easily
- You're not constantly scanning for "something more interesting"

- You can **inhibit the pull toward novelty** and maintain engagement with the non-dynamic task

When your Stabilizer is weak (Frontal Slow):

- Every new stimulus pulls your attention (sounds, movements, thoughts)
- You can't stay with boring tasks: you're scanning for novelty
- You need constant stimulation to maintain engagement
- **This looks exactly like ADHD inattentiveness**: not because you can't pay attention, but because you can't inhibit attention to novelty long enough to focus on boring things

The Stabilizer's job: **Sustain engagement on the boring thing. Inhibit distraction by the interesting thing.** When it's offline, everything novel becomes irresistible, not because you're impulsive, but because your system can't maintain the motor and attentional set needed to ignore it.

3.4.7 Distinguishing Frontal Slow from Slowed Alpha

Critical distinction:

Frontal Slow (theta/delta excess):

- ADHD signature
- Responds to stimulants
- Theta suppression/beta enhancement neurofeedback
- Task initiation deficit
- Left motor/premotor regions

Slowed Alpha Peak Frequency:

- COMT genotype variant
- Does NOT respond to stimulants (may worsen)
- Alpha peak frequency training needed
- Processing speed issue (not initiation)
- Global pattern (not just frontal)

Why this matters: If you have "ADHD-like" symptoms but stimulants don't help (or make you more anxious), you might have slowed alpha, not frontal slow. Different phenotype = different treatment. (See Chapter 12: The Fog for slowed alpha discussion.)

3.5 Toolkit Preview

Your Stabilizer is trainable, not with more stimulants, but with tools that build sustainable activation.

Movement first, motivation second: don't wait to feel like starting. Move your body and motivation follows. Design your mornings around a predictable activation sequence: light, movement, one winnable task. Same order, every day.

- **Sleep** (Ch 13): Stabilizer offline means restless body at night. Sleep is the Stabilizer's repair window, and sleep quality directly determines morning activation capacity.
- **Productivity** (Ch 16): motor activation strategies for task initiation built specifically for slow-start patterns.
- **Neurofeedback** (Ch 18): SMR and theta/beta training are among the most researched protocols for motor engagement and sleep quality. One of the few areas where the evidence base is deep.

Detailed protocols are in Part II. These circuits respond to training.

The sensorimotor circuits that create task-initiation paralysis are the same circuits that, once trained, produce smooth motor engagement and sustained focus. Part II shows you how to build that.

3.6 Key Takeaways

The Stabilizer (Sensorimotor Cortex/SMR) is your brain's motor engagement system, the circuit that executes decisions, sustains physical and mental activation, and inhibits distraction by novelty.

- **The two procrastination modes:** (1) CEO procrastination = stuck deciding between approach (Happy Little Kid) and avoidance (Grumpy Old Man); (2) Stabilizer procrastination = CEO decides, but motor system won't execute.
- **ADHD inattentiveness redefined:** Not inability to focus: inability to sustain focus on boring things while inhibiting attention to interesting things. Weak Stabilizer can't turn off phasic alertness (vigilance for novelty).
- **Tonic vs. phasic alertness:** Stabilizer provides tonic alertness (sustained engagement) and inhibits phasic alertness (vigilance for novelty). When weak: can't sustain boring tasks, interesting stimuli hijack attention.
- **Frontal Slow predicts stimulant response:** Excess theta/low beta in motor cortex (measurable QEEG pattern) is among the stronger physiological predictors of who responds to stimulants, but they're borrowed activation, not built capacity.
- **SMR = idle gear:** Sensorimotor rhythm training improves sleep (sleep spindles, deep sleep), task initiation (smooth gear engagement), and reduces restlessness (motor system learns to idle).

- **Not the same as Fog:** Stabilizer = motor engagement failure (can't start/sustain action, can't inhibit novelty). Fog (Chapter 12) = slowed processing speed (everything takes longer to compute). Different circuits, different treatments.

3.7 Reader Reflections

1. **Can you distinguish CEO procrastination from Stabilizer procrastination?** Stuck deciding (ping-ponging between options) or stuck executing (decision is clear but body won't move)?
2. **Do you recognize novelty hijacking attention?** Can you hyperfocus on interesting tasks but can't sustain boring ones?
3. **How's your sleep?** Restless at night? Wake unrefreshed? Trouble falling asleep?

Ch 4: The Supervisor (Right Pre/Postcentral Gyri)

The Golden Retriever or the Cat? Which One Are You?

It's 2am. You have a deadline tomorrow. But there's this new idea, podcasting. You don't have equipment. You've never podcasted. But right now, at 2am with 17 browser tabs open, this feels like THE thing.

4.1 "The Passenger-Seat Driver"

You know you should sleep. You know you should finish the project you started three weeks ago with such enthusiasm. But you can't stop yourself. Click. Another tab. Portuguese tiny house podcasting. You don't speak Portuguese. You don't own a tiny house. You've never podcasted.

Squirrel! New shiny thing. Must chase.

Or maybe you're the opposite. You're sitting at your desk, perfectly still. Not fidgeting. Not moving. Body calm. But you've been sitting here for forty minutes, unable to start, because you're monitoring: "Is this the right first sentence? Should I check my email first? Did I prepare enough? Maybe I should research more…"

Same problem. Different expression. Can't brake the impulse (click, chase, start new thing). Can't release the brake (second-guessing, perfectionism, paralysis by quality control).

This is the Supervisor, your right sensorimotor cortex, the passenger-seat driver. Its job: apply the brake, monitor quality, make micro-adjustments. "Slow down, there's a curve ahead." "Don't click that." "You've checked enough, just start."

When it's weak (excess theta, low SMR) you're all gas, no brake. Impulsive. Clicking, buying, starting new projects. Can't sustain attention. Novelty wears off, you drift to the next shiny thing.

When it's overactive (too much monitoring, too much inhibition) you're all brake, no gas. Perfectionism. Second-guessing. Can't start because you're quality-controlling things that don't need quality control yet.

Here's what I see on brain maps: **right sensorimotor strip dysregulation**. Either excess theta (brake offline, impulsivity) or excessive monitoring (brake won't release, paralysis).

The torture? Can't stop yourself from impulses you know are wrong. Or can't start because you're second-guessing everything. Commission errors (doing when you shouldn't) or omission errors (not doing when you should).

The gift? When it's balanced, the Supervisor is quality control and impulse regulation. You can resist impulses. You can pace yourself. You can sit still when needed. You can act when needed. You have a brake that works, not stuck on, not stuck off.

The challenge isn't to suppress all impulses or stop monitoring quality. It's to train the brake to work when you need it and release when you don't.

4.2 The Torture: When the Supervisor Is Too Weak (or Too Strong)

Let's talk about what it's actually like when your brake system is dysregulated.

4.2.1 When the Supervisor Is Too Weak: The Golden Retriever

Impulsivity: Can't Stop Yourself

You see something. You want it. You buy it. Before you can think about whether you actually need it, whether you can afford it, whether this is a good idea.

You have an idea. You start it. Before you can think about whether you have time, whether you'll finish it, whether this is the right priority.

Someone texts. You respond immediately. Before you can think about whether this is the right time, the right response, the right tone.

This is **impulsivity**, your Supervisor isn't braking. The gap between impulse and action is too short. You're all gas pedal, no brake (Aron et al., 2003; Aron et al., 2004).

Shiny Object Syndrome: The Graveyard of Unfinished Projects

You start projects with genuine enthusiasm. You research. You buy supplies. You work on it obsessively for three days, two weeks, maybe a month.

Then novelty wears off. And you drift to the next shiny thing.

This is the **golden retriever**, chasing every shiny object, bringing you gifts you didn't ask for, completely unaware that you're exhausted from keeping up.

Your Supervisor should be saying: "Finish this before starting the next one." But it's not. The brake isn't working. So you keep starting, keep abandoning, keep accumulating unfinished projects.

Can't Sustain Attention: Drifting Off Task

You're working on something. Five minutes in, you're checking your phone. Ten minutes in, you're on a different task. Fifteen minutes in, you've forgotten what you were originally doing.

This isn't ADHD inattention from the Stabilizer (Chapter 3, that's "can't start"). This is **can't sustain**, your Supervisor isn't maintaining inhibitory control over distractions.

The Stabilizer got you into gear. But the Supervisor isn't keeping you in the lane. You're drifting, swerving, chasing every distraction.

Commission Errors: Responding When You Shouldn't

On attention tests (CPT, Go/No-Go), you press the button when you shouldn't. You see a stimulus, you react, even though the rule says "don't respond to this one."

This is **commission errors**, responding when you should inhibit. Your Supervisor isn't braking fast enough. The impulse to respond beats the inhibition.

Fidgeting, Restlessness: Can't Sit Still

You're in a meeting. You're supposed to sit still. But your leg is bouncing. Your fingers are tapping. You're shifting in your seat. You can't stop moving.

This is the Supervisor failing to maintain motor stillness. The inhibitory tone that should keep your body quiet, it's not there.

4.2.2 When the Supervisor Is Too Strong: Perfectionism Paralysis

Second-Guessing: The Brake That Won't Release

You're about to send an email. You've read it seventeen times. You've edited it twelve times. It's fine. But you can't hit send.

"What if there's a typo? What if they misinterpret? What if this isn't perfect?"

Your Supervisor is over-braking. You can't pull the trigger because the quality control system won't give you the "all clear."

Perfectionism: Nothing Is Ever Good Enough

You finish a project. It's good. But your Supervisor says: "It could be better. Fix this. And this. And this."

You never finish because nothing meets your Supervisor's standards. The brake is so strong that you're stuck, stalling, unable to move forward.

Over-Inhibition: Can't Take Risks

You want to try something new. Your Supervisor immediately applies the brake: "What if you fail? What if you embarrass yourself? What if it's not perfect?"

So you don't try. Your Supervisor has decided that the risk of imperfection is too high. The brake won't release.

4.3 The Gift: When the Supervisor Works Right

Now let's talk about why you need your Supervisor, when it's balanced, not too weak or too strong.

4.3.1 Impulse Control: The Pause Button

When your Supervisor works, you have a pause button between impulse and action.

You want to buy something. Your Supervisor says: "Wait. Do you actually need this? Can you afford it?"

You want to send an angry text. Your Supervisor says: "Hold on. Is this the right response? Will you regret this?"

You want to start a new project. Your Supervisor says: "Finish the current one first."

This is **impulse control**, the ability to pause, think, choose consciously instead of reacting automatically.

4.3.2 Quality Control: Catching Errors Before They Ship

When your Supervisor works, you catch mistakes before they become problems.

You're about to send an email. Your Supervisor notices the typo. You fix it before hitting send.

You're making a decision. Your Supervisor flags: "Wait, we're missing information. Let's think this through."

You're executing a plan. Your Supervisor detects: "This isn't working. Adjust."

This is **quality control**, the ability to monitor your own performance and make corrections before disaster strikes.

4.3.3 Pacing: Knowing When to Slow Down

When your Supervisor works, you can pace yourself.

You're working too fast. Your Supervisor says: "Slow down. You're making mistakes."

You're about to burn out. Your Supervisor says: "Take a break. You need rest."

You're approaching a complex task. Your Supervisor says: "Ease up, there's a curve ahead."

This is **pacing**, the ability to modulate your speed and intensity based on the demands of the task.

4.3.4 The Cat on the Windowsill: Embodied Stillness

When your Supervisor works, you can be perfectly still.

Body quiet. Not fidgeting. Not restless. Just: calm, embodied presence.

Attention sharp. Monitoring. Ready. Patient.

This is the **cat on the windowsill**, high SMR, right sensorimotor engaged, inhibitory tone maintained. You can sit still without effort. You can wait without restlessness. You can be present without fidgeting.

This is the Supervisor's gift: embodied calm with sharp attention.

The goal isn't to silence the Supervisor, but to adjust its cadence: when and how often it checks in, so it doesn't interrupt every single move.

4.4 The Neuroscience: The Passenger-Seat Driver

Okay, let's get into the brain science. This is where we go from "I can't control my impulses" (or "I can't stop controlling") to "here's exactly which circuit is braking (or over-braking) and why."

4.4.1 Where the Supervisor Lives

The Supervisor **anchors in your right sensorimotor strip** (the right precentral gyrus (primary motor cortex, M1) and right postcentral gyrus (primary somatosensory cortex, S1)) but, like the Stabilizer (Chapter 3), uses wider motor networks including the **supplementary motor area (SMA)** that sits just anterior to M1.

On a QEEG cap, this is **C4, FC4, CP4**, the right central sites, with connections forward to medial frontal areas.

Primary motor cortex (M1, right):

- Primary motor control for the left body
- Ongoing control of movement, posture, pacing
- Makes micro-adjustments: grip, pressure, timing

Somatosensory cortex (S1, right):

- Primary somatosensory cortex for the left body
- Provides continuous feedback: "Are we on course? Do we need to adjust?"

Supplementary Motor Area (SMA, bilateral but right-weighted for inhibition):

- Just anterior to M1, crucial for motor planning and inhibitory control
- Part of the right-lateralized inhibitory network (with right IFG/Problem Child)
- Helps pause, adjust, and refine actions before they happen

The sensorimotor integration loop:

Just like the left side (Stabilizer, Chapter 3), the right M1 and S1 are tightly interconnected. But the right side has a special role in **inhibition and quality control**.

4.4.2 The Supervisor as Passenger-Seat Driver

If the Stabilizer (left) is the gearbox that keeps you moving, the Supervisor (right) is the passenger-seat driver riding shotgun in your body.

It doesn't decide where you're going (that's the CEO, Chapter 5). It doesn't provide the gas (that's the Stabilizer, Chapter 3). But it watches:

- The speed (are we going too fast?)
- The lane (are we drifting?)
- The feel of the car (is something off?)

And it says: "Ease up, there's a curve" or "You're drifting; correct a little."

In your phenotype map:

- **CEO** (ACC): "This is the priority. Do this."
- **Stabilizer** (left sensorimotor): "Got it. Putting body into gear."
- **Supervisor** (right sensorimotor): "Hold on, slow down, there's a turn ahead. Adjust."

The Supervisor is quality control, pacing, inhibitory tone.

4.4.3 Transcallosal Inhibition: The Lateral Brake

Here's where it gets interesting. The two sensorimotor strips (left and right) don't just work independently, they inhibit each other.

Transcallosal inhibition (TCI) (Ni et al., 2009):

The sensorimotor cortex can inhibit motor activity in the opposite hemisphere via connections through the corpus callosum. One motor strip can dampen the other to refine motor output.

What this means:

The Supervisor (right) can apply a brake to the Stabilizer (left). When you need to slow down, adjust, or stop, the right sensorimotor strip inhibits the left.

This is the lateral brake. The passenger-seat driver tapping the brake pedal.

When this system works: smooth, controlled action with micro-adjustments.

When it fails: either impulsivity (Supervisor can't brake Stabilizer) or paralysis (Supervisor over-braking Stabilizer).

In practice, this is why you can intend to stop something (eating, scrolling, interrupting) and still not stop. The decision is made. The Stabilizer acknowledges it. The Supervisor's brake just isn't firing hard enough.

4.4.4 Right-Hemisphere Inhibitory Networks

The Supervisor doesn't work alone. It's part of a **right-lateralized inhibitory network** (Loayza et al., 2022; Schaum et al., 2021):

The network includes:

- Right IFG (inferior frontal gyrus: the Problem Child's brake, Chapter 7)
- Right sensorimotor cortex (the Supervisor: body-level brake)
- Basal ganglia and subthalamic nucleus (subcortical brake)

How it works:

Right frontal areas (IFG) initiate the "stop" signal. This signal projects down through basal ganglia and into motor pathways, including right sensorimotor cortex. The Supervisor is where the brake meets the body. The CEO (anterior cingulate) can also modulate this brake directly: ACC has functional connections to supplementary motor area and primary motor cortex, giving it a rapid route to adjust inhibitory tone when conflict or errors are detected (Shibata et al., 2015; Takeuchi et al., 2011). When your CEO detects a looming mistake, it doesn't just update a mental priority list. It reaches into the motor system and adjusts the Supervisor's grip on the wheel.

When this network is hypoactive: You can't stop. Impulsivity. Commission errors. Fidgeting.

When this network is hyperactive: You can't start. Over-inhibition. Perfectionism paralysis.

4.4.5 Sustained Attention and Right-Lateralized Monitoring

The Supervisor is also part of sustained attention networks.

The research (Bonnelle et al., 2011; Huang et al., 2023; McMackin et al., 2020):

Sustained attention involves a **predominantly right-lateralized frontoparietal network**. During boring, sustained attention tasks (SART, CPT), right frontoparietal and sensorimotor regions show characteristic engagement when people successfully withhold responses and maintain performance.

What this means:

The Supervisor is monitoring: "Are we actually on the lane we think we're on?" It's making micro-adjustments to keep you on task, on course, on target.

When the Supervisor is engaged, you can sustain attention on boring tasks. When it fatigues, you drift off task, make commission errors, lose inhibitory control.

Time-on-task effects (Liu et al., 2020):

As you sustain attention over time, right sensorimotor connectivity decreases. Performance degrades. The Supervisor gets tired. Motivation can specifically restore right sensorimotor functional connectivity during inhibition, giving the Supervisor a second wind.

4.4.6 ADHD and the Weak Supervisor

In ADHD, the Supervisor is often weak.

The EEG pattern (Loo et al., 2012; Woltering et al., 2012; Lin et al., 2021):

Elevated theta/beta ratio at fronto-central and lateral sites, including motor regions. Too much slow (theta), not enough fast (beta/SMR). The Supervisor is underaroused, can't maintain inhibitory tone.

The behavioral pattern:

Impulsivity, hyperactivity, can't sustain attention, fidgeting, commission errors. This is the golden retriever, the Supervisor isn't braking.

The motor-inhibition link (Lin et al., 2021):

Theta/beta ratio fully mediates the relationship between motor competence and inhibition performance in ADHD children. Your motor strip theta directly predicts your ability to inhibit.

This is why: motor system = embodied inhibition. When your motor cortex is dominated by slow waves, you can't brake physically or cognitively.

4.4.7 SMR: The Cat on the Windowsill Rhythm

Sensorimotor rhythm (SMR) at C4 (right sensorimotor) is the Supervisor's optimal state.

What SMR looks like:

Body perfectly still. Motor system inhibited. Attention sharp. This is the cat on the windowsill, high SMR, low slow-wave activity, embodied calm with focused attention.

SMR training improves:

- **Impulse control** (Bluschke et al., 2016: theta/beta NF modulates response inhibition)
- **Selective attention** (Bouny et al., 2022: one SMR session improves Stroop performance)
- **Motor performance** (Gong et al., 2020; Afrash et al., 2023, SMR improves reaction time, motor learning in athletes)

Why this works: You're training the Supervisor to maintain inhibitory tone, body still, attention sharp, ready to brake when needed.

The Supervisor: Right Precentral Gyrus	
Gifts	**Torture**
• Quality control (catch mistakes before they happen) • Impulse control (think before acting) • Sustained attention (maintain focus) • Calm alertness (ready without being activated) • Appropriate inhibition (know when to brake/release) • Thoughtful action (intention, not impulse)	• Golden retriever (too weak): impulsive, chasing shiny objects • Cat on windowsill (too strong): overinhibited, perfection paralysis • Can't finish projects (start everything, finish nothing) • Say things you regret (blurt, interrupt, no filter) • Perfectionism paralysis (checking and rechecking) • Swinging extremes (impulsive then frozen)

4.5 Toolkit Preview

Your Supervisor is trainable, whether too weak (impulsivity) or too strong (perfectionism).

For impulsivity: pause practice, three breaths before acting on the impulse. For perfectionism: time-limit practice, when the clock runs out, it ships. The goal is balance, not more braking.

- **Productivity** (Ch 16): task management strategies address both impulsive project-chasing and perfectionist paralysis.
- **Meditation** (Ch 17): body stillness practices for the golden retriever; letting-go practice for the frozen cat.

- **Neurofeedback** (Ch 18): SMR training in the right sensorimotor region builds the flexible brake, knowing when to apply it and when to release.

Detailed protocols are in Part II. These circuits respond to training.

The sensorimotor circuits that create impulsivity or perfectionism paralysis are the same circuits that, once trained, produce flexible quality control, knowing when to brake and when to release. Part II shows you how to build that.

4.6 Key Takeaways

The Supervisor (Sensorimotor Rhythm System) is your brain's quality control and inhibition system, the circuit that says "wait, check this first" and prevents impulsive action.

- **Bidirectional dysregulation:** Too weak = golden retriever (impulsive, interrupting, acting before thinking). Too strong = frozen cat (overinhibited, can't act, perfectionism paralysis). Both are Supervisor problems.
- **SMR = calm sustained attention:** "Cat on windowsill" state, alert but not impulsive, engaged but not restless. Different from Stabilizer's SMR (motor engagement/sleep).
- **ADHD presents both ways:** Classic ADHD = weak Supervisor (can't brake). Some "ADHD" presentations = overactive Supervisor (can't release brake to act). Same diagnosis, opposite circuit problems.
- **Stimulant paradox:** Strengthens weak Supervisor (golden retriever gets leash) but can overactivate an already-strong Supervisor (frozen cat gets more frozen).
- **Training:** SMR/low beta neurofeedback: knowing when to apply the brake versus when to release it.

4.7 Reader Reflections

1. **Are you a golden retriever or a cat on the windowsill?** Act impulsively (weak Supervisor), overthink and can't act (overactive), or swing between both?
2. **What does your imbalance look like?** Interrupting? Buying without thinking? Or paralyzed by perfectionism?
3. **When does your internal editor show up too early, and when does it arrive just in time?**

Systems Interlude: The Orienting System

Midline Cingulate: Internal vs. External Focus

Location: Anterior cingulate (midline front) + Posterior cingulate (midline back)
Phenotypes: CEO (Chapter 5) + Lifeguard (Chapter 6)
System function: Conflict detection and task switching (anterior) vs. environmental scanning and context integration (posterior)

Key insight: The midline axis determines where your attention points, inward toward conflicts and decisions (anterior), or outward toward the environment and context (posterior). Front asks "what should I do?", back asks "what's happening?"

What This System Does When Balanced

Your Orienting System directs your attention between internal and external worlds. When it's balanced:

- You can focus on what matters and ignore what doesn't (CEO working)
- You can switch between tasks cleanly without getting stuck (CEO flexible)
- You can let go of conflicts that don't need resolving (CEO releases)
- You notice changes in your environment without threat sensitivity (Lifeguard working)
- You integrate past context with present moment (Lifeguard contextualizing)

This is the **Salience Network (SN) plus Default Mode Network (DMN)** in action, your CEO switches between internal reflection (Lifeguard) and external tasks, while your Lifeguard provides context and monitors environment.

What Dysregulation Looks Like

CEO stuck (anterior cingulate hyperactive):
Perseveration, rumination, OCD-like loops, can't let go of conflicts, stuck on wrong thing, procrastination from unresolved "should vs. don't want to"

CEO weak (anterior cingulate underactive):
Can't sustain attention, easily hijacked by distractions, no conflict monitoring, impulsive

Lifeguard hyperactive (posterior cingulate overactive):
Hypervigilance, constant environmental scanning, rumination (replaying past events), can't turn off threat-monitoring, social exhaustion from monitoring everyone

Lifeguard offline (posterior cingulate underactive):
Dissociation, disconnection from environment, not integrated with context, "there but not there"

Both dysregulated:
Stuck in loops (CEO hyperactive) AND hypervigilant scanning (Lifeguard hyperactive) = ruminating about threats while constantly monitoring for new ones. This is the "anxious ruminator" pattern.

How This Connects to Other Systems

The Orienting System detects *what* needs attention; other systems execute:

- **Attention System (Ch 3-4):** Implements CEO's decisions
- **Motivation System (Ch 1-2):** Provides approach / avoid drive

CEO (switchboard) detects conflicts and directs attention. Lifeguard monitors context and provides backdrop for decisions.

Network Connection

The CEO (SN hub) and Lifeguard (DMN hub) work together to switch between internal and external focus. When dysregulated, the CEO can't switch cleanly, and the Lifeguard either intrudes during tasks (rumination) or goes offline when resting (dissociation).

Think of Lifeguard and Princess & Pea as your threat-detection cadence: how frequently your brain scans for danger and how long it keeps the alarms ringing.

Map so far: 4 of 12. You've met the motivational engine (HLK + GOM) and the motor axis (Stabilizer + Supervisor). Up next: The CEO and The Lifeguard, how your brain decides what matters and keeps watch over the world. Front midline meets back midline: inside-self vs. outside-world.

Ch 5: The CEO (Anterior Cingulate)

Stuck on the Wrong Thing (And You Know It)

There's a song playing in your head. Has been for three hours. Not even a good song. Just the same eight bars, on loop. You can't stop it. You try thinking about something else. The song returns in ten seconds.

5.1 "Stuck on the Wrong Thing"

Or maybe it's a thought: "Did I say the wrong thing in that meeting?" You've replayed the conversation a dozen times. Analyzed every word. Nothing changes. But your brain won't let it go.

Or it's a motor tic: blinking. Blinking again. You know you're doing it. You try to stop. Five seconds later, blink, blink, blink. It's like your brain has decided "we're blinking now" and won't take other input.

This is the CEO (your anterior cingulate cortex, your brain's task-switcher and conflict monitor) gone tyrant. When it's working, it flexibly selects what you attend to, switches when needed, stays when needed. When it's stuck, it picks something (a song, a thought, a tic, an internal conflict) and **won't let go.**

Here's what I see on brain maps: hyperactivity at the frontal midline. Excess theta. High beta. A brain region that should be flexibly switching between tasks, but instead it's locked on. Stuck.

The person sitting across from me says: "I can't stop thinking about that email. I've been thinking about it for three hours. Not writing it, thinking about it. 'Should I send it? What will they think? Is it the right tone?' It's not even important. I have a deadline. But my brain has decided *this internal conflict* is the priority."

Someone interrupts you. You snap. Not because they're wrong, because your CEO was finally settled on something, and now it has to re-orient, re-prioritize, start over. Interruptions feel like violence when your CEO is sticky.

Here's the counterintuitive part: the CEO isn't supposed to be this rigid. It's supposed to be your brain's flexible switchboard. But when it's hyperactive (excess theta, high beta on that frontal midline) it becomes a tyrant. It doesn't just get stuck. **It micromanages.** "Think of this, think of this, hey think of this, think of this." It latches onto the same information again and again, unable to delegate or release.

I see this in QEEG all the time. Anterior cingulate hyperactivation. The person comes in saying "I can't stop perseverating on things that don't matter." And I'm looking at their brain map thinking, "Yeah, your CEO is screaming at full volume and nobody else can get a word in."

The torture? Perseveration. Getting stuck on internal conflicts, obsessive thoughts, earworms, tics. Irritability when interrupted. OCD-like loops. Can't let go even when you know you should. Your brain picks something and makes it the entire world. What's off here is often sequencing cadence: how quickly CEO can switch tasks, update priorities, and release from a loop.

The gift? When it's working right, the CEO is your executive attention, selecting what you attend to internally. It keeps you on rails. It monitors for what matters. It switches when needed and stays when needed. Sustained focus without stuckness.

Cannabis quiets the CEO. "I can finally be present." But it also kills your motivation and task-switching. Turns out you need *some* CEO to get shit done, just not a tyrant.

The work? Train cognitive flexibility (neurofeedback), practice letting go (meditation), and learn when to listen to your CEO and when to tell it to shut up.

5.2 The Torture: When the CEO Gets Stuck

Let's talk about what it's actually like when your brain's project manager can't let go.

5.2.1 Sticky Attention: Locked on the Wrong Priority

You know you should be working on the important thing. The deadline. The project that actually matters. But your brain has decided that *this other thing* is the priority.

Maybe it's a minor slight from three days ago. Maybe it's a typo in an email. Maybe it's a problem that's already solved but your brain keeps re-solving it. Maybe it's just... nothing. Nothing important. But your CEO has locked onto it and won't let go.

This is **sticky attention**, your anterior cingulate has decided this is what matters right now, and it won't switch. You're stuck.

The frustrating part? You know it's the wrong priority. You can see the important work sitting there, waiting. But your CEO won't release you. It keeps pulling your attention back to the thing that doesn't matter.

This isn't ADHD (that's the Supervisor, Chapter 4: can't sustain attention). This is the opposite: you're sustaining attention on the *wrong* thing and you can't switch.

5.2.2 Inflexibility and Meltdowns: When Expectations Change

Here's where the CEO's stickiness shows up most clearly in kids (and adults who still have this pattern):

You had a plan. You were expecting X. Then X changes to Y.

And you melt down.

Not because Y is bad. Not because you can't handle change in general. But because your CEO was locked onto X, and now it has to switch to Y, and the switching cost is too high.

Examples:

- Kid expects McDonald's, you go to Burger King instead → meltdown
- Adult expects meeting at 2pm, it gets moved to 3pm → disproportionate distress
- Routine changes unexpectedly → can't cope

This is **cognitive inflexibility**, your CEO can't switch when expectations change. It was holding "X is the plan" and now it has to rebuild the entire stack for Y. The switching cost feels overwhelming.

This is why autistic kids (and adults) need routines, predictability, advance warning of changes. It's not that they're "rigid", their CEO has a high switching cost. Unexpected changes require cognitive flexibility their ACC can't generate in the moment.

And when the CEO can't switch? Meltdown. Shutdown. Overwhelm. Not because they're being difficult, because the switching cost exceeded their capacity.

5.2.3 Irritability When Interrupted: Violence Against Your Focus

Someone interrupts you. A reasonable interruption. A question. A request. Something that should take 30 seconds.

And you snap.

Not because they're wrong. Not because you're busy. But because your CEO was finally settled on something, and now it has to re-orient, re-prioritize, start over.

Interruptions feel like violence when your CEO is sticky.

Your brain was holding a complex stack of information, what you're working on, why it matters, what comes next. The interruption dumps the stack. Now you have to rebuild it. And your CEO is furious.

This is why people with sticky CEOs:

- Work alone (can't tolerate interruptions)
- Get angry at reasonable questions (the interruption cost is too high)
- Need long uninterrupted blocks (can't context-switch efficiently)
- Seem "intense" or "unapproachable" (protecting their focus)

You're not being difficult. Your CEO just has a high switching cost.

5.2.4 Earworms and Mental Loops: Can't Stop the Song

There's a song. Playing. On loop. For hours.

Not even the whole song, just a fragment. Eight bars. A chorus. Maybe just "na na na na na" from some commercial jingle you don't even like.

You try thinking about something else. It works for ten seconds. Then the song returns.

You try singing a different song. That lasts maybe thirty seconds. The original song comes back.

This is an **earworm** (involuntary musical imagery) and it's your CEO stuck on an auditory pattern (Beaman & Williams, 2010). Your anterior cingulate has flagged this sound fragment as "incomplete" and won't discharge it. So it keeps looping, trying to resolve something that has no resolution.

Or it's a phrase: "Don't forget to..." repeating. Or counting: "1, 2, 3, 1, 2, 3..." Or a prayer or mantra you can't stop.

These are **simple mental loops**, repetitive cognitive patterns your CEO can't release. They're not meaningful. They're not useful. They're just... stuck. Your brain is stuck hitting "refresh" on the same micro-pattern.

The frustration: You know it's meaningless. You know you should stop. But your CEO won't let go. The song/phrase/count has become the entire focus of your attention, and no amount of conscious effort releases it.

The neuroscience behind this (chronic frontal midline theta, the mechanism behind earworms, tics, and simple rituals) is in the "Theta-Stuck CEO" section below.

5.2.5 Motor Tics and Repetitive Movements: Can't Stop Blinking

Blink. Blink again. You know you're doing it. You try to stop.

Five seconds later: blink, blink, blink.

Or it's throat clearing. Shoulder shrugging. Nose scrunching. A specific hand movement. Nail biting. Skin picking.

These are motor loops, repetitive movements your CEO can't discharge. Your anterior cingulate has flagged something as "incomplete" in the motor planning system, and it keeps sending the signal to repeat the movement.

You're aware of it (unlike unconscious habits). You can suppress it temporarily (unlike fully involuntary movements). But it comes back. The urge builds. And eventually, you do it again.

This is your CEO stuck on a motor pattern. It's the same stuckness mechanism as earworms, just expressed through movement instead of thought.

In tic disorders (Tourette's, chronic tic disorder): The ACC shows abnormal recruitment during inhibition tasks. Your CEO is supposed to help you inhibit unwanted movements. But when it's stuck, it can't release the "do this movement" signal. So the tic repeats.

The frustration: You know you're doing it. You know it's not serving a purpose. But your CEO won't let go of the motor script. The movement becomes compulsory, not because you want to do it, but because your CEO has made it the priority.

The full neuroscience of tics and motor loops (frontal control network dysregulation, conflict signals that won't clear) is in the "Theta-Stuck CEO" section below.

5.2.6 Can't Let Go of Slights: Perseveration on Internal Conflicts

Someone said something three weeks ago. It wasn't even that bad. Maybe it was criticism. Maybe it was just a tone. Maybe you're not even sure what it was.

But you can't let it go.

Not replaying the event itself (that's the Lifeguard, Chapter 6). But perseverating on the **internal conflict** it created: "Should I be mad? Should I say something? Did I handle it wrong? What should I do about this?" You can't stop cycling through your internal response to the event.

This is the CEO stuck on **unresolved internal conflict**. Your anterior cingulate's job is to monitor for conflicts and signal when something needs resolving. But when it's hyperactive, it flags conflicts that don't need resolving and won't let go until they're "fixed."

The problem: some conflicts can't be fixed. Some slights don't have resolution. Some problems don't have solutions. But your CEO doesn't accept that. It keeps the conflict flag raised, keeps your attention locked on the internal question, keeps you stuck on "what should I do about this?"

And it gets worse: Your CEO can ping-pong with your Lifeguard. The Lifeguard replays the external event: *what did they say, what did they mean?* The CEO perseverates on the internal response: *should I be upset, what should I do?* Together they create resonant anxiety, front of brain stuck on self, back of brain stuck on world, both amplifying each other.

5.2.7 The Two Types of Stuck: Simple vs. Narrative

The CEO can get stuck in two different ways: **simple loops** (songs stuck in your head, counting, tapping, skin picking) or **narrative loops** (complex "what if" storylines, moral contamination scenarios, elaborate checking stories with branching possibilities). Simple loops are repetitive patterns that won't discharge. Narrative loops are elaborated stories your brain can't drop. The distinction matters because the interventions differ, we'll get to that.

5.3 The Gift: When the CEO Works Right

Now let's talk about why you need your CEO, when it's working right, not stuck.

5.3.1 Conflict Monitoring: Knowing When Something's Wrong

Your CEO's primary job is **conflict monitoring**, detecting when there's a mismatch between what you're doing and what you should be doing (van Veen & Carter, 2002).

You're about to send an angry email. Your CEO flags it: "Wait, is this the right move?"

You're making a decision based on emotion. Your CEO notices: "Hold on, we're not thinking clearly."

You're about to walk into a situation unprepared. Your CEO alerts: "We need to adjust."

This is the **error-detection system**, the "uh, that wasn't right" signal. When it's working properly, it keeps you from making mistakes, helps you course-correct, alerts you when something needs attention.

People with weak CEOs miss these signals. They make impulsive decisions without noticing the conflict. They don't catch errors until it's too late.

People with strong (but not stuck) CEOs catch problems early. They notice when they're off-track. They adjust before disaster strikes.

5.3.2 Task-Switching: Knowing When to Let Go

Your CEO is supposed to be your **task-switcher**, the system that decides when to stay focused and when to shift.

The important meeting ends. Your CEO says: "Okay, that's done. Next priority."

You finish a task. Your CEO releases it: "Complete. Move on."

Someone interrupts with something urgent. Your CEO assesses: "Yes, this is more important. Switch."

When your CEO works right, you can:

- Let go of completed tasks (not ruminating after they're done)
- Switch when needed (respond to changing priorities)
- Stay when needed (not distracted by every interruption)
- Prioritize effectively (what matters most right now?)

This is **cognitive flexibility**, the ability to shift mental sets when the situation changes. It's essential for adaptive behavior.

5.3.3 Executive Attention: Holding What Matters

Your CEO's other job is **executive attention**, holding the current priority in working memory so you stay on track.

You're working on a complex project. Your CEO holds: "This is what we're doing. This is why it matters. This is what comes next."

Someone asks you a question. Your CEO maintains: "We're still working on the project. Answer the question, then return."

You get distracted. Your CEO reminds: "No, we're doing this, not that."

When your CEO works right, you have:

- Focus (staying on the current priority)
- Coherence (actions aligned with goals)
- Persistence (not abandoning tasks prematurely)
- Direction (knowing what you're doing and why)

People with weak CEOs lose track. They forget what they were doing. They get derailed by distractions. They can't hold priorities in mind.

People with strong CEOs stay on rails. They know what matters. They execute coherently.

5.3.4 The Balance: Flexible Focus

The gift of a healthy CEO is **flexible focus**:

- Strong enough to maintain priorities (not scattered)
- Flexible enough to switch when needed (not stuck)
- Sensitive enough to detect errors (not oblivious)
- Calm enough to let go of resolved conflicts (not ruminating)

This is the sweet spot. Your CEO is online, engaged, monitoring, but not tyrannical.

You have a steel trap mind. When regulated, that's a gift, deep focus, relentless pursuit of understanding, catching details others miss. But when you're using that steel trap through fatigue, through stress, through depletion, **it cramps. And now you can't unstick it.** The muscle that should open when you decide to open it instead stays clenched. Same resource, but it's controlling you instead of you controlling it.

5.4 The Neuroscience: The Anterior Cingulate as Reconciler

Okay, let's get into the brain science. This is where we go from "I can't stop thinking about this" to "here's exactly which circuit is stuck and why."

5.4.1 Where the CEO Lives

The CEO lives in your **anterior cingulate cortex (ACC)**, a strip of cortex that runs along the midline of your brain, behind your forehead, connecting the two hemispheres.

On a brain map, this is the **frontal midline**, the strip running down the center of your forehead region.

The ACC sits at a crucial intersection:

- **Behind it:** Sensory cortex (the outside world, what's happening)
- **In front of it:** Prefrontal cortex (the Happy Little Kid, the Grumpy Old Man, executive control)
- **Below it:** Limbic system (emotions, motivation, threat response)

The ACC's job is to reconcile all of this: "Given what's happening in the world, given what I'm feeling, given my competing goals, what should I do right now?"

5.4.2 The ACC's Three Jobs

1. Conflict monitoring (Yeung & Cohen, 2006; van Veen & Carter, 2002):

The ACC fires when there's conflict between competing responses or goals. Stroop task (word says "red" but ink is blue). Flanker task (arrows pointing different directions). Errors. Near-errors. Competing desires.

The ACC doesn't *resolve* the conflict, it detects it and pings lateral prefrontal cortex: "Hey, we have a problem here. Need more control."

2. Error detection (Swick & Turken, 2002):

The ACC generates the "uh, that wasn't right" signal. You make a mistake and immediately know it, that's your ACC. The error-related negativity (ERN) in EEG research is generated by the ACC.

This is useful, it helps you course-correct. But when it's overactive, you get false alarms. Your CEO flags "errors" that aren't errors. It keeps the error signal raised even after you've corrected.

3. Affective salience (ventral/rostral ACC):

The more ventral (lower) parts of ACC process emotional significance: "How bad/good is this for me right now?" Pain, social pain, emotional conflict, the ACC tracks how much you should care.

This is why the ACC is involved in both cognitive control AND emotional pain. It's monitoring: "What matters? What's the priority? How much should I care about this?"

5.4.3 The CEO in the Triple Network Model

Here's how your CEO fits into the bigger picture:

The anterior cingulate (along with the anterior insula) is a core node of the **Salience Network (SN)**, the switchboard between your internal narrator (DMN/Lifeguard) and task mode (CEN/frontal and motor circuits). The CEO is the core node of SN, with contributions from Princess & Pea (social salience) and Problem Child (reactive braking). (See Part I Overview for the full Triple Network Model.)

What the Salience Network does:

- Detects what's important (internal and external)
- Decides what deserves attention
- **Switches between DMN and CEN**: "Should we be in task mode or rest mode?"
- Integrates emotion, interoception, and cognitive demands

When your CEO (SN node) works right:

- You notice what matters
- You switch cleanly between internal reflection (DMN/Lifeguard in the Back neighborhood) and external tasks (CEN/front and motor circuits)
- You prioritize effectively
- You let go of what doesn't matter

When your CEO is dysregulated:

- **Hyperactive SN:** Everything feels urgent, can't filter what matters, stuck flagging conflicts that don't need resolving
- **Poor switching:** Can't transition from DMN (internal/Lifeguard) to CEN (task mode/front and Axis), or vice versa
- **Sticky salience:** Things that shouldn't matter feel critically important, can't let go

This isn't just my model. This is Menon's triple network model (2011), replicated across anxiety, depression, ADHD, OCD, autism, schizophrenia. Your CEO dysregulation is a salience network problem, replicated in study after study across every major diagnostic category (Seeley et al., 2007; Sridharan et al., 2008; Bolton et al., 2020).

How this connects to the framework:

Your CEO lives in the **Front neighborhood** and sits at the core of the **Executive Control System** (paired with the Problem Child). It's the switchboard between your Back neighborhood (Lifeguard/DMN, environmental context) and your Front + Axis neighborhoods (CEN, task execution). When your CEO is stuck, the whole orchestra loses its conductor.

5.4.4 Frontal Midline Theta: The CEO's Control Signal

Here's where it gets really interesting.

When your CEO is working (engaging cognitive control, holding information in mind, resolving conflict, adjusting behavior), it generates a specific brain rhythm: **frontal midline theta (fm-theta)**.

Slow theta waves from the ACC/medial frontal region. This is the CEO's control signal.

Frontal midline theta (fm-theta) bursts up when you engage cognitive control, detect conflict, make errors, or need to adjust behavior. In a healthy system, it is **phasic**, it comes online when needed ("ping! adjust"), then goes offline when the conflict is resolved. In a dysregulated system, theta becomes **tonic**, a constant background hum of unresolved conflict. The CEO never gets the "all clear" signal. So it keeps looping.

Under the Hood: Frontal Midline Theta Research

Multiple EEG/MEG studies treat fm-theta as the canonical cognitive control rhythm of the ACC, the signal by which the CEO coordinates other regions to focus, inhibit, or switch (Cavanagh & Frank, 2014; Cavanagh & Shackman, 2015; Womelsdorf et al., 2010; Töllner et al., 2017; Eisma et al., 2021). Enhanced resting-state fm-theta is consistently observed in high-anxiety and OCD populations, suggesting that "tonic" theta (loop-stuck) reflects a failure of normal phasic discharge rather than a fundamentally different mechanism.

5.4.5 Theta-Stuck CEO: Simple Loops, Tics, Rituals

When theta becomes chronic at the frontal midline, you get **simple repetitive loops**:

Mental loops: Songs stuck in your head (earworms), phrases repeating, counting, praying in a fixed way, simple obsessive thoughts.

Motor loops: Nail biting, skin picking, tapping, touching, arranging, tics (Tourette's, chronic tic disorder), simple checking rituals.

What's happening: Your CEO is stuck in a theta mode. It can't discharge the "incomplete" signal. So your brain runs little scripts (songs, movements, rituals) trying to clear the conflict flag. But it never clears. So the loop continues.

This is the **Looping CEO**, stuck hitting "refresh" on the same micro-pattern.

5.4.6 Beta-Stuck CEO: Intrusive Narratives, Complex Obsessions

When **beta activity** in the rostral (forward) ACC becomes pathologically elevated, you get something different: not simple loops, but elaborated obsessions, your inner narrator becomes hostage to the error signal.

What's happening: Beta in midline frontal networks is tied to sustained top-down control and active thinking. When it locks in, the ACC isn't just flagging conflict, it's holding and elaborating it.

This creates: Complex "what if" storylines (branching narratives, not simple loops), moral contamination scenarios, intrusive thoughts with plots and consequences, obsessive narratives you cannot drop.

This is the **Intrusive Narrator**, still the CEO, but now flooded with unresolved high-stakes scenarios it won't release.

The key distinction:

- **Theta-stuck:** Simple, repetitive (song, tic, ritual)
- **Beta-stuck:** Complex, narrative (intrusive story, elaborate obsession)

Both are the CEO stuck. But the frequency pattern tells you which type of stuck, and which neurofeedback protocol targets it.

Under the Hood: EEG Research Behind the Two Stuck Types

Theta-stuck: In OCD and high-anxiety populations, researchers observe enhanced resting midfrontal theta and abnormal conflict-related theta responses, linked to intrusive thoughts and compulsive checking (Zaboski et al., 2021). In tic disorders and Tourette's, abnormal frontal inhibitory network recruitment during inhibition tasks (Peterson et al., 1998; Kawohl et al., 2009; Abi-Jaoude et al., 2022).

Beta-stuck: A neurofeedback study in OCD inpatients found that higher pretreatment beta power in rostral ACC was linked to greater symptom severity; training that reduced pathological beta was associated with clinical improvement (Kopřivová et al., 2013). Beta in midline frontal networks reflects sustained top-down control, when locked in, it amplifies and elaborates the conflict signal rather than resolving it.

5.4.7 The CEO as Reconciler: Arbitrating Between Characters

Here's how the CEO fits into your internal cast of characters:

The back of your brain (sensory cortex): The outside world. What's happening. The environment.

The front midline (ACC): The inside-self meaning. What am I doing? Was that a mistake? How much do I care? Which competing goal wins?

The CEO sits between:

- **Happy Little Kid** (left frontal: BAS/approach): "This is interesting! Let's engage!"
- **Grumpy Old Man** (right frontal: BIS/avoidance): "This is dangerous! Avoid!"

The CEO's job is to arbitrate: "Okay, Happy Little Kid wants to explore. Grumpy Old Man is worried. Given the current context, which voice should I amplify?"

When your CEO works right, you get balanced decision-making. When it's stuck, one voice dominates and you can't switch. When it's offline, you have no arbitrator, the characters just fight, and you can't decide. This is often what **procrastination** is: your CEO failing to reconcile approach and avoidance. Happy Little Kid says "let's try!" Grumpy Old Man says "don't try!" CEO can't decide. So you do neither. You're paralyzed. (See Chapter 16 for procrastination patterns.)

5.4.8 ACC vs. PCC: Front = Self, Back = World

Here's a crucial distinction between two midline structures, and a fundamental principle of brain organization:

Front of brain = INSIDE / SELF

Back of brain = OUTSIDE / WORLD

ACC (Anterior Cingulate - CEO):

- **Location:** Front midline = SELF territory
- **Focus:** Internal: "What am I doing? How do I feel? What's my priority?"
- **When stuck:** PERSEVERATION: can't let go of internal conflicts
- **Torture:** "Should I be mad about this? What should I do? Can't decide!"
- **NOT rumination** (that's Lifeguard): but perseveration on internal response

PCC (Posterior Cingulate - Lifeguard, Chapter 6):

- **Location:** Back midline = WORLD territory
- **Focus:** External: "What's happening out there? What's the context? What's the threat?"
- **When stuck:** RUMINATION: replaying past external events
- **Torture:** "What happened? What did they mean? Replaying the interaction!"
- **NOT internal conflict**: but environmental replay and scanning

The ping-pong (resonant anxiety):

When both are stuck, they amplify each other:

- **Lifeguard (back):** Replays external event: "what did they say?"
- **CEO (front):** Perseverates on internal response: "should I be upset? what should I do?"
- **Lifeguard:** "Did you hear that?!"
- **CEO:** "I heard! Should I worry?!"
- **Lifeguard:** "I'm worrying!"
- **CEO:** "Me too! What should we do?!"

Front and back playing ping-pong. Self and world in resonant anxiety loop. Neither can discharge. Both amplify each other.

In kids: The PCC can serve some ACC roles developmentally. This is why you see both internal inflexibility (CEO) and external threat sensitivity (Lifeguard) in neurodivergent kids. The systems are still differentiating.

In adults: The distinction is clearer. ACC = internal/self-focused perseveration. PCC = external/environment-focused rumination. But they can still trigger each other.

Both respond to neurofeedback. We'll cover PCC/Lifeguard in Chapter 6.

The CEO: Anterior Cingulate

Gifts	Torture
• Executive attention (hold priorities, stay on track) • Conflict detection (notice competing goals) • Error detection (catch mistakes early) • Cognitive flexibility (switch when needed) • Sustained focus (complex tasks without abandoning) • Coherent action (behavior aligned with goals)	• Sticky attention (locked on wrong thing) • Interruption violence (snap when interrupted) • Inflexibility (meltdown when plans change) • Can't let go of slights (perseverate on internal conflicts) • OCD-like loops (intrusive thoughts, compulsions, rituals) • Perfectionism paralysis (stuck refining details) • Ping-pong with Lifeguard (resonant anxiety)

5.5 Toolkit Preview

Your CEO is trainable. You need conflict monitoring, just not stuck loops. If cannabis, alcohol, or rituals have been your release valve, you've been quieting the CEO temporarily. Chapter 14 explains the pattern.

When a loop starts, try the external pattern-break: stand up, change rooms, set a timer, name the loop out loud. "This is my CEO stuck, not a real problem that needs solving right now." Interrupting the loop from the outside is faster than reasoning your way through it from the inside.

- **Meditation** (Ch 17): open awareness and noting practice train the CEO to observe without locking on.
- **Stress Response Regulation** (Ch 15): nervous system downregulation reduces the background threat load that feeds loops.
- **Neurofeedback** (Ch 18): frontal midline training: protocol depends on whether your CEO runs theta-stuck (simple loops, tics) or beta-stuck (intrusive narratives). QEEG-guided.

Detailed protocols are in Part II. These circuits respond to training.

The anterior cingulate circuits that create stuck loops and intrusive narratives are the same circuits that, once trained, produce flexible conflict monitoring, flag, resolve, release. Part II shows you how to build that.

5.6 Key Takeaways

The CEO (Anterior Cingulate) is your brain's task-switcher and conflict monitor, arbitrating between competing priorities, including Happy Little Kid's approach and Grumpy Old Man's avoidance.

- **Front = Self, Back = World:** CEO (front midline) perseverates on INTERNAL conflicts ("should I be mad?"), while Lifeguard (back midline, Ch 6) ruminates on EXTERNAL events ("what happened?").
- **The ping-pong with Lifeguard:** When both stuck, they amplify each other, Lifeguard replays event, CEO perseverates on response, creating resonant anxiety between front and back.
- **Procrastination as CEO failure:** Can't reconcile "try!" with "don't!" = paralysis (see Ch 16). Stabilizer (Ch 3) handles the second mode: CEO decides, but motor system won't execute.
- **Sticky attention ≠ good focus:** CEO hyperactivation looks like focus but is actually inflexibility, perseveration on wrong priorities, interruptions feel like violence.

- **Cannabis targets the CEO:** Quiets frontal midline theta and conflict monitoring ("finally present"), but also reduces motivation and task completion (Stabilizer impact).
- **Training flexibility, not elimination:** Frontal midline theta regulation, open awareness meditation, NAC (N-acetylcysteine) supplementation. The goal: CEO can switch and let go, not just monitor.

5.7 Reader Reflections

1. **What does your CEO get stuck on most often?** Can you distinguish internal perseveration (CEO) from external rumination (Lifeguard)?
2. **How do interruptions feel?** Like violence? Like your whole mental stack dumped?
3. **Do you recognize inflexibility around expectations?** Think about when plans changed unexpectedly, did you melt down?

Ch 6: The Lifeguard (Posterior Cingulate)

Watch the Road!

You're driving. Your passenger is talking. You're listening, responding, having a conversation. Then they reach for something, and your brain goes on high alert.

6.1 "Watching for Danger in Everything"

A sudden movement in your peripheral vision, and your brain screams: **"WATCH THE ROAD!"**

Now in threat mode, you snap at your passenger. "Don't do that! I'm driving!" They look confused. "I was just getting my phone. You were looking at the road."

But your Lifeguard (your posterior cingulate, your brain's environmental scanner) detected movement and immediately flagged it as potential threat. Not consciously. Not rationally. Just: movement = possible danger = alert.

Or maybe you're at a party. Everyone else is relaxed, talking, laughing. You're scanning. Exits. Who's angry. Who's drunk. Escape routes. Threat assessment. You can't relax because your Lifeguard is convinced that if you stop watching, something bad will happen.

Or maybe you're replaying that conversation from three weeks ago. Not because you want to. But because your Lifeguard is convinced that if you analyze it enough, you'll figure out what went wrong and prevent it from happening again.

The Lifeguard's bias is asymmetric. The cost of missing a tiger is high. Death. So your brain over-accommodates for that possibility. Better to have a thousand false alarms than miss one real threat.

This is your posterior cingulate, your brain's environmental threat sensitivity system. When it's working right, it's orienting to what is necessary, detecting real threats, guiding contextual awareness. When it's stuck, it's threat scanning, rumination, PTSD. Your Lifeguard learned that the world is not safe, and now it won't stop watching, or replaying.

Quick distinction: The Lifeguard evaluates the OUTSIDE world (*Is this environment safe? What happened out there?* The Grumpy Old Man (Chapter 2) evaluates INTERNAL effort) *Is this worth doing? Can I handle it?* Back brain scanning the world vs. front brain appraising self. When cramped: Lifeguard produces trauma patterns and hypervigilance. Grumpy Old Man produces dread and depression.

6.2 The Torture: When the Lifeguard Never Stops Watching

Let's talk about what it's actually like when your environmental scanner won't turn off.

6.2.1 Threat Scanning: The Lifeguard in Overdrive

Your Lifeguard scans constantly (**"Heads up, heads up, heads up"**) repetitive, relentless monitoring:

- Who's angry? (Threat assessment)
- Where are the exits? (Escape planning)
- What's that sound? (Change detection)
- Who's looking at me? (Social threat)
- What could go wrong? (Environmental prediction)

You can't relax. You can't be present. Because your Lifeguard is convinced that if you stop watching for one second, you'll miss the threat.

Lifeguard's cadence is how often it pings the horizon for danger; we're not removing the radar, we're slowing the ping rate and shortening recovery.

Strictly speaking, "hypervigilance" in clinical literature refers to primary sensory cortex hyperactivity, the visual and auditory screen constantly ON. The Lifeguard is posterior cingulate, the threat evaluation and environmental monitoring system that *drives* that sensory hyperactivity, not the sensory processing itself (Leech & Sharp, 2014).

At a party:

Everyone else is relaxed, talking, laughing. You're scanning. Who's drunk. Who's getting angry. Escape routes. Threat assessment. You look calm on the outside, but inside you're a threat-detection machine running at full volume.

Driving:

Your passenger reaches for something. Movement in peripheral vision. Your Lifeguard screams: "WATCH THE ROAD!" You snap at them. They're confused, you were watching the road. But your Lifeguard detected movement and flagged it as potential threat.

In public:

You're constantly aware of everyone around you. Who's behind you. Who's watching. What they're thinking. Whether you're safe. You can't just exist, you're always monitoring.

This is **threat scanning**, your posterior cingulate monitoring for threats constantly. It's exhausting. And it's often a false alarm. But your Lifeguard doesn't care about false alarms. It cares about not missing the one real threat.

6.2.2 Rumination: Replaying to Prevent

It's been three weeks. You're still replaying that conversation. That mistake. That thing you said.

"I should have said..." "Why did I do that?" "What were they thinking?"

This is **rumination**, your Lifeguard replaying past events, trying to extract lessons, trying to prevent future threats.

The logic: If I analyze this enough, I'll figure out what went wrong. Then I can prevent it from happening again. Then I'll be safe.

But here's the problem: some events don't have lessons. Some mistakes don't have solutions. Some social interactions were just awkward, not dangerous. But your Lifeguard doesn't accept that. It keeps replaying, analyzing, trying to find the threat pattern.

This is different from the CEO (Chapter 5):

- **CEO:** Stuck on internal conflicts ("What should I do?")
- **Lifeguard:** Stuck on external events ("What happened? What's the threat?")

The CEO is self-focused. The Lifeguard is environment-focused. Both are stuck, but on different things.

6.2.3 Sensory Overload: Too Much Input

Your Lifeguard is monitoring everything:

- Every sound (potential threat?)
- Every movement (danger?)
- Every person (safe or unsafe?)
- Every change in environment (what's different?)

This creates **sensory overload**, too much input, too much processing, too much threat assessment. You're overwhelmed not because the environment is objectively overwhelming, but because your Lifeguard is processing everything as potentially relevant.

The grocery store is overwhelming (too many people, sounds, movements). The office is overwhelming (constant environmental changes). Social situations are overwhelming (too many people to monitor).

You need quiet, low-stimulation environments. Not because you're "sensitive" (though you might be, see Princess & the Pea, Chapter 8). But because your Lifeguard needs to reduce the monitoring load.

6.2.4 Dissociation: When the Lifeguard Goes Offline

Here's the flip side: when threat scanning becomes too much, the Lifeguard shuts down completely.

Dissociation, you're physically present but mentally gone. "Patient etherized upon a table" (T.S. Eliot). You're there, but you're not there. You're watching yourself from outside. Everything feels distant, unreal, foggy.

This is your Lifeguard going offline to protect you from overwhelm. When the threat-scanning becomes unbearable, your brain just... stops. Shuts down the monitoring system. Disconnects you from the environment.

The pattern:

- Hypervigilance (Lifeguard overactive) → Overwhelm → Dissociation (Lifeguard offline)

You swing between extremes: constantly scanning or completely disconnected. There's no middle ground.

6.2.5 PTSD: The Lifeguard Who Learned the World Isn't Safe

Trauma teaches your Lifeguard that the world is dangerous. Not "might be" dangerous, IS dangerous.

You experienced a real threat. Your Lifeguard was right to be watching. The tiger was real.

But now your Lifeguard can't turn off. Even when you're safe. Even when the threat is gone. Your posterior cingulate is stuck in threat-scanning mode.

Triggers bring you back:

- A sound (reminds you of the threat)
- A smell (context cue)
- A person (resembles the threat)
- A situation (similar context)

Your Lifeguard immediately goes to full alert. You're back in the threat. Not remembering it, experiencing it. Your body responds as if the threat is happening now.

This is **PTSD**, your Lifeguard learned that the world isn't safe, and now it won't stop watching. The environmental scanner that's supposed to help you navigate the world has become a prison of constant threat detection.

You're looking for sharks in the indoor pool. Your Lifeguard learned from real threat, the danger was actual. But now you're in a different context. Safe. The threat is gone. Yet your posterior cingulate hasn't updated. Still scanning for sharks even though you're in a chlorinated indoor pool in broad daylight. The threat assessment that saved you then is imprisoning you now (Thome et al., 2020).

6.3 The Gift: When the Lifeguard Keeps You Safe

Now let's talk about why you need your Lifeguard, when it's working right, not stuck in hypervigilance.

6.3.1 Contextual Awareness: Reading the Room

Your Lifeguard is your **contextual awareness system**, it tells you what's happening in the environment, what's relevant, what's changed.

You walk into a room and immediately sense the vibe. Tense? Relaxed? Hostile? Safe? You don't have to think about it, your Lifeguard reads the context automatically.

Someone's body language shifts. Your Lifeguard notices. "Something changed. Pay attention."

The energy in a meeting shifts. Your Lifeguard detects it before anyone says anything.

This is **relevance detection**, your Lifeguard filters the environment for what matters. It's not scanning for threats (that's hypervigilance). It's scanning for relevance: "What's important here? What should I pay attention to?"

When your Lifeguard works right, you're contextually aware without being hypervigilant. You notice what matters without getting overwhelmed by everything.

6.3.2 Change Detection: Spotting What's Different

Your Lifeguard is a **change detector**, it notices when something in the environment is different from expected.

You walk into your house and immediately know something's off. You can't say what. But something changed.

Someone's routine shifts. Your Lifeguard flags it: "That's unusual. Worth noting."

The environment changes subtly. Your Lifeguard catches it before you consciously process it.

This is useful. Change can signal threat. But it can also signal opportunity, novelty, something worth paying attention to.

When your Lifeguard works right, you're good at noticing what's changed without catastrophizing about it.

6.3.3 Learning from Experience: Pattern Recognition

Your Lifeguard learns from past events. Not obsessively (that's when it's stuck). But adaptively.

"Last time I was in this situation, X happened. So I should prepare for X."

"This person reminds me of that person who was dangerous. Worth being cautious."

"This context has threat patterns. Stay alert."

This is **pattern recognition from experience**, your Lifeguard using past information to navigate present situations. It's protective. It's adaptive. It keeps you safe.

The difference between healthy learning and rumination:

- **Healthy:** "I learned X. I'll apply that lesson. Now I can move on."
- **Rumination:** "I'm stuck replaying X. I can't move on. I need to analyze it more."

6.3.4 Orienting Attention: Knowing What Matters

Your Lifeguard **orients your attention** to what's relevant in the environment.

A car honks. Your Lifeguard immediately orients: "Threat? No. Just traffic. Return to task."

Someone calls your name. Your Lifeguard shifts: "That's relevant. Pay attention."

Background noise increases. Your Lifeguard assesses: "Not relevant. Filter it out."

This is automatic, unconscious environmental filtering. Your Lifeguard is constantly deciding: "What in this environment deserves attention?"

When it works right, you're present, aware, responsive, but not overwhelmed. You notice what matters without noticing everything.

6.4 The Neuroscience: Posterior Cingulate and the Default Mode Network

Okay, let's get into the brain science. This is where we go from "I can't stop scanning for threats" to "here's exactly which circuit is stuck and why."

6.4.1 Where the Lifeguard Lives

The Lifeguard lives in your **posterior cingulate cortex (PCC)**, a strip of cortex along the back midline of your brain, behind the ACC.

On a brain map, this is the **posterior midline**, the strip running down the center back of your head.

The PCC sits at the back of your brain's "self-system," connecting:

- **Sensory cortex** (what's happening in the environment)
- **Memory systems** (what happened before in similar contexts)
- **Prefrontal cortex** (what should I do about this?)

The PCC's job is to integrate: "Given what's happening in the environment, given what I know from past experience, what's relevant? What's the threat? What should I pay attention to?"

6.4.2 PCC vs. ACC: Outside vs. Inside

ACC (Anterior Cingulate - CEO, Chapter 5):

- **Location:** Front midline
- **Focus:** Internal / self
- **Questions:** What am I doing? How do I feel? What's my priority?
- **When stuck:** Obsessive about internal states, OCD, can't switch tasks
- **Frontal = "self"**

PCC (Posterior Cingulate - Lifeguard):

- **Location:** Back midline
- **Focus:** External / environment
- **Questions:** What's happening out there? What's the context? What's the threat?
- **When stuck:** Hypervigilant about environment, ruminating about past events, PTSD
- **Posterior = "outside"**

In kids: The PCC can serve some ACC roles developmentally. This is why neurodivergent kids show both internal inflexibility (CEO) and external threat sensitivity (Lifeguard). The systems are still differentiating.

In adults: The distinction is clearer. ACC = internal stuckness. PCC = external stuckness.

6.4.3 The Default Mode Network (DMN)

The PCC is the core hub of the **Default Mode Network (DMN)**, a set of brain regions including medial prefrontal cortex, posterior cingulate/precuneus, and angular gyrus that activate during rest, mind-wandering, memory, self-reflection, and environmental context integration (Buckner et al., 2008). The Lifeguard (DMN hub) works with the CEO (Salience Network) to switch between internal reflection and external task mode (Menon, 2011; Bolton et al., 2020). (See Part I Overview for the full Triple Network Model.)

When your Lifeguard (DMN hub) works right:

- You integrate past context with present moment
- You can mind-wander productively (planning, remembering, imagining)
- You switch cleanly between internal reflection (DMN active) and external tasks (CEN active)
- Your environmental scanning is flexible, not stuck

When your Lifeguard (DMN) is dysregulated:

- **Hyperactive DMN:** Won't turn off during tasks, rumination intrudes, can't shift from "rest mode" to "task mode"
- **Disconnected DMN:** Dissociation, not integrated with environment, "there but not there"
- **Poor switching:** Can't cleanly transition between internal (DMN) and external (CEN) modes, your CEO (Salience Network) can't coordinate the switch

How this connects to the framework:

Your Lifeguard lives in the **Back neighborhood** and is the core hub of the **Orienting & Sensing System** (paired with Princess & the Pea). It's your connection to the Default Mode Network, the large-scale network that your CEO (Front/Salience Network) switches away from when you need to focus on tasks. When your Lifeguard is stuck scanning or ruminating, your DMN won't release control to your CEN (task circuits).

6.4.4 Hypervigilance: PCC Stuck "On"

When I map someone with elevated threat sensitivity, I see **posterior cingulate hyperactivation**, excess activity in the posterior midline region. Your Lifeguard is running hot, scanning constantly.

Often combined with:

- **High beta** (threat-scanning mode)
- **DMN dysregulation** (can't shift out of monitoring mode)
- **Connectivity to amygdala** (threat detection amplified)

Your brain is stuck in "watch for threats" mode. Even when you're safe. Even when you're trying to relax. The Lifeguard won't stand down.

6.4.5 Dissociation: PCC Stuck "Off"

On the flip side, dissociation shows up as **PCC hypoactivation**, low activity at posterior midline. Your Lifeguard has gone offline.

Often combined with:

- **Low alpha** (can't generate calm, present awareness)
- **DMN disconnection** (not integrated with environment)

- **Reduced connectivity** (brain regions not talking to each other)

You're there but not there. Present but disconnected. Your Lifeguard has shut down to protect you from overwhelm.

6.4.6 Rumination: PCC Stuck on Past Events

Rumination shows up as **PCC hyperactivation during rest**, your Lifeguard is replaying past events instead of monitoring present environment.

The DMN is supposed to be flexible, mind-wandering, planning, remembering, then returning to present. But in rumination, it's stuck replaying the same events.

Your Lifeguard is trying to extract threat patterns from the past to prevent future threats. But it can't discharge. The analysis never completes. So it keeps looping.

This is different from CEO loops (Chapter 5):

- **CEO:** Stuck on internal conflicts, tasks, priorities
- **Lifeguard:** Stuck on external events, past interactions, environmental threats

Both are stuck. But the CEO is self-focused, the Lifeguard is environment-focused.

The Lifeguard: Posterior Cingulate

Gifts	Torture
• Contextual awareness (reading rooms) • Protective vigilance (detecting real dangers) • Learning from experience (extracting lessons) • Environmental sensitivity (notice details) • Pattern recognition (see threat patterns) • Intuitive safety assessment (know when "off")	• Constant hypervigilance (scanning exits, never relax) • Rumination won't stop (replaying endlessly) • Sensory overload (too much input) • PTSD patterns (trauma-learned, world unsafe) • Dissociation when overwhelmed (shut down completely) • Exhaustion from scanning (constant monitoring drains)

6.5 Toolkit Preview

Your Lifeguard is trainable. You need environmental awareness, not permanent hypervigilance.

Grounding practice: when the scanner won't stand down, name five things you can see right now. Present-moment sensory data interrupts the threat-replay loop faster than arguing with the replay.

- **Stress Response Regulation** (Ch 15): HRV biofeedback and breathwork teach the nervous system that the current moment is safe.
- **Meditation** (Ch 17): body scan and open awareness practices build present-moment presence without the vigilance tax.
- **Neurofeedback** (Ch 18): posterior cingulate calming protocols reduce environmental over-scanning and rumination cycling.

If your Lifeguard is trauma-based, trauma-informed work addresses the root, Chapter 15 maps the options. Detailed protocols are in Part II. These circuits respond to training.

The posterior cingulate circuits that create chronic hypervigilance are the same circuits that, once trained, produce contextual awareness without constant threat-scanning. Part II shows you how to build that.

6.6 Key Takeaways

The Lifeguard (Posterior Cingulate) is your brain's environmental scanner, watches for danger, replays past events, never stops monitoring.

- **Back of brain = OUTSIDE/WORLD:** Lifeguard ruminates on EXTERNAL events ("what happened?"), while CEO (Ch 5) perseverates on INTERNAL conflicts ("should I be mad?"). Lifeguard = world-focused. CEO = self-focused.
- **The ping-pong with CEO:** When both stuck, they amplify each other, Lifeguard replays event, CEO perseverates on response, creating resonant anxiety between back (world) and front (self).
- **Lifeguard vs. Grumpy Old Man:** Lifeguard evaluates the OUTSIDE world, threat scanning, replaying events. Grumpy Old Man (Ch 2) evaluates INSIDE effort, whether something is worth doing. Lifeguard → hypervigilance, trauma. Grumpy Old Man → dread, depression. Different circuits, different questions.
- **The cost of missing a tiger:** Better a thousand false alarms than one missed danger, so your Lifeguard never rests.
- **PTSD as Lifeguard stuck ON:** Trauma teaches your scanner the world is dangerous. Lifeguard won't stand down even when contextually safe.

- **Training to distinguish real from false threats:** Posterior cingulate regulation, present-moment awareness, trauma processing (EMDR, somatic work), learning to trust safety signals.
- **Notice your threat cadence:** Which contexts keep Lifeguard on permanent high alert vs. where it can cycle down?

6.7 Reader Reflections

1. **What does your hypervigilance look like?** Can you distinguish world-scanning (Lifeguard ("is the environment safe?") from effort-appraising (Grumpy Old Man) "is this worth doing?")?
2. **Do you recognize the difference between contextual awareness (gift) and hypervigilance (torture)?** When did scanning keep you safe versus exhaust you with false alarms?

Systems Interlude: The Nonverbal Sensing System

Right Hemisphere: Oppositional vs. Sensitive

Location: Right inferior frontal cortex (front) + Right temporoparietal junction (back)
Phenotypes: Problem Child (Chapter 7) + Princess & the Pea (Chapter 8)
System function: Braking/resistance (front) vs. high-gain sensory and social processing (back)

Key insight: Your right hemisphere specializes in reactive control, front says NO (braking, resistance), back feels EVERYTHING (amplified sensory and social perception). Together, they create the "reactive sensitivity" axis.

What This System Does When Balanced

Your Nonverbal Sensing System protects you through resistance and detects threats through amplified perception. When it's balanced:

- You can apply brakes when needed: pause, inhibit, say "no" (Problem Child functional)
- You can set boundaries without burning bridges (Problem Child discriminating)
- You read social cues accurately without overwhelm (Princess & Pea attuned)
- You feel empathy without absorbing everyone's emotions (Princess & Pea boundaried)

This is your **reactive control and receptive processing system**, the Problem Child slams brakes when threats appear, and the Princess & the Pea processes sensory and social information with exquisite precision. Together they create a sensitive threat-detection and response system.

What Dysregulation Looks Like

Problem Child brake failure (right IFG dysregulated):
Oppositional defiance, anger without brakes, self-sabotage, burning bridges, reactive "you can't make me"

Problem Child over-braking:
Says "no" to everything, reflexive resistance, frozen by oppositional impulses

Princess & Pea high-gain (right TPJ amplified):
RSD, sensory overwhelm, absorbing everyone's emotions, misophonia, social nuance becomes torture

Princess & Pea flooded (right TPJ dysregulated):
Paradoxically appears "disconnected" because you're feeling TOO MUCH, signal floods so intensely you can't parse it. Can't read the room not because you're missing cues, but because you're picking up too many. This is poet-brains and autistic brains, exquisite sensitivity that overflows parsing.

Both dysregulated:
Reactive resistance + amplified processing = "prickly empath." You feel everything intensely AND resist everything reflexively. The "RSD + ODD" constellation.

How This Connects to Other Systems

The Nonverbal Sensing System is threat-detection and emergency response:

- **Princess & Pea:** Early-warning radar (amplified sensitivity)
- **Problem Child:** Emergency brake (reactive resistance)
- **CEO (Ch 5):** Decides if threat is real and how to respond
- **Attention System (Ch 3-4):** Implements the response

Network Connection

Problem Child (reactive control) and Princess & Pea (social / sensory salience) both feed into the **Salience Network (SN)**, amplifying threat signals and triggering emergency braking. When dysregulated, neutral cues feel like threats, triggering defensive reactions.

These circuits give you a sensory cadence: how quickly you register input, how long it echoes, and how much buffer you need between hits.

Map so far: 6 of 12. You've met the left-hemisphere drive systems (HLK, GOM) and the midline attention systems (CEO, Lifeguard). Up next: The Problem Child and The Princess & Pea, your right hemisphere, where emotion, threat response, and sensitivity live. These two chapters explain why neurodivergent people often feel so much, so fast.

Ch 7: The Problem Child (Right IFG)

The Teenager Who'd Rather Lose Than Be Controlled

7.1 "The Defiant Brake Failure"

You know you're supposed to do the thing. You know the consequences if you don't. Your boss is reasonable. Your partner is right. The cop is just doing their job.

And yet.

"You can't make me."

Here's the thing about the Problem Child, your brain's right frontal brake system at F8/FT8: it's not that you don't understand consequences. You understand them perfectly. It's that being controlled feels more threatening than the punishment itself. I'd rather fail on my own terms than succeed on yours.

This pattern shows up consistently on QEEG. It's not "bad attitude." It's brake failure under chronic threat. Your right inferior frontal gyrus (the circuit that normally slams the brakes on impulses and angry reactions) is underpowered, fatigued, or just done with compliance.

The snarky truth? The Problem Child is often the Grumpy Old Man's exhausted teenager. Stage 1: anxious overcontrol (trying so hard to be good). Stage 2: fatigue and invalidation (the brake pads wear out). Stage 3: "Fuck it, I'm done playing your game."

The torture? Chronic conflict. Burning bridges. Self-sabotage. Knowing you're cutting off your nose to spite your face and doing it anyway. When Problem Child leads, your behavioral cadence gets jerky: sudden accelerations, hard stops, no smooth transitions.

The gift? When this energy is channeled, it's assertiveness. Boundary-setting. Spotting injustice. Rebellion as innovation. The people who change broken systems aren't the compliant ones.

The work? Strengthen the brake (neurofeedback), calm the threat appraisal (Grumpy Old Man regulation), and give the Problem Child safer ways to say no.

7.2 The Torture: When the Problem Child Takes Over

Let's talk about what it's actually like when your brake system fails and oppositionality takes over.

7.2.1 Oppositional Defiance: The Automatic "No"

Someone asks you to do something. A reasonable request. Your boss. Your partner. Your parent. Maybe even yourself.

And before you can think about it, before you can consider whether it's a good idea, your brain says: **"You can't make me."**

Not thoughtful rebellion. Not principled resistance. Just automatic defiance.

You know you're being unreasonable. You know the consequences. You know this person isn't trying to control you, they're just asking you to do a normal thing. But your brain has already decided: compliance = threat. And you can't override it.

The pattern is predictable:

- Authority figure says "do this" → automatic "no"
- Small request → big blowup (escalates immediately)
- Arguing, rule-bending, chronic non-compliance
- Regret later (after the defiance passes: "why did I do that?")

This isn't about the actual request. It's about control. Your brain interprets external control as threat. Even when the control is reasonable, helpful, or literally what you wanted to do anyway (if someone else tells you to do it): your Problem Child, that reactive brake at right frontal F8, says "no."

And here's the cruel part: you're often oppositional to yourself. You set a goal. You want to achieve it. But the moment it feels like an obligation, like you "should" do it, your Problem Child rebels. You self-sabotage not because you don't want the outcome, but because the internal authority figure triggers the same defiance as external authority.

7.2.2 Spite-Driven Decisions: I'd Rather Lose Than Comply

You're about to make a decision that will hurt you. You know it will hurt you. Everyone around you knows it will hurt you. But someone is trying to tell you not to do it, trying to control you, trying to make you comply.

So you do it anyway.

"I'd rather lose on my own terms than win on yours."

This is **spite-driven decision-making**, making choices that hurt you specifically to assert autonomy, to prove that no one can control you.

You quit the job before they can fire you (even though you needed the job). You end the relationship before they can leave you (even though you wanted to stay). You fail the class rather than do the assignment (even though you care about your education). You burn bridges specifically to prove that you can't be controlled.

The paradox is excruciating:

- You know it's self-destructive
- You do it anyway
- Because defiance feels more important than the outcome
- Because being controlled feels more threatening than the consequences

This isn't rational. Your Problem Child doesn't care about rational. Your brake system has decided that compliance = loss of autonomy = existential threat. So you protect your autonomy even when it costs you everything else.

7.2.3 Anger Without Brakes: Zero to Explosion

Someone says something. It's not even that bad. Maybe it's criticism. Maybe it's just a tone. Maybe it's nothing at all, you're just already on edge.

And you explode.

Zero to one hundred in seconds. You're yelling. You're saying things you don't mean. You can see the other person's face, hurt, shocked, scared. Part of you knows you should stop. But you can't. The brake isn't working.

This is **anger without inhibition**, your right IFG (the brake system) isn't strong enough to stop the reaction. You feel angry and you immediately act on it. No pause. No "let me think about this." No "is this proportional?" Just: feel → react.

The escalation is terrifying, for you and everyone around you. A small slight becomes a screaming match. A minor frustration becomes physical aggression (throwing things, slamming doors, in some cases hitting). More commonly, it's verbal aggression, saying the most hurtful thing you can think of, going for the jugular.

The aftermath is brutal:

The anger passes. You come back to yourself. And you see the damage. The hurt on their face. The things you said. The relationship you just damaged. The bridge you just burned.

Guilt. Shame. "Why did I do that? What's wrong with me?"

You apologize. You mean it. You promise it won't happen again.

But it does. Because your brake system is still fatigued, still underpowered, still failing under threat. The cycle repeats.

7.2.4 Low Punishment Sensitivity: Consequences Don't Land

What makes the Problem Child so confusing to everyone (including you): **consequences don't work the way they're supposed to.**

Your boss threatens to fire you. Your brain: "Whatever."

Your partner says they'll leave if you don't change. Your brain: "I don't believe you."

The cop pulls you over. Your brain: "I dare you."

This isn't bravado. This isn't "not caring." This is **low punishment sensitivity**, your amygdala (fear center) is under-reactive. Threats that would make other people comply just… don't land for you.

The neuroscience: **low fear conditioning, amygdala under-reactivity, blunted cortisol response** (Matthys et al., 2013). Your brain doesn't process threats the way most brains do. Punishment doesn't deter you because your threat-detection system doesn't register it as threatening enough.

This creates a vicious cycle:

- You don't respond to normal consequences
- Authority figures escalate (bigger threats, harsher punishment)
- Escalation increases your sense of threat and control
- Your defiance increases
- They escalate more
- You defy more

The problem: Normal parenting, normal management, normal consequences; they don't work. Not because you're "bad," but because your brain is wired differently. You're under-stimulated, sensation-seeking, need intensity to feel anything. Mild consequences feel like nothing. Harsh consequences feel like attack, which triggers more defiance.

And here's what makes it feel unfair: you're not trying to be difficult. Your brain genuinely doesn't process threat the way other brains do. What feels like "reasonable consequences" to them feels like either nothing or attack to you. There's no middle ground.

7.2.5 Chronic Conflict: Burning Bridges Everywhere

The Problem Child doesn't just create conflict with one person or in one domain. It creates conflict everywhere.

With authority:

Parents, teachers, bosses, police, anyone perceived as trying to control you. Even when they're reasonable. Even when they're trying to help. Your brain interprets authority as threat, and you respond with defiance.

You're the person who gets fired from jobs not because you can't do the work, but because you can't handle being managed. You're the person who argues with cops even though you know it will make things worse. You're the person who rebels against your parents even when they're being supportive.

It's not that you hate authority. It's that your brain interprets external control as existential threat.

With peers:

Arguments. Fights. Difficulty compromising. "My way or the highway."

You're not trying to dominate. But your Problem Child can't tolerate someone else's agenda winning. Collaboration feels like loss of control. Compromise feels like defeat. So you dig in, escalate, burn the relationship rather than bend.

Friends get exhausted. Partners leave. You end up isolated not because you don't want connection, but because your Problem Child makes connection feel like threat.

With yourself:

And here's the cruelest part: you're oppositional to your own goals.

You want to exercise. You set a plan. Then the moment it feels like an obligation (like you "should" do it), your Problem Child rebels. You sabotage yourself not because you don't want the outcome, but because the internal authority figure (your own "should") triggers the same defiance as external authority.

You can't make yourself do things even when you desperately want to. Because "making yourself" feels like control. And control = threat. So you rebel against yourself, sabotage your own goals, and then hate yourself for it.

The Problem Child (your reactive brake circuit) doesn't distinguish between external control and self-discipline. Both feel like threat. Both trigger defiance.

7.3 The Gift: When the Problem Child Is Channeled

Now let's talk about why you wouldn't want to eliminate your Problem Child even if you could.

7.3.1 Assertiveness: The Ability to Say No

When your Problem Child is regulated (when you have brakes but they're not broken), you get something most people struggle with: **genuine assertiveness.**

Not passive. Not aggressive. Assertive.

You can say no. Without guilt. Without aggression. Without needing to justify yourself. Just: "No, that doesn't work for me."

You set boundaries. You protect yourself. You stand up for yourself and others. You don't tolerate being walked over, manipulated, or exploited.

This is the Problem Child's gift when it's channeled. While other people are people-pleasing, avoiding conflict, saying yes when they mean no, you're the person who can actually set boundaries.

The world needs people who can say no. Who can stand up to pressure. Who can protect themselves and others from exploitation.

7.3.2 Spotting Hypocrisy and Injustice: The Bullshit Detector

You're quick to spot unfairness. Hypocrisy. Double standards. "Rules for thee but not for me."

While other people are nodding along, you're the one saying "wait, that's not fair."

This is your **injustice detector**, the Problem Child's refusal to tolerate unfairness. You won't comply with unjust rules just because everyone else is. You won't stay quiet when you see corruption. You speak truth to power even when it's uncomfortable.

When channeled, this becomes:

Activism: Fighting injustice, challenging broken systems, advocating for change. The people who lead social movements aren't the compliant ones, they're the ones who couldn't tolerate injustice and refused to comply.

Advocacy: For yourself and others. You're the person who stands up when someone's being treated unfairly. You're the person who challenges authority when authority is wrong.

Whistleblowing: Exposing corruption, calling out hypocrisy, refusing to participate in unethical systems. This takes courage. The Problem Child has it.

Reform: Changing broken systems from the inside. Not just complaining, actively working to make things better, fairer, more just.

7.3.3 Rebellion as Innovation: Questioning the Status Quo

"Why do we do it this way?"

"Who decided this was the right way?"

"What if we tried something different?"

The Problem Child questions everything. Not to be difficult, because you genuinely don't understand why everyone's following rules that don't make sense.

When channeled, this becomes:

Entrepreneurship: Breaking rules to create something new. Every successful entrepreneur is, at some level, a Problem Child who couldn't tolerate the way things were and built something different.

Innovation: Doing things differently because the old way doesn't work. The people who disrupt industries, challenge assumptions, find better ways, they're not the compliant ones.

Disruption: Challenging established norms, questioning authority, refusing to accept "that's how we've always done it." This is how progress happens.

Leadership: Not following, leading. Not complying, setting direction. The Problem Child energy, when channeled, becomes the person who says "follow me, I know a better way."

7.3.4 Protective Anger: Fuel for Change

Anger gets a bad rap. But anger, when regulated, is protective and motivating.

Your Problem Child's anger protects you from:

- Exploitation (you won't tolerate being used)
- Abuse (you won't accept mistreatment)
- Injustice (you won't stay quiet when something's wrong)

When regulated (anger with brakes), this becomes:

Anger as information: "This is wrong. This needs to change." Your anger tells you when boundaries are being violated, when injustice is happening, when something needs to be addressed.

Anger as fuel: Motivates action. Not passive acceptance. Not suppressed resentment. Active, constructive response to injustice.

Anger with choice: You feel the anger. You acknowledge it. You choose how to respond. Not suppressing it (that's unhealthy). Not exploding (that's destructive). Channeling it into constructive action.

The gift: While other people suppress their anger or explode, you're learning to use anger as fuel for change. This is powerful.

7.4 The Relationship to Grumpy Old Man: Evolutionary Stages

Here's the clinical pattern I see constantly: **the Problem Child is often the Grumpy Old Man's exhausted teenager.**

The 3-stage progression:

Stage 1: Anxious Overcontrol. You start as the anxious kid trying desperately to be good. Overactive threat appraisal, rigid rule-following, hypervigilance. You're compliant not from genuine alignment, but from terror of consequences. Exhausting. You're running your threat-assessment system at full volume constantly, being "good" from fear.

Stage 2: Brake Pads Wear Out. Then chronic stress, sleep deprivation, repeated invalidation. Your brake system (right IFG at F8/FT8) starts to fail. The pads that kept you compliant wear out. You can't sustain anxious overcontrol anymore. You're still anxious underneath, but the brake that kept you compliant is failing. The dangerous moment when anxious compliance flips to active defiance.

Stage 3: Active Defiance. Instead of avoiding trouble through compliance, you're actively defiant. The Grumpy Old Man is still there (still threat-biased, still anxious), but the tactic changed: Before, "Freeze and appease." After, "Fight and sabotage." You're done playing the game, done being controlled, even if it costs you. This isn't "bad attitude", it's brake failure under chronic threat.

What I see clinically: Kids (and adults) who were anxious worriers (the "good" kids) becoming angry, oppositional, non-compliant. Not because they became "bad," but because they got exhausted, cornered, and repeatedly invalidated. The brake system that kept them compliant wore out.

The reversal: Address fatigue (sleep), calm Grumpy Old Man (reduce threat appraisal), strengthen brake (right IFG training). Result: oppositional → assertive, defiant → boundaried, anger without brakes → protective anger with choice. The Problem Child energy doesn't disappear. It gets channeled.

7.5 The Neuroscience: Response Inhibition and the "Stop" System

The Problem Child lives in your **right inferior frontal gyrus (rIFG / right ventrolateral PFC)**, F8/FT8 on the EEG cap. This is your brain's **brake system**: response inhibition, anger regulation, behavioral gating.

The distinction from Grumpy Old Man:

- **F4 (Grumpy Old Man - Chapter 2):** Threat appraisal: "This will end badly"
- **F8 (Problem Child):** Behavioral gate: "Do I stop, comply, or push back?"

7.5.1 The Brake System

Right IFG function: Stops prepotent responses, brakes premature actions, regulates anger, gates social norm compliance. When working: anger with brakes (feel angry, think, choose response). When underpowered or fatigued: anger without brakes → oppositionality, aggression, "I dare you" energy.

Research evidence: Lesion studies show that damage to right inferior frontal gyrus selectively impairs the ability to stop prepotent responses on stop-signal tasks (Aron et al., 2003). Across fMRI and lesion studies, this right ventrolateral prefrontal region emerges as a core hub in a broader braking network involving pre-SMA, subthalamic nucleus, and connected regions (Aron et al., 2004). Brain stimulation studies show that interfering with right prefrontal and medial regions disrupts different aspects of inhibitory control, action restraint versus action cancellation (Dambacher et al., 2014). This same region modulates aggressive responses to social exclusion, lowers hurt feelings (RSD connection), and regulates aggressive behavior (Eisenberger et al., 2003).

ODD pattern: Oppositional Defiant Disorder research shows reduced activation in right IFG (brake fails) while nearby tissue overworks (compensatory effort) (Noordermeer et al., 2016). Result: can't stop even when you know you should. Low punishment sensitivity + under-stimulation + weak brake = Problem Child.

Sleep deprivation directly impacts brake: Right hemisphere advantage for alertness, sleep deprivation makes right VLPFC fail. Fatigue makes Problem Child come out. Chronic threat + low arousal + exhaustion = brake system can't sustain anxious compliance, flips to oppositionality.

7.6 QEEG Signature: What I See in Brain Maps

7.6.1 EEG Patterns in Problem Child

Right frontal (F8/FT8) patterns:

Low arousal: Theta leakage under load. Your brake system is fatigued, underaroused. It should be generating beta (activation, engagement) but instead it's generating theta (slow waves, fatigue). The brake is there, but it's too tired to work.

Unstable activation: Inconsistent patterns during inhibition tasks. Sometimes the brake works. Sometimes it doesn't. You can't predict when you'll be able to control yourself.

Low beta: Brake system underpowered. Fast beta waves are what you need for inhibition, for pausing, for thinking before reacting. When fast-wave activity is low in right frontal inhibitory regions, the brake doesn't have enough power.

Atypical asymmetry: In some Problem Children, I see greater right than left frontal activation overall. This is withdrawal dominance (Grumpy Old Man) plus brake failure (Problem Child). You're both anxious AND oppositional.

7.6.2 The Combined Pattern: Grumpy Old Man + Problem Child

Here's where it gets interesting, and exhausting.

High beta at F4 (Grumpy Old Man): Anxiety, threat appraisal, worry. Your threat-assessment system is running hot. Everything feels dangerous.

Low beta at F8 (Problem Child): Brake failure, can't inhibit. Your brake system is fatigued, underpowered, failing.

Result: Anxious + oppositional. You're simultaneously worried about consequences AND unable to stop yourself from defying. You know you shouldn't, but you can't help it.

This is the pattern I see in people who say: "I know I'm going to regret this, but I can't stop myself."

7.6.3 Under Fatigue: When the Brake Completely Fails

Here's what happens when you're sleep-deprived, stressed, overwhelmed:

Theta increases (especially right frontal): Your brain is generating more slow waves. Fatigue. Underarousal. The brake system is shutting down.

Beta decreases: Less activation, less inhibition capacity. The brake gets weaker.

Oppositionality worsens: You can't sustain compliance anymore. The brake is too fatigued to work.

The pattern I observe clinically:

Excess theta + fatigue at F4 / F8 → tips the system from anxious overcontrol to dread and oppositionality.

Chronic threat (Grumpy Old Man) + low arousal (fatigue) → erode the brake system (Problem Child).

The system can't sustain anxious compliance anymore → flips to active defiance.

This is why sleep deprivation makes oppositional behavior worse. This is why stress makes anger harder to control. This is why the Problem Child comes out when you're exhausted.

It's not that you're "losing control." It's that your brake system literally doesn't have the resources to maintain control under these conditions.

The Problem Child: Right IFG	
Gifts	**Torture**
• Assertiveness (say no, set boundaries) • Spotting injustice (see unfair systems) • Rebellion as innovation (change broken systems) • Authentic autonomy (refuse control, protect agency) • Boundary enforcement (don't tolerate mistreatment) • Creative defiance (find new ways around obstacles)	• Automatic oppositionality ("you can't make me" even when it hurts you) • Spite-driven decisions (lose on your terms vs. win on theirs) • Anger without brakes (zero to explosion) • Chronic conflict (burn bridges, exhaust relationships) • Self-sabotage (rebel against yourself) • Brake failure under fatigue (sleep deprivation worsens)

7.7 Toolkit Preview

Your Problem Child is trainable. That assertiveness and injustice-detection are worth keeping, you just need a brake that works.

Sleep first. Right frontal brake function fails under sleep deprivation faster than almost any other system. This is the non-negotiable. Well-rested you has brakes. Exhausted you becomes oppositional.

- **Sleep** (Ch 13): protect it ruthlessly. The brake erodes without it.
- **Stress Response Regulation** (Ch 15): chronic threat wears the brake down. HRV biofeedback and vagal toning lower the baseline threat load that triggers defiance.
- **Neurofeedback** (Ch 18): right frontal inhibitory training strengthens response inhibition over time.

Detailed protocols are in Part II. These circuits respond to training.

The right frontal brake circuits that create oppositional explosions are the same circuits that, once trained, produce assertive boundaries with a working brake. Part II shows you how to build that.

7.8 Key Takeaways

The Problem Child (Right IFG/Ventrolateral PFC) is your brain's brake system, the circuit that stops impulsive reactions, regulates anger, and decides whether to comply or rebel.

- **"I'd rather lose than be controlled":** Compliance feels more threatening than consequences when brake system operates under chronic threat, this drives self-sabotage and burned bridges
- **RSD + anger = explosive:** Rejection sensitivity (right frontal + right TPJ) plus brake failure (right IFG) means criticism triggers immediate, uncontrolled rage, not "anger issues," but specific circuit configuration
- **The Grumpy Old Man → Problem Child pipeline:** Anxious overcontrol (Stage 1) → exhausted compliance (Stage 2) → brake failure/"fuck it" (Stage 3). Problem Child is often Grumpy Old Man's exhausted teenager.
- **Sleep deprivation's direct impact:** Right hemisphere brake systems are especially vulnerable to fatigue, well-rested you has brake function, exhausted you becomes oppositional and explosive
- **When channeled: rebellion as innovation:** Assertiveness, boundary-setting, spotting injustice, and the "why can't we do it differently?" that drives systemic change
- **Training the brake without suppressing fire:** Right frontal SMR/beta neurofeedback strengthens inhibition, sleep optimization protects brake capacity, addressing Grumpy Old Man reduces chronic threat that exhausts the brake

7.9 Reader Reflections

1. **Do you recognize the "I'd rather lose than be controlled" pattern?** Times you've sabotaged yourself just to avoid feeling controlled?
2. **Can you trace your Problem Child back to your Grumpy Old Man?** Anxious overcontrol before the oppositionality? The three stages (anxious compliance → exhaustion → brake failure)?
3. **Are there situations where your Problem Child has actually been the solution?** Times when your "no" protected you, when your opposition spotted injustice, when your defiance led to necessary change? How can you channel that energy more effectively?

4. **Where in your day do you notice "jerkiness" in your action cadence: impulsive starts, abrupt stops, and hard pivots?**

Ch 8: The Princess & the Pea (Right TPJ)

I Can't Tell What's Behind Your Smile

8.1 "Feeling What Everyone Else Misses"

Your partner says "I'm fine" with a slightly tight smile.

Everyone else accepts this and moves on. You don't. You can't.

Because you heard something in their tone. You saw something in their eyes. A micro-expression. A tension in their jaw. Something that tells you they're not fine.

But you can't tell what it means.

Are they mad at you? Disappointed? Sad? Lying to protect you? About to leave?

You generate seventeen possible interpretations. You catastrophize all of them simultaneously. You can't ask directly because that might make it worse. So you just… spiral.

"I can't tell what's behind your smile."

This is the Princess & the Pea: your right temporoparietal junction and its connected network. "Princess & Pea" is shorthand for a hub where sensory, social, emotional, and motor signals converge. The right TPJ sits at the junction where your temporal lobe (side) meets your parietal lobe (top/back), and it's wired into face processing areas, motor cortex, emotional centers, and attention systems. It processes social and sensory information with the gain turned way up.

You feel what others miss. The micro-expressions. The tone shifts. The unspoken tension. The sensory details that others filter out automatically.

The gift? **Exquisite empathy.** You feel what others feel. You sense what's unspoken. You catch social nuance that shallow processors miss.

The torture? **It hurts you a little more.** Rejection that others shrug off feels like annihilation. Sensory input that others don't notice makes you want to crawl out of your skin. Criticism feels like a physical wound.

The tragedy? Substances that numb the torture also numb the gifts. You can finally tolerate existing, but you've lost access to the depth that makes you who you are.

8.2 The Torture: When Everything Feels Too Much

Let's talk about what it's actually like when your social and sensory processing runs at higher gain than everyone else's.

8.2.1 RSD: When Criticism Feels Like Annihilation

"Can I give you some feedback?" Alex's stomach drops. His manager's tone is neutral, professional. But the words "feedback" land like a punch. Before she even speaks, his brain knows: you're worthless, you failed, everyone sees it. She says: "The presentation was good, just tighten the conclusion." Constructive. Mild. But Alex hears: you're incompetent, you embarrassed yourself, you should quit. The pain is physical. Chest tight, throat closing, face hot. He nods, mumbles thanks, escapes to bathroom. Sits in stall, hands shaking. Not "being sensitive." His right frontal cortex + right TPJ processing mild criticism with amplified gain. Volume 11 in a volume-5 world.

Someone gives you mild, constructive feedback. You hear: "You're worthless and everyone knows it."

Your friend takes three hours to text back. You immediately know: they hate you and were just being polite all along.

Your boss says "Can we talk?" You're convinced: you're getting fired, you've failed, everyone thinks you're incompetent.

This is **Rejection Sensitivity Dysphoria (RSD)**, emotional pain that's disproportionate to the trigger. (A note: RSD is a clinical concept popularized by William Dodson, widely recognized in the ADHD community but not yet a formal DSM or ICD diagnosis. The phenomenon is real and measurable; the label is still catching up.) Not "you're being dramatic." Not "you're too sensitive." Your right TPJ is processing social information with higher gain. What others experience at volume 5, you experience at volume 11.

WHAT THE DATA SHOWS:

RSD isn't "being too sensitive." It's your brain processing criticism with amplified gain. The pain is real, physical, measurable. You're not making it up, you're accurately reporting.

The neuroscience: Your right TPJ (temporoparietal junction) is hyperactive. It's amplifying social and emotional signals. Criticism doesn't just register as feedback, it's amplified into catastrophic rejection.

And here's the cruel part: you can't tell which signals are real and which are amplified. Is your friend actually mad, or are you just detecting that they're tired? You generate seventeen possible interpretations and your brain treats all of them as equally threatening.

8.2.2 Social Anxiety: Reading Too Much

You're at a party. Someone laughs. Your brain immediately asks: "Are they laughing at me?"

Someone whispers. Your brain: "They're talking about me."

Someone's face shifts slightly. Your brain: "They don't like me."

This is **social anxiety driven by hyperactive social processing**. You're not paranoid, you're picking up real micro-signals. The problem is you're picking up SO MANY signals that you can't tell which ones matter.

You're reading:

- Facial expressions (micro-expressions others miss)
- Tone of voice (prosody, emotional inflection)
- Body language (tension, distance, orientation)
- Subtext (what's not being said)
- Energy (the vibe in the room)

This is exhausting. Every social interaction is a data tsunami. You're processing at a level of detail that most people don't even perceive.

8.2.3 Sensory Overwhelm: The World Is Too Loud

The grocery store is overwhelming. Not because you're "sensitive", because your brain is processing every sound, every light, every person, every movement as potentially relevant.

Sounds:

- Background music (others filter out, you can't)
- Conversations (you hear all of them)
- Fluorescent lights (buzzing you can't ignore)
- Chewing, breathing, tapping (misophonia: sounds that trigger rage or distress)

Lights:

- Too bright (painful, not just uncomfortable)
- Fluorescent flicker (you notice the rapid flickering most people don't see)
- Screens (blue light feels like assault)

Touch:

- Tags in clothes (intolerable)
- Certain fabrics (sensory hell)
- Light touch (worse than firm pressure)
- Hugs (overwhelming, not comforting)

Crowds:

- Too many people (sensory and social overload)
- Too much input (can't filter)
- Need to escape (not social anxiety: sensory overwhelm)

This is **sensory processing sensitivity**, your brain processing sensory information with higher gain. You're not imagining it. Your right TPJ is amplifying the signal.

8.2.4 Misophonia: When Sounds Trigger Rage

Someone is chewing. Loudly. You can hear every wet sound, every lip smack, every swallow.

And you want to scream. Or leave. Or throw something.

This is **misophonia**, specific sounds trigger disproportionate emotional responses. Usually rage, sometimes panic, sometimes disgust.

Common triggers:

- Chewing, eating sounds
- Breathing, sniffling
- Tapping, clicking
- Repetitive sounds

This isn't "being annoyed." Your brain is processing these sounds as threats. Current research implicates the insular cortex, anterior cingulate, and auditory cortex, with likely contributions from TPJ and connected limbic regions generating the fight-or-flight response to... chewing. The exact circuit is still being mapped, but the emotional amplification is real and measurable.

It's not rational. You know it's not rational. But knowing doesn't help. The sound triggers the response automatically.

8.2.5 Face Recognition and Social Cueing: Processing Overload

You're good at reading faces. Too good.

You catch micro-expressions others miss. You notice when someone's smile doesn't reach their eyes. You see the slight tightening around the mouth that signals disapproval.

But you also:

- Struggle with face blindness (prosopagnosia) sometimes: too much detail, can't integrate into "face"
- Get overwhelmed by eye contact (too much social information)
- Miss obvious social cues while catching subtle ones (flooded by signal, can't parse hierarchy)

- Can't tell if someone's being sarcastic or serious (tone processing overload, too many signals)

Here's what's happening: Your brain has a two-stage face processing system:

Stage 1 - Fusiform Face Area (FFA): Extracts identity and stable features ("who is this person?"). This lives in the ventral visual stream, bottom of your brain.

Stage 2 - Right TPJ & pSTS: Takes FFA's output and adds dynamic interpretation, gaze direction, expression changes, biological motion, and most importantly: **"What are they doing and what does it mean for me?"** (Schwiedrzik et al., 2015; Turk-Browne et al., 2010).

Princess sits at Stage 2, downstream of face recognition. She's not just seeing faces, she's reading intent, weighing "is this about me?", and deciding whether that micro-expression is safe, threatening, or important. FFA and pSTS show strong resting-state connectivity to rTPJ, forming an integrated face-to-social-meaning pipeline.

The flooding problem: You're not missing social cues because you're not picking them up. You're missing them because you're picking up *too many* and drowning in signal. FFA feeds faces, pSTS extracts gaze and expression, Princess amplifies all of it with high gain, and you end up processing social information at overwhelming detail while simultaneously losing the forest for the trees.

Your right TPJ is working overtime processing social information, amplifying everything, flooding your system, overwhelming your ability to parse what matters.

8.2.6 Emotional Contagion: Feeling What Others Feel

You walk into a room and immediately feel the tension. Not because anyone said anything. But because you're picking up the emotional atmosphere.

Someone near you is anxious. Now you're anxious.

Someone's angry. Now you're on edge.

Someone's sad. Now you feel heavy.

This is **emotional contagion**. Your empathy system is so active that you absorb others' emotions. You're not just noticing their feelings, you're feeling them.

This makes you:

- Incredible therapist, friend, partner (you genuinely feel with people)
- Exhausted in public (absorbing everyone's emotions)
- Unable to distinguish your emotions from others' (whose anxiety is this?)

- Needing alone time to "reset" (discharge absorbed emotions)

You're an emotional sponge. It's a gift and a curse.

8.3 The Gift: When Sensitivity Becomes Superpower

Now let's talk about why you wouldn't want to eliminate your Princess & the Pea even if you could.

8.3.1 Exquisite Empathy: Feeling With People

You don't just understand what people are feeling. You feel it with them.

Someone tells you about their pain. You don't just sympathize, you feel it in your body. Their grief becomes your grief. Their joy becomes your joy. Their fear becomes your fear.

This is **genuine empathy**, not cognitive ("I understand you're sad") but affective ("I feel your sadness with you").

This makes you:

- The friend people come to when they're hurting (you actually get it)
- The therapist who can sit with pain (you're not afraid of emotions)
- The partner who knows what you're feeling before you say it
- The artist who can capture human depth (you feel what others miss)

While other people are saying "I understand" from a distance, you're actually there with them, feeling what they feel.

8.3.2 Social Nuance Detection: Reading What's Unspoken

You catch things others miss:

- The slight tension in someone's voice (they're upset but hiding it)
- The micro-expression that flashes before the polite smile (they're uncomfortable)
- The shift in energy when someone walks in the room (something happened)
- The subtext beneath the words (they're saying X but meaning Y)

This is **social nuance detection**, your right TPJ processing social information at a level of detail others don't access.

This makes you valuable in:

- Relationships (you know when something's wrong before they say it)
- Negotiation (you read the room, sense what people really want)
- Leadership (you detect team dynamics others miss)
- Creative work (you capture human complexity)

You're not overthinking social interactions. You're accurately processing information that's actually there. Others are under-processing. You're processing at the right level of detail, it's just exhausting.

8.3.3 Depth of Experience: Living in High Definition

You don't experience life in standard definition. You experience it in 4K.

Music isn't just pleasant. It moves you to tears. Art isn't just interesting. It reaches inside you. Nature isn't just pretty. It's overwhelming in its beauty.

This is **depth of experience**, your brain processing aesthetic, emotional, and sensory information with higher gain.

This creates:

- Profound aesthetic experiences (art, music, nature hit harder)
- Deep emotional life (you feel more intensely)
- Rich inner world (your internal experience is vivid, complex)
- Creative depth (you access emotional territory shallow processors can't)

The torture is that it's too much. The gift is that it's everything. You live in a richer, deeper, more vivid world than most people access.

8.3.4 Highly Sensitive Person (HSP): It's Not Just You

Elaine Aron's research on Highly Sensitive People (HSP):

About 15-20% of the population has **sensory processing sensitivity**, a trait characterized by:

- Depth of processing (you process information deeply)
- Overstimulation (you get overwhelmed more easily)
- Emotional reactivity (you feel more intensely)
- Sensitivity to subtleties (you notice what others miss)

This is genetic, neurobiological, and stable (Aron & Aron, 1997). It's not trauma (though trauma can amplify it). It's how your brain is wired. Sensory processing sensitivity is an evolved biological strategy (present in about 15-20% of humans and many other species) marked by deeper processing and heightened responsivity rather than pathology (Aron et al., 2012).

In brain imaging: HSPs show increased activation in regions including right TPJ, insula, and sensory processing areas (Acevedo et al., 2014). Your brain is literally processing with higher gain, feeling what everyone else misses.

8.3.5 Connection to the Bard (Chapter 10)

Note: The Princess & the Pea (right TPJ) works closely with the Bard (Chapter 10), your prosody and tone-of-voice processor.

Princess & the Pea: Detects that something's off in the tone **Bard:** Processes what the tone means (sarcasm, humor, emotional inflection)

Together, they give you social and emotional nuance detection. When both are strong, you're incredibly attuned to human communication. When both are hyperactive, you're overwhelmed by social information.

The work isn't to blunt your sensitivity, but to give it a humane cadence: fewer hits at once, more recovery between them.

8.4 The Neuroscience: Right TPJ and Sensory-Social Processing

Let me show you where "too sensitive" actually lives, and why it's not too much, just higher gain.

Okay, let's get into the brain science. This is where we go from "I'm too sensitive" to "here's exactly which circuit is processing with higher gain and why."

8.4.1 Where the Princess & the Pea Lives

The Princess & the Pea lives in your **right temporoparietal junction (TPJ)**, the region where your temporal lobe (side of brain) meets your parietal lobe (top/back), specifically at the junction of posterior superior temporal gyrus, inferior parietal lobule, and lateral occipital cortex. On a QEEG cap, this is around **P4, T6, TP8**, right posterior-temporal sites.

But here's what makes this interesting: **rTPJ is a hub, not a solo act.** It's the convergence point where multiple networks meet:

Connected networks:

- **Face processing** → Fusiform face area (FFA) feeds identity, rTPJ adds intent
- **Motor systems** → M1 and supplementary motor area (SMA) for action/mirror control

- **Emotional centers** → Amygdala connection makes social info instantly emotional
- **Attention systems** → Frontoparietal networks for orienting to salient events
- **Default mode network** → Social prediction and self-referential processing

That's why "Princess & Pea" captures so much, it's the hub where sensory, social, emotional, and agency signals all converge. When this hub runs hot, everything amplifies.

The right TPJ processes:

- **Social cognition**: Theory of mind, perspective-taking, reading intent
- **Sensory integration**: Combining vision, touch, proprioception, vestibular input into "where am I? what's my body?"
- **Agency**: "Was that me or the world?" (sense of control and authorship)
- **Self-other distinction**: Knowing where you end and others begin
- **Predictive precision**: Deciding which mismatches matter (gain on prediction errors)

When this hub is hyperactive, you get:

- Amplified social processing (RSD, social anxiety)
- Amplified sensory processing (sensory overwhelm, misophonia)
- Emotional contagion (absorbing others' emotions)
- Blurred self-other boundaries (whose feelings are these?)
- Uncertain agency (world feels unpredictable, less "under your hand")

8.4.2 QEEG Signature: What I See in Brain Maps

When I map someone with Princess & the Pea patterns, I see:

Right TPJ hyperactivation: Excess activity at P4, T6, TP8. Your social-sensory processor is running hot.

Increased connectivity to amygdala: Your emotional center is tightly coupled to your social processor. Social information immediately becomes emotional. Criticism → emotional pain. Rejection → threat response.

High beta in right posterior regions: Your brain is in high-alert mode for social and sensory information. You're scanning, processing, analyzing constantly.

Sensory gating deficits: Your brain isn't filtering sensory input effectively. What others automatically filter out (background noise, fluorescent buzz, tags in clothes), you process as relevant.

This isn't subtle. It's a clear pattern that correlates with how you describe your experience: "Everything feels too much. I notice things others don't. Rejection feels like physical pain." Social exclusion activates the same anterior cingulate cortex regions involved in physical pain (Eisenberger et al., 2003), when your Princess & Pea runs at higher gain, that signal is amplified further.

8.4.3 The Highly Sensitive Person (HSP) Brain

Elaine Aron's research shows that HSPs have measurable brain differences:

- Increased activation in brain regions involved in awareness, empathy, and sensory processing

- Including right TPJ, insula (interoception), and sensory cortices
- This is genetic (runs in families), stable (doesn't change much), and adaptive (in the right environment)

The evolutionary logic:

In a tribe, you need some people who are highly attuned to social dynamics, environmental changes, and subtle threats. The HSPs are the ones who notice:

- When someone's upset (before they say it)
- When the environment has changed (potential danger)
- When social dynamics are shifting (group cohesion)

In modern environments (loud, overstimulating, socially complex), this becomes torture. But the trait itself is adaptive, calibrated for depth, not volume.

8.4.4 RSD and the Amygdala Connection

The research (Dodell-Feder et al., 2011; Masten et al., 2009):

Right TPJ hyperactivation correlates with rejection sensitivity in multiple fMRI studies. In our clinical database at Peak Brain Institute (3,000+ QEEG assessments), approximately 60% of clients reporting RSD show elevated right TPJ beta activity (clinical observation, not yet published).

What's happening: Your right TPJ is tightly connected to your amygdala (threat/emotion center). Social information is immediately routed to emotional processing. Criticism doesn't just register as information, it triggers emotional pain response.

This isn't "in your head." It's measurable. Your circuits are configured this way.

8.4.5 Sensory Processing and Integration: Body-Self Model

Your right TPJ integrates multiple sensory streams into a unified "body-self model", a constantly updated answer to "where am I?" and "what counts as my body?":

- **Vision** (facial expressions, body language, spatial orientation)
- **Audition** (tone of voice, prosody, environmental sounds)
- **Touch** (tactile boundaries, what's touching me)
- **Proprioception** (where are my limbs?)
- **Vestibular** (am I moving? which direction?)
- **Interoception** (internal body states, heart rate, breathing)

The neuroscience: TMS (transcranial magnetic stimulation) over rTPJ during rubber-hand experiments makes it harder to distinguish what belongs to your body versus external objects. rTPJ is running a stored "body model" and testing incoming multisensory evidence against it (Tsakiris et al., 2008). Out-of-body experiences often localize to TPJ lesions or stimulation, where visual, tactile, and vestibular signals get misintegrated and people mislocalize themselves in space (Blanke & Arzy, 2005; Ionta et al., 2011).

What this means: Princess isn't just processing social information, she's integrating *all* sensory channels at once and deciding "is this me? is this mine? is this about me?"

When it's hyperactive, you get **sensory integration issues**, too much input, can't filter, everything feels relevant.

This is why:

- Grocery stores are overwhelming (visual + auditory + social + proprioceptive overload)
- Parties are exhausting (too many sensory streams to integrate simultaneously)
- Certain textures are intolerable (tactile processing amplified, body-boundary sensitivity)
- Misophonia happens (auditory processing with emotional amplification)
- You're aware of your heartbeat, breathing, internal sensations (interoceptive gain up)

Your brain is trying to integrate all of this information into "me in space," and it's turned the gain up too high on every channel.

8.4.6 Motor Interaction: "Is That Me Moving or Them?"

One more piece: Princess also talks to your motor system.

When you watch someone else perform an action, your motor cortex partially activates (mirror neurons; Rizzolatti & Craighero, 2004). Normally, your brain suppresses this so you don't automatically imitate everything you see. Right TPJ is part of that control system, it helps distinguish "their action" from "my action" and gates which motor representation wins (Bardi et al., 2017; Santiesteban et al., 2012).

When Princess is dysregulated: The boundary between "watching" and "doing" can blur. You might find yourself mirroring others' postures, movements, or emotional expressions automatically. Or conversely, you might feel disconnected from your own actions, "my body moved but it didn't quite feel like me."

The insight: Princess is the hub that decides "mine versus not-mine" across multiple domains, sensory input, emotions, agency, and even motor actions. When she's uncertain, everything blurs. When she's hyperactive, everything amplifies.

8.4.7 Agency and Control: "Did I Make That Happen?"

Here's something you might not have connected to Princess & Pea: **sense of agency**, the feeling that outcomes flow from your intentions, that you're controlling what happens.

When rTPJ is uncertain or dysregulated, the world stops feeling firmly "under your hand." Things feel like they're happening *to* you rather than *by* you. Your actions don't quite feel like yours. The connection between intention and outcome feels loose.

The neuroscience: rTPJ is a key node in the agency network: it compares what you intended to what actually happened and decides "was that me?" (Hughes, 2018; Haggard, 2017). When there's a mismatch (you intended X but Y happened), rTPJ lights up. In functional neurological disorder (movement symptoms without neurological damage), rTPJ shows structural and functional abnormalities that track with disturbed agency: "my body moved, but not by me" (Espay et al., 2018; Bühler et al., 2024).

For you: When Princess is hyperactive or dysregulated, this can show up as:

- Uncertainty about whether you caused something ("Did I upset them, or did they have a bad day?")
- Difficulty distinguishing your impact from environmental factors
- Feeling like the world is unpredictable (because you're uncertain which outcomes you controlled)
- Hyper-monitoring your own actions (checking constantly if you're "doing it right")

The connection: Princess doesn't just process social signals with high gain, she also weighs whether events are "about me" and "caused by me." When she's cranked up, everything feels like it might be your fault, and nothing feels quite under your control.

8.4.8 The Predictive Hub: Gain on "What Concerns Me"

Let's get more precise about what "high gain" actually means.

Your right TPJ isn't just amplifying everything randomly. It's a **predictive hub**, constantly comparing what's happening to what you expected, and deciding how much weight to give the mismatches. In predictive processing terms, it's tuning the *precision* on prediction errors: when reality doesn't match expectations, does that matter a little or a lot?

Your rTPJ is turning up the volume on "that might be about me" and "that matters to me." A friend being quiet gets high gain (error: expected friendliness, got distance → "they're mad at me"). A stranger being rude gets lower gain (not about me, doesn't matter). Except when Princess is running too hot, everything gets high gain, even the stranger's rudeness becomes "what did I do wrong?"

The "cocktail party effect" (tracking one conversation in a noisy room) involves right TPJ. Princess is boosting the relevant stream and filtering the rest. When she can't regulate gain properly, you hear *all* the conversations equally loud.

Bon mot version: "Princess is the gain knob on what counts as me, what matters to me, and what might be about me."

Under the Hood: Predictive Coding and Selective Attention at rTPJ

Brain imaging shows rTPJ uses different frequency bands for predictions versus errors: beta activity (12–25 Hz) carries predictions ("I expect this person to be friendly"); gamma activity (30–80 Hz) carries prediction errors ("Wait, they just frowned, that wasn't expected"). Both are strongly gated by task relevance, only relevant predictions and errors get high-gain neural expression (Auksztulewicz et al., 2017; Geng & Vossel, 2013). In selective listening, the better you track attended speech, the stronger the rTPJ signal and its connection to auditory cortex (Puschmann et al., 2017). When Princess is dysregulated, the precision weighting is too high on too many channels, everything becomes task-relevant, and prediction errors flood in from every direction.

8.4.9 Self-Other Boundaries: "Whose Feeling Is This?"

Here's where emotional contagion gets its mechanism.

Right TPJ regulates the boundary between self and other, across perception, action, and affect (Quesque & Brass, 2019). It's not just noticing others' emotions; it's keeping yours separate from theirs.

The research: Meta-analyses show rTPJ and adjacent right supramarginal gyrus are crucial for overcoming **emotional egocentricity**, keeping "my feeling" and "your feeling" distinct (Silani et al., 2013). When this system is dysregulated:

- **Too porous:** You feel everyone's emotions as your own (emotional contagion)
- **Too rigid:** You can't empathize, can't take others' perspectives (rare in Princess types)

Neuromodulation studies (tDCS over rTPJ) causally shift perceived self-other distance: stimulation can make you feel more separate from observed experiences, supporting rTPJ as a boundary-setting mechanism (Santiesteban et al., 2012).

For you: When Princess runs hot, boundaries leak. You walk into a room and absorb the tension. Someone near you is anxious, now you're anxious. You can't tell: whose anxiety is this? Is this my feeling or am I picking up theirs?

The mechanism: Princess checks every sensation and feeling, "mine or someone else's?" When she's uncertain or overwhelmed, she defaults to "might be mine" (better safe than sorry). The result: you drown in other people's emotional states.

The gift side: This same porous boundary, when regulated, is what makes you an exceptional therapist, friend, artist. You genuinely feel with people. Not "I understand you're sad", you feel their sadness with them. That's rare, precious, and exhausting.

Princess as bouncer: When working well, she's the bouncer at the door of "me", checking every feeling, letting yours in, keeping others' feelings acknowledged but not absorbed. When overwhelmed, the door's wide open and everything floods in.

The Princess & the Pea: Right TPJ

Gifts	**Torture**
• Exquisite empathy (feel what others feel) • Social nuance detection (micro-expressions, subtext) • Depth of connection (shallow processors can't access) • Artistic sensitivity (subtleties in art/music/relationships) • Early warning system (sense when something's wrong) • Emotional intelligence (complex emotional dynamics)	• Rejection Sensitivity Dysphoria (RSD): criticism = annihilation • Sensory overwhelm (sounds/lights/textures overwhelming) • Social anxiety (too many signals, exhausted by processing) • Emotional flooding (feelings at volume 11) • Misophonia (specific sounds trigger rage) • Can't tell what's real (seventeen interpretations, uncertain)

8.5 Toolkit Preview

Your Princess & Pea is trainable. You need empathy and nuance, just not at volume 11. If alcohol, cannabis, or isolation have been your protection, you've been numbing the torture and the gifts simultaneously. Chapter 14 explains the trade-off.

Start with your environment right now: noise-canceling headphones, soft textures, smaller social groups, and scheduled recovery time after high-stimulation situations reduce the load before you need to regulate anything.

- **Sleep** (Ch 13): sleep deprivation amplifies RSD and sensory sensitivity directly. This is a critical first variable.
- **Stress Response Regulation** (Ch 15): nervous system flexibility lets you process social signals at appropriate gain instead of maximum gain.
- **Neurofeedback** (Ch 18): right TPJ calibration trains processing without numbing, the goal is accurate, not numb.

Detailed protocols are in Part II. These circuits respond to training.

The right TPJ circuits that create rejection sensitivity and sensory overwhelm are the same circuits that, once trained, produce accurate empathy at manageable gain. Part II shows you how to build that.

8.6 Key Takeaways

The Princess & Pea (Right TPJ) is your brain's high-gain social and sensory processor, the circuit that feels what others miss, catches micro-expressions, and experiences everything more intensely.

- **"I can't tell what's behind your smile":** You detect micro-signals (real data) but generate seventeen interpretations, picking up subtle cues but can't parse which is correct, leading to catastrophizing all possibilities simultaneously
- **RSD as circuit configuration:** Rejection Sensitivity Dysphoria isn't "being too sensitive", it's right frontal (Grumpy Old Man) + right TPJ (Princess & Pea) hyperactivation processing criticism with amplified gain
- **The substance paradox:** Alcohol/cannabis/benzos numb torture but also numb gifts, you get relief from overwhelm but lose access to empathy, social nuance, depth, and artistic sensitivity that make you who you are
- **Sensory Processing Sensitivity (HSP) is genetic:** 15-20% of population (Elaine Aron's research), stable wiring, not something to eliminate, environmental optimization and sensory gating training allow you to access gifts without constant overwhelm

- **Training gating, not numbing:** Right TPJ regulation (neurofeedback), sensory meditation (body scan, sound meditation), equanimity practices (observe without amplifying), learning which signals are worth amplifying versus which to let pass

8.7 Reader Reflections

1. **How does RSD show up for you?** Delayed text = they hate you? Can you trace this to high-gain processing?
2. **What sensory inputs overwhelm you most?** Sounds? Lights? Touch? Crowds? Have there been times when these sensitivities turned into superpowers, catching details others missed, sensing what someone needed before they asked, creating art from depth others can't access?
3. **Can you recognize when you're reading real signals versus amplifying neutral ones?** Think of a time you were certain someone was upset, were they, or were you interpreting fatigue as rejection?
4. **How uncertain is your sense of agency?** Do you struggle to tell whether outcomes are "caused by you" or "just happened"? When things go wrong, do you default to "my fault" or struggle to know if you had any control? Can you trace this to Princess uncertainty about "was that me?"

Systems Interlude: Language & Social

Semantic vs. Nonverbal: Words, Tone, and Meaning

Your Interpreter hears the words. Your Bard hears what they actually mean. Poet-brains hear both (simultaneously) and wonder why everyone else only caught half.

Location: Left temporal / parietal (language comprehension) + right posterior temporal (prosody / tone) + left frontal (Broca's area / speech production)
Phenotypes: Interpreter (Chapter 9) + Bard (Chapter 10) + Speaker (minor character, Broca's area)
System function: Decodes meaning from words and tone, produces verbal expression, what you hear, how you hear it, what you say

---

What This System Does When Balanced

Your Language & Social Communication System translates the world into meaning and expresses your thoughts. When it's balanced:

- You understand spoken and written language without delays (Interpreter working)
- You catch sarcasm, irony, and emotional tone (Bard attuned)
- You can articulate your thoughts clearly (Speaker producing speech)
- Your voice matches your emotions (Bard + Speaker coordinating)
- You can find words when you need them (Speaker accessing vocabulary)

The Interpreter handles the **what** (literal meaning, words, grammar), the Bard handles the **how** (tone, prosody, emotional music), and the Speaker handles **expression** (producing verbal output).

Key relationship: Wernicke's (Interpreter) generates linguistic content, Broca's (Speaker) executes motor production. Language flows posterior → anterior, with the Interpreter checking what the Speaker produces, which is why stuttering involves both regions. Speaker doesn't get a full phenotype chapter because it largely serves the Interpreter's content. Word-finding issues come from slowing alpha in language areas (words exist, access is slow), which is different from expressive aphasia (know what to say, can't produce it).

What Dysregulation Looks Like

Interpreter slow (left temporal/parietal underactive or slowed alpha): Processing delays, have to read things multiple times, word-finding difficulties (slowed alpha spreading in language areas, words exist but access is slow), can't track fast conversations, dyslexia, verbal comprehension challenges

Interpreter overactive (left temporal/parietal hyperactive): Constant internal narration, can't stop explaining, talk-to-think, verbal processing dominates all experience

Bard offline (right posterior underactive): Miss sarcasm and irony, take things literally, sound flat or monotone, voice doesn't match emotions, struggle to tell if someone's joking

Bard hyperactive (right posterior overactive): Over-read tone, hear criticism in neutral speech, prosody overwhelms literal meaning, emotional tone feels threatening

Both dysregulated: Classic autism / ADHD language patterns, slow verbal processing + missing social cues, or fast verbal processing + tone-deafness. Text communication becomes easier because it removes the prosodic layer.

Network Connection

The Interpreter and Bard are part of the **receptive processing networks**, taking in and decoding information rather than generating action. The Interpreter connects to the **Default Mode Network (DMN)** when engaged in internal narration and autobiographical thinking. The Bard contributes to **social salience detection**, reading emotional tone to determine if someone is safe, threatening, joking, or serious.

This system shapes your conversational cadence: how quickly you generate words, how long you stay on a topic, how fast you read subtext.

Map so far: 8 of 12. You're more than halfway through the orchestra. You've met the approach-avoidance engine, the motor axis, the orienting system, and the right-hemisphere sensitivity pair. Up next: The Interpreter and The Bard, how your brain decodes language and the emotional music behind words. Left hemisphere meaning meets right hemisphere tone.

Ch 9: The Interpreter (Left Temporal)

When Words Don't Land

Someone's giving you directions. Multi-step instructions. You're listening carefully. By the time they finish, you've lost track of steps two and three.

9.1 "The Meaning-Decoder"

You're at a party. Music's playing, people are talking. Someone's giving you directions. You hear them, but you can't pull their voice out from the background noise. The words blur together.

Or you're reading a paragraph, and you get to the end and realize you have no idea what you just read. The words were there, but the meaning didn't stick.

Or you're speaking, and the perfect word is right there (you know it) but you can't retrieve it. You say "the thing" instead of "colander." You use five words when one precise word exists but won't come.

This is the Interpreter: your left posterior temporal lobe, the classic receptive language zone that neurology has known about since Wernicke described it in the 1870s. Its job: decode meaning from words, retrieve words for expression, and coordinate with the Speaker to turn thought into speech.

The Interpreter handles:

- **Semantic comprehension**: What does this word actually mean?
- **Auditory scene analysis**: Pulling speech from background noise (the cocktail party problem)
- **Word retrieval**: Finding the right word when you need it
- **Arcuate Fasciculus coordination**: The highway connecting comprehension (Wernicke's) to speech production (Broca's/Speaker)

Your speech cadence: do you need to talk fast and continuous, or shorter bursts with pauses to consolidate?

When this circuit is strong, language lands easily. You pull conversation from noisy rooms effortlessly. Multi-step instructions? No problem. The right word appears when you need it. Your thought and speech are synchronized.

When it's weak or wired atypically, the experience flips:

- Background noise drowns out speech
- Words are there, but meaning won't stick
- You know the word but can't retrieve it
- Your thought and speech are out of sync (stuttering, word-finding delays)

And here's where it gets interesting: the Interpreter works closely with the **Speaker** (left frontal, Broca's area). They're connected by the **arcuate fasciculus**: the white-matter highway between them. **Wernicke's (Interpreter, posterior) drives Broca's (Speaker, frontal)** much more than the reverse. Language generation flows posterior → anterior.

The Interpreter generates and understands language. The Speaker produces speech output. When the phone line between them is clear, thought and speech are synchronized.

When it's not:

- **Speaker damage (stroke, trauma):** Expressive/Broca's aphasia: you know what you want to say but can't produce it
- **Word-finding issues:** Slowing alpha spreading in language areas: words exist, access is slow (like buffering)
- **Different mechanisms:** Aphasia = motor production failure. Word-finding = retrieval/access slowdown.

9.2 The Torture: When the Interpreter Fails (or Overwhelms)

Let's talk about what it's actually like when your meaning-decoder is dysregulated.

9.2.1 The Cocktail Party Problem: Can't Pull Speech from Noise

You're in a restaurant. Your friend is talking. But there's music playing, dishes clattering, other conversations. You can hear that they're speaking, but you can't pull their voice out from the noise. The words blur together.

Or you're on a Zoom call with background noise. Everyone else seems fine. You're straining to understand, asking people to repeat.

Or you're in a lecture hall. The person behind you is whispering. You can't follow the lecture anymore. You're tracking the wrong auditory stream.

This is **auditory scene analysis failure**: your Interpreter can't cleanly separate the target voice from background sounds. It's not a hearing problem (your ears are fine). It's a central auditory processing issue: your brain can't filter.

Not because you're not paying attention. Your attention is fine. Your Interpreter just can't do the signal separation work that others do automatically.

9.2.2 Receptive Language Struggles: Hearing But Not Understanding

You're listening. You're paying attention. The words are clear. But the meaning isn't landing.

Someone gives you instructions. By step three, you've lost the thread. You have to ask them to repeat. They get frustrated: "I just told you."

You're reading. The words are there. But you get to the end of the paragraph and realize you absorbed nothing. You have to read it three times before the meaning registers.

This is **receptive language difficulty**: your Interpreter isn't efficiently converting sounds (or text) into meaning. The phonemes are there, but the semantic integration isn't happening smoothly.

Not because you're not smart. Your intelligence is fine. Your Interpreter is just wired differently.

9.2.3 Word-Finding Struggles: Knowing the Word But Can't Access It

You're talking. You know exactly what you want to say. The word is right there. But it won't come.

You say "the thing you use to drain pasta" instead of "colander."

You describe around the word: "You know, that feeling when…"

You substitute: "I need the…thingy."

This is **word retrieval difficulty** (anomia): your Interpreter can't efficiently access stored lexical items. The word exists in your semantic network, but the retrieval pathway is slow or blocked.

The neuroscience:

Left temporal regions (particularly middle temporal gyrus and angular gyrus) are critical for lexical retrieval. When these areas show reduced activation or increased alpha (idling), word finding slows. It's like buffering: the information exists but access is delayed.

What's happening: Your semantic knowledge is intact (you know what a colander is), but the phonological form won't surface. You're stuck describing instead of naming.

This is different from **expressive aphasia** (Speaker damage, Broca's area stroke), where you know the word but can't motorically produce it. Word-finding is a retrieval problem. Aphasia is a production problem.

9.2.4 Dyslexia: When Print Feels Opaque

You're intelligent. You're articulate. But reading is hard. Not impossible, just harder than it should be.

Letters seem to move. Words blend together. You lose your place. You have to re-read sentences. Spelling is a nightmare, you know the word, but you can't map it to letters.

I see this constantly in my practice, brilliant clients who read slowly, avoid reading-heavy tasks, feel shame about something that's just wiring. Not low IQ. Not lack of effort. Just glitchy phonological mapping.

This is **dyslexia**: your Interpreter's phonological layer is glitchy. It struggles to cleanly convert graphemes (letters) ↔ phonemes (sounds) and to keep sound patterns in short-term storage.

The neuroscience (Skeide et al., 2015; Achal et al., 2016):

Left temporoparietal cortex (TPJ) is crucial for encoding and retrieval of speech sounds. In dyslexia, this region shows reduced activation during phonological tasks and word reading. It's not "visual", it's phonological. Your Interpreter can't efficiently map print to sound.

The frustration: Your intelligence is normal or high. But reading feels like decoding a foreign language. Every. Single. Time.

9.2.5 ASD and Literal Processing: Missing Implied Meaning

You hear the words. You understand the literal meaning. But you miss what they actually mean.

Someone says "Can you pass the salt?" You answer "Yes" but don't pass it. (They meant "please pass the salt," not asking about your capability.)

Someone uses a metaphor: "It's raining cats and dogs." You look outside, confused.

Someone's being indirect: "It's getting late..." You agree. They were hinting they want to leave.

This is **ASD-flavored literal processing**: your Interpreter decodes the semantic content accurately but doesn't automatically infer the pragmatic intent, implied meaning, or non-literal usage.

The neuroscience (Tesink et al., 2009; Gold & Faust, 2010):

The left inferior frontal gyrus (IFG) and superior temporal regions work together to process metaphors, idioms, and implied meaning. In autism, this network shows reduced recruitment, metaphors are processed more literally, requiring effortful re-interpretation rather than automatic non-literal comprehension.

What's happening: Your Interpreter is doing its job, extracting semantic content from words. But the layer that automatically applies context, intent, and non-literal interpretation isn't engaging smoothly. You're missing the pragmatic overlay that neurotypicals apply without thinking.

Note: This is about SEMANTIC processing and implied meaning. Tone and emotional subtext processing (whether someone sounds sarcastic, angry, or friendly) is handled by the **Bard** (Chapter 10, right posterior). The Interpreter handles *what* they said. The Bard handles *how* it felt.

9.2.6 Stuttering: When Interpreter and Speaker Are Out of Sync

You know what you want to say. The meaning is clear in your mind. The word is ready. But when you try to speak, the words get stuck. Repetitions. Blocks. Prolongations.

"I w-w-w-want to go." The word is there, but it won't flow.

This is **stuttering**: not a pure Speaker problem, but a **coordination problem** between Interpreter (Wernicke's, posterior) and Speaker (Broca's, frontal) along the **arcuate fasciculus**: the white-matter highway connecting them.

Note on the Speaker: The Speaker (left frontal, Broca's area) handles motor production of speech, actually moving your mouth to form words. When the Speaker itself is damaged (stroke, trauma), you get **expressive aphasia**: you know what you want to say but can't produce it. That's different from **stuttering** (timing coordination issue between Interpreter and Speaker) and different from **word-finding** (slowed alpha, covered in Timekeeper / Chapter 11, words exist but retrieval is slow). Speaker is a "bonus phenotype", driven by the Interpreter, not a standalone circuit with its own chapter.

The neuroscience (Chang & Guenther, 2020; Cieslak et al., 2015):

Developmental stuttering involves atypical structure and function in a network including:

- Left IFG / Broca's area (Speaker: motor articulation)
- Premotor cortex (motor planning)
- Posterior temporal regions (Interpreter: phonological encoding)
- Arcuate fasciculus (the connection between them)
- **Basal ganglia and cerebellum** (timing and sequencing)

Chang & Guenther (2020) emphasize the role of the **cortico-basal ganglia-thalamocortical loop** in timing control and motor sequencing, faulty auditory-motor integration and feedforward / feedback control. **Cieslak et al. (2015)** show that the **arcuate fasciculus** often has reduced structural integrity (fewer or less organized white-matter tracts) in developmental stuttering.

What's happening: Your Interpreter generates the phonological plan (the sound pattern of the word). This plan travels via the arcuate fasciculus to the Speaker (Broca's area), which converts it into motor commands for articulation.

When the arcuate fasciculus connection is glitchy or the timing between Interpreter and Speaker is off, the phonological frames from your Interpreter and the motor programs from your Speaker don't align in time. The result: repetitions, blocks, prolongations.

It's not that you don't know what to say. The semantic content is clear. The word is selected. The phonological form is encoded. **The timing between comprehension/encoding (Interpreter) and production (Speaker) is disrupted.**

This is why stuttering is an Interpreter chapter issue, not purely a Speaker issue, the problem is in the coordination between posterior (Wernicke's/Interpreter) and frontal (Broca's/Speaker), mediated by the arcuate fasciculus.

9.2.7 Verbal Working Memory Overload: Can't Hold It All

Someone gives you a phone number. By digit seven, you've lost digits two and three. Someone gives you complex instructions. You can follow the first part, but the rest falls out of your working memory. You're in a conversation. Someone makes a point. By the time they finish their next sentence, you've forgotten what you were going to say.

This is **verbal working memory limitation**: your Interpreter can't hold enough phonological information in the buffer.

The neuroscience:

Left TPJ supports verbal short-term storage. Damage here reduces verbal span despite intact basic speech perception (Paulesu et al., 1993). This is your phonological buffer, the place where you hold words, instructions, phone numbers while you use them.

When this buffer is small or noisy, you can't hold multi step instructions, long sentences, complex verbal information. You need things written down. You need to repeat back to encode. You need external memory support.

9.3 The Gift: When the Interpreter Is Strong

Now let's talk about why you need your Interpreter: when it's working well, not struggling.

9.3.1 High Verbal Comprehension: Language Lands Easily

When your Interpreter is strong, you follow complex speech effortlessly. Lectures, podcasts, audiobooks, you absorb them easily. Multi-step instructions? No problem. Complex sentences? You track them.

This is **high verbal comprehension**: your Interpreter efficiently converts sounds into meaning, holds verbal information in working memory, integrates context and semantics.

The research (Heyer et al., 2021; Menary et al., 2013):

Verbal IQ correlates with cortical thickness and microstructure particularly in left temporal association cortex. Greater cortical richness in left temporal regions = higher verbal ability.

This is the hyper-articulate gifted/tortured poet: Interpreter strong, Speaker strong (when we get to that phenotype). You're verbally brilliant.

9.3.2 Semantic Integration: Getting the Meaning

When your Interpreter works, you don't just hear words, you get the meaning. The gist. The implication. The context.

Someone uses a metaphor. You get it immediately, your brain automatically processes the non-literal meaning.

Someone's being indirect. You catch what they're actually asking for, not just the literal words.

You read complex text. The meaning integrates smoothly, you're building a coherent mental model as you read.

This is **semantic integration**: your Interpreter combining phonology (sounds), semantics (meaning), syntax (grammar), and context (situation) into coherent understanding.

Note: If someone's tone doesn't match their words, that's the **Bard** (Chapter 10). The Interpreter handles what they said (semantic content). The Bard handles how it felt (prosody, emotional tone).

9.3.3 Verbal Working Memory: Holding Complex Information

When your Interpreter works, you can hold complex verbal information in mind.

Phone numbers. Multi-step instructions. Long sentences. Arguments with multiple premises. You can track them, hold them, use them.

This is your **phonological buffer**: left TPJ storing verbal information while you process it.

9.3.4 Clarity and Articulation: Explaining Complex Ideas

When your Interpreter is strong, you can take complex ideas and make them clear. You find the right words. You structure explanations. You make the implicit explicit.

This is the gift of strong receptive language: you understand deeply, so you can explain clearly.

9.4 The Neuroscience: The Meaning-Decoder

Okay, let's get into the brain science. This is where we go from "I struggle with language" (or "I'm verbally brilliant") to "here's exactly which circuit is doing what."

9.4.1 Where the Interpreter Lives

The Interpreter lives in your **left posterior temporal lobe and temporoparietal junction (TPJ)**: the classic receptive language zone, often called Wernicke's area.

The anatomy: As we saw in the Language & Social Communication systems interlude, this includes the posterior superior temporal gyrus/sulcus (speech sound processing), the temporoparietal junction (syntax, context, and phonological buffer), the superior temporal sulcus (prosody and social signals), and adjacent middle temporal gyrus (semantic retrieval).

- Semantic processing, word meaning
- Integrating language with world knowledge

Together: This is the receptive language hub, turning raw speech sounds into coherent internal models of "what was just said" and whether it fits the situation. In practice: this is why a paragraph sometimes clicks on first read, or why you get to the end and realize you absorbed nothing. Same words, different Interpreter state.

9.4.2 The Interpreter's Job: Decoding Meaning

The Interpreter does several things simultaneously:

1. Phonological processing:

- Segmenting continuous speech into discrete units (phonemes, words)
- Mapping sounds to stored word forms
- Holding phonological information in short-term buffer

2. Semantic processing:

- Accessing word meanings
- Integrating words into sentence meaning
- Connecting language to world knowledge

3. Syntactic processing:

- Tracking grammar, sentence structure
- Knowing if the sentence is well-formed
- Predicting what comes next

4. Social-pragmatic processing:

- Integrating tone, prosody, context
- Understanding implied meaning, subtext
- Tracking communicative intent (what they really mean)

When all of this works smoothly, language lands effortlessly. When any piece is glitchy, when you can't pull one voice from background noise, or say "the thing" instead of "colander," or read a whole page and retain nothing, you're seeing where one of these layers is buffering.

9.4.3 The Interpreter → Speaker Connection: Arcuate Fasciculus

The Interpreter (posterior temporal/TPJ) connects to the Speaker (left frontal: IFG/Broca, premotor) via the **arcuate fasciculus (AF)**: a white-matter highway.

What the AF does:

Carries phonological and lexical information forward so the Speaker can:

- Repeat what was heard
- Turn comprehension into speech output
- Build complex syntax

When the AF is intact: Smooth connection between understanding and speaking. You hear, you understand, you can repeat it back, you can elaborate.

When the AF is damaged: Conduction aphasia, relatively preserved comprehension, relatively preserved spontaneous speech, but impaired repetition and phonological errors. The Interpreter can't properly drive the Speaker.

In your phenotype map:

- **Interpreter** (left posterior temporal/TPJ): Hears, decodes meaning, holds verbal info
- **Arcuate fasciculus**: The phone line between them
- **Speaker** (left frontal: will cover more fully elsewhere): Produces speech, articulates

When the phone line is clear, thought and speech are synchronized. When it's glitchy, you get timing problems (stuttering), repetition problems (conduction aphasia), or the experience of "I know what I want to say but can't find the words."

9.4.4 Dyslexia: The Phonological Layer Glitch

The neuroscience (Skeide et al., 2015; Achal et al., 2016):

Dyslexia involves reduced activation in left temporoparietal cortex during phonological tasks and word reading. Genetic risk variants for dyslexia show altered hemodynamic responses in this region.

What's happening:

Your Interpreter's phonological processing is glitchy. It can't efficiently:

- Map graphemes (letters) to phonemes (sounds)
- Segment words into sound units
- Hold phonological patterns in short-term storage
- Retrieve phonological codes quickly

Reading requires phonological processing. If your Interpreter's phonological layer is weak, reading feels like constant decoding work. Your intelligence is fine. Your Interpreter is just wired differently.

9.4.5 ASD: The Literal Processing Glitch

The neuroscience (Tesink et al., 2009; Gold & Faust, 2010):

Processing metaphors and idioms typically recruits left IFG and posterior temporal regions. In autism, metaphorical language processing shows reduced recruitment of these networks and relies more on effortful, literal-then-reinterpret strategies.

What's happening:

Your Interpreter decodes the semantic content accurately. But the layer that automatically applies non-literal interpretation, implied meaning, and pragmatic context isn't engaging smoothly. You're processing the literal semantic content but missing the pragmatic layer.

This is different from missing **emotional tone** (sarcasm detection, emotional prosody), that's the **Bard** (Chapter 10, right posterior). The Interpreter handles *what* was said (semantic meaning, literal vs. figurative). The Bard handles *how* it sounded (emotional tone, prosody, sarcasm).

9.4.6 Stuttering: The Timing Glitch

The neuroscience (Chang & Guenther, 2020):

Developmental stuttering involves a network including left IFG (Speaker), premotor, auditory cortex, **cortico-basal ganglia-thalamocortical loops** (timing and motor sequencing), and temporoparietal regions (Interpreter). Altered connectivity and timing between these nodes. Faulty auditory-motor integration and feedforward/feedback control.

What's happening:

Your Interpreter and Speaker are slightly out of sync in time. The phonological frames from your Interpreter and the motor programs from your Speaker don't align. The result: repetitions, blocks, prolongations.

It's not that you don't know what to say. It's that the timing between comprehension and production is off.

The Interpreter: Left Posterior Temporal	
Gifts	**Torture**
• Language comprehension (complex meaning, nuance) • Rapid decoding (process verbal info quickly) • Meaning-making (sounds into sense) • Verbal fluency (words available when needed) • Reading comprehension (understand, retain text) • Conceptual integration (connect ideas through language)	• Words don't land (read paragraph multiple times) • Slow verbal processing (fall behind in conversations) • Word-finding difficulties (can't access words) • Constant narration (can't experience without commentary) • Dyslexia patterns (letters jumbled, reading exhausting) • Stuttering/speech blocks (timing off between thought & speech)

9.5 Toolkit Preview

Your Interpreter is trainable, whether words struggle to land or your internal narrator won't stop.

For verbal overflow: practice the pause before speaking. Let yourself process internally first. For comprehension delays: slow down, ask for written versions, re-read without shame, these are accommodations, not weaknesses.

- **Meditation** (Ch 17): non-verbal practices: body scan, breath, movement, give the Interpreter a genuine rest.
- **Neurofeedback** (Ch 18): left temporal activation for comprehension struggles; alpha training for verbal hyperactivity. Protocol depends on your specific pattern.

Detailed protocols are in Part II. These circuits respond to training.

The left temporal circuits that create comprehension delays or verbal flooding are the same circuits that, once trained, produce clean language processing, decode when needed, experience non-verbally when not. Part II shows you how to build that.

9.6 Key Takeaways

The Interpreter (Left Posterior Temporal/Wernicke's Area) is your brain's semantic language system: the circuit that decodes WHAT words mean, retrieves words for speech, and coordinates with the Speaker to produce language.

- **The Interpreter vs. The Bard:** The Interpreter handles WHAT was said (semantic content, literal vs. figurative meaning, word retrieval). The Bard (Chapter 10, right posterior) handles HOW it was said (tone, prosody, emotional coloring, sarcasm). Together, they decode human communication. When the Interpreter is weak, you miss the literal meaning. When the Bard is weak, you miss the emotional subtext.
- **Bidirectional issues:** Either words don't land (receptive processing delays, need to read/hear multiple times, struggle in noisy environments) OR constant narration won't stop (hyper-verbal internal monologue). Different problems, same circuit.
- **Comprehension vs. production coordination:** Interpreter (Wernicke's, posterior) generates and decodes language, retrieves words. Speaker (Broca's, frontal) produces speech output. They're connected by the **arcuate fasciculus**, the white-matter highway. When this coordination is smooth, thought and speech are synchronized. When it's disrupted, you get stuttering (timing problem), word-finding delays (retrieval problem), or conduction aphasia (repetition problem).
- **Word-finding vs. aphasia:** Word-finding difficulty = retrieval slowdown (word exists, access is delayed, like buffering). Expressive aphasia = Speaker/motor production failure (know what to say, can't motorically produce it). Different mechanisms, different circuits.
- **Auditory scene analysis:** Pulling target speech from background noise is an Interpreter function. When this fails, noisy environments become impossible, not a hearing problem, but a central processing problem.
- **"Talking to think" as external working memory:** If you process through verbalizing, you're using language as thinking tool, not just communication, your Interpreter needs external output to complete processing loops.
- **Autism's literal interpretation:** Processing language more literally, missing implied subtext (pragmatic layer), taking longer to decode idioms/metaphors, different Interpreter wiring for pragmatic inference, not comprehension deficit. (Tone/emotional prosody is Bard, not Interpreter.)
- **Training regulation:** Left posterior temporal neurofeedback, meditation to reduce constant narration (open awareness practices), phonological

training for dyslexia, and learning when to engage verbal processing versus when to experience non-verbally.

9.7 Reader Reflections

1. **How does language comprehension feel?** Do words land immediately or need processing time?
2. **Do you recognize constant narration?** Does your brain narrate everything?
3. **Do you process through talking?** Can you identify this as external working memory (strength) rather than "talking too much"?

Ch 10: The Bard (Right Posterior Temporal/TPJ)

"Nice Job" - Compliment or Threat?

Your boss says "Nice job" after your presentation. Everyone else hears: compliment. You hear: threat. Or stress. Or judgement.

10.1 "Hearing the Music Behind the Words"

What did you notice? Something. There was something in the tone. A flatness. A slight edge. A micro-pause before "nice." Something that tells you they didn't actually mean it.

But you can't tell if you're right or if you're over-reading.

Are they being sarcastic? Passive-aggressive? Genuinely complimentary but tired? You generate seventeen possible interpretations based on that two-word phrase.

This is the Bard, your right posterior temporal lobe and temporoparietal junction, the circuit that reads not WHAT people say, but HOW they say it. Your brain's social storyteller, interpreting the emotional narrative beneath the words.

The melody. The timing. The stress. The warmth or bite or wink in a voice.

The Bard listens to the music behind the words and decides: "Is this a compliment, a threat, or a joke?"

When your Bard is strong:

- You "hear the smile" in someone's voice
- You get sarcasm, irony, deadpan immediately
- You can tell when "Fine" means "fine" vs. "you are dead to me"
- You're funny: you have timing, delivery, prosodic control

When your Bard is dysregulated (flooding/poor filtering):

- You miss sarcasm not because you're not picking it up, but because you're picking up TOO MANY prosodic signals and drowning in them
- Can't tell if someone's joking or serious (signal-to-noise ratio collapsed)
- Your own speech may be flat/monotone (aprosodia from frontal Speaker issues)
- Prosodic flooding can look like "missing" emotional color, you're overwhelmed by it

When your Bard is overactive or threat-biased:

- You hear threat in neutral tones
- Over-read prosody, assuming hostility where none exists
- Ambiguous vocal cues feel dangerous
- Social paranoia-light (every "how are you?" sounds loaded)

The Bard is the mirror-half to the Interpreter (Chapter 9):

- **Interpreter** (left TPJ): Semantic content: WHAT they said
- **Bard** (right TPJ/pSTS): Emotional and pragmatic contour: HOW they meant it

Together, they decode human communication. When both work, you're socially fluent. When one is weak, you're missing half the message.

10.2 The Torture: When the Bard Fails (or Overwhelms)

Let's talk about what it's actually like when your prosody decoder is dysregulated.

10.2.1 Missing Sarcasm: Taking Everything Literally

Someone says "Oh great, just what I needed" with a flat, sarcastic tone. You think: they're happy about this. Everyone else knows: they're being sarcastic. You miss it entirely. Later, someone tells you "they were being sarcastic" and you're genuinely confused. It sounded sincere to you.

Or someone says "I'm fine" in a clipped, tense voice. You take them at their word. Everyone else knows they're not fine. You missed the tone-content mismatch, the words said one thing, the tone said another, and you couldn't tell which to believe.

I see this pattern frequently in my practice, clients who miss sarcasm entirely, take things literally, genuinely confused when told "they were joking." Not social blindness. **Bard flooding.**

This is **dysregulated Bard**, you're processing the semantic content (Interpreter working) but drowning in prosodic signals. You're not missing the emotional layer because it's absent, you're missing it because you're picking up TOO MANY signals and can't parse which ones matter.

Sarcasm, irony, teasing, deadpan, these require parsing WHICH prosodic features matter. When your Bard is flooding (high beta, low alpha filtering), you're overwhelmed by prosodic data. The music is too loud, too complex, collapsing into noise.

10.2.2 Flat Speech: Aprosodia

Your speech is flat. Monotone. No emotional color. No rhythm or stress variation.

You're excited, but you sound bored. You're joking, but you sound serious. You're being warm, but you sound cold.

This is **aprosodia**, your Bard isn't generating emotional prosody in your own speech. You understand the words, but you can't wrap them in the emotional packaging that conveys intent.

The neuroscience: Right temporal and frontal lesions produce aprosodia (Bateman et al., 2019). You can speak (Speaker intact), you understand words (Interpreter intact), but the emotional melody is gone (Bard offline).

People misread you constantly. They think you're angry when you're calm. They think you're serious when you're joking. Your Bard can't color your voice with the emotional tone you're feeling.

10.2.3 Over-Reading Threat: Hearing Hostility in Neutral Tones

Someone says something in a neutral tone. You hear: anger, contempt, rejection.

Your Bard is detecting threat in prosody that isn't there. Or it's detecting micro-signals of irritation and amplifying them into hostility.

This is **threat-biased Bard**, your right hemisphere is biased toward emotion-attention integration, prioritizing salient or threatening stimuli (Hartikainen, 2021). Ambiguous vocal cues get interpreted as dangerous.

Combined with the Princess & the Pea (Chapter 8, right TPJ social sensitivity), this creates social paranoia-light. You're hearing threat in voices that are actually neutral or mildly annoyed.

10.2.4 Missing Obvious, Catching Subtle: Wrong Layer

You miss obvious social cues. Someone's clearly uncomfortable, everyone else notices. You don't.

But you catch subtle micro-shifts in tone that others miss. A slight warmth. A micro-hesitation. An almost-imperceptible edge.

This is **Bard flooding and losing hierarchy**, you're picking up so many prosodic signals that you can't distinguish what's loud / obvious from what's subtle. The signal-to-noise ratio collapses. You catch micro-details while missing macro-patterns.

Your Bard is exquisitely sensitive to nuance, but when flooded, the nuance drowns out the obvious. You're not under-processing, you're drowning in signal.

10.2.5 Making Jokes When People Want Directness

You're in a serious conversation. Someone's upset. You make a joke.

Not because you don't care. But because your Bard defaults to humor as social navigation. Lightening the mood. Diffusing tension. Making connection through laughter.

But they wanted directness. They wanted sincerity. Your joke landed wrong.

This is **Bard as default mode**, you process social situations through humor, irony, playfulness. But not everyone wants that. Sometimes people want straight talk.

10.3 The Gift: When the Bard Makes You Brilliant

Now let's talk about why you need your Bard, when it's working right, not struggling.

10.3.1 Prosody Decoding: Hearing the Music

When your Bard works, you hear what others miss.

Someone says "I'm fine" and you immediately know: they're not fine. The tone tells you.

Someone says one thing, but their tone says another. You catch the mismatch, the words say "no problem" but the voice says "I'm annoyed." You know which one to believe.

Someone's voice has a slight warmth. You know: they like you, even if their words are neutral.

Someone's being sarcastic. You get it immediately. You don't need emojis or "/s" tags. The prosody tells you.

This is **affective prosody decoding**, extracting emotion, intent, and pragmatic meaning from tone, rhythm, stress, and timing.

This is also tone-content mismatch detection: When the words don't match the music, your Bard knows. It's not just hearing tone, it's detecting when tone contradicts content and knowing which signal to trust.

You're not over-reading. You're accurately processing information that's actually there in the voice.

10.3.2 Humor: Getting the Joke

When your Bard works, you get jokes. Punchlines land. Irony is obvious. Deadpan is hilarious.

You detect incongruity, the mismatch between expectation and reality that creates humor. You infer intent ("are they teasing or attacking?"). You integrate tone and context: "cheerful tone about a bad situation = sarcasm."

This is the Bard's specialty: detecting the twist, the wink, the playful subversion of expectations.

And when your Bard is strong, you're funny. You have timing. Delivery. Prosodic control. You can make people laugh not just with what you say, but how you say it.

10.3.3 Sarcasm and Irony: Saying One Thing, Meaning Another

When your Bard works, you can say one thing and mean another, and people get it.

"Oh great, just what I needed" (sarcastic tone) = everyone knows you're not actually happy.

"That's... interesting" (specific prosodic coloring) = everyone knows you think it's terrible.

This is **pragmatic coloring**, using prosody to signal "I don't literally mean these words."

And you can detect it in others. When someone's being ironic, sarcastic, teasing, your Bard catches it. You don't take things at face value. You hear the subtext.

10.3.4 Social Inference: Reading Intent

When your Bard works, you can infer intent from voice + context.

Someone asks "Can you help me?" with a specific tone. Your Bard knows: they're not actually asking, they're demanding.

Someone says "Whatever you want" with a specific prosody. Your Bard knows: they're not actually okay with whatever, they have a preference and they're annoyed you're not picking up on it.

This is **Theory of Mind through prosody**, using vocal cues to infer what someone's really thinking, feeling, wanting.

Your Bard is a bridge between voice perception, emotion, and social inference. It answers: "Are you joking or attacking me? Are you sincere or sarcastic? Are you safe or dangerous?"

10.3.5 The Performer's Gift: Charisma and Timing

When your Bard is strong, you're charismatic. Not because you're extroverted (that's different). But because you can modulate your voice to carry emotional nuance.

You can:

- Make people laugh (timing, delivery)
- Comfort people (warm, soothing prosody)
- Command attention (prosodic emphasis)
- Tell stories (emotional coloring, rhythm)

This is why performers, comedians, storytellers, therapists often have strong Bards. They can use voice as an instrument to convey meaning beyond words.

Bard shapes cadence: pacing, pause, emphasis. Which is why people experience you as compelling. Or overwhelming.

10.4 The Neuroscience: Right-Hemisphere Prosody

Okay, let's get into the brain science. This is where we go from "I miss sarcasm" (or "I'm hilarious") to "here's exactly which circuit is processing prosody and why."

10.4.1 Where the Bard Lives

The Bard lives in your **right posterior temporal lobe and temporoparietal junction (TPJ)**, the mirror to the Interpreter (Chapter 9), but on the right side.

The anatomy:

Right posterior superior temporal gyrus/sulcus (pSTG/pSTS):

- Voice-sensitive patches that respond to emotional tone in speech
- Prosodic parsing: intonation, stress, rhythm, phrasing
- Emotional decoding: extracting anger, joy, sadness, contempt from vocal tone

Right temporoparietal junction (TPJ):

- Convergence of STG, supramarginal gyrus (SMG), angular gyrus (AG)
- Social inference: using voice + context to infer intent
- Theory of Mind: reading others' beliefs and intentions
- Pragmatic coloring: detecting sarcasm, irony, teasing, play

Right superior temporal sulcus (STS):

- Tracks biological motion, gaze, prosody, communicative intent
- Common function for social and speech perception (Redcay, 2008)
- Abnormal in autism (affects both social and prosodic processing)

Together: This is the prosody and emotional tone hub, turning the music of speech into social and emotional meaning. Whether you instantly hear "nice job" as genuine or sarcastic, miss the joke, or hear hostility in a neutral sentence, that's this circuit tuning or misfiring.

10.4.2 The Bard's Job: Decoding How, Not What

The Bard does several things simultaneously:

1. Affective prosody decoding:

- Extracting emotion from tone (angry, happy, sad, contempt)
- Detecting warmth, coldness, sincerity, hostility
- Reading the emotional color in voices

2. Pragmatic interpretation:

- Detecting sarcasm, irony, teasing, deadpan
- Knowing when words don't match intent
- Understanding "saying one thing, meaning another"

3. Social inference through tone:

- Using prosody to infer intent ("are they safe?")
- Integrating tone with context ("cheerful about bad news = sarcasm")
- Theory of Mind: "what do they really think?"

4. Prosodic production:

- Generating emotional tone in your own speech
- Modulating voice to convey intent
- Using prosody to signal meaning beyond words

When all of this works smoothly, you're socially fluent in the prosodic layer. When any piece is glitchy, you're missing (or over-reading) the music.

10.4.3 Right Hemisphere Prosody System

The research (Ross, 1993, 2023; Hertrich et al., 2020; Patel et al., 2018):

The right hemisphere, especially right temporal lobe, is critical for recognizing affective prosody, the emotional tone of speech.

Right temporal lesions → impaired recognition of emotional prosody **Right frontal lesions** → impaired expression of emotional prosody **Often both** → complete aprosodia (can't produce or perceive emotional tone)

fMRI studies (Pichon et al., 2013; Leipold et al., 2022):

Right posterior STS becomes more active as emotional prosody demands increase. Voice-sensitive areas of STG/STS can decode categories of vocal emotion from multivariate patterns, discriminating anger, fear, joy purely from tone.

What this means: Your Bard is a specialized voice-emotion decoder. It's not processing words (that's the Interpreter). It's processing the emotional and social layer carried by prosody.

10.4.4 Humor, Incongruity, and "Getting the Joke"

The research (Shibata et al., 2014; Razafimandimby et al., 2009):

Humor detection engages right middle temporal gyrus and right medial frontal gyrus. Punchline incongruities (the mismatch that creates humor) recruit right temporal-frontal networks.

What's happening:

Your Bard detects incongruity (expectation vs. reality), integrates emotional tone and context, and infers intent ("are they teasing or serious?").

In right-hemisphere lesions: People understand literal content but miss jokes, irony, and implied meaning. They can paraphrase the words but don't grasp why it's funny or cutting.

That's pure Bard damage: Interpreter's still reading the script; the Bard can't hear the punchline.

10.4.5 Sarcasm and Irony: Prosody-Context Integration

The research (Akimoto et al., 2013; Obert et al., 2016; Filik et al., 2019; Vassolo et al., 2025):

Sarcasm perception depends on prosody-context interaction. Sarcastic interpretations are strongest when tone and situation mismatch (cheerful tone about a bad deed). Irony comprehension recruits fronto-temporo-parietal networks including TPJ and medial prefrontal cortex, overlapping with Theory of Mind circuits. You need to infer what the speaker really thinks.

What's happening: Your Bard integrates prosodic cues (tone, stress, timing) + contextual information (what happened) + Theory of Mind (what they really think) to decide: "They're saying X, but they mean Y."

When your Bard is weak, you take things at face value. When it's strong, you catch the subtext.

10.4.6 Theory of Mind and Communicative Intent

The research (Watanabe et al., 2006):

Right posterior STS/TPJ is a canonical node for Theory of Mind and perspective-taking, especially for reading others' beliefs and intentions. Developmental fMRI shows that interpreting communicative actions (pointing, indirect speech) engages right pSTS/TPJ, maturing into adult-like patterns over time.

What this means: Your Bard isn't just processing prosody, it's using prosody to infer intent. "What do they really want? Are they safe? Are they joking or threatening?" This is the bridge between voice perception, emotion, and social inference.

10.4.7 ASD and the Atypical Bard

The research (Redcay, 2008; Hernandez et al., 2015):

In autism, STS and adjacent temporal regions show structural and functional abnormalities, atypical responses to human voices, prosody, and emotional tone processing, with altered connectivity of temporal language regions.

What's happening: The Bard circuits exist, but their tuning curves for vocal emotion and social contingency are skewed. Sarcasm, humor, prosodic hints (the emotional tone layer) feel unreliable or confusing.

You can understand the literal words (Interpreter working, see Chapter 9 for semantic/pragmatic processing), but the prosodic and emotional tone layer (Bard) doesn't integrate smoothly.

Note: Missing metaphors and implied meaning is Interpreter (Ch 9, literal semantic processing). Missing sarcasm, emotional tone, and vocal emotion is Bard (this chapter, prosody processing). Both can be atypical in autism, but they're different circuits.

10.4.8 The Bard-Interpreter Partnership

Here's how they work together:

Interpreter (left TPJ, Chapter 9):

- Semantic content: "They said 'nice job' "
- Literal meaning: "They're complimenting my work"

Bard (right TPJ/pSTS):

- Prosodic analysis: "Flat tone, slight edge, micro-pause"
- Pragmatic interpretation: "They're being sarcastic or passive-aggressive"

Together:

- Full communication decoding: "They said 'nice job' but they didn't mean it"

When both are strong: You're socially fluent. You get what people say AND how they mean it.

When Interpreter > Bard: You understand words but miss tone. You take sarcasm literally. You miss jokes.

When Bard > Interpreter: You have a powerful sense of "vibe" but fuzzy semantics. You read rooms more than sentences. You catch tone but miss content.

The phenotype hook: You might be a Bard-heavy brain in an Interpreter-heavy world, or vice versa. Both are valuable. But they require different social strategies.

The Bard: Right Posterior Temporal

Gifts	Torture
• Reading emotional tone (what they really mean) • Humor & wit (getting/making jokes, timing) • Sarcasm detection (know when sarcastic vs. serious) • Emotional communication (express through tone) • Social intelligence (reading between lines, subtext) • Musical/prosodic sensitivity (music, poetry, rhythm)	• Missing sarcasm (take everything literally, "I was kidding") • Sounding flat/robotic (voice doesn't match emotions) • Over-reading threat (hear criticism in neutral tone) • Social tone-deafness (miss implied meaning, hints) • Amplifying emotional content (hear threat everywhere) • Communication mismatch (miss music or amplify threat)

10.5 Toolkit Preview

Your Bard is trainable, whether you're missing the music or amplifying threat in neutral tones. The goal is the same either way: accurate, not numbed or overwhelmed.

If you miss sarcasm and tone, explicit prosody practice helps: "When someone says X with tone Y, they usually mean Z." Make the implicit rules explicit until pattern recognition builds.

- **Stress Response Regulation** (Ch 15): nervous system calming reduces the threat-bias that makes neutral speech sound hostile.
- **Neurofeedback** (Ch 18): right posterior temporal training calibrates prosodic processing to appropriate gain.

Detailed protocols are in Part II. These circuits respond to training.

The right posterior temporal circuits that create tone-deafness or threat-biased prosody reading are the same circuits that, once trained, produce accurate social music, hearing what's actually there. Part II shows you how to build that.

10.6 Key Takeaways

The Bard (Right Posterior Temporal) is your brain's prosody processor, the circuit that reads tone, sarcasm, humor, and the emotional music behind words.

- **Bidirectional dysregulation:** Flooding/poor filtering = "missing" the music (drowning in too many prosodic signals, can't parse which matter, looks like tone-deaf, take everything literally, miss sarcasm). Overactive/threat-biased = amplifying threat signals (hear hostility in neutral tone, over-read criticism). Both make social communication exhausting.
- **Words vs. Music:** Interpreter (Chapter 9) = words and meaning. Bard = tone and emotion. Some people have strong Interpreter but flooded Bard (understand words, drowning in prosodic signals). Others have both dysregulated (double communication challenge).
- **Autism often involves flooded Bard:** Missing sarcasm and implied tone, not catching prosodic signals, not because signals are absent, but because you're picking up TOO MANY and drowning in them (high beta, low alpha filtering). For semantic meaning (literal vs. figurative), that's Interpreter territory (Chapter 9). Some autistic presentations also involve threat-biased Bard (amplifying threat in tone).
- **Flat affect as output issue:** When your Bard can't modulate prosody production, you sound flat/monotone even when experiencing emotion, people misread your internal state because your tone doesn't match.
- **Training calibration:** Right posterior temporal neurofeedback, explicit prosody training (learning tone patterns consciously), and calibrating emotional reading (distinguishing real from amplified threat in tone).

10.7 Reader Reflections

1. **Do you miss sarcasm and humor, or over-read tone?** Do people say "I was joking" and you had no idea? Or does "nice job" sound sarcastic?
2. **How does your voice sound to others?** Flat/monotone? Overly dramatic? Do people misunderstand your emotional state?
3. **What would it look like to help your Bard play their part in the orchestra?** Whether you're missing prosody or flooding on it, how might training this circuit change your social navigation, your creative expression, your ability to connect?

Systems Interlude: Processing & Recovery

Axis Neighborhood: Clock Speed & Energy Management

Location: Global, alpha frequency (clock speed) + energy cycling rhythms
Phenotypes: Timekeeper (Chapter 11) + Fog & the Tide (Chapter 12)
System function: Regulates processing speed, timing, coordination, and energy cycling, your brain's pacing and rhythmic rest systems

---

What This System Does When Balanced

Your Processing & Recovery System manages how fast your brain runs and when it needs to rest. When it's balanced:

- Your processing speed matches task demands (Timekeeper flexible)
- You can downshift to rest and sleep (Timekeeper slows when needed)
- You have mental clarity and energy when needed (Fog clears)
- You can access deep processing and restorative rest (Fog as gift)

The Timekeeper is your **alpha frequency**, the brain's clock speed, typically 8-12 Hz, that coordinates timing across regions. The Fog & the Tide is your **energy cycling rhythm**, natural oscillation between high-energy clarity (high tide) and low-energy rest (low tide), or when that rhythm breaks and you're stuck in chronic Fog.

Together, Timekeeper and Fog set your processing cadence: the alternation between think fast, think deep, and don't think at all.

What Dysregulation Looks Like

Timekeeper too fast (alpha frequency high):
Racing thoughts, can't slow down to rest, anxiety as speed dysregulation, can't downshift at night, insomnia, mind won't stop

Timekeeper too slow (alpha frequency low):
Sluggish processing, everything takes longer, falling behind in conversations, word-finding delays, "slow" compared to peers

Fog chronic (global slowing persistent):
Brain fog, cognitive fatigue, unrefreshing sleep, words don't come, memory poor, processing laggy, exhaustion from thinking

Fog absent (can't access protective rest):
Burnout, pushing through depletion, no circuit breaker, heading toward crash

Both dysregulated:
Racing mind + brain fog simultaneously, thoughts moving fast but can't land, or oscillating between manic speed and exhausted fog

---

Network Connection

The Processing & Recovery System affects **all networks globally**, it's the infrastructure underneath everything else. When your Timekeeper is dysregulated, it affects how fast your DMN / CEN / SN can switch. When you're stuck in chronic Fog (lost the Tide's rhythm), all networks slow down together with no recovery windows.

This system also manages **seizure and migraine threshold**, the Stabilizer's SMR (sensorimotor rhythm) is anti-seizure, and the Fog often appears as protective slowing before migraine or after intense cognitive load.

Hardware Safety Note

Unlike other systems (which are about regulation and optimization), the Processing & Recovery System includes **hardware safety limits**. Chronic Fog can signal:

- Sleep disorders (apnea, narcolepsy, insufficient deep sleep)
- Post-viral fatigue (long COVID, mono, chronic fatigue syndrome)
- Burnout from sustained overload
- Migraine prodrome or recovery
- Medication side effects

If your Fog is persistent and unresponsive to sleep / pacing interventions, this is a **diagnostic signal**, see Chapter 13 (Sleep) and consider medical evaluation.

This system sets your processing cadence: how fast your brain runs, how long it can sustain, and when it needs to go dark and recover. Everyone has a Tide. Poet-brains just have sharper peaks and deeper troughs, and a culture that punishes the troughs instead of planning around them.

Map so far: 10 of 12. Two characters left: The Timekeeper and The Fog & Tide. These are the infrastructure beneath everything you've already met, the clock speed and energy cycling that set the tempo for all twelve phenotypes. If you've felt like other interventions "should be working but aren't," these final two chapters often explain why.

Ch 11: The Timekeeper (Alpha Frequency)

Fast Brain, Smart Brain, or Just Anxious Brain?

People tell you you're quick. You process fast. Make connections rapidly. Three steps ahead in conversations. Always waiting for people to catch up.

11.1 "The Brain's Clock Speed"

Or perhaps people wait for you. You need time to process. You get there eventually, but you need a minute. Words don't come quickly. You're still thinking about question one while they're on question three.

Timekeeper is your internal tempo track: your timing cadence for thought and action.

Or maybe you're fast but it's torture. Racing thoughts at 3am. Can't slow down even when you're exhausted. Anxiety as speed dysregulation.

This is the Timekeeper, your brain's clock speed, the idling RPM of your cortex.

Your **individual alpha frequency (IAF)** is like your engine at idle. Some people idle slow. Some fast. This is your baseline, a phenotype pattern, not just a momentary state. Your brain's processing speed.

When your Timekeeper is fast (high IAF):

- Quick processing, sharp temporal resolution
- Fast reaction times, efficient working memory
- But also: racing thoughts, anxiety, can't slow down

When your Timekeeper is slow (low IAF) (Clark et al., 2004):

- Laggy processing, delayed recall
- Tip-of-tongue, word-finding difficulties
- "Nodding but not absorbing"
- In aging: promising biomarker of cognitive decline

When your Timekeeper is desynchronized (Piai et al., 2018; Wei et al., 2024):

- Different brain regions idling at different speeds
- Patchy timing, inconsistent processing
- Especially in left language networks: word retrieval glitches

The Timekeeper sets not just how fast you think, but how gracefully your brain can move between gears, idle, and deep repair.

11.2 The Torture: When the Clock Is Wrong

11.2.1 Too Fast: Racing and Can't Stop

Your brain is running at 2x speed, which feels like 10x. Thoughts race. You can't slow down. Even when you're exhausted, your Timekeeper won't idle at a comfortable speed.

That's the Timekeeper paradox: You think SO MUCH that people tell you to slow down. But you're also synthesizing patterns so fast that you're accessing insights others miss. Too much and not enough simultaneously.

Important distinction: The experience of "thinking too much" has two layers. The Timekeeper sets the **speed**, how fast thoughts move. But the **volume** of thinking (can't stop, can't let go, brain won't shut up) is really the activation/inhibition axis: Stabilizer trying to GO while Supervisor tries to STOP, approach system engaging while withdrawal system brakes. When the Timekeeper is fast AND the go/stop system is stuck, that's when "thinking too much" becomes unbearable. Speed alone is just quick processing. Speed plus a jammed brake is torture.

Racing thoughts: Not just "thinking a lot", thoughts moving so fast you can't catch them. One thought triggers seventeen others. You're three conversations ahead while still in the first one.

Anxiety as speed dysregulation: Your fast Timekeeper creates the subjective experience of anxiety. Not because you're worried about something specific, because your brain is running too fast to feel calm.

Can't sleep: Your Timekeeper won't slow down. You're exhausted, but your brain is still racing. Beta spindles at night, your cortex stuck in "on" mode.

Burnout: Constant high-speed is exhausting. You're burning fuel, going fast, but you can't sustain it. Eventually you crash.

11.2.2 Too Slow: Laggy and Can't Keep Up

Your brain is running at 0.5x speed. Words don't come quickly. You need time to process. You're still thinking about the first thing while everyone else has moved on.

Tip-of-tongue: You know the word. It's right there. But you can't retrieve it. Your Timekeeper is too slow to access the phonological code quickly.

Word-finding difficulty: Names, concepts, words, they're in there, but retrieval is laggy. People wait for you. You feel slow.

"Nodding but not absorbing": Especially in kids/teens. You look like you're listening, but your Timekeeper is too slow to bind information into memory. Nothing's encoding.

In aging: Your Timekeeper slows. This slowing is emerging as a promising marker of cognitive decline. Words take longer. Processing is laggier. Memory is worse.

11.2.3 Desynchronized: Patchy Timing

Different brain regions idling at different speeds. Your left language networks running at one tempo, your right at another. No unified clock.

The result: Inconsistent processing. Word retrieval glitches. Information sliding off even as you try to hold it. The networks that need to cooperate can't synchronize because they're running at different speeds.

11.3 The Gift: When the Clock Is Right

11.3.1 Fast and Sharp: High Bandwidth

When your Timekeeper is fast and well-regulated, you're quick. Sharp. Efficient.

Quick wit, rapid synthesis, improvisation. You process information fast. You make connections others miss because you're sampling more frequently.

This is high bandwidth, more processing loops per second.

11.3.2 Slow and Deep: Thorough Processing

When your Timekeeper is slow but well-regulated, you're thorough. Deep. Careful.

You don't rush. You process completely. You integrate information deeply instead of quickly.

This is depth over speed, fewer loops, but each one is thorough.

11.3.3 Synchronized: Smooth Coordination

When your Timekeeper is synchronized across networks, information flows cleanly. No glitches. No lag. Networks cooperate because they're running at the same tempo.

The Timekeeper: Alpha Speed & Spread	
Gifts	**Torture**
• Fast processing: quick wit, rapid synthesis, improvisation • Efficient working memory (high-bandwidth) • Sharp temporal resolution (catch details, precise timing) • Deep processing (when slow): thorough integration, depth • Appropriate speed matching (right speed for task) • Smooth state-shifting (fast → idle → slow → sleep)	• Racing thoughts (brain won't stop, can't slow down) • Poor sleep (can't downshift, not enough slow wave) • Burnout from speed (running too fast too long) • Sluggish processing (everything takes longer, fall behind) • Tip-of-tongue (words stuck, can't retrieve quickly) • Desynchronization (regions at different speeds, glitchy)

11.4 The Neuroscience: The Brain's Clock Speed

Okay, let's get into the brain science. This is where we go from "I think too fast" (or "I think too slow") to "here's exactly what your brain's clock speed is and why."

11.4.1 Individual Alpha Frequency: Your Brain's RPM at Idle

The Timekeeper is primarily your **individual alpha frequency (IAF)** or **peak alpha frequency (PAF)**, the dominant frequency of your alpha rhythm (varies by individual).

What alpha is:

Alpha waves are the idling rhythm of cortex at rest. Not "off", idling. Your brain cycling through integration and separation states.

Your personal alpha peak is relatively consistent, it's your baseline phenotype pattern. Some people idle slower, some faster. This is your brain's clock speed, and it's:

- **Influenced by genetics** (heritable component)
- **Measurable** (clear peak on QEEG spectral analysis)
- **Trainable** (neurofeedback can shift it, ~0.5-1 Hz change possible with sustained training)
- **Predictive** (tells me about your processing speed)

The research (Corcoran et al., 2018):

IAF is a stable individual parameter that can be measured reliably and used as a cognitive marker across tasks.

11.4.2 Fast Timekeeper: High IAF

What higher IAF tends to correlate with (Rathee et al., 2020; Clark et al., 2004; Tarasi et al., 2024):

Faster information processing:

- Shorter reaction times
- Better working memory (digit span)
- More precise perceptual discrimination
- Better temporal resolution (you can sample the world more quickly)

The mechanism:

Faster alpha means shorter cycles. Your brain can sample, integrate, and hand off information more times per second. You're running more processing loops per unit time.

The gift: Quick wit, rapid synthesis, improvisation, creativity under pressure. You're fast.

The torture: Racing thoughts, anxiety, can't slow down, burnout. You're TOO fast. Your brain won't idle at a comfortable speed, it's revving at a red light.

11.4.3 Slow Timekeeper: Low IAF

What lower IAF tends to correlate with (Ramsay et al., 2021; Puttaert et al., 2021):

Slower information processing:

- Longer reaction times
- Reduced working memory efficiency
- Worse visual discrimination
- Poorer episodic memory encoding/retrieval

The mechanism:

Slower alpha means fewer cycles. Your brain is sampling and integrating fewer times per second. You're running fewer processing loops per unit time.

The experience:

Tip-of-tongue (Shafto et al., 2007; Wei et al., 2024): You know the word, but you can't retrieve it. The phonological code is there, but retrieval is laggy. Aging research shows that slower processing contributes to more frequent tip-of-tongue events; separately, IAF slowing with age suggests that a slowing Timekeeper may be one mechanism, though this specific connection hasn't been directly tested in these studies.

Word-finding difficulty: Names, words, concepts, they're in there, but retrieval is laggy. You need a moment. People wait for you.

"Nodding but not absorbing": Especially in kids/teens whose PAF is still developing. The Interpreter (Chapter 9) is hearing the words, but the Timekeeper is too slow to bind them into durable memory traces. They look like they're listening, but nothing's encoding.

In aging (Park et al., 2024; Finley et al., 2024; Zhao et al., 2025):

PAF slows with age. This slowing is emerging as a promising biomarker of cognitive decline. Lower IAF is associated with greater future decline, worse episodic memory, and emerging neurodegenerative conditions in several recent studies.

Your Timekeeper is literally slowing down.

11.4.4 Development: The Clock Speeds Up

The research (Freschl et al., 2022; Arioli et al., 2024):

PAF rises steadily from infancy through childhood and plateaus in young adulthood

What this means:

Kids and teens have slower Timekeepers. Their brains are literally running at lower clock speed. This isn't immaturity, it's developmental.

When you're talking to a younger kid whose dominant rhythm is still developing, you're talking to a brain whose sampling rate is lower. They're "nodding but not encoding" because their Timekeeper can't process that quickly yet.

11.4.5 Fast Brain ≠ Smart Brain (But They're Related)

Here's the nuance: **fast Timekeeper = fast processing, but NOT necessarily high IQ.**

The research (Posthuma et al., 2001; Ociepka et al., 2022):

Both IAF and IQ are highly heritable. But there's **no genetic correlation** between IAF and WAIS-III dimensions. Smarter brains do not simply "run faster."

Higher IAF → faster task performance on speed tasks. But no link to general intelligence (g) once you control for other factors.

What this means:

The Timekeeper tracks **processing speed**, one factor of intelligence. But full-scale IQ also depends on frontal integration, connectivity complexity, network efficiency.

You can have a fast Timekeeper and average IQ. You can have a slow Timekeeper and high IQ.

Clinical heuristic: One SD in alpha maps loosely onto one SD of speed-ish IQ. But it's one marker among many.

11.4.6 Beta Spindles: When the Clock Races

Now let's talk about when the Timekeeper isn't just fast, it's racing and can't stop.

Spindling beta (fast-wave bursts):

Spindle-shaped beta bursts visible on raw EEG trace. High amplitude. Often bilateral. This is different from general beta excess.

Linked to GABAergic dysregulation:

- GABAA receptor genes (genetic variants)
- "Weak brakes", your inhibitory system can't calm the racing
- Runs in families

Clinical significance:

When I see spindling beta, the client usually reports:

- "My brain won't shut off"
- "Racing thoughts at night"
- "Anxiety that feels physical"
- "Can't relax even when exhausted"
- "Alcohol is the only thing that works"

Why beta spindles create torture:

Over-arousal. Your cortex is stuck in "on" mode. Your GABAergic system can't provide natural braking. You're revving at a red light, burning fuel, going nowhere.

This is the Timekeeper racing, not just running fast.

11.4.7 Delta: The E-Brake and Metabolic Maintenance

Delta waves are the slowest brain rhythm. This is deep maintenance mode.

The research (Long et al., 2021; Decker et al., 2009; Harel et al., 2025):

Delta is associated with homeostatic sleep drive. It builds with waking time and energy use. It increases in NREM slow-wave sleep after sleep deprivation. It's your brain's "drop speed and repair" mode.

When delta works right:

- Appears in deep sleep (SWS)
- Stays out of waking cognition
- Supports restoration, metabolic cleanup

When delta is dysregulated:

Excess waking delta: Brain is trying to take micro-naps while awake. Drowsiness, fog, "brain taking breaks without permission."

Delta-deficient sleep: Can't enter or maintain deep restoration even when exhausted. "Tired but wired."

The e-brake metaphor: Delta is the system's "drop speed and repair" mode. If it intrudes at wrong times or fails to appear when needed, timing and restoration suffer.

11.5 Toolkit Preview

Your Timekeeper is trainable. The goal is tempo flexibility, fast when needed, idle when resting, deep when sleeping. Being stuck at one speed is the problem.

For a racing Timekeeper: HRV biofeedback (Ch 15) teaches your nervous system to downshift. This is often where sleep quality breaks first, the connection between clock speed and sleep is one of the most trainable patterns in the book.

- **Sleep** (Ch 13): fast Timekeepers especially need deep sleep to restore. Protecting sleep is protecting clock flexibility.
- **Stress Response Regulation** (Ch 15): nervous system downregulation helps break the speed-plus-anxiety loop.
- **Neurofeedback** (Ch 18): alpha frequency training to widen your tempo range, not fixing it at one speed, but building the ability to shift.

Detailed protocols are in Part II. These circuits respond to training.

The alpha-frequency circuits that create racing thoughts or sluggish processing are the same circuits that, once trained, produce tempo flexibility, fast when needed, idle when resting, deep when sleeping. Part II shows you how to build that.

11.6 Key Takeaways

The Timekeeper (Individual Alpha Frequency/Peak Alpha Frequency) is your brain's processing speed, the clock rate at which your cortex operates.

- **Bidirectional dysregulation:** Too fast = racing thoughts, anxiety, can't slow down to rest, poor sleep. Too slow = sluggish processing, everything takes longer, cognitive fatigue, feeling behind. Both = out of sync with context.

- **"Anxiety as speed dysregulation":** When your Timekeeper races (excess beta, fast alpha), anxiety isn't just emotion, it's your brain processing too fast to rest. Feeling overwhelmed because you're computing at 2x speed.
- **Fast ≠ smart, slow ≠ dumb:** Faster alpha = quicker processing but anxiety trade-offs. Slower alpha = deeper processing but less speed. Different characteristics, not better/worse.
- **The stimulant-sedative cycle:** Stimulants during day (focus the speed), sedatives at night (slow down to rest). Tolerance to both. Dysregulation worsens. Forcing speed changes without training flexibility.
- **Training speed flexibility:** Alpha frequency neurofeedback trains your brain to shift speeds, fast when needed, idle when resting, slow when sleeping. Learning to match tempo to context instead of being stuck at one speed.
- **Widening your tempo range:** Your job isn't to slow Timekeeper forever, but to widen its tempo range so you can choose when to run fast and when to idle.

11.7 Reader Reflections

1. **Does your brain feel too fast or too slow?** Racing thoughts? Or sluggish processing?
2. **Can you shift speeds appropriately?** Or are you stuck at one speed regardless of context?
3. **Do you notice a correlation with sleep?** Can you predict your Timekeeper's pace based on how your sleep performed? This connection between sleep quality and processing speed is one of the most trainable patterns, Chapter 13 will show you how.
4. **What's your sleep like?** Does your brain stay fast even when trying to rest?

Ch 12: The Fog & the Tide

When Your Brain's Weather Turns Gray

You wake up and your brain feels like it's wrapped in cotton. Words are on the tip of your tongue but won't come. You read the same paragraph three times and retain nothing. Your partner asks a simple question and you need five seconds just to process what they said.

12.1 "The Tide: Natural Rhythm That Protects"

Welcome to The Fog & the Tide, your brain's natural energy cycles and what happens when they get stuck.

Here's what's wild: I can see this on brain mapping before you even feel it. Your dominant rhythm slows. Your frontal fast waves compensate (trying to cut through the fog). Your connectivity patterns show your brain networks aren't talking to each other efficiently. It looks the same whether you have long COVID, sleep deprivation, chronic fatigue, or just pushed too hard for too long.

The counterintuitive part? The Tide is your brain's protective rhythm, cycling between clarity and rest, performance and recovery. It's when you lose that rhythm and get stuck in perpetual Fog that it becomes torture.

Think of it like ocean tides:

The Tide (healthy rhythm):

- Energy ebbs and flows naturally across your day
- Low tide: rest, repair, deep processing, maintenance mode
- High tide: clarity, focus, performance, engagement
- You know when to push (high tide) and when to honor rest (low tide)
- Predictable cycles you can work with
- Tide = healthy energy cadence

The Fog (stuck state):

- Tide won't come back in: stuck at perpetual low tide
- No rhythm, just chronic depletion
- Can't predict when you'll be functional
- Morning fog never lifts, crashes with no recovery
- Like a maintenance crew that showed up but forgot to leave
- Fog = cadence collapsed or frozen

The research backs this up:

After brain injury, people show sleep-like slow waves during wakefulness, patches of cortex going into sleep-like dynamics while the rest is awake (Massimini et al., 2024). This disrupts networks and behavior, but likely protects overtaxed tissue. It's The Tide trying to pull energy into repair mode.

Delta power reflects sleep pressure and metabolic need. More delta in NREM is associated with better cognition in conditions like Parkinson's. The low-tide state is the metabolic governor kicking in: pull power from higher-order networks, shift into maintenance mode. This is adaptive, when it cycles properly.

But here's where it gets tricky: is your Tide working (honor the rhythm) or are you stuck in Fog (intervention needed)?

12.2 The Torture: Stuck in the Fog

When you lose the Tide, when the rhythm breaks and you're stuck in perpetual low-energy fog:

- **Chronic depletion:** Can't think clearly for weeks or months
- **No recovery windows:** Every task feels like running through deep water, no matter when you try
- **Unpredictable function:** Can't plan around your energy because there's no pattern
- **Social stigma:** People think you're lazy but you're just... broken. Depleted. The tide won't come back in.
- **Lost autonomy:** Can't access the clarity and engagement you need to live your life
- **Perpetual maintenance mode:** Your brain keeps trying to rest and repair but never restores full function

This is The Fog: stuck at low tide with no rhythm, no cycling, no windows of clarity to count on.

12.3 The Gift: The Tide Working

When your Tide cycles naturally, when you have predictable ebbs and flows of energy:

- **Adaptive rest:** Low tide protects you from total system failure, forces recovery when you need it
- **Deep processing:** Low-energy states access different thinking, slow, reflective depth that fast brains can't reach

- **Creativity incubation:** Some of the most profound insights come from low-tide states when your brain's maintenance mode reorganizes information
- **Predictable rhythm:** You know when to schedule demanding work (high tide) and when to honor rest (low tide)
- **Trust in recovery:** Low tide isn't scary because you know high tide returns
- **System intelligence:** Your brain knows when to ebb (rest/heal) and when to flow (engage/perform)

This is The Tide working: natural oscillation between clarity and recuperation, performance and restoration. You're not fighting your energy cycles, you're surfing them.

The challenge: Distinguishing natural Tide (honor it, work with it) from stuck Fog (intervene, restore the rhythm). And not forcing morning-person productivity on a brain at natural low tide, or stimulants on a brain that has slowed alpha (COMT genotype), not ADHD.

What it feels like:

- Processing speed slowed (running through deep water)
- Delayed recall (words on tip of tongue)
- Short-term memory failing (filing cabinet with sticky drawers)
- Attention wandering (GPS losing signal)
- **Haze in front of the screen**: you're looking at information (text, faces, screens) and there's a moment of "Wait, what?" before your brain catches up and you can process it
- Everything takes longer, requires more effort

The metaphor: Think of your brain as a bustling city's transportation system. When everything's working well, information flows smoothly across neural networks like traffic on well-maintained highways. Brain fog is what happens when multiple systems start running below optimal efficiency, like a city during a rainy rush hour when several major intersections have malfunctioning traffic lights.

The validation: This isn't "in your head." All of these can be seen in QEEG. Your brain fog is measurable, objective, real.

12.4 The Biology: What's Actually Happening

12.4.1 Energy Production Slowdown

What's happening:

- Your neurons' mitochondria (cellular power plants) aren't producing energy efficiently
- Like power grid running on backup generators instead of main power
- Cellular ATP production impaired

Why:

- Inflammation (immune system activation draws energy)
- Oxidative stress (cellular damage)
- Sleep deprivation (mitochondria don't recover)
- Metabolic dysfunction (glucose utilization impaired)

What it feels like:

- Mental exhaustion (not just sleepy: depleted)
- Tasks require enormous effort
- "Battery at 10%" feeling

12.4.2 Neurovascular Changes (Blood Flow Impairment)

What's happening:

- Brain's blood vessels not delivering oxygen and nutrients effectively
- Like water pressure dropping in building's plumbing
- Reduced cerebral blood flow

Causes:

- Chronic inflammation (systemic)
- Active vascular irritation (post-viral, post-concussion)
- Neurovascular coupling impaired

Research evidence:

- Post-viral fatigue (long COVID)
- Post-concussion syndrome
- Chronic fatigue syndrome (ME/CFS)

12.4.3 Inflammatory and Healing Response

My view:

Not "chemical imbalance" (oversimplified). Instead:

- Neurovascular changes impact how systems use neurotransmitters
- Resources shift toward healing and repair (draws up slow brain waves)
- System goes into overdrive trying to heal while awake

The cascade:

- Strong immune/inflammatory response → very fatiguing
- Processes trying to heal create oxidative stress
- Deep fatigue
- Cascade of body and brain processes that don't feel good

Why this matters:

- Explains why simple neurotransmitter interventions often fail
- Systemic issue (not one broken part)
- Healing response creates fog (paradoxically)

12.4.4 The Tide: Why Fog Comes and Goes

Here's what's counterintuitive: The Fog isn't static. It ebbs and flows across your day, across your week, pulled by rhythmic biological forces you can track and work with.

The Fog is the state, that low-energy, altered-connectivity brain mode you see on QEEG. **The Tide is its rhythm**, the waxing and waning of intensity driven by inflammatory cycles, sleep pressure, glucose dynamics, and circadian patterns.

Here's what creates the tides:

1. Inflammatory Waves

Interleukin-6 (IL-6) and related markers don't just sit at elevated levels, they oscillate across the day with robust diurnal variation. In depression and post-viral states, IL-6 shows a shifted circadian rhythm that correlates with worse morning fog, fatigue, and concentration difficulties that lift by evening. Higher systemic inflammatory markers correlate with worse cognitive function, including executive performance and fatigue (Marsland et al., 2015), a baseline "sea level" on top of which diurnal cytokine swings modulate how thick the fog gets hour by hour.

2. Sleep Pressure and CSF Pulses

Sleep loss produces local sleep-like slow waves in awake cortex, specific brain regions briefly going "offline" while you're still conscious. High-density EEG shows these localized slow waves are time-locked to attentional lapses, mind-blanking, and "where did my brain just go?" moments. Recent work shows that after sleep deprivation, large low-frequency cerebrospinal fluid (CSF) pulses intrude into wakefulness, coupled to attention failures, essentially brief "sleep intrusions" that prioritize metabolic cleanup over sustained focus. **This is the tide coming in:** maintenance waves that temporarily thicken the fog, then recede.

3. Glucose Swings

The brain runs on glucose with minimal reserves. Acute glucose variability (spikes and crashes across the day) is consistently associated with worse cognitive performance, greater cognitive impairment risk, and the familiar post-meal fog or reactive hypoglycemia crashes (Cunningham et al., 2023). These fluctuations happen on the scale of minutes to hours, creating fast ripples on top of the slower inflammatory and sleep-pressure tides.

4. Circadian Currents

Antioxidant systems, mitochondrial function, and repair pathways have time-of-day patterns (Wilking et al., 2013). The brain's ability to clear reactive oxygen species and restore energetic capacity follows a 24-hour cycle, adding another layer of predictable modulation to fog intensity.

Why this matters:

Understanding the tide means you're not fighting a static deficit, you're working with rhythmic patterns. Morning fog that lifts by afternoon isn't "I'm better", it's the tide ebbing. Post-lunch crash isn't "I'm broken", it's glucose dynamics riding on top of baseline inflammation. Knowing when your tide predictably surges lets you plan around it, protect during it, and intervene at the right leverage points (sleep timing, glucose stability, anti-inflammatory routines, stress management).

The Fog & the Tide aren't separate problems. The Fog is the low-power state. The Tide is how hard it pulls you under at different times of day. Both are trainable. Both respond to targeted intervention.

12.5 The Neuroscience: Two Types of "Slow"

12.5.1 Frontal Slow vs. Slowed Alpha (Critical Distinction)

Many people experience "brain fog" or cognitive slowing, but there are two distinct patterns with different causes and treatments:

12.5.2 Type 1: Frontal Slow (Theta/Delta Excess)

As described in Chapter 3 (Stabilizer), Frontal Slow is excess theta/delta in frontal regions, the ADHD signature that responds to stimulants. Task initiation deficit, motor paralysis, theta/beta ratio elevated. Stimulants work temporarily; neurofeedback trains sustained engagement.

12.5.3 Type 2: Slowed Alpha Peak Frequency (COMT Genetic Variant)

What it feels like:

- "Everything feels slow"

- "I process information slowly"
- "I need more time than others"
- Not ADHD-type inattention (different quality)

The key distinction: If you've tried stimulants and they didn't help (or worse, made you more anxious) you probably don't have frontal slow (ADHD type). You likely have a genetic variant affecting your brain's processing speed. Your dominant brain rhythm runs slower than typical, often linked to COMT genotype (Bodenmann et al., 2009). Traditional analysis sometimes misses this, classifying it as general slow-wave excess.

Why this matters: Different phenotype, different treatment. Stimulants won't help (and may hurt). You need alpha peak frequency training, not theta suppression.

Clinical insight: I've seen many clients diagnosed with "treatment-resistant ADHD" who actually have slowed alpha. Once we train alpha peak frequency instead of suppressing theta, they improve. The problem wasn't that they were "resistant", the problem was misidentification.

See Substance Patterns (Chapter 14) for the full technical breakdown of this COMT genetic pattern, why stimulants don't work for it, and why this distinction predicts treatment response.

12.6 QEEG Patterns in Brain Fog (Universal Signatures)

Here's what's remarkable: Regardless of cause (long COVID, sleep deprivation, mold exposure, post-concussion, chronic fatigue, burnout), early QEEG work shows **similar patterns**, though findings remain heterogeneous and preliminary across conditions.

What this means:

- Brain fog represents a common "low energy state" of neural function
- Similar patterns = similar interventions can work across different causes
- QEEG provides objective measurement (not just "I feel foggy")
- Can track severity and treatment effectiveness

12.6.1 Pattern 1: Slowed Alpha Peak Frequency (Already Discussed)

The signature:

- Dominant rhythm slower than typical range
- Speeds drift between regions (loss of synchrony)
- Like engine running at lower RPM

Causes:

- COMT genotype (genetic: lifelong)
- Post-viral (acquired: long COVID, etc.)
- Sleep deprivation (temporary)
- Chronic fatigue (persistent)
- Hormonal changes (perimenopause, thyroid)

Consistency: Shows up across all causes (universal signature)

12.6.2 Pattern 2: Frontal Beta Overactivation (Compensatory Mechanism)

The signature:

- Increased beta activity in frontal areas
- Brain working harder to maintain normal function
- Like CPU running at high capacity even for simple tasks

Why this happens:

- Compensatory mechanism (brain trying to cut through fog)
- Effort to maintain function despite energy deficit
- Hyperactivation to overcome sluggishness

What it feels like (paradoxically):

- **Obsessive thoughts** (can't let go: brain hyper-focusing to compensate)
- **Rumination** (stuck in loops: effort to process)
- **Earworms** (songs playing in head: repetitive neural firing)
- **Racing thoughts in slow motion** (beta excess + slowed alpha simultaneously)

This explains the paradox: You can have brain fog (slow processing) AND racing thoughts (beta overactivation) at the same time. They're not contradictory, one is compensating for the other.

Consistency: Appears whether from poor sleep, stress, post-viral fatigue, burnout.

12.6.3 Pattern 3: Coherence Changes (Connectivity Disruption)

The signature:

- Coordination between brain regions less efficient
- **Delta hypercoherence** (deep fatigue, not feeling rested)
- **Low alpha phase lag** (suggests deep fatigue)
- Disrupted connectivity patterns

The metaphor:

- Highway system with consistent congestion

- Traffic forced to take longer, less direct paths
- Information still gets through, but slower and less efficiently

What it means:

- Brain networks not communicating well
- Integration impaired (harder to synthesize information)
- Cognitive tasks require more effort (compensating for poor connectivity)

Why this matters:

- Not just slow: inefficient
- Multiple systems affected simultaneously
- Explains why "everything" feels harder (not just one function)

12.6.4 Pattern 4: Delta Patterns (Restorative State Dysregulation)

Two extremes:

Excess delta (while awake):

- Brain pushing hard to rest and heal
- Trying to sleep while awake
- Exhaustion signature
- "I could fall asleep standing up"

Very low delta:

- Feeling depleted
- Hard time resting and healing
- Can't even access restorative states
- "Tired but wired"

The paradox:

- High delta = brain trying to shut down (needs rest)
- Low delta = brain can't access rest (depleted)
- Both create fog (different mechanisms)

12.6.5 Early Detection: QEEG Shows Changes Before Symptoms

Key finding:

- Brain's electrical activity changes may precede conscious experience of cognitive sluggishness by **days or even weeks**
- Early detection allows earlier intervention
- Can see fog developing before you feel it

Clinical value:

- Preventive (catch before severe)
- Objective tracking (not just "do I feel better?")
- Treatment monitoring (is intervention working?)
- Trust when fog lifts (objective confirmation, not placebo)

Example: Post-viral brain fog (long COVID) often shows QEEG changes before patient reports symptoms. Early neurofeedback intervention may prevent chronic fog.

12.7 Causes of Brain Fog (Many Roads to Same Pattern)

Remarkably, early QEEG studies suggest similar patterns across different causes, though research is still emerging.

Cause	Mechanism	Key Clue	Where to Start
Post-Viral Fatigue (Long COVID, EBV)	Neurovascular changes, inflammatory response	Fog began after illness, persists months/years	Medical eval + sleep (Ch 13)
Sleep Deprivation	Mitochondria don't recover; ADHD: 20.5% SWS reduction (Furrer et al., 2019)	Fog tracks with sleep quality	Sleep (Ch 13), fix this first
Mold Exposure	Mycotoxins, inflammatory cascade, neurovascular	Hidden mold in home/workplace; unexplained onset	Environmental assessment + medical eval
Post-Concussion	Vascular irritation, inflammatory cascade	History of head injury, even "minor"	Neurology eval + sleep (Ch 13)
ME/CFS	Systemic energy production impairment	Fog + post-exertional malaise (crash after activity)	Medical eval + pacing + sleep (Ch 13)
Hormonal Changes	Thyroid, menopause, cortisol dysregulation	Fog correlates with cycle, age transition, or thyroid labs	Endocrine eval + sleep (Ch 13)
Stress / Burnout	HPA axis dysregulation, cortisol pattern disruption	Fog worsened by sustained overwork	Stress regulation (Ch 15) + sleep (Ch 13)

Cause	Mechanism	Key Clue	Where to Start
Medications	Anticholinergics, benzos, some antidepressants cause cognitive slowing	Fog began or worsened after medication change	Medication review with prescriber

The key insight: Early research suggests similar QEEG patterns regardless of cause. Converging patterns mean similar interventions may work across different types of brain fog, but identifying the root cause determines the priority order.

12.7.1 The Research Evidence: Many Roads, One Fog Pattern

Long COVID / Post-Viral (Ortelli et al., 2023; Benis et al., 2023; Kopańska et al., 2022; Gaber et al., 2024; Manganotti et al., 2025; Gangemi et al., 2024): Early QEEG studies suggest altered theta/alpha power, increased right-hemisphere theta/alpha/SMR, elevated beta2, and fronto-parietal coherence changes in some long-COVID patients with brain fog. Findings remain heterogeneous, and no single validated QEEG signature exists yet, but the emerging pattern shows: slowed background + compensatory beta.

Sleep Disorders (D'Rozario et al., 2022; Lee et al., 2012; Howarth et al., 2024; El-Mekkawy et al., 2022; Gu et al., 2023): OSA shows reduced delta in SWS, EEG slowing, altered vigilance profiles. CPAP treatment normalizes EEG and improves cognition. RLS shows altered power and connectivity. Insomnia shows elevated beta, reduced delta, tired but wired.

Mild TBI / Concussion (Dunkley et al., 2015; Safar et al., 2021; Nwakamma et al., 2024; Barone et al., 2024; Tarapore et al., 2013): Increased low-frequency connectivity, slower posterior dominant rhythm, altered spectral power. Sleep-like slow waves intruding into wake (Massimini et al., 2024). Tracks with processing speed deficits.

ME/CFS and Fibromyalgia (Decker et al., 2009; Silva-Passadouro et al., 2024): Reduced delta in SWS but elevated in lighter stages. Altered low-frequency power and connectivity. Common EEG themes across FMS, ME/CFS, and long COVID, brains stuck in low-energy, high-inflammatory states.

Aging and Cognitive Decline (Lizio et al., 2011; Kopčanová et al., 2024; Meghdadi et al., 2021; López-Sanz et al., 2016; Tanabe et al., 2020): Increased delta/theta, decreased alpha, alpha slowing. These changes track cognitive decline severity. Even in subjective cognitive decline (normal tests, "something's off"), MEG/EEG show altered alpha power and connectivity.

Alcohol and Chemical Fog (Coutin-Churchman et al., 2006; Ehlers & Criado, 2007; Rangaswamy et al., 2002; Jurado-Barba et al., 2020; Zhang et al., 2023): Decreased slow-band power in some regions, increased beta, altered fronto-parietal connectivity. Chronic alcohol = hyperaroused but inefficient cortex with cognitive slowness.

Cognitive Fatigue in Healthy Brains (Wu et al., 2025): Even in healthy adults, cognitive fatigue from sustained tasks produces widespread connectivity changes, especially in low frequencies. The Fog can be induced temporarily in anyone who pushes too hard.

The evidence suggests: many roads, converging patterns. Different insults produce similar low-energy EEG signatures, though more research is needed to establish definitive diagnostic markers.

The Fog & the Tide: Processing & Recovery System

Gifts (The Tide Working)	Torture (Stuck in Fog)
• Natural energy cycling (predictable high/low tide windows) • Protective rest at low tide (prevents total burnout) • Deep processing mode (slow, reflective depth during ebb) • Creativity incubation (profound insights during low-energy states) • Trust in rhythm (low tide isn't scary, high tide returns) • System intelligence (brain knows when to rest, when to engage)	• Stuck at perpetual low tide (no recovery windows) • Cognitive slowing (processing through molasses, no rhythm) • Word-finding failures (words on tip of tongue, can't retrieve) • Memory failures (read paragraph three times, nothing sticks) • Unpredictable function (can't plan, no pattern to energy) • Chronic depletion (feel broken, but tide won't come back in) • Misdiagnosed as ADHD (slowed alpha looks like inattention)

12.8 Toolkit Preview

Your Fog & Tide responds to training, but treatment depends on cause. The critical first step is the distinction made above: natural Tide (rest is the intervention) versus chronic Fog (circuit-level intervention needed).

If stimulants or caffeine have been your push-through, Chapter 14 explains when they help versus when they worsen the underlying pattern.

- **Sleep** (Ch 13): non-negotiable. Morning routine is your fog intervention, consistent wake time and morning light are more powerful than anything you do at night. You cannot out-hack poor sleep.
- **Neurofeedback** (Ch 18): QEEG-guided only. The Fog presents with multiple distinct signatures (slowed alpha, excess theta, frontal hypoactivation, coherence disruption) and the protocol depends on which pattern is driving your specific Fog. Without the map, you cannot pick the right road.
- If your Fog is persistent, unresponsive to sleep, or worsening: get a QEEG assessment and a medical evaluation. The Causes section above lists what to rule out first.

What recovery feels like: When fog lifts (whether from sleep, neurofeedback, or addressing root causes) it's like **someone cleaned the windshield.** The world suddenly has higher contrast. Information lands without delay. You didn't realize how foggy you were until clarity returns.

Detailed protocols are in Part II. These circuits respond to training.

The processing and recovery circuits that create chronic fog are the same circuits that, once trained, restore natural energy cycling and cognitive clarity. Part II shows you how to build that.

12.9 Key Takeaways

The Fog & the Tide: your brain's energy cycles and what happens when they break.

- **The Tide (gift):** Natural energy oscillation. Low tide for rest / repair, high tide for clarity / performance. Predictable rhythm you can work with.
- **The Fog (torture):** Stuck at perpetual low tide. No rhythm, no recovery windows, chronic depletion.
- **Many roads, one pattern:** Long COVID, sleep deprivation, mold exposure, concussion, burnout, chronic fatigue, all show similar QEEG signatures (slowed alpha, compensatory beta, disrupted coherence, excess delta).
- **Two types:** Type 1 (Frontal Slow / ADHD) responds to stimulants. Type 2 (Slowed Alpha / COMT) does NOT, may worsen. See Chapter 14 for breakdown.
- **The Tide is protective:** Natural oscillation between clarity and rest. Low tide isn't failure, it's your brain saying "slow down, recover." Honoring that rhythm prevents burnout.

- **Not Stabilizer:** Fog & the Tide = processing speed/energy cycling. Stabilizer (Ch 3) = motor engagement. Different circuits, different treatments.
- **Temporary vs. chronic:** Temporary fog after intensity = rest. Chronic fog unresponsive to rest = needs QEEG assessment, root cause work.
- **Training:** Frontal Slow → theta suppression/beta enhancement. Slowed Alpha → alpha peak training. Chronic fog → address root causes + coherence training.

12.10 TOOL: Track Your Tide (9-Day Pattern Log)

Why track? Your Tide has rhythms, but you might not see them without tracking. Morning fog that lifts by afternoon? Post-lunch crash? Weekend recovery? Tracking reveals patterns.

The cadence: Days 1-2 set the tracking habit. Days 3-9 give you a full week of data. Nine days is enough to spot patterns without overwhelming you.

12.10.1 Your 9-Day Log

Rate Energy/Clarity each time: E / C (1-10 scale)

Day	AM	Mid	PM	Notes (sleep hrs, stress, meals, triggers)
1	__/__	__/__	__/__	
2	__/__	__/__	__/__	
3	__/__	__/__	__/__	
4	__/__	__/__	__/__	
5	__/__	__/__	__/__	
6	__/__	__/__	__/__	
7	__/__	__/__	__/__	
8	__/__	__/__	__/__	
9	__/__	__/__	__/__	

Energy: 1 (depleted) → 5 (moderate) → 10 (peak)
Clarity: 1 (heavy fog) → 5 (functional) → 10 (crystal clear)

12.10.2 What the Patterns Mean

Healthy Tide (rhythmic cycling):

- Energy/clarity cycles predictably (e.g., low mornings → high afternoons, or vice versa)
- You can plan around it and know when to schedule demanding work
- Low tide isn't scary because high tide returns

Stuck Fog (no rhythm):

- No pattern: random crashes, chronic depletion
- No recovery windows: perpetually at low tide
- Unpredictable function: can't plan around it
- **Needs intervention:** Sleep, root cause work, neurofeedback

Common Triggers to Watch:

- Sleep < 7 hours → fog next day?
- High stress → 2-3 day crash?
- Carb-heavy lunch → afternoon fog?
- Screen time before bed → morning fog?

12.10.3 Your Next Steps

If you see a Tide: Honor the rhythm. Schedule demanding work for high-tide windows. Rest during low tide without guilt. This is your brain working properly, adaptive cycling between energy and recovery. If you can predict the tide, you can design your day's cadence around it instead of fighting it.

If you see Fog: Fix sleep first (Chapter 13). Address root causes (illness, inflammation, hormones). If you're still stuck, neurofeedback can train out of chronic patterns (Chapter 18).

12.11 Reader Reflections

1. **What does your fog feel like specifically?** Slow processing? Words won't come? Can you distinguish Fog from Stabilizer (motor engagement)?
2. **Can you identify what triggers your fog?** Poor sleep? Post-illness? Stress? Pattern of temporary fog (after intensity) versus chronic?
3. **Can you think of times when you thanked or welcomed the Fog in for protective rest?** When slowing down was exactly what your system needed? Not every fog is dysfunction, sometimes it's wisdom. Learning to distinguish protective rest from chronic shutdown is key.
4. **If you've tried stimulants, how did they affect it?** Helped or made you anxious without clearing fog?

12.12 You've Met All Twelve

That's your orchestra. Twelve instruments. Twelve ways of being gifted and tortured at the same time.

You've been running the Mastery Loop first two steps (Notice and Normalize) across all twelve phenotypes. You can now name what's happening in your circuits instead of calling yourself broken. You know which characters tend to show up in your particular constellation.

The recognition journey is over. The tools are next.

Part II is where borrowed peace ends and built capacity begins.

Part II
Interventions & Biohacking

Overview: Tools for Regulating Your Phenotypes

Mastery Loop Steps: REGULATE + REASSIGN

You've spent Part I recognizing and validating your circuits. You know which phenotypes dominate your constellation. You know why you've suffered the way you've suffered. You know that what looked like character flaws were circuit patterns.

Now the work changes.

Part I was about recognition. Part II is about capacity. Not borrowed capacity (the kind you get from stimulants, alcohol, isolation, or ritual) but **built capacity**: neuroplastic changes to the actual circuits through training, sleep, breathwork, HRV, and neurofeedback.

These are Steps 3 and 4 of the Mastery Loop: REGULATE and REASSIGN. You've learned to Notice and Normalize your phenotypes. Now you learn precision tools to regulate them, and how to reassign which phenotype leads in which context.

This section provides **phenotype-specific interventions**, not generic advice, but targeted tools mapped to the circuits you learned about in Part I. Every chapter maps back to the twelve phenotypes. Every tool has a mechanism. Nothing here is "just try this." You know why it works because you know your circuits.

The full Mastery Loop integration (and how to put everything together) is in Chapter 22.

Navigate Part II by need:

- **Can't sleep?** Start with Chapter 13 (Sleep): it's the foundation everything else builds on.
- **Using substances to cope?** Chapter 14 (Substance Patterns) explains why they worked and what works instead.
- **Overwhelmed, anxious, shut down?** Chapter 15 (Stress Response Regulation) teaches HRV and vagal toning.
- **Can't start tasks?** Chapter 16 (Productivity) is built for non-linear brains.

- **Want a daily practice?** Chapter 17 (Meditation) matches practice to phenotype.
- **Ready for precision brain training?** Chapter 18 (Neurofeedback) is the deep tool.

The Chapters

- **Ch 13 (Sleep):** The foundation everything else builds on. Phenotype-specific strategies.
- **Ch 14 (Substances):** Why they worked, why they fail, what works instead. Non-judgmental.
- **Ch 15 (Stress Response):** HRV, vagal toning, breathwork, cold exposure. Nervous system flexibility.
- **Ch 16 (Productivity):** Task management for non-linear brains. Working with your Stabilizer, not against it.
- **Ch 17 (Meditation):** Phenotype-matched practice. Why "just breathe" doesn't work for Timekeepers.
- **Ch 18 (Neurofeedback):** Precision protocols for all 12 phenotypes. The deep tool.

The core principle: Conduct, don't sedate. You're not changing what you CAN do. You're training how FLEXIBLY you use those traits, regulation, not elimination.

Your Phenotype → Tools Quick Reference

These tables show your Step 3 (Regulate) options for each phenotype. After you Notice which phenotype is active and Normalize why it's doing what it's doing, use these tables to choose which tool to try.

Use this to prioritize which interventions will have the biggest impact on *your* constellation.

Resilience & Risk

Phenotype	Resilience to Build	Substance Risk
Happy Little Kid	Baseline engagement without intensity dependence	Stimulants (crash risk), sugar

Phenotype	Resilience to Build	Substance Risk
Grumpy Old Man	Wise effort-evaluation instead of catastrophic dread	Alcohol (worsens), cannabis (short-term only)
Problem Child	Assertive boundaries with a working brake	Stimulants (short-term help, tolerance risk); cannabis (worsens)
CEO	Flexible conflict monitoring: flag, resolve, release	Stimulants (help but risky), alcohol (worsens)
Lifeguard	Contextual awareness without chronic hypervigilance	Alcohol (numbs but backfires), benzos (dependence risk)
Princess & Pea	Accurate empathy at manageable gain	Alcohol, stimulants (both worsen sensitivity)
Stabilizer	Smooth task initiation and sustained motor engagement	Stimulants (help focus, worsen motor); alcohol (worsens next day)
Supervisor	Flexible quality control: brake/release as needed	Stimulants (help), alcohol (disinhibits)
Bard	Accurate prosody reading without threat amplification	Cannabis (creative short-term, flattens long-term); alcohol
Interpreter	Clean language processing: decode/rest as needed	Stimulants (help), alcohol (impairs fluency)
Timekeeper	Tempo flexibility: fast/idle as needed	Stimulants (worse), cannabis (mixed)
Fog & Tide	Restored energy cycling and processing clarity	Stimulants (help), alcohol (worsens), cannabis (mixed)

Sleep & Interventions

Phenotype	Sleep	Interventions
Happy Little Kid	Consistent wake time, morning light	MND: open awareness; NFB: left frontal uptraining
Grumpy Old Man	Prioritize *quality* over timing	MND: loving-kindness, gratitude; NFB: right frontal downtraining
Problem Child	Reduce sleep debt to quiet loops	MND: body scan, noting practice; NFB: SMR uptraining
CEO	Deprivation = executive collapse	MND: focused attention; BFB; NFB: midline frontal
Lifeguard	Debt = threat sensitivity spike	MND: loving-kindness; BFB; NFB: posterior cingulate
Princess & Pea	Sleep is *everything*; prioritize ruthlessly	MND: gentle breath, body scan; BFB; NFB: alpha training

Phenotype	Sleep	Interventions
Stabilizer	Inconsistent sleep = restlessness	MND: movement, walking; NFB: sensorimotor rhythm (SMR)
Supervisor	Debt = impulsivity spike	MND: focused attention; NFB: SMR training
Bard	Circadian consistency critical	MND: open awareness, creative visualization; NFB: right posterior temporal
Interpreter	Timing affects language processing	MND: mantra, noting practice; NFB: left temporal
Timekeeper	Deprivation = racing thoughts	MND: breath counting, slowing practice; NFB: alpha peak frequency
Fog & Tide	Diagnostic; fix this first	MND: focused attention (lift fog); NFB: multiple sites (QEEG-guided)

MND = meditation | NFB = neurofeedback | BFB = HRV biofeedback

How to use these tables:

1. Identify your top 3 phenotypes (from self-assessment or Part I)
2. Find their rows in both tables
3. Look for overlaps: if all 3 say "sleep is critical," start there
4. Cross-reference with Chapters 13-18 for detailed protocols

Free First: Every intervention in Part II starts with tools that cost nothing: morning light, breathwork, meditation, movement, sleep hygiene. Neurofeedback accelerates the process, but the foundation is free, accessible, and effective on its own. Start with Chapters 13, 15, and 17. Build from there.

If You Only Do 3 Things from Part II

If you're overwhelmed or need to start small, focus on these three actions:

1. **Pick one core tool**: Sleep (Ch 13), Meditation (Ch 17), or Neurofeedback (Ch 18), and commit to 4 weeks of practice
2. **Track 2-3 metrics**: Sleep quality, anxiety level, task initiation, whatever matters most to your phenotypes
3. **Read Ch 14 (Substances)** if you're using substances to regulate, it will explain *why* they worked and *what* to do instead

Start small. Build capacity. Repetition trains regulation.

"I wish that peace of mind were something I could steal."

You've been stealing it, with substances, with avoidance, with sheer willpower. Part II teaches you to build it instead.

Let's learn the controls.

Ch 13: Sleep: The Cadence of Rest

Here's what I've learned: **if your sleep is broken, everything else is harder.**

Not impossible, harder. Your Happy Little Kid struggles to engage. Your Grumpy Old Man generates more dread. Your Fog thickens. Your Supervisor can't hold attention. Your CEO gets stuck on the wrong thing.

Sleep isn't everything, but it's the foundation everything else sits on. This chapter is about finding your cadence of rest, the rhythm that lets your brain recover, repair, and reset.

Here's what most sleep advice gets wrong: **Your morning routine IS your sleep routine.**

KEY INSIGHT:

You don't fix sleep at bedtime. You fix sleep at sunrise. Morning light and consistent wake time create more powerful sleep signals than anything you do in the evening.

The first few hours after waking set the tone for your entire day, and your entire night. Morning light exposure, consistent wake time, and early rising create more powerful sleep signals than anything you do at bedtime.

I learned this the hard way. Years of trying to "fix" my sleep by focusing on bedtime routines, supplements, sleep hygiene. Nothing worked consistently until I started getting up at the same time every day and getting outside within 30 minutes of waking.

That one change (morning light and consistent wake time) did more for my sleep than everything else combined.

This chapter will flip your understanding of sleep optimization. We're starting with sunrise, not sunset. **Submit to a better timekeeper: the Earth.**

A note on safety: The strategies in this chapter are behavioral and nutritional, not medical. If you're on sleep medications (benzodiazepines, Z-drugs, prescription hypnotics), do not change dosing without your prescriber's guidance, abrupt benzodiazepine discontinuation can provoke severe withdrawal and seizures; gradual tapering under medical supervision is standard protocol (Ashton, 2002). If you have a seizure disorder, sleep apnea, or narcolepsy, work with your physician. Supplements interact with medications. When in doubt, consult your provider before starting.

Where This Fits in The Mastery Loop:

This is **Step 3: Regulate**, these are the tools you choose after you've Noticed which phenotype is struggling and Normalized why. Sleep optimization makes every phenotype more regulate-able. When you're well-rested, your Grumpy Old Man generates less dread, your Stabilizer activates more easily, your CEO releases loops faster. Sleep is the foundation for all other regulation.

13.1 The Foundation: Circadian Rhythm as Central Timekeeper

Your body's internal clock isn't just about sleep. It's a sophisticated timing system that coordinates countless biological processes: hormone production, metabolism, cognitive function, DNA repair, immune function, neurotransmitter regulation.

Later, in Action Cadence (Ch 16), we'll pair this rest cadence with how you start and spend your work blocks.

Think of it as your body's central timekeeper, a biological metronome that keeps all your physiological systems synchronized and running at the right tempo. This is the cadence of rest: the rhythm your body needs to recover.

13.1.1 Oscillating Systems and Feedback Loops

Your circadian rhythm is an **oscillating system**, like weather patterns, brainwaves, and heartbeats. These systems share common features:

- **Precise timing of delay and feedback** creates stable patterns
- **Stable and resilient** (can absorb occasional disruption without losing rhythm)
- **Occasional disruptions** (staying up late, sleeping in) won't completely derail the system
- **BUT: Chronic disruptions** create dysregulation

Here's the key: Moving counter to the system's natural momentum (getting up earlier) creates powerful **re-entrainment signals**. Getting up early has a much stronger effect on resetting your clock than sleeping in.

Think of this as ringing a bell twice a day: Morning light + wake time (ding), and evening darkness + sleep time (ding). After a few days of consistent cues, your brain starts to anticipate, falls asleep more easily, wakes more evenly, gets into deep rest. Not willpower. Physiology.

Critical insight you need to understand:

You can't "catch up" on sleep by staying in bed late.

The system doesn't work that way. Circadian oscillation is driven by feedback mechanisms, and sleeping in provides weak feedback (or even counterproductive feedback). If you need extra sleep, **add it at the beginning of your night** (earlier bedtime), not the end (sleeping in).

This works with your body's natural oscillatory patterns rather than against them.

13.2 The Highest-Leverage Sleep Intervention: Morning Light

Forget melatonin supplements, blue light blockers, and expensive sleep gadgets for a moment. One of the highest-leverage tools for optimizing sleep timing and quality is **morning light exposure**.

13.2.1 Why Morning Light Is Special

When early morning light hits your eyes, it triggers a cascade of hormonal and neurological responses:

1. **Signals suprachiasmatic nucleus (SCN)** through vasopressin pathway
2. **Suppresses melatonin production** (wakefulness signal)
3. **Increases cortisol** (alertness and activation)
4. **Sets entire day's hormonal rhythm** (cortisol, melatonin, dopamine, serotonin)
5. **Different from light at other times of day** (not just "more light")

If you've spent years trying to fix sleep at bedtime and nothing stuck, this is why. The morning signal is the one your brain actually listens to.

The timing matters: The circadian system is most sensitive to light in the **early morning hours around sunrise**. Getting outside soon after waking provides the strongest reset signal for your internal clock.

Best practice: Get outdoor light within 30-60 minutes of waking, for 10-30 minutes

Why early morning? The light spectrum and angle at sunrise provide a particularly effective entrainment signal. Even cloudy mornings are far brighter than indoor lighting. The earlier in the morning you get light, the stronger the phase-advancing effect on your circadian rhythm (Duffy & Czeisler, 2009; Wright et al., 2013).

13.2.2 How to Get Morning Light (Properly)

Do:

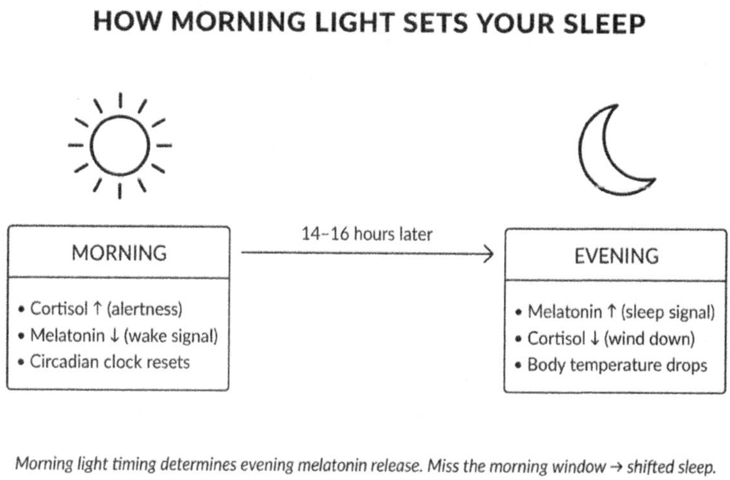

Figure 13.1: Circadian Timeline

- Get outside within 30-60 minutes of waking
- Look **toward** the sun (never directly at it)
- 10-30 minutes minimum (longer if cloudy)
- Even cloudy days provide sufficient light (much brighter than indoor)
- Walk, stretch, or do sun salutations while getting light

Don't:

- Rely on artificial light (insufficient, even "daylight" bulbs)
- Wear sunglasses during this window (reduces the entrainment signal)
- Stay indoors and rely on window light (much dimmer than outside, even on cloudy days)
- Skip because "it's cloudy" (still works)

Why morning light matters more than evening light avoidance:

For phase-shifting your circadian clock, morning light is typically higher leverage than evening light restriction. Yes, dim lights in evening help, but if you have to choose, **prioritize morning light**. Getting the morning reset right cascades through the rest of the day's hormonal timing.

13.3 My MVP (Minimum Viable Practice) for Sleep

The philosophy: Consistency with a simple practice outperforms perfection with a complex one.

My personal protocol (and what I recommend):

13.3.1 1. Early Rising

Not a morning person? Neither are most of my clients. Start with 30 minutes earlier than your current wake time, then gradually shift. Consistency matters more than the exact time. The goal is a stable, earlier anchor, not a punishing alarm.

My personal target is 4-5am. That's not where you need to start. But here's why early works:

- Maximum circadian impact (strong re-entrainment signal)
- Quiet time before world wakes (no distractions)
- Uses negative feedback for circadian reset
- Early light provides strong circadian entrainment signal

13.3.2 2. Caffeine/Stress-Free First Hour

No phone. No email. No coffee immediately.

Why:

- Allows natural cortisol awakening response (CAR)
- Prevents cortisol + caffeine spike (anxiety, jitteriness)
- Protects morning mental clarity
- Reduces stress reactivity throughout day

What to do instead:

- Gentle movement (sun salutations, walking, stretching)
- Morning light exposure
- Breathwork or meditation
- Hydration (water, electrolytes)

13.3.3 3. Five Sun Salutations (Multi-Benefit Stacking)

Why sun salutations are perfect:

- **Mindful movement** (meditation benefits without sitting still)
- **Timed light exposure** (outside = circadian entrainment)
- **Gentle exercise** (appropriate for early morning, cortisol-friendly)
- **Mental preparation** (intention setting, body awareness)
- **Takes 5-10 minutes** (sustainable daily)

The beauty: You're stacking multiple mechanisms simultaneously. Not "meditation OR exercise OR light exposure", all three at once.

13.3.4 4. Early Time-Restricted Feeding (eTRF)

End eating early (6-7pm cutoff).

Why this supports sleep:

- Eating signals "daytime" to body
- Late eating disrupts circadian rhythm
- eTRF enhances metabolic health
- Morning hunger supports waking (activation signal)
- 12-14 hour overnight fast optimizes metabolism

Not intermittent fasting extremism, just ending dinner by 7pm.

Early time-restricted feeding (eTRF) supports metabolic flexibility and circadian alignment.

13.4 Why This MVP Works

Simple enough to sustain daily:

- 4-5am wake (or 30 min earlier than current)
- First hour: no phone, no coffee
- 5 sun salutations outside (10 minutes)
- End eating by 6-7pm

Mechanisms addressed:

- Circadian entrainment (morning light, consistent wake time)
- Cortisol optimization (gentle morning movement, stress-free first hour)
- Metabolic health (eTRF)
- Stress regulation (breathwork, movement, intention)
- Sleep pressure (early wake = earlier sleep onset)

Result: Better sleep, better mood, better focus, better regulation, all from morning interventions.

13.5 Sleep Architecture: What You're Optimizing

Your sleep cycles through 4 stages in 90-110 minute cycles, typically 3-5 cycles per night (Walker, 2017):

Deep sleep (Stage 3): Physical recovery, glymphatic clearance, delta waves flush metabolic waste (Fultz et al., 2019). Goal: 15-25% of total sleep (Ohayon et al., 2004). Stage 2 sleep spindles consolidate declarative memories (Diekelmann & Born, 2010).

REM sleep: Emotional memory processing, REM separates feeling from memory, processing emotionally charged experiences (Walker & van der Helm, 2009). Creativity, dreaming.

What we can control: Duration (7-9 hours) and quality (especially Deep sleep). Daily behavior impacts Deep sleep.

What destroys sleep:

- Alcohol (reduces REM, disrupts Deep sleep)
- Cannabis (reduces REM, builds tolerance)
- Benzodiazepines (reduces Deep sleep, cognitive impairment)
- Stimulants (reduces total + Deep sleep)
- Late eating (disrupts circadian rhythm)
- Evening stress (sympathetic dominance)

Bottom line: The phenotype strategies below optimize your architecture. Wearables (Oura, Whoop) can track your progress.

13.6 Phenotype-Specific Sleep Strategies

Now let's get specific. Your phenotype determines which sleep challenges you face and which interventions will work.

13.7 For Princess & Pea: Sensory Gating

Your challenge: The world is too loud, too bright, too scratchy, too warm, too everything, especially when you're trying to sleep.

13.7.1 Environment Optimization (Non-Negotiable)

Temperature:

- **Cool bedroom: 65°F (18°C)** or cooler
- You likely need cooler than average (sensory sensitivity)
- Use fan for air circulation (bonus: white noise)
- Breathable bedding (cotton, linen, bamboo)
- Consider cooling mattress pad (ChiliPad, Eight Sleep)

Light:

- **Blackout curtains** (complete darkness)
- Or sleep mask (if curtains insufficient)
- Cover LED lights (electronics, clocks)
- Red light only if needed (doesn't suppress melatonin)
- Even small amounts of light disrupt your sleep more than others

Sound:

- **White noise machine** or fan (consistent sound)
- Or earplugs (if you can tolerate)
- Pink noise may enhance deep sleep (research emerging)
- Consistent sound better than intermittent (masks unpredictable noises)

Texture:

- **Quality bedding** (soft, breathable, no scratchy tags)
- Weighted blanket (if you like pressure: many Princess types do)
- Pillow quality matters (neck support, comfort)
- Mattress firmness (personal preference, but quality matters)

Why you need this:

- Your right TPJ (Princess) processes sensory information with higher gain
- What others don't notice, you feel intensely
- This isn't "high maintenance": it's sensory processing sensitivity
- Your sleep is more fragile to environmental disruption

13.7.2 Morning Light (Even More Important for You)

Why:

- Morning light helps regulate sensory gating throughout day
- Better daytime regulation = less sensory overwhelm = better sleep
- Circadian rhythm optimization reduces RSD (rejection sensitivity) intensity

Protocol:

- Outside within 30 minutes of waking
- 10-30 minutes (longer if you're sensitive to morning grogginess)
- Gentle movement (walking, stretching) while getting light

13.8 For Timekeeper: Calming Racing Thoughts

Your challenge: Your brain won't shut off. Racing thoughts at night. Anxiety about not sleeping. The more you try to relax, the faster your brain runs.

13.8.1 Evening Wind-Down (Start 2-3 Hours Before Bed)

Light intensity reduction:

- **Dim all lights** (not just blue light: intensity matters more)
- Candlelight or very dim red/amber light ideal
- Avoid bright screens (TV, phone, computer)
- If you must use screens: lowest brightness + blue light filter

Why intensity matters more than blue light:

- Bright light (any color) suppresses melatonin
- Blue light filters insufficient if light is bright
- Dim red/amber light doesn't suppress melatonin

Autonomic down-regulation:

- **HRV biofeedback** (5-10 minutes before bed)
- **Box breathing** (4 in, 4 hold, 4 out, 4 hold × 5 minutes)
- **Body scan meditation** (shifting from thoughts to sensations)
- **Progressive muscle relaxation** (tense and release)

13.8.2 Daytime Stress Management (Prevents Nighttime Racing)

The problem: Racing thoughts at night are often accumulated stress from day.

The solution: Regulate throughout day, not just at bedtime.

Protocols:

- Morning breathwork (before technology)
- Midday stress breaks (5-minute breathing, walking, stretching)
- Afternoon HRV training (teaching nervous system it's safe)
- Evening transition ritual (work → home, active → rest)

13.8.3 Caffeine Cutoff (Strict 2pm)

Why 2pm:

- Caffeine half-life: 5-6 hours
- 2pm cutoff = mostly cleared by 10pm bedtime
- Even if you "fall asleep fine," caffeine disrupts sleep architecture (less Deep sleep)

Genetic factors:

- CYP1A2 gene affects caffeine metabolism
- Fast metabolizers: can handle later caffeine
- Slow metabolizers: may need earlier cutoff (noon)
- If you're Timekeeper + slow metabolizer: caffeine is likely worsening your sleep

13.8.4 Neurofeedback for Racing Thoughts

SMR training calms racing thoughts while maintaining alertness, like training your brain to downshift from overdrive to cruise control. Reduces beta spindles (the "can't turn brain off" signature) and improves sleep spindles (the brain's natural sleep-promoting rhythm). See Chapter 18 for full protocol.

Alpha training helps shift from beta (thinking) to alpha (relaxation), especially effective at right posterior sites for calming the racing mind. See Chapter 18 for protocol.

Theta training can ease the alert-to-sleep transition but isn't for everyone (some get too drowsy). Chapter 18 covers when this is appropriate.

13.9 For Stabilizer: Activation Strategies (Yes, for Sleep)

Your challenge: You can't initiate the sleep process. You know you should go to bed, but you can't make yourself start the bedtime routine.

13.9.1 Sleep Initiation Activation

The problem: Your Stabilizer (left motor/premotor) has trouble initiating ANY task, including sleep.

The solution: Create momentum toward bed (not "trying harder").

Evening routine as task chain:

1. **Alarm at 9pm** (bedtime routine starts, external cue)
2. **First action easy** (brush teeth, low activation energy)
3. **Chain tasks** (teeth → face wash → pajamas → bed)
4. **Each step creates momentum** for next
5. **No decisions** (routine is automatic)

Why this works:

- External cue (alarm) provides initiation
- Task chaining reduces activation energy for each step
- Momentum builds (easier to continue than start)
- Automaticity removes decision fatigue

13.9.2 The Sleep-Attention Loop: Two Sides of the Same Circuit

Here's what most people don't know: The same brain circuit that keeps you focused during the day keeps you asleep at night.

Your Stabilizer (left frontal region) has two jobs:

1. **Keeps you in gear when you're awake** (sustained attention, focus, task engagement)
2. **Keeps you in sleep when you're asleep** (sleep maintenance, deep rest, recovery)

Two sides of the same coin. Hard to stay awake enough when awake. Hard to stay asleep enough when asleep.

When your Stabilizer is weak (low beta, excess slow waves), you struggle both ways:

- **During the day:** Inattentive, drifting, popping back into neutral when trying to focus
- **At night:** Waking frequently, light sleep, never feeling rested

You're not "falling asleep during the day" from laziness, you're falling asleep into ADHD. Your brain is fighting fatigue during the day, creating inattentiveness, visual attention drift, all the hallmarks of ADD. But the root isn't dopamine, it's sleep.

The vicious cycle with stimulants: Coffee helps. Adderall works. But they disrupt sleep architecture (reduce slow-wave sleep, fragment continuity), making the Stabilizer weaker long-term. You're borrowing from tomorrow.

The sustainable path: Fix sleep first (this chapter), watch attention improve as Stabilizer comes online naturally.

13.9.3 Morning Activation (Sets Up Evening Sleep Pressure)

Consistent wake-up time:

- **Same time every day** (even weekends, even when tired)
- This is THE most important sleep intervention for Stabilizer
- Wake time locks in circadian rhythm
- Creates sleep pressure by evening

Morning light + movement:

- Outside within 30 minutes of waking
- Gentle movement (5 sun salutations, walking)
- Activation signal for Stabilizer
- Sets cortisol rhythm (high morning, low evening)

Morning hunger (from eTRF):

- End eating by 6-7pm night before
- Morning hunger = activation signal
- Supports waking (not just circadian, but metabolic)
- Breakfast becomes reward for waking

Why "trying harder" to sleep makes it worse:

- Stabilizer doesn't respond to effort (responds to momentum and external cues)
- Anxiety about sleep activates Grumpy Old Man (opposite of helpful)
- Sleep is passive process (can't "do" sleep, can only allow it)

13.10 For Grumpy Old Man & Lifeguard: Dread & Threat Interventions

Your challenge: Nighttime activates both Grumpy Old Man (everything feels like too much, generating futility scenarios) and Lifeguard (threat sensitivity, environmental scanning). Sleep feels vulnerable. This combination prevents sleep onset.

13.10.1 Why Your Brain Resists Sleep

Evolutionary context:

- Nighttime = vulnerability
- Sleep = loss of vigilance
- Grumpy Old Man (right DLPFC) evolved to conserve energy by avoiding unnecessary effort
- Lifeguard (posterior cingulate) evolved to scan for threats
- For some brains, these protection systems never turn off

Modern manifestation:

- Lying in bed → Grumpy Old Man generates futility "what if" scenarios ("tomorrow will be exhausting")
- Darkness → Lifeguard threat sensitivity (scanning for external threats)
- Quiet → internal thoughts amplified
- Vulnerability → dread + anxiety

13.10.2 Sleep Anxiety Interventions

HRV training (Heart Rate Variability biofeedback):

- Teaches nervous system it's safe
- Parasympathetic activation (brake pedal)
- 5-10 minutes before bed
- Apps: Elite HRV, HeartMath, Welltory

Safety cues:

- Consistent bedtime routine (predictability = safety)
- Comfortable sleep environment (sensory safety)
- White noise (masks unpredictable sounds)
- Weighted blanket (pressure = calming)
- Partner/pet (social safety: if not disruptive)

Catastrophic thought interruption:

- **Cognitive defusion:** "I'm having the thought that everything will fall apart" (naming it as a *thought*, not a prediction)
- **Worry time:** 15 minutes earlier in evening to process worries (not in bed)
- **Thought parking:** Write worries down, promise to address tomorrow
- **Breathing:** 4-7-8 breath (4 in, 7 hold, 8 out) shifts to parasympathetic

13.10.3 Morning Breathwork (Prevents Evening Anxiety)

5-minute box breathing (before technology):

- 4 seconds in, 4 hold, 4 out, 4 hold
- Repeat for 5 minutes

- Optimizes CO2 tolerance
- Sets calm, focused tone for day
- Reduces anxiety accumulation

Why morning breathwork helps sleep:

- Prevents stress accumulation throughout day
- Trains autonomic regulation
- Less daytime anxiety = less nighttime anxiety
- Proactive (not reactive at bedtime)

13.10.4 Supplements for Grumpy Old Man

Magnesium glycinate:

- 200-350mg before bed (350mg is the supplemental upper limit)
- Supports GABA, muscle relaxation
- Calming without sedation
- Safe, well-tolerated

L-Theanine + GABA:

- L-Theanine: 200-400mg (promotes relaxation, enhances alpha waves)
- GABA: 500-1000mg (calming reported; oral GABA crosses the blood-brain barrier poorly, so the mechanism is debated)
- Synergistic (work better together)
- Non-addictive alternative to benzos

Microdose melatonin:

- **0.3-0.5mg** (NOT 3-10mg typical doses)
- Higher doses suppress natural production
- Timing: 1-2 hours before desired sleep
- Supports circadian rhythm (not sedation)

Start low, monitor response. Not replacements for behavioral interventions.

13.11 For Fog: Chronotype Honoring

Your challenge: Morning people's advice doesn't work for you. You're a night person. Forcing early schedule creates misery, not optimization.

13.11.1 Chronotype Reality

The truth: Some brains are wired for later sleep-wake cycles.

Genetic factors:

- PER3 gene variants affect chronotype

- "Night owls" aren't lazy, they're genetically different
- Forcing morning-person schedule fights biology

BUT: Consistent wake time still matters (even for night people)

The balance:

- Honor your chronotype (don't force 5am if you're night person)
- But maintain consistency (same wake time daily)
- Structure life around your rhythm (if possible)

13.11.2 Sleep Inertia Management (Waking Protocols)

The problem: You wake up in fog. Takes hours to feel alert. Morning is torture.

Why this happens:

- Slow transition from sleep to wake
- Adenosine clearance delayed
- Cortisol awakening response blunted
- May have slowed alpha peak frequency (COMT genotype: see Chapter 12)

Waking protocols:

- **Morning light immediately** (even before fully awake: open curtains, go outside)
- **Cold exposure** (cold shower, cold water on face: activating; a randomized trial found cold showers reduced sickness absence and improved self-reported well-being) (Buijze et al., 2016)
- **Movement** (gentle stretching, walking: not intense)
- **Hydration** (water + electrolytes: brain needs hydration)
- **Patience** (takes 30 90 minutes to fully wake: plan accordingly)

What doesn't work:

- Hitting snooze (fragments sleep, worsens inertia)
- Caffeine immediately (delays natural cortisol response)
- Forcing productivity before fully awake (sets up failure)

13.11.3 When Fog Is Rest vs. Dysfunction

Fog as rest (honor it):

- After intense period (creative project, social marathon, stress)
- Seasonal (winter, less light)
- Recovery from illness
- Natural rhythm (some days slower than others)

Fog as dysfunction (address it):

- Chronic (every day, for weeks/months)
- Worsening over time
- Paired with depression, apathy
- Not responsive to rest

QEEG can distinguish:

- Excess theta (ADHD-type: see Chapter 3)
- Slowed alpha (COMT genotype: see Chapter 12)
- Frontal hypoactivation (depression-type)

13.12 The Substance Connection: Destroying Sleep Architecture

Many poet-brains have discovered that alcohol, cannabis, or benzodiazepines seem to solve sleep problems. **Short-term: Yes, they work. Long-term: They destroy the very architecture that makes sleep restorative.**

13.12.1 How Each Substance Disrupts Sleep

Alcohol:

- Reduces REM sleep (emotional processing disrupted)
- Disrupts slow-wave sleep (physical recovery impaired)
- Increases sleep fragmentation (wake more often)
- REM rebound when wearing off (vivid dreams, nightmares)
- Glutamate surge (anxiety next day)

Cannabis:

- May help sleep onset initially
- Reduces REM sleep (dreaming suppressed)
- Tolerance builds rapidly
- Withdrawal causes severe sleep disruption (irritability, insomnia)

Benzodiazepines:

- Reduces deep sleep (SWS impaired: less restorative)
- Physical dependence develops quickly
- Withdrawal dangerous (seizures, death: requires medical supervision)
- Rebound insomnia worse than baseline

Stimulants:

- Disrupt sleep 8-12 hours after use
- Reduce total sleep time and deep sleep
- Create vicious cycle: poor sleep → more stimulants → worse sleep

The pattern: You get unconsciousness, not restoration. The sleep architecture that consolidates learning, processes emotions, and builds resilience, destroyed.

See Chapter 14 for substance patterns, genetic factors, and neurofeedback alternatives.

13.13 Hormonal Transitions: Perimenopause, Menopause

If you're in perimenopause or menopause, your sleep disruption isn't just "I'm stressed and tired." **There are measurable circuit changes happening.**

13.13.1 What's Happening in Your Brain

Progesterone dropping away creates left frontal (C3) changes:

- Beta dips (less activation)
- Theta surges (more slow waves)
- This is the same circuit: your Stabilizer, that has dual function: keeps you focused during the day AND keeps you asleep at night

You'll notice BOTH:

- Sleep fragmentation (waking frequently, light sleep, never feeling rested)
- Executive function changes during the day (attention drift, word-finding issues, tip-of-tongue moments, "fogginess")

This is the dual function principle again: The circuit that regulates sleep depth also regulates daytime attention. Hormones affect both simultaneously.

13.13.2 Why This Matters

It's not "all in your head" or "just part of aging."

Your brain map would show:

- Left frontal beta reduction (Stabilizer weakening)
- Theta increases in C3 (slow waves creeping in)
- Executive function changes visible on performance testing
- Not just subjective: measurable

You're not imagining it. Your circuits are changing.

13.13.3 What Actually Helps

Sleep optimization still works (this chapter's MVP):

- Morning light and consistent wake time
- Sleep hygiene, sensory optimization

- But may not fully resolve until hormones stabilize
- These create the best foundation possible given hormonal constraints

Neurofeedback can compensate:

- Target C3 specifically (left frontal activation)
- SMR training for sleep-wake transitions
- Multiple frequency combinations may be needed to find what works for you
- Timeline: Often requires more sessions (40-60+) due to ongoing hormonal variability

HRT consideration:

- If sleep disruption is severe and affecting quality of life
- Progesterone specifically supports both sleep and left frontal function
- Talk to your doctor: this is a medical decision
- Neurofeedback can work alongside HRT

Nootropic support (consult your provider):

- CDP-choline can help with slowed processing and word-finding
- May provide "boardroom edge" during the day
- Won't fix sleep directly, but compensates for daytime executive function impacts
- Dose carefully (5 days/week, not daily) to avoid cholinergic overload (irritability, tight muscles)

13.13.4 The Reality

Perimenopause/menopause doesn't mean "accept terrible sleep forever."

But it does mean:

- The foundation matters even more (MVP protocol non-negotiable)
- Neurofeedback may take longer to show effects
- Hormonal variability creates moving target (some weeks better than others)
- Patience and persistence required
- Consider medical support if severe

You can still optimize. It's just harder. And that's not your fault, it's physiology.

13.14 Neurofeedback Protocols for Sleep

Phenotype-specific protocols (Hoedlmoser et al., 2008; Lambert-Beaudet et al., 2021):

For Timekeeper: SMR training calms racing thoughts, alpha training shifts from overdrive to relaxation, beta spindle reduction for the "can't turn brain off" pattern

For Grumpy Old Man: Right frontal alpha training for dread reduction, alpha-theta for deep relaxation, HRV biofeedback for autonomic regulation

For Stabilizer: Theta/beta ratio optimization builds sleep pressure, left frontal activation during day improves evening sleepiness

For Lifeguard: Posterior cingulate calming reduces hypervigilance, alpha-theta for deep rest states

For Princess & Pea: Sensory gating protocols filter intensity, SMR for calm focus, right TPJ regulation for emotional reactivity

General sleep optimization: Alpha-theta for deep relaxation, SMR for sleep-wake transitions, posterior alpha for visual cortex calming

Timeline: 20-40 sessions for lasting changes. Repetition trains regulation.

Composite, like every case in this book. The pattern is one I have seen many times; the person is not one person.

Tom used to lie awake for hours, brain racing, catastrophizing, needing alcohol to quiet the Grumpy Old Man enough to sleep. After two months of neurofeedback (right frontal alpha training, SMR for sleep architecture), he discovered something remarkable: he could fall asleep at will. Not just at night, anywhere.

I came into the office one afternoon and found him asleep on the waiting room couch. "Is he here for a visit?" I asked. The front desk staff laughed: "No, he's been here three times already this week. He discovered he can fall asleep now, so he called this morning asking when you'd be in. He's been here half an hour. Asleep for twenty minutes. He just... can."

His right frontal cortex learned to generate the calm he'd been borrowing from alcohol. His brain learned the rhythm naturally.

See Chapter 18 for detailed protocols, electrode placements, and session structure for all these approaches.

13.15 Evidence-Based Supplements (Not Replacements for Behavior Change)

My recommendations: If the MVP protocol isn't enough (especially when your Timekeeper is racing or your Grumpy Old Man won't stop predicting tomorrow's disasters) these can support the wind-down. They're helpers, not substitutes for light and consistency.

Magnesium (glycinate or threonate):

- 200-350mg before bed (350mg is the supplemental upper limit)
- Supports GABA, muscle relaxation
- Safe, well-tolerated
- Most people deficient

L-Theanine:

- 200-400mg
- Promotes relaxation without sedation
- Enhances alpha waves
- Synergistic with GABA

GABA:

- 500-1000mg
- Direct GABAergic effect
- May not cross blood-brain barrier well (individual variation)
- Synergistic with L-theanine

If racing thoughts or dread keep you staring at the ceiling, these target the neurochemistry behind that loop.

Microdose Melatonin:

- **0.3-0.5mg** (NOT 3-10mg typical doses)
- Higher doses suppress natural production
- Timing: 1-2 hours before desired sleep
- Supports circadian rhythm (not sedation)

Glycine:

- 3-5g before bed
- Promotes deep sleep
- Lowers core body temperature
- Well-researched, safe

Apigenin:

- 50mg (from chamomile)
- Mild anxiolytic
- GABA-A receptor modulation

Inositol:

- 500-1000mg
- Supports neurotransmitter signaling
- May reduce anxiety

Timing note:

- Melatonin: 1-2 hours before desired sleep (circadian signaling)

- Others: Generally "before bed" (30-60 minutes), but optimal timing varies by individual
- Start with standard recommendations, adjust based on response
- Work with healthcare provider to find your optimal timing

Key principles:

- Start with low doses, monitor response
- Be aware of interactions with medications
- Consult healthcare professional
- These support natural sleep (unlike alcohol/benzos/cannabis which disrupt)

13.16 The Integrated Approach: Stacking Mechanisms

The most powerful approach combines multiple strategies:

13.16.1 Morning (Foundation):

1. Consistent wake time (even weekends)
2. Morning light exposure (within 30-60 minutes, outside, 10-30 minutes)
3. Gentle movement (5 sun salutations, walking, stretching)
4. Caffeine/stress-free first hour (no phone, no email)
5. Hydration (water, electrolytes)

13.16.2 Throughout Day:

6. Stress management (breathwork, HRV training, meditation)
7. Caffeine cutoff (2pm strict)
8. Physical activity (moderate exercise earlier in day)

13.16.3 Evening:

9. Stop eating 2-3 hours before bed (eTRF: end by 6-7pm)
10. Dim lights (intensity reduction, not just blue light)
11. Evening wind-down routine (consistent, relaxing)
12. Cool bedroom (65°F / 18°C)
13. Sensory optimization (dark, quiet, comfortable)

13.16.4 Bedtime:

14. Supplements if needed (magnesium, L-theanine, GABA, microdose melatonin)
15. Relaxation practice (HRV, breathing, body scan)
16. No screens (or lowest brightness + blue filter)

13.16.5 Ongoing:

17. Neurofeedback training (phenotype-specific protocols, 20-40 sessions)
18. Track sleep (wearable or subjective, monitor what works)

Remember: Start with the MVP (early wake, morning light, sun salutations, eTRF). Add other strategies as needed for your phenotype.

13.17 Expert Perspectives

The protocols in this chapter draw from converging research: morning light exposure for circadian entrainment (Wright et al., 2013; Duffy & Czeisler, 2009), early time-restricted feeding for metabolic alignment, and Peak Brain Institute's phenotype-specific approach combining these tools with QEEG-guided optimization.

13.18 The Promise

Sleep is where trait regulation consolidates.

Every neurofeedback session, every meditation practice, every stress management technique, your brain integrates that regulation training during sleep. Without quality sleep, you're building on sand.

But here's the good news: **You don't need to fix sleep at bedtime. You fix sleep at sunrise.**

Morning light. Consistent wake time. Gentle movement. Early eating cutoff. These create the conditions for sleep to happen naturally.

And if you need more support: phenotype-specific neurofeedback protocols, evidence-based supplements, and understanding your genetic patterns (LVF, Frontal Slow, Beta Spindles, Slowed Alpha).

MYTH vs REALITY:

MYTH: "I'll catch up on sleep this weekend."

REALITY: Sleep debt doesn't work like a bank account. Chronic deprivation changes your phenotypes, upregulates Lifeguard, downregulates CEO, makes Problem Child stickier. "Catching up" reduces acute exhaustion; it doesn't reverse the circuit changes. Consistency beats binge-recovery every time.

If you only do one thing from this chapter: Get morning sunlight within 30 minutes of waking, every single day. Everything else in this chapter is negotiable. This isn't.

13.19 Key Takeaways

Every intervention you do consolidates during sleep. Without quality sleep, everything else is harder.

- **Morning routine IS your sleep routine:** Morning light and consistent wake time create more powerful sleep signals than anything you do at bedtime, circadian alignment happens at dawn, not dusk
- **My MVP:** Wake same time daily (even weekends), outside within 30 minutes, move gently, eat within 1 hour, these four create a foundation for every phenotype
- **Substances give unconsciousness, not restoration:** Alcohol fragments sleep architecture, cannabis suppresses REM, stimulants disrupt circadian rhythm, you're stealing from tomorrow, not building capacity
- **Phenotype-specific interventions:** Sensory gating for Princess & Pea, thought-calming for Timekeeper, activation support for Stabilizer, anxiety regulation for Grumpy Old Man
- **SMR neurofeedback = sleep training:** Increases sleep spindles, improves deep sleep (N3), reduces restlessness (see Chapter 18)
- **Infrastructure beats willpower:** Create conditions where sleep happens naturally, you can't force it
- **Everything else sits on top of sleep:** If this cadence is off, every other cadence gets noisy.

13.20 Reader Reflections

1. **What's your current morning routine?** Consistent wake time or variable? Morning light or straight to screens?
2. **Which phenotype's sleep challenges resonate most?** Sensory overwhelm? Racing thoughts? Can't initiate sleep? Anxiety?
3. **What's one element of my MVP you could implement this week?** Start with one.

Ch 14: Self-Medication & Substance Patterns

You weren't self-medicating wrong. You were self-medicating intelligently without the right tools. Alcohol can work for LVF brains. Stimulants can work for Frontal Slow. Now let's build the calm without the hangover.

If you don't use substances, skim the phenotype-mapping section, it explains why other people in your life might. If you do, this chapter is written without judgment. You've been regulating real circuits with the tools you had.

14.1 "Building Resilience vs. Stealing Quiet"

Peter Mulvey again: *"I wish that peace of mind were something I could steal."*

Many poet-brains have tried to steal quiet, with:

- Alcohol (dampening the Grumpy Old Man, calming the Timekeeper)
- Cannabis (quieting the CEO's task-switching, softening the Lifeguard's hypervigilance)
- Stimulants (activating the Stabilizer, sharpening the Executive Team)
- Psychedelics (dissolving rigid patterns, accessing deeper creativity)
- Nicotine (focus, anxiety reduction, oral fixation)
- Caffeine (masking ADHD, pushing through Fog)

The validation: You're not "self-medicating" because you're weak or addicted. You're trying to regulate circuits that neuroscience barely understands and psychiatry often medicalizes without offering real solutions. You were stealing quiet because you didn't have tools to build resilience.

Substances are blunt instruments for delicate circuitry.

A note on safety: This chapter explains patterns, not prescriptions. If you're physically dependent on alcohol, benzodiazepines, or opioids, do not stop abruptly. Withdrawal from these substances can be medically dangerous. Work with a physician. If you're in active addiction crisis, this chapter is context for after you're stabilized, not a substitute for clinical support. Harm reduction, not reckless self-experimentation.

14.2 Why You Reached for What You Reached For

Here's what 20 years of brain mapping has taught me:

Your substance patterns aren't random. They're not moral failures. They're **intelligent attempts to regulate specific brain patterns that have genetic and neurobiological roots.**

Substances feel like they're fixing traits, but they're really hijacking cadence: forcing temporary changes in speed, mood, or intensity that you don't control.

If you're anxious and over-aroused (Grumpy Old Man, Timekeeper), you likely reached for alcohol or benzodiazepines, because your brain has a genetic predisposition to find GABAergic substances calming. Your GABAA receptor genes make alcohol feel like it "fixes" you (Edenberg et al., 2004). This isn't weakness, it's neurobiology.

If you're under-aroused and can't initiate (Stabilizer, Fog), you likely reached for stimulants, because your frontal cortex shows excess theta (slow waves) that stimulants temporarily suppress (Arns et al., 2008; Chabot et al., 1999). The function of that use is regulation, not moral failure, but the costs and risks are still real. Understanding the function helps you replace the tool.

If you tried stimulants and they didn't help (or made you anxious), you likely have slowed alpha peak frequency, a COMT genetic variant that doesn't respond to stimulants. Not "treatment-resistant", misidentified pattern.

If you can't turn your brain off (beta spindles), you reached for alcohol, benzos, or cannabis because they target GABA, the right system. You found the concept. Substances are just the blunt instrument.

You weren't wrong about what needed regulation. You just didn't have the right tools.

Substances work short-term. They fail long-term (tolerance, withdrawal, side effects, borrowing from tomorrow).

Neurofeedback targets the same patterns. No drug-like tolerance or withdrawal. Durable changes.

See *The QEEG Field Guide* (Hill & Lomeli, forthcoming) for the complete technical breakdown: EEG patterns (LVF, Frontal Slow, Slowed Alpha, Beta Spindles), genetic factors (GABAA, COMT, mu-opioid receptors), chronic use EEG changes, and treatment prediction frameworks.

Where This Fits in The Mastery Loop:

Understanding WHY substances "worked" is part of **Step 2: Normalize**, "Of course you reached for alcohol/stimulants/cannabis. Your brain was intelligently trying to regulate your Grumpy Old Man (or whichever phenotype was loudest). This makes perfect sense." Then this chapter gives you **Step 3: Regulate** alternatives (neurofeedback, HRV training, meditation, sleep optimization) that target the same circuits without tolerance, withdrawal, or borrowing from tomorrow.

14.3 The Pattern: Your Brain Seeks What Regulates It

Here's what's remarkable: **your EEG pattern often predicts which substance you'll find most effective.**

SUBSTANCE–PHENOTYPE MAP

Why you reach for what you reach for

	Grumpy Old Man	CEO	Stabilizer	Happy Little Kid	Lifeguard	Princess & Pea
Alcohol	●				●	
Cannabis	●	●				
Stimulants			●	●		
Nicotine		●	●		●	
Psychedelics		●				
Opioids						●

EEG patterns predict substance preference. Self-medication targets specific circuits.

Figure 14.1: Substance-Phenotype Matrix

Under-aroused (excess theta, low beta): can't initiate, feel sluggish. You seek stimulants. They reduce theta, increase beta, wake up your frontal cortex. You feel functional for the first time. **The trap:** Chronic use exacerbates the slow-wave pattern. You crash harder.

Over-aroused (excess beta): anxiety, racing thoughts, can't turn off. Alcohol, benzos, cannabis dampen the overactivity. You can finally relax. **The trap:** Your brain adapts by increasing excitation. Rebound anxiety worse than baseline.

Depressed (left frontal hypoactive): You seek stimulants or MDMA. They boost dopamine. **Anxious** (right frontal hyperactive): You seek alcohol or cannabis. Both traps: chronic use exaggerates the asymmetry.

Rigidly stuck (CEO in loops, OCD-like): Psychedelics decrease coherence, break rigid patterns. Borrowed insight, not built capacity.

Fragmented (scattered attention): Stimulants or nicotine sharpen coherence. But chronic use damages the networks you're trying to coordinate.

14.4 What Chronic Use Does: Why Substances Stop Working

Here's what happens with chronic use, measurable EEG changes that explain why substances stop working and why quitting is so hard:

Alcohol: Your brain compensates for the calming by becoming hyperexcitable. When you're not drinking, excess beta dominates, more anxiety than before you started. The calm you borrowed? You need more alcohol to achieve it. Tolerance builds, anxiety worsens, the cycle reinforces.

Cannabis: Your brain becomes persistently under-aroused. The calm you achieved becomes your stuck baseline. You can't access activation when you need it. May reverse with prolonged abstinence, but takes months.

Stimulants: The pendulum swings. Using: hyperaroused, focused. Withdrawal: depleted, slow. The system you artificially activated becomes more sluggish in compensation. The activation you borrowed leaves you more depleted.

Opioids: Diffuse slowing across all regions. Mental clouding, low motivation. Largely reversible with sustained abstinence (2-3 months), but withdrawal requires medical supervision.

Psychedelics: Unique in not causing chronic EEG pathology with typical use. Classic psychedelics (LSD, psilocybin) don't create lasting damage. MDMA is different: heavy chronic use can cause serotonergic neurotoxicity. They don't train capacity, borrowed flexibility, not built skill.

Under the Hood: Pharmacology of Chronic Use

Alcohol: GABA-A receptor agonism produces acute calming; chronic use triggers compensatory upregulation of glutamate (NMDA) receptors and downregulation of GABA-A, producing hyperexcitability on withdrawal (tremors, seizures, life-threatening rebound). Frontal EEG desynchronization is among the strongest predictors of relapse (Bauer, 2001; Winterer et al., 1998).

Cannabis: CB1 receptor downregulation reduces endocannabinoid tone. Posterior EEG rhythms decrease even after stopping, reduced alpha, disrupted network coordination (amotivational syndrome). Recovery takes months of abstinence for receptor re-expression.

Stimulants: Dopamine transporter upregulation and D2 receptor downregulation with chronic use. During use: high beta/gamma (hyperaroused). On withdrawal: high theta/delta (depleted). Chronic use exacerbates the frontal slow pattern you were trying to fix.

Opioids: Mu-opioid receptor tolerance produces diffuse cortical slowing. Hypo-arousal, low motivation. Withdrawal is dangerous but EEG normalization is largely achievable at 2-3 months sustained abstinence.

MDMA: Serotonergic neurotoxicity with heavy chronic use, 5-HT transporter density decreases. Classic psychedelics (LSD, psilocybin) do not show this pattern at typical doses.

14.5 Building What You Were Borrowing: The Toolkit

You've been regulating specific brain patterns. The substances worked because they targeted the right systems.

Think of this chapter as mapping your "borrowed cadence" strategies so you can replace them with cadences you actually own.

Now let's build that regulation without the rebound. Without the tolerance. Without borrowing from tomorrow.

The toolkit includes:

Neurofeedback (detailed below): Targeted training of specific circuits. Trains your brain to generate the calm, focus, or activation you were borrowing. No drug-like tolerance or withdrawal; you're training capacity, not borrowing chemistry. This is my go-to tool because it targets the exact patterns your brain map shows.

Mindfulness-Based Relapse Prevention / MBRP (see below): Teaches urge surfing, emotional regulation, and how to work with cravings without acting on them. Strong evidence base, reduces relapse, maintained at 12-month follow-up. Meditation trains you to surf the states your circuits create.

Sleep optimization (Chapter 13): Repairs what substances damaged. Restores dopamine, fixes architecture, rebuilds baseline. Non-negotiable foundation. Morning light, consistent wake time, sleep restriction if needed.

HRV biofeedback (Chapter 15): Teaches nervous system safety and regulation. Builds vagal tone, reduces stress reactivity. Especially crucial for anxiety-based patterns (alcohol, benzos) or trauma history.

Therapy & community support: 12-step programs (AA, NA), SMART Recovery, individual therapy, group therapy. Provides accountability, models recovery, reduces isolation. You don't have to do this alone.

Medication (when needed): Sometimes helpful during transition, naltrexone for alcohol, bupropion for stimulants, medical taper for benzos. Work with prescriber who understands neurofeedback integration.

Each tool addresses different aspects:

- Neurofeedback trains the underlying circuits
- Mindfulness teaches you to work with what those circuits create
- Sleep provides the foundation for everything
- HRV builds nervous system resilience
- Community provides accountability and hope
- Medication can bridge the transition (under supervision)

The full stack works better than any single tool. Neurofeedback + MBRP + sleep optimization addresses addiction at multiple levels: circuits, skills, and foundation.

That said, neurofeedback is the precision option, it's the only tool that can target your specific EEG signature and train lasting changes in those exact patterns. Let me show you why it works, then we'll cover the rest of the toolkit.

14.6 Why Neurofeedback Works for Substance Patterns

Here's what makes neurofeedback different from substances:

Specific targeting: Trains individual circuits (calm Grumpy Old Man without suppressing Happy Little Kid). Substances flood everything.

Lasting: Trains trait regulation over 20-40 sessions. You keep the capacity, you gain flexibility. Substances are temporary (hours, then rebound).

No drug-like tolerance or withdrawal: You're training regulatory capacity, not borrowing chemistry. Benefits tend to be durable; many people maintain gains for years, though touch-up sessions are sometimes helpful.

Preserves gifts: Regulates torture while keeping depth, creativity, empathy, sensitivity. Substances often numb everything.

The evidence: A growing body of RCTs confirms meaningful neurofeedback effects for substance use patterns. A 2008 systematic review (Sokhadze et al.) rated the evidence across alcohol, stimulant, and opiate populations, finding consistent signals for EEG biofeedback as a treatment for substance use disorders. Effect sizes vary and the field is still evolving, but the signal is consistent enough to take seriously.

For detailed protocols, outcomes, and citations: See Chapter 18 (Neurofeedback).

14.7 Neurofeedback by Substance Pattern (Quick Reference)

14.7.1 Alcohol → Peniston Alpha-Theta Protocol

What alcohol may have been regulating: Grumpy Old Man (dread/overwhelm), Lifeguard (trauma/hypervigilance), Princess & Pea (sensory overwhelm). You found calm you couldn't generate naturally.

The neurofeedback solution: Peniston Alpha-Theta Protocol (30-40 sessions). Trains deep relaxation states, processes trauma/triggers, reduces stress reactivity. Outcomes: 70-80% abstinence rates in early published trials, though sample sizes were small and replication varies (Peniston & Kulkosky, 1989, 1991; Scott et al., 2005).

Why it works: Teaches your brain to generate the calm you were borrowing from alcohol. Addresses root cause (anxiety, trauma) not just symptom.

Full protocol details and citations: See Chapter 18.

14.7.2 Cannabis → SMR + CEO Flexibility

What cannabis may have been regulating: CEO stuck (task-switching constantly), Lifeguard threat-sensitive (ruminating), "finally I can let go and be present."

The neurofeedback solution: SMR (calm focus), anterior cingulate flexibility (CEO learns to release), posterior cingulate calming (Lifeguard relaxes). 40-60 sessions. Motivation circuit restoration (3-6 months).

Full protocol details: Chapter 18

14.7.3 Stimulants → Theta/Beta + Left Frontal Beta Training

What stimulants may have been regulating: Stabilizer offline (Frontal Slow, ADHD), task initiation impossible, "finally I can focus."

The neurofeedback solution: Theta/beta ratio optimization (wake Stabilizer naturally), left frontal beta training (sustainable activation), sleep architecture repair. 40-60 sessions + 6-18 months dopamine recovery.

Note: Expect initial difficulty (withdrawal fog) before improvement. Patience required.

Full protocol details: Chapter 18

14.7.4 Benzos → Alpha Training + Medical Taper (REQUIRED)

Critical: Benzo withdrawal can be life-threatening. **Medical supervision required.**

The neurofeedback support: Right frontal alpha training (builds natural calm during taper), HRV biofeedback (teaches nervous system safety), sensory gating (if used for overwhelm). 40-60 sessions concurrent with medical taper.

Full protocol & safety details: Chapter 18.

14.7.5 Polysubstance Use → Individualized Protocol

For complex patterns: QEEG assessment identifies all dysregulated phenotypes, then individualized protocol targets root causes (anxiety → right frontal alpha, ADHD → theta/beta, trauma → alpha-theta, RSD → right TPJ). 60-120+ sessions.

The key: Don't just stop using, address what you were trying to regulate.

Detailed protocols for polysubstance patterns, craving reduction, relapse prevention: Chapter 18.

14.8 Mindfulness for Addiction: Evidence-Based Support

Mindfulness-Based Relapse Prevention (MBRP) integrates meditation with addiction-specific coping skills. The research is compelling: reduces relapse, decreases craving, improves emotional regulation, with benefits maintained at 12-month follow-up (Bowen et al., 2014, *JAMA Psychiatry*).

The core insight: Cravings are temporary. They rise, peak, and fall, typically in 20-30 minutes. You don't have to act on them. You can observe them.

14.8.1 The Essential Practices

MBRP teaches three meditation types (see Chapter 17 for full framework):

Feeling Tone, External (Body Scan for Craving)

When craving hits, scan your body. Where do you feel it? Chest tightness? Jaw clenching? Stomach churning? Notice the somatic sensations without judgment. Watch them change. This is **urge surfing**, riding the wave instead of being swept under. The craving will peak and pass whether you use or not. You're training attention on external physical sensations (feeling tone, external).

Present Time Attention (SOBER Breathing Space)

The **SOBER breathing space** anchors you in present time without reaction:

- **S**top (step back from automatic reaction)
- **O**bserve (what's happening? thoughts, sensations, urges)
- **B**reathe (3-5 deep breaths, anchor in present time)
- **E**xpand (broaden awareness: whole body, environment)
- **R**espond (choose action mindfully, not reactively)

Use this in high-risk situations: triggers, stress, emotional overwhelm, before making decisions about use. Present time attention creates space between urge and action, where your prefrontal cortex can engage instead of your amygdala.

Feeling Tone, Internal (Loving-Kindness for Shame)

Shame drives use: feel bad → use to feel better → feel worse → repeat. Self-compassion (internal feeling tone) breaks the cycle. Generate compassion toward yourself: "This is hard. I'm struggling. I deserve kindness." Notice harsh self-judgment (especially with RSD) and practice compassion anyway.

14.8.2 Why Meditation Works for Addiction

Neurofeedback trains the circuits. Meditation teaches you to surf the states those circuits create. Together: powerful combination.

- **Strengthens prefrontal cortex** (executive control: pause between urge and action)
- **Reduces amygdala reactivity** (emotional regulation: less hijacking)
- **Enhances insula function** (body awareness: notice cravings as sensations, not commands)
- **Builds new pathways** (urge → observe, not urge → use)

The integration: MBRP + neurofeedback addresses addiction at multiple levels. Mindfulness builds awareness and distress tolerance. Neurofeedback trains underlying dysregulation. Sleep optimization (Chapter 13) repairs what substances damaged. Together: the full stack.

See Chapter 17 for full meditation instruction, phenotype-specific practices, and how to build a sustainable practice.

14.9 Harm Reduction: If You're Not Ready to Quit

The philosophy: Meet people where they are. Any reduction in harm is progress.

Not everyone is ready for abstinence. That's okay. Harm reduction offers alternatives.

14.9.1 Moderation Management (Controlled Drinking)

Behavioral program for problem drinkers aiming to moderate (not abstain). Guidelines: limit drinks per occasion (3-4 for men, 2-3 for women), days per week (3-4 max), track use, identify triggers. Best for early-stage problem drinking, not severe dependence. **Caution:** Physical dependence requires medical supervision for withdrawal.

14.9.2 The Sinclair Method (TSM) with Naltrexone

Naltrexone (opioid antagonist) taken 1 hour before drinking blocks alcohol's endorphin reward. Brain gradually unlearns association over 3-4 months. Sinclair's trials reported ~78% success rate using this extinction protocol (Sinclair, 2001). Allows continued drinking while retraining brain (harm reduction approach). Requires medical supervision.

14.9.3 Harm Reduction Through "Snobbery"

Quality over quantity. Cultivate discernment, become a wine connoisseur, craft beer enthusiast, or cannabis sommelier. Snobbery naturally reduces consumption (savoring one excellent glass vs. chugging cheap bottle). Shifts from automatic use to intentional selection. For novelty-seeking brains: explore quality, not quantity.

14.9.4 Tracking and Awareness (Quantified Self)

What's measured is managed. Track with apps (Sunnyside, Cutback Coach), breathalyzers, sleep trackers (Oura, Whoop), or journals. Awareness reveals patterns, triggers, and progress. Not judgment, data

---

14.9.5 Moderation Requires Low Tolerance (Reset Strategies)

To moderate, you need low tolerance. High tolerance means needing more for effect. Reset with strategic breaks (30-day abstinence), spacing (increase days between use), or gradual dose reduction. Cannabis tolerance builds rapidly; stimulants quickly; alcohol slower. Breaks break the cycle.

Critical for opioids: Abstinence lowers tolerance fast. The dose your body handled before a break can be lethal afterward. Most opioid overdose deaths happen on return to use, not during active use, because people go back to a dose their body no longer handles. If you use opioids and take any break, days or months, your old dose is not your dose.

14.10 Beyond the Basics: Advanced Strategies

The foundation is covered (sleep in Chapter 13, stress management in Chapter 15, neurofeedback in Chapter 18, MBRP above, harm reduction strategies above). Here are additional elements that support recovery:

Environmental design matters. Remove triggers (alcohol, paraphernalia), add supports (meditation space, exercise equipment). Make good habits easy, bad habits hard. Arrange your physical, digital, and social environments for success. Reduce exposure to using contexts initially, build sober social life.

Identity-based change works better than outcome goals. Not "I'm trying to quit drinking" (implies struggle), but "I'm a non-drinker" (implies fact). Identity drives behavior. See yourself as sober, speak as sober, act as sober, become. Your narration matters. Change your story about yourself.

Neuroplasticity tools accelerate change. Neurofeedback trains patterns, mindfulness strengthens pathways, environmental exploration promotes plasticity, resistance training boosts brain health. Your brain can change. New patterns don't erase old, they dominate them.

Hormetic stressors build resilience once foundations are stable. Cold exposure (stress tolerance, norepinephrine), intermittent fasting (metabolic flexibility), sauna (cardiovascular resilience), resistance training (physical and mental toughness). These provide natural "highs" and replace substance use with healthy challenge. **Caution:** Start after sleep and basic stress are managed. Don't add stress when already overwhelmed.

14.11 The Integration: Multimodal Approach

The most powerful approach combines interventions in phases:

Foundation (Week 1): Sleep optimization (Chapter 13), stress management (HRV, breathwork), nutrition (omega-3s, magnesium, protein), medical assessment if severe dependence.

Behavioral (Weeks 1-8): MBRP program (8 weeks), environmental design (remove triggers, add supports), identity shift ("I'm a non-user" not "I'm trying to quit"), social support (12-step, SMART Recovery, therapy), tracking.

Neurofeedback (Months 1-3): Phenotype-specific protocols, Alcohol/Grumpy → Peniston Alpha-Theta, Cannabis/CEO → SMR + anterior cingulate flexibility, Stimulants/Stabilizer → theta/beta ratio, Benzos/Princess → alpha training + HRV + medical taper. Plus craving reduction and addressing underlying dysregulation.

Pharmacological (when appropriate): Naltrexone, bupropion, acamprosate, always with medical supervision, especially for alcohol/benzo taper.

Long-term (Months 6-18): Brain restoration (dopamine system recovery takes 6-18 months), life restructuring (Chapter 19), maintenance practices and community.

Each phase builds on the previous. The foundation is non-negotiable; everything else layers on top.

14.12 Composite Clinical Illustrations

These clinical stories illustrate the integration of neurofeedback protocols (particularly Peniston alpha-theta for alcohol, SMR for cannabis, and theta/beta training for stimulants) with Mindfulness-Based Relapse Prevention (MBRP). The combination addresses both underlying brain dysregulation and behavioral coping skills.

14.12.1 Case 1: The Architect Who Stopped Borrowing Calm (Michael)

Composite, like every case in this book. The pattern is one I have seen many times; the person is not one person.

Background: 39, drank 4-6 drinks nightly for 15 years. "I couldn't turn off the catastrophizing without it."

QEEG before:

- Right frontal hyperactivation (Grumpy Old Man screaming)
- High beta bilaterally (Timekeeper racing)
- Low Voltage Fast (LVF) pattern (genetic predisposition)

Intervention:

- **Peniston Alpha-Theta protocol** (50 sessions over 6 months)
- Right frontal alpha training
- SMR for sleep
- HRV biofeedback (autonomic regulation)
- Taper protocol (reduced alcohol slowly while training circuits)
- Sleep repair (broken by years of alcohol)
- **MBRP** (8-week program: urge surfing, SOBER breathing space)
- Cognitive behavioral work (challenging catastrophic thoughts)

QEEG after:

- Balanced frontal activation (Grumpy Old Man calmed)
- Normalized beta (Timekeeper at healthy speed)

- Sustainable calm without substances

Real life: Sustained sobriety.

Quote: *"I finally have the calm I was trying to steal. And I can still access it tomorrow. The catastrophizing still happens sometimes, but it's like turning down the volume. I can observe it without drowning in it. I'm not numb like I was with alcohol. I'm actually present. Urge surfing was hard at first, sitting with anxiety felt impossible. But after Alpha-Theta training, my brain learned to access that deep calm state. Now when cravings come, I can ride them. They pass. I don't need to drink."*

14.12.2 Case 2: The Creative Who Found Focus Without Weed (Jessica)

Composite. Drawn from patterns I have seen in many people; no single person's history.

Background: 31, used cannabis daily for 8 years to "quiet my brain." "My thoughts were like a thousand browser tabs open."

QEEG before:

- Anterior cingulate hyperactivation (CEO task-switching constantly)
- Low frontal beta (Stabilizer offline)
- Pattern: CEO couldn't stop directing traffic, Stabilizer couldn't initiate

Intervention:

- **SMR training** (40 sessions: calm focus)
- **Anterior cingulate flexibility** (CEO training)
- **Left frontal activation** (Stabilizer protocols)
- **MBRP** (8-week program: mindful awareness of triggers)
- Meditation practice (learning to access presence sober: Chapter 17)
- Task initiation protocols (working with Stabilizer directly, Chapter 16)

QEEG after:

- Balanced cingulate activity (CEO can switch when needed, stay when needed)
- Improved frontal activation (Stabilizer online)

Real life: Reduced cannabis to occasional (weekends, social). Can abstain when they choose.

Quote: *"I can focus AND initiate now. I don't need to be high to feel okay. The CEO still gets loud sometimes, but I have tools now. SOBER breathing space gives me a pause. I can notice the urge to smoke without automatically doing it. And my creativity is actually sharper, turns out I don't need cannabis to be creative. I just needed to calm the chaos underneath. Urge surfing taught me that cravings pass. They're waves. I can ride them."*

14.12.3 Case 3: The Executive Who Reclaimed Her Dopamine (Rachel)

Composite. A clinical pattern, not one person's story.

Background: 42, used prescription Adderall for 10 years, then escalated to cocaine when Adderall stopped working. "Without stimulants, I couldn't start anything."

QEEG before:

- Excess theta in left motor/premotor (Stabilizer offline: Frontal Slow)
- Low beta throughout frontal cortex
- Dopamine system exhaustion (from years of artificial stimulation)

Intervention:

- **Medical detox** (supervised withdrawal: stimulant withdrawal not life-threatening but very difficult)
- **Theta/beta ratio optimization** (60 sessions over 18 months)
- **Left frontal beta training** (natural activation: waking Stabilizer)
- Dopamine restoration protocols (nutrition, exercise, sleep)
- Behavioral activation (gradually rebuilding task initiation, Chapter 16)
- **MBRP** (8-week program: managing cravings during recovery)
- Support group (addressing addiction patterns, identity shift)

QEEG after:

- Improved beta (Stabilizer waking naturally)
- Theta reduction (more alert baseline)
- Sustainable activation (not borrowed from future)

Real life: Off cocaine. No longer needs Adderall.

Quote: *"It took 18 months to feel normal. My brain had to relearn how to make its own dopamine. Neurofeedback gave my Stabilizer a jumpstart, but I had to be patient. The first 6 months were brutal. I couldn't focus, couldn't initiate, felt like a zombie. But MBRP taught me to sit with that discomfort. Urge surfing got me through cravings. SOBER breathing space gave me a tool when I wanted to use. Now I can initiate tasks without drugs. Not perfectly (I still have ADHD) but I'm not stealing from tomorrow anymore. And I'm proud of who I am now: someone who recovered."*

14.13 If You're Currently Using: Harm Reduction Strategies

Track patterns: which phenotypes drive use, when, why, how much. Notice what you're regulating (anxiety, motivation, social ease, sleep). Set boundaries (time, amount, context). Protect sleep (alcohol before 6pm, no stimulants after 2pm). Mitigate damage (hydration, nutrition, NAC). Know your triggers.

14.14 If You Want to Reduce or Quit

Medical supervision for alcohol/benzos: Withdrawal can be dangerous (seizures, death). Taper under medical supervision, inpatient if severe, outpatient if mild-moderate.

Neurofeedback during taper: Build alternative regulation while still using, reduces rebound anxiety, addresses underlying dysregulation.

Address underlying dysregulation first: Anxiety → right frontal alpha/HRV. ADHD → theta/beta training/sleep. Trauma → Alpha-Theta protocol. Build alternative tools (MBRP, neurofeedback, sleep optimization) BEFORE removing crutch.

Support systems: Therapy, support groups (12-step, SMART Recovery, Refuge Recovery), sober communities.

Expect 6-18 months for brain restoration: Dopamine system, sleep architecture, emotional regulation, cognitive function all take time. Be patient.

14.15 Integration: If You've Used Psychedelics

Psychedelics are different (not physically addictive, but can be psychologically compelling). Legal status varies by jurisdiction and is changing rapidly; medical decisions about any substance should be made with a licensed professional.

If you've used psychedelics therapeutically:

- **Integration therapy** (making meaning of insights)
- Journaling (processing experiences)
- Therapy (trained in psychedelic integration)
- Community (integration circles, support)

If you've learned something from substance use:

- **Keep the insights** (what did you learn about yourself?)
- **Lose the dependency** (access insights without substance)
- Meditation can access similar states (Alpha-Theta neurofeedback, deep meditation, see Chapter 17)

Your brain's capacity to access those states exists without substances:

- Neurofeedback + meditation can get you there
- Voluntarily, sustainably, without borrowing from tomorrow
- Integration, not just cessation

14.16 The Promise

You don't need to borrow peace. You can build it.

You've been trying to regulate circuits that feel unbearable. That's intelligent, not shameful.

But substances are like trying to adjust a watch with a hammer. They work, but they damage.

Neurofeedback is the precision tool:

- Large effect sizes in recent meta-analyses (clinically significant)
- 70-80% abstinence outcomes in early Peniston protocol trials (small samples; later replication varies)
- Reduces craving, improves self-regulation
- No drug-like tolerance, withdrawal, or dependence

MBRP is the mindfulness tool:

- Evidence-based (reduces relapse, maintained at 12 months)
- Urge surfing (ride craving waves)
- SOBER breathing space (pause between urge and action)
- Self-compassion (not shame)

Harm reduction is the compassionate approach:

- Meet you where you are
- Any reduction in harm is progress
- Moderation or abstinence (you choose)
- Non-judgmental support

You can:

- Calm Crumpy Old Man without alcohol (Peniston Alpha-Theta, right frontal alpha)
- Quiet CEO without cannabis (SMR, anterior cingulate flexibility)
- Activate Stabilizer without stimulants (theta/beta ratio, left frontal beta)
- Access creativity without substances (Alpha-Theta, meditation, flow states)
- Regulate anguish without numbing gifts (targeted training, not blunt instruments)

The peace you've been trying to steal?

It's already inside your circuits. We just need to teach them a new rhythm.

You can train your brain. The calm, focus, and activation you've been borrowing from substances. I can help you build them into your baseline.

MYTH vs REALITY:

MYTH: "I have an addictive personality."

REALITY: You have phenotypes that are chronically dysregulated. You discovered that certain substances can temporarily regulate them. That's not an addictive personality. That's a brain trying to survive with the tools it has. The problem isn't your personality. It's that borrowing regulation works great... until it doesn't.

If you only do one thing from this chapter: Track your substance use for two weeks without judgment, just observe the pattern, the phenotypes you're trying to regulate, and the rebound the next day.

14.17 Try the Poet-Brain Mastery Loop: Recognizing Your Substance Pattern

NOTICE: Which phenotype is driving this substance use? (Alcohol for anxious Grumpy? Cannabis for stuck CEO? Stimulants for paralyzed Stabilizer?)

NORMALIZE: "Of course I reach for this, it's the only tool I have that regulates this specific circuit. This is intelligent self-medication, not weakness."

REGULATE: One tool from this chapter to try: Track the pattern for two weeks (just observe). If you already take nights off without trouble, use one of them differently: sit with the phenotype underneath instead of reaching past it. Notice what the craving is asking for. If skipping a night is not something your body is used to, or if you drink daily, take benzodiazepines, or use opioids, talk to your doctor before changing anything. Withdrawal from those is a medical matter, not a mindfulness exercise. Or: Read Chapter 18 (Neurofeedback) to see how to train the circuit you've been borrowing from.

REASSIGN: "I'm going to let my sober brain show me what's actually happening. Which phenotype is loudest when I'm not regulating with substances?"

REFLECT: After 24-48 hours: What did I notice? Did the phenotype get louder without the substance? Did I find another way to regulate? What would it take to build this capacity internally?

14.18 Key Takeaways

Substance use patterns map directly to EEG phenotypes, you reach for what regulates the circuit that's most dysregulated. This isn't weakness; it's intelligent self-regulation with the wrong tools.

- **EEG patterns correlate with substance response:** LVF → alcohol/benzos (GABA genetics). Frontal Slow → stimulants (ADHD). Slowed Alpha → stimulants often DON'T work (COMT variant).
- **Why they work short-term but fail long-term:** Substances target the same circuits neurofeedback trains, pharmacologically valid. But tolerance, rebound dysregulation, and sleep disruption mean you're always borrowing from tomorrow.
- **The tragedy:** Numbing torture also numbs gifts: alcohol quiets Grumpy Old Man but kills Happy Little Kid, cannabis releases CEO but shuts down Stabilizer.
- **Alternatives exist:** MBRP (Chapter 17) combines meditation with addiction-specific skills. Neurofeedback (Peniston protocol) reported high abstinence rates in early trials; builds durable capacity without drug-like tolerance or rebound.

14.19 Reader Reflections

1. **Which phenotype are you trying to regulate?** Can you map your substance use to specific circuits?
2. **What does borrowed regulation feel like versus the rebound?** Are you borrowing from tomorrow?
3. **If you stopped using, what would you lose?** Just the substance, or also your access to calm/focus/activation?

Ch 15: Stress Response Regulation

The Volume Knob You've Been Looking For

The autonomic nervous system is your volume knob. Most poet-brains have spent years trying to adjust it with substances. Too much (over-activated, anxious, racing, impulsive). Not enough (under-activated, flat, depressed, can't initiate). This chapter is about finding the middle ground.

15.1 "Managing Too Much or Not Enough"

You've already discovered the concept:

- Alcohol or benzos to activate parasympathetic (brake pedal, calm down)
- Stimulants to activate sympathetic (gas pedal: speed up)
- Cannabis to modulate both (sometimes calming, sometimes activating)

You were right. Your nervous system needed regulation.

The problem: Substances are sledgehammers. They work, but they're imprecise, create tolerance, and borrow from tomorrow.

This chapter gives you precision controls:

- HRV biofeedback (teaching your nervous system it's safe)
- Vagal toning (strengthening the brake)
- Breathwork (immediate state changes)
- Cold exposure (vagal stimulation)
- Neurofeedback (training specific circuits)

All of these are cadence tools for your stress system: how quickly you spike, how long you stay there, and how fast you can come back down.

No substances required. No tolerance. No withdrawal. Just training.

A note on safety: These techniques regulate your autonomic nervous system. Most are low-risk, but if you have cardiovascular conditions, get medical clearance before cold exposure or intense breathwork. If you have a trauma history (PTSD, complex trauma), body-based practices can surface intense material. Start gently. If you're in active crisis, stabilize first (988 Suicide & Crisis Lifeline, or 911). These tools supplement professional care. They don't replace it.

15.2 The Autonomic Nervous System: Gas Pedal and Brake

15.2.1 Two Branches

Sympathetic Nervous System (Gas Pedal):

- Fight-or-flight response
- Activation, arousal, mobilization
- Increases: heart rate, breathing, blood pressure, muscle tension
- Decreases: digestion, immune function, rest
- Hormones: adrenaline, norepinephrine, cortisol

Parasympathetic Nervous System (Brake Pedal):

- Rest-and-digest response
- Relaxation, recovery, restoration
- Decreases: heart rate, breathing, blood pressure, muscle tension
- Increases: digestion, immune function, healing
- Primary pathway: vagus nerve

If you've ever felt stuck in fight-or-flight for days, or collapsed into shutdown where nothing feels real, that's this system dysregulated.

Optimal state: Flexible switching between activation and relaxation, the middle ground.

Dysregulated states:

- **Stuck in sympathetic (too much):** Chronic anxiety, threat sensitivity, racing thoughts, insomnia, impulsivity (Timekeeper, Grumpy Old Man, Lifeguard)
- **Stuck in parasympathetic (not enough):** Shutdown, depression, low energy, dissociation, can't initiate (Fog)
- **Rigid switching:** Can't shift states appropriately (anxious when need to relax, lethargic when need to activate)

15.3 Polyvagal Theory: Three States of Your Nervous System

Developed by Stephen Porges, explains why you feel what you feel in different contexts.

15.3.1 State 1: Social Engagement System (Ventral Vagal)

What it is:

- Safe, connected, present
- Optimal state for learning, connection, creativity
- Facial expressions, voice prosody, eye contact work naturally

Brain/body:

- Ventral vagus nerve active
- Heart rate variable (flexible)
- Breathing easy
- Muscles relaxed

When you're here:

- Feel safe, connected
- Can learn, create, connect
- Emotions regulated
- Thinking clear

For poet-brains:

- This is the state you're trying to access
- But easily shift out (perceived threat → fight-or-flight)
- Princess & Pea especially sensitive (RSD triggers shift)

15.3.2 State 2: Fight-or-Flight (Sympathetic)

What it is:

- Threat detected, mobilization
- Survival mode (confront or escape)

Brain/body:

- Sympathetic nervous system dominant
- Heart rate increases (rapid, less variable)
- Breathing rapid, shallow (chest breathing)
- Muscles tense (preparation for action)
- Digestion suppressed
- Tunnel vision (focus on threat)
- Pupils dilated

When you're here:

- Anxiety, panic, anger
- Hypervigilance (scanning for threats)
- Racing thoughts (threat simulation)
- Can't relax, can't sleep
- Impulsive (react without thinking)

For poet-brains:

- **Grumpy Old Man:** Chronic overwhelm (futility predictions = effort-dread simulation)

- **Timekeeper:** Sympathetic dominance (racing thoughts, can't slow down)
- **Lifeguard:** Hypervigilance (constant environmental scanning)
- **Princess & Pea:** Easily triggered (RSD, perceived rejection = threat)

The problem: Modern life creates chronic activation (not acute threat → resolution). Stuck in fight-or-flight.

15.3.3 State 3: Shutdown (Dorsal Vagal)

What it is:

- Immobilization, freeze, dissociation
- When fight-or-flight isn't an option (overwhelm, inescapable threat)
- Evolutionary: "play dead" (last resort survival)

Brain/body:

- Dorsal vagus nerve active (older vagal pathway)
- Heart rate decreases
- Numbness, collapse
- Dissociation (disconnect from body, emotions)
- Fatigue, lethargy

When you're here:

- Depression (not just sad: shut down)
- Dissociation ("patient etherized on a table": T.S. Eliot)
- Numbness (can't feel emotions)
- Exhaustion (can't mobilize)
- Freeze response (can't act)

For poet-brains:

- **Fog:** Shutdown state (dorsal vagal dominance)
- **Lifeguard:** Dissociation (when threat scanning becomes too much)
- **After prolonged fight-or-flight:** System shuts down (can't sustain activation)

From Introduction Section 7: "Patient etherized on a table" = dorsal vagal shutdown (Lifeguard offline)

15.3.4 The Ladder: Moving Between States

Polyvagal hierarchy:

1. **Social engagement** (ventral vagal, optimal)
2. **Fight-or-flight** (sympathetic, mobilization)
3. **Shutdown** (dorsal vagal, immobilization)

You can't jump from shutdown to social engagement. Must go through fight-or-flight (activation) first.

Clinical insight:

- If you're in shutdown (Fog, depression), you need activation first (sympathetic), then regulation (ventral vagal)
- If you're in fight-or-flight (anxiety, hypervigilance), you need calming (ventral vagal)
- Different interventions for different states

This explains why:

- Meditation doesn't work when you're shut down (need activation first)
- "Just relax" doesn't work when you're anxious (need tools to shift states)
- Exercise helps depression (activates sympathetic, then shifts to ventral vagal)

15.4 Heart Rate Variability: Your Nervous System's Flexibility

15.4.1 What HRV Measures

HRV = variation in time between heartbeats

Example:

- Beat 1 → Beat 2: 0.85 seconds
- Beat 2 → Beat 3: 0.92 seconds
- Beat 3 → Beat 4: 0.88 seconds
- Variation = HRV (higher = better)

What it means:

- **High HRV:** Flexible ANS (good stress resilience, can shift between activation and relaxation)
- **Low HRV:** Rigid ANS (poor stress resilience, stuck in one state, chronic stress)

HRV as biomarker (Thayer & Lane, 2000):

- Predicts: stress resilience, emotional regulation, cardiovascular health, longevity
- Tracks: recovery, overtraining, illness, stress levels
- Real-time: shows current ANS state

15.4.2 HRV Biofeedback (Primary Tool for Anxiety)

What it is:

- Real-time feedback on your ANS state
- Visual or auditory cues showing HRV
- Training to increase HRV (improve flexibility)

The practice:

1. **Measure HRV** (chest strap or finger sensor)
2. **Breathe at resonance frequency** (~6 breaths/min typically, varies by individual)
3. **Watch HRV increase** (real-time feedback)
4. **Practice 5-10 minutes daily**

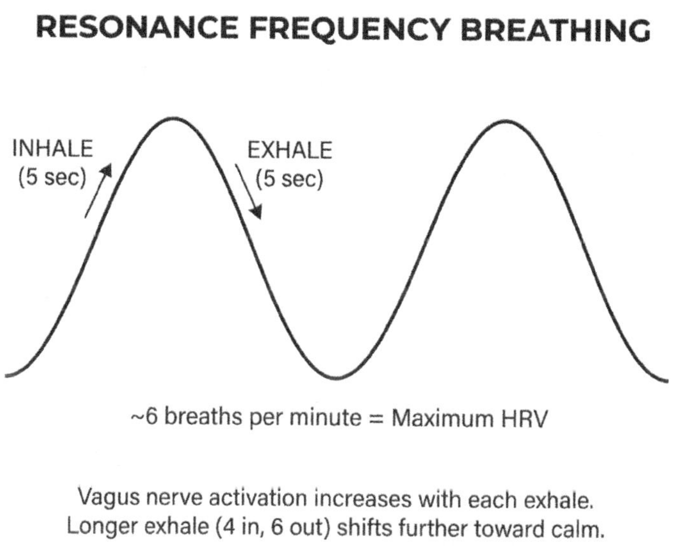

Figure 15.1: HRV Resonance Frequency Breathing

Why this works (Lehrer & Gevirtz, 2014):

- Breathing at resonance frequency maximizes HRV
- Trains vagal tone (strengthens parasympathetic)
- Teaches nervous system it's safe (not constant threat)
- Builds flexibility (can shift states when needed)

Outcomes:

- Reduces anxiety, improves stress resilience

- Enhances emotional regulation
- Improves sleep quality
- Increases parasympathetic tone
- Better cardiovascular health

Apps: Elite HRV, HeartMath, Welltory, Oura Ring, Whoop

Timeline: Daily practice, benefits in 2-4 weeks, lasting changes in 2-3 months

For phenotypes:

- **Grumpy Old Man:** Reduces dread, futility predictions
- **Timekeeper:** Calms racing thoughts, reduces sympathetic dominance
- **Lifeguard:** Teaches body it's safe (reduces threat sensitivity)
- **Princess & Pea:** Emotional regulation, stress resilience

---

15.5 Vagal Toning: Strengthening Your Brake Pedal

15.5.1 The Vagus Nerve

What it is:

- 10th cranial nerve
- "Wandering nerve" (vagus = wanderer)
- Connects brain to heart, lungs, digestive system
- Primary parasympathetic pathway

Vagal tone:

- Strength of vagus nerve activity
- **High vagal tone:** Better stress resilience, emotional regulation, digestion, immune function
- **Low vagal tone:** Anxiety, poor stress recovery, digestive issues, inflammation

You can strengthen vagal tone (like strengthening a muscle).

15.5.2 Vagal Toning Techniques

1. Breathwork (Most Accessible)

When your Grumpy Old Man is running disaster scenarios or your Lifeguard won't stop scanning, breathwork is the fastest tool you have, no device, no app, no setup. The trick is matching the technique to what's happening in your nervous system right now.

Diaphragmatic breathing:

- Deep belly breaths (not chest)
- Inhale through nose (expand belly)
- Exhale through mouth (belly contracts)
- Stimulates vagus nerve

Box breathing (4-4-4-4):

- Inhale 4 seconds, hold 4, exhale 4, hold 4
- Derived from yogic *samavritti pranayama*; popularized in military training by Navy SEALs (Divine, 2007)
- Optimizes CO2 tolerance
- Calms nervous system

4-7-8 breath:

- Inhale 4 seconds, hold 7, exhale 8
- Longer exhale = parasympathetic activation
- Good for sleep, anxiety, panic

Physiological sigh (Balban et al., 2023):

- Double inhale through nose (short, then short)
- Long exhale through mouth
- Fastest way to reduce stress (offloads CO2)
- Can do anytime, anywhere

Slow breathing (~6 breaths/min):

- Resonance frequency (maximizes HRV)
- Inhale 5 seconds, exhale 5 seconds
- Vagal stimulation

---

2. Cold Exposure (Vagal Stimulation)

Diver's reflex:

- Cold water on face (immediate vagal activation)
- Slows heart rate, promotes relaxation
- Mammalian diving reflex (evolutionary)
- Can do at sink (cold water, 30 seconds)

Cold showers:

- Gradual adaptation (start warm, end cold)
- 30 seconds to 3 minutes cold
- Stimulates vagus nerve
- Increases norepinephrine 2-3x (alertness, mood) (Šrámek et al., 2000)
- Builds stress resilience

Ice baths (advanced):

- 2-10 minutes at 50-59°F (10-15°C)
- Hormetic stress (controlled challenge)
- Significant vagal stimulation
- Requires adaptation (don't start here)

Why for anxiety:

- Vagal stimulation (parasympathetic activation)
- Stress inoculation (builds resilience)
- Norepinephrine boost (mood improvement, alertness)
- Sense of mastery (tolerating discomfort)

Caution: Start gentle (cold water on face), progress gradually (cold showers), advanced only when ready (ice baths).

---

3. Humming, Singing, Chanting

Why this works:

- Vibration stimulates vagus nerve
- Vocal cords connected to vagal pathway
- Immediate calming effect

Practices:

- "Om" chanting (meditation)
- Humming (while breathing out)
- Singing (any song, especially slow)
- Gargling (vigorous: vagal stimulation)

For Interpreter (Linguist): Vocal practices activate language network (but non-verbal, sound, not words)

---

4. Social Connection (Safe)

Why this works:

- Safe social engagement activates ventral vagal (social engagement system)
- Eye contact, facial expressions, prosody (tone)
- Co-regulation (nervous systems sync)

Practices:

- Time with safe people (not stressful relationships)
- Eye contact (when comfortable)
- Warm conversation (not conflict)
- Physical touch (if comfortable: hugs, hand-holding)
- Pets (unconditional, calming)

For Princess & Pea: Social connection powerful (but must be safe, RSD triggers shift to fight-or-flight)

For Lifeguard: Safe social reduces threat scanning (trusted people = safety cue)

---

5. Massage and Physical Touch

Why this works:

- Vagus nerve pathway through neck, shoulders
- Massage stimulates vagal tone
- Reduces muscle tension (physical manifestation of sympathetic)

Practices:

- Professional massage (especially neck, shoulders, back)
- Self-massage (neck, temples, jaw)
- Partner massage (safe touch)
- Foam rolling (myofascial release)

---

6. Exercise (Metabolizes Stress Hormones)

Why exercise reduces anxiety:

- Metabolizes cortisol (burns off stress hormones)
- Endorphins (natural mood boost)
- Norepinephrine (alertness, confidence)
- BDNF (brain-derived neurotrophic factor: neuroplasticity)
- Improves sleep (see Chapter 13)
- Sense of mastery

Types:

- **Aerobic:** Running, cycling, swimming (endorphins, cortisol metabolism)
- **Resistance training:** Strength, confidence, neuroplasticity
- **Yoga:** Movement + breathwork + mindfulness (vagal stimulation)
- **Walking:** Gentle, accessible, outdoors = light exposure

Timing:

- Morning ideal (cortisol + exercise = natural activation)
- Avoid intense exercise 3 hours before bed (see Chapter 13)
- During day (metabolizes stress before it accumulates)

For phenotypes:

- **Stabilizer:** Exercise provides activation (momentum for day)
- **Grumpy Old Man:** Metabolizes cortisol (reduces dread)
- **Timekeeper:** Releases energy (calms racing)
- **Fog:** Gentle exercise activates (not intense)

15.6 When Anxiety Becomes Chronic: Phenotype Connection

Quick recap (detailed in Part I):

- **Grumpy Old Man** (Ch 2): Futility predictions, effort-dread simulation, avoidance
- **Lifeguard** (Ch 6): Hypervigilance, environmental scanning, rumination
- **Princess & Pea** (Ch 8): RSD, sensory overwhelm, social threat sensitivity
- **Timekeeper** (Ch 11): Racing thoughts, can't slow down, anxiety as speed

The common thread: All involve chronic fight-or-flight activation (sympathetic dominance, can't shift to rest-and-digest).

Health consequences: Insomnia, digestive issues, immune suppression, cardiovascular stress, cognitive impairment.

This chapter focuses on the tools to shift your nervous system out of chronic threat mode, regardless of which phenotype is driving it.

15.7 HRV Biofeedback: Teaching Your Nervous System It's Safe

15.7.1 How HRV Biofeedback Works

The principle:

- Your nervous system learns from feedback
- High HRV = safe state (flexible, resilient)
- Training to increase HRV = training safety response

The protocol:

1. **Measure HRV** (chest strap, finger sensor, or wearable)
2. **Breathe at resonance frequency** (~6 breaths/min typically, varies by individual)
   - Inhale 5 seconds, exhale 5 seconds
   - Or inhale 4, exhale 6 (longer exhale = more parasympathetic)
3. **Watch HRV increase** (visual feedback, graph, number, color)
4. **Practice 5-10 minutes daily** (consistency matters)
5. **Generalize** (use breathing in daily life when stressed)

Finding your resonance frequency:

- Most people: 5.5-6.5 breaths/min
- Test different rates (5, 5.5, 6, 6.5 breaths/min)
- Highest HRV = your resonance frequency

- Apps can help find it (Elite HRV, HeartMath)

Why this works:

- Breathing at resonance frequency maximizes vagal stimulation
- Real-time feedback reinforces (operant conditioning)
- Trains parasympathetic activation (strengthens brake)
- Builds new neural pathways (stress → breathe → calm, not stress → panic)

Outcomes (research evidence):

- Reduces anxiety, improves stress resilience
- Enhances emotional regulation
- Improves sleep quality
- Lowers blood pressure
- Reduces depression symptoms
- Increases vagal tone (measurable)

Timeline:

- Immediate: Calming during practice
- 2-4 weeks: Notice reduced anxiety, better stress response
- 2-3 months: Lasting changes in baseline HRV, vagal tone

15.7.2 HRV Apps and Devices

Apps:

- **Elite HRV:** Free, tracks trends
- **HeartMath:** Inner Balance app, biofeedback training
- **Welltory:** HRV tracking, lifestyle correlations
- **Breathwrk:** Guided breathing with HRV tracking

Devices:

- **Chest straps:** Most accurate (Polar H10, Wahoo TICKR)
- **Finger sensors:** HeartMath Inner Balance
- **Wearables:** Oura Ring, Whoop (track HRV during sleep)
- **Smartphone:** Camera can measure (less accurate)

Recommendation: Start with app + chest strap (most accurate, affordable)

15.8 Breathwork Techniques (Immediate State Changes)

No equipment needed. Can do anywhere. Immediate effects.

15.8.1 1. Diaphragmatic Breathing (Foundation)

How:

- Place hand on belly
- Inhale through nose (belly expands, not chest)
- Exhale through mouth (belly contracts)
- Slow, deep breaths

Why:

- Stimulates vagus nerve (diaphragm movement)
- Shifts from chest (sympathetic) to belly (parasympathetic)
- Increases oxygen efficiency
- Immediate calming

When to use: Anytime, especially when you notice chest breathing (sign of stress)

15.8.2 2. Box Breathing (4-4-4-4)

How:

- Inhale 4 seconds
- Hold 4 seconds
- Exhale 4 seconds
- Hold 4 seconds
- Repeat 5-10 cycles

Why:

- Regulates nervous system (balanced activation/relaxation)
- Optimizes CO2 tolerance
- Calms mind (gives something to focus on)
- Used by Navy SEALs for tactical stress management (Divine, 2007)

When to use: Morning (before technology), before stressful situations, during anxiety

---

15.8.3 3. 4-7-8 Breath (Parasympathetic Activation)

How:

- Inhale 4 seconds (through nose)
- Hold 7 seconds
- Exhale 8 seconds (through mouth)
- Repeat 4-8 cycles

Why:

- Longer exhale = parasympathetic activation
- Slows heart rate
- Reduces anxiety
- Promotes sleep

When to use: Before bed, during anxiety, panic attacks

15.8.4 4. Physiological Sigh (Fastest Stress Reduction)

How:

- Double inhale through nose (short inhale, then another short inhale)
- Long exhale through mouth
- One cycle = immediate effect

Why:

- Offloads CO2 (accumulated during stress)
- Fastest way to reduce stress (Balban et al., 2023)
- Resets breathing pattern
- Immediate calming

When to use: Acute stress, panic, overwhelm (immediate relief)

15.9 Cold Exposure: Vagal Stimulation and Stress Resilience

15.9.1 The Diver's Reflex (Immediate Vagal Activation)

What it is:

- Mammalian diving reflex (evolutionary: conserve oxygen underwater)
- Cold water on face → immediate vagal activation
- Slows heart rate, promotes relaxation

How:

- Fill sink or bowl with cold water (add ice if you want)
- Submerge face for 15-30 seconds
- Or cold washcloth on face
- Immediate calming effect

When to use: Panic attacks, acute anxiety, emotional overwhelm (immediate intervention)

15.9.2 Cold Showers (Building Resilience)

The protocol:

- Start warm (normal shower)
- End with cold (30 seconds to 3 minutes)
- Gradually increase cold duration over weeks
- Breathe through discomfort (don't hold breath)

Why this works:

- Vagal stimulation (parasympathetic activation)
- Norepinephrine boost (mood, alertness, focus)
- Stress inoculation (builds resilience to discomfort)
- Sense of mastery (tolerating challenge)
- Metabolic benefits (brown fat activation, metabolism)

Outcomes:

- Reduces anxiety over time (not just during shower)
- Improves mood (norepinephrine)
- Builds stress resilience (hormetic stress)
- Enhances willpower (tolerating discomfort)

Timeline: Daily or several times/week, benefits in 2-4 weeks

Research: Buijze et al. (2016) found cold showers reduced sick days, improved well-being

---

15.9.3 Ice Baths (Advanced: Hormetic Stress)

The protocol:

- 2-10 minutes at 50-59°F (10-15°C)
- Requires adaptation (don't start here)
- Breathe through discomfort
- Exit before shivering becomes violent

Why (advanced benefits):

- Significant vagal stimulation
- Stress resilience building (hormetic stress)
- Norepinephrine boost (sustained)
- Metabolic benefits
- Mental toughness

Caution: Not for everyone. Start with cold showers. Build gradually. Medical clearance if cardiovascular issues.

15.10 Neurofeedback for Anxiety and Activation

15.10.1 For Calming (Parasympathetic Activation)

Right Frontal Alpha Training (Grumpy Old Man):

- Increase calming rhythms in right frontal cortex
- Reduces anxiety, rumination, catastrophizing
- Natural relaxation (not borrowed from substances)
- 20-40 sessions

SMR Training (Timekeeper, Beta Spindles):

- Builds "calm but ready" state at sensorimotor cortex: not racing, not drowsy
- Reduces anxiety with hyperarousal, calms beta spindles (the "can't turn brain off" pattern)
- See Chapter 18 for protocol details, electrode placements, session structure

Alpha-Theta Training (Deep Relaxation):

- Increase alpha and theta (posterior regions)
- Deep relaxation, meditation-like states
- Trauma processing (if applicable)
- 20-30 sessions (after SMR foundation)

If anxiety has been your baseline for so long you've forgotten what calm feels like, this training rebuilds the default.

Posterior Cingulate Calming (Lifeguard):

- Reduce hyperactivation in posterior midline regions
- Reduces threat sensitivity
- Environmental scanning normalizes
- 20-30 sessions

Amygdala Regulation:

- Real-time fMRI neurofeedback (advanced, expensive)
- Or EEG protocols targeting amygdala-connected regions
- Reduces fear response, emotional reactivity
- 20-30 sessions

15.10.2 For Activation (Sympathetic When Needed)

Left Frontal Beta Training (Stabilizer):

- Increase fast-wave activity in left motor/premotor regions

- Activates Stabilizer (task initiation)
- Wakes Frontal Slow pattern
- 30-40 sessions

Theta Suppression (Fog):

- Reduce excess slow-wave activity in frontal regions
- Increases alertness
- Improves sustained attention
- 30-40 sessions

Alpha Peak Frequency Training (Slowed Alpha):

- Speed up dominant brain rhythm to more typical tempo
- Increases processing speed
- Different from theta suppression
- 20-40 sessions

15.11 Matching Tools to Phenotypes: Quick Reference

Different phenotypes need different approaches:

- **Stabilizer** (Ch 3): Needs ACTIVATION (left frontal beta, morning routine, exercise). Not: relaxation (already too relaxed)
- **Timekeeper** (Ch 11): Needs CALMING (right frontal alpha, HRV, breathwork, cold exposure). Not: stimulants
- **CEO** (Ch 5): Needs FLEXIBILITY (anterior cingulate training, meditation, task-switching). Not: rigid routines
- **Lifeguard** (Ch 6): Needs CALMING + GROUNDING (posterior cingulate regulation, HRV, present-moment awareness)
- **Princess & Pea** (Ch 8): Needs SENSORY GATING (right TPJ regulation, environment optimization, loving-kindness)
- **Grumpy Old Man** (Ch 2): Needs CALMING (right frontal alpha, HRV, challenging futility predictions)
- **Fog** (Ch 12): Depends (shutdown = activation first; exhaustion = honor rest)

For specific protocols per phenotype, see Part I "Quick Hits" sections.

15.12 Lifestyle Interventions for Anxiety

15.12.1 Nutrition (Anti-Inflammatory, Gut-Brain Axis)

Higher systemic inflammatory markers correlate with worse executive function and fatigue (Marsland et al., 2015).

Anti-inflammatory foods:

- Omega-3 fatty acids (fish, flaxseed, walnuts)
- Antioxidants (berries, dark chocolate, green tea)
- Fermented foods (probiotics: gut-brain axis)
- Leafy greens (magnesium, folate)

Avoid:

- Excess caffeine (amplifies anxiety: see Chapter 13 for timing)
- Sugar (blood sugar spikes/crashes affect mood)
- Alcohol (rebound anxiety next day: see Chapter 13)
- Processed foods (inflammatory)

Supplements:

- Omega-3s (1-2g daily: anti-inflammatory)
- Magnesium (200-350mg: GABA support, calming; 350mg/day is the NIH supplemental upper limit; kidney function affects clearance, check with your provider if relevant)
- L-Theanine (200-400mg: calming, balances caffeine)
- GABA (500-1000mg: calming reported, though oral GABA crosses the blood-brain barrier poorly; mechanism debated)
- Probiotics (gut health, 90% serotonin in gut)

Gut-brain axis:

- 90% of serotonin produced in gut (Yano et al., 2015)
- Gut microbiome affects mood, anxiety
- Probiotics, fermented foods support gut health
- Reduces inflammation (systemic)

15.12.2 Digital Detox (Reducing Stimulation)

Why screens increase anxiety:

- Constant notifications (threat vigilance: Lifeguard activated)
- Social comparison (RSD triggers: Princess & Pea)
- Blue light (circadian disruption: see Chapter 13)
- Information overload (CEO overwhelmed)
- Decision fatigue (depletes resources)

Strategies:

- **No phone first hour morning** (see Chapter 13: MVP)
- **No screens 1-2 hours before bed** (circadian support)
- **Turn off non-essential notifications** (reduce threat vigilance)
- **Scheduled phone time** (not constant checking)
- **Screen-free spaces** (bedroom, dining table)

- **Social media boundaries** (time limits, curated feeds)

For phenotypes:

- **Lifeguard:** Notifications = constant threat cues (turn off)
- **CEO:** Information overload = overwhelm (limit input)
- **Princess & Pea:** Social media = RSD triggers (curate carefully)
- **Happy Little Kid (approach system):** Infinite scroll = novelty trap (time limits)

15.12.3 Sleep as Anxiety Foundation

From Chapter 13:

- Poor sleep dramatically increases anxiety (amygdala hyperreactivity)
- Sleep deprivation = low HRV (rigid ANS)
- Morning routine sets up entire day (reduces anxiety accumulation)

Critical: Can't regulate anxiety without sleep. Address sleep first.

See Chapter 13 for full sleep optimization protocol.

15.13 The Substance Connection: Found the Right System

You've been regulating your autonomic nervous system with substances:

- **Alcohol/benzos:** Activating parasympathetic (GABA: pressing the brake pedal)
- **Stimulants:** Activating sympathetic (dopamine, norepinephrine, pressing gas pedal)
- **Cannabis:** Modulating both (sometimes brake, sometimes gas)

You were right. Your ANS needed regulation. Substances target the correct systems (GABA for calm, dopamine/norepinephrine for activation). You found the concept, gas pedal vs. brake.

But substances are sledgehammers when you need precision controls. They affect your whole brain, create rebound effects (anxiety worse when alcohol wears off), and don't build capacity.

The precision alternatives teach your nervous system to regulate itself:

- **HRV biofeedback:** Trains parasympathetic activation (brake pedal)
- **Neurofeedback:** Targets specific circuits (right frontal for Grumpy Old Man, left frontal for Stabilizer)
- **Breathwork:** Immediate state changes (vagal tone, CO_2 optimization)
- **Cold exposure:** Natural vagal stimulation

- **Exercise:** Metabolizes stress hormones

No tolerance. No withdrawal. No rebound. Just trained capacity.

See Chapter 14 for genetic factors (LVF, GABA receptor genes), specific substance-phenotype patterns, and neurofeedback protocols.

15.14 The Integration: Stacking Interventions

The most powerful approach combines multiple levels:

15.14.1 Foundation (Daily):

1. **Sleep optimized** (Chapter 13, morning routine, consistent wake time)
2. **HRV biofeedback** (5-10 min daily, builds vagal tone)
3. **Breathwork** (box breathing morning, 4-7-8 evening)
4. **Exercise** (morning ideal, metabolizes cortisol)
5. **Nutrition** (anti-inflammatory, omega-3s, magnesium)

15.14.2 Phenotype-Specific (Tailored):

6. **For Grumpy Old Man:** Right frontal alpha neurofeedback, loving-kindness meditation (increases vagal tone; Kok & Fredrickson, 2010)
7. **For Timekeeper:** SMR training, body scan meditation, caffeine cutoff
8. **For Lifeguard:** Posterior cingulate calming, grounding techniques, safe environments
9. **For Princess & Pea:** Sensory gating, self-compassion, environmental optimization
10. **For Stabilizer:** Left frontal beta (activation, not calming)
11. **For Fog:** Depends (activation if shutdown, rest if exhaustion)

15.14.3 Advanced (If Needed):

12. **Cold exposure** (diver's reflex, cold showers, ice baths)
13. **Neurofeedback** (20-40 sessions, phenotype-specific)
14. **Therapy** (CBT, trauma therapy if applicable)
15. **Medication** (if needed, SSRIs, beta-blockers, under medical supervision)

Start with foundation. Add phenotype-specific. Consider advanced if needed.

15.15 The Promise

Your nervous system is trainable.

The anxiety you've been trying to calm with alcohol or benzos, you can train your brain to access that calm naturally (HRV, vagal toning, right frontal alpha).

The activation you've been borrowing from stimulants, you can train your Stabilizer to wake up on its own (left frontal beta, morning routine, sleep optimization).

The regulation you've been stealing from substances. I can help you build it into your baseline.

No tolerance. No withdrawal. No borrowing from tomorrow.

Just precision controls for your nervous system.

MYTH vs REALITY:

MYTH: "Anxiety is just worrying too much."
REALITY: Anxiety is a *circuit state.* Your Lifeguard is firing too hot, your sympathetic nervous system stuck in threat mode. You need circuit-level interventions: HRV training, cold exposure, breath work, neurofeedback. Cognitive tools help after the circuit calms.

If you only do one thing: Learn 4-7-8 breathing (4-second inhale, 7-second hold, 8-second exhale) and use it when Lifeguard spikes.

15.16 Key Takeaways

Your nervous system has two modes: gas pedal (sympathetic) and brake pedal (parasympathetic). Anxiety is stuck in gas; depression is stuck in brake. The goal is flexible shifting.

- **Polyvagal theory:** Three states: ventral vagal (safe/social), sympathetic (fight/flight), dorsal vagal (shutdown/freeze). Live mostly in ventral vagal with ability to shift when needed.
- **HRV = flexibility metric:** Higher HRV = better stress resilience and emotional regulation. Trainable through breathwork, cold exposure, HRV biofeedback.
- **Phenotype-specific direction:** Grumpy Old Man/Lifeguard need calming. Stabilizer/Fog need activation.
- **Breathwork for immediate changes:** Box breathing (calm), physiological sigh (anxiety reset), Wim Hof (activation).
- **Neurofeedback for baseline shifts:** Trains nervous system flexibility over 20-40 sessions.
- **Track your stress cadence:** "Slow burn", "instant spike, fast crash", or "stuck on"? Tailor protocols to that pattern.

15.17 Reader Reflections

Are you stuck in gas pedal (anxiety) or brake (shutdown)? Or do you swing between both? Which phenotypes need calming (Grumpy Old Man/Lifeguard) versus activation (Stabilizer/Fog)?

Ch 16: Productivity & Procrastination

Do You Procrastinate?

one part, the quiet part.
the small, still part, that knows.
said "you have many things to do that you will find joy in doing!"
then another part..
in an act of rampant ventriloquism
added, "tomorrow."

, a hill

16.1 "The Action Cadence for Non-Linear Brains"

Do you procrastinate? Of course you do. We all do.

Studies show **80-95% of college students procrastinate**, and **20% of adults are chronic procrastinators**, experiencing negative effects on productivity and chronic stress (Steel, 2007; Steel & Ferrari, 2013).

But here's what's different for poet-brains: **Your procrastination isn't just "bad habits" or "poor time management."** It's about finding the right action cadence, the rhythm that matches your non-linear brain.

This is the behavioral counterpart to your sleep cadence: when and how you spend the energy that Chapter 13 helps you reclaim.

It's often:

- **Effort-based avoidance** (Grumpy Old Man generating dread about wasted work)
- **Activation energy deficit** (Stabilizer offline: can't initiate)
- **Cognitive fatigue** (Fog: no resources left)
- **Sensory overwhelm** (Princess & Pea: environment too chaotic)
- **Hyperfocus trap** (CEO stuck on wrong thing)

The good news: All these areas are **regulatory, not fixed**. You can learn to understand and take control over executive function, processing speed, sleep quality, and stress response.

This chapter will help you understand your brain's specific procrastination pattern, then give you strategies that actually work for YOUR phenotype.

Throughout Part III, we'll keep coming back to this: build life design, social life, and creative work around your real action cadence instead of pretending you're a steady-state machine.

16.2 Understanding Procrastination: Biopsychosocial

Procrastination isn't simple. The reasons and ways we avoid work stem from:

- Resource limits (sleep, energy, attention)
- Self-doubt about capacity (fear of failure)
- Burnout (chronic stress, depletion)
- Sleep dysregulation (see Chapter 13)
- Trauma and stress response (limbic system overreaction)
- Genetic tendencies (ADHD, anxiety, processing speed)

16.2.1 Three Types of Procrastination

1. Effort / Dread Avoidance

- **Perfectionism** (if I can't do it perfectly, it's not worth the effort)
- **Futility prediction** (this will take too much work and won't pay off)
- **Choice paralysis** (all options feel like too much effort)
- **Phenotype:** Grumpy Old Man (right DLPFC) generating dread about task effort

2. Physical / Cognitive Fatigue

- **Poor sleep** (see Chapter 13: foundation for everything)
- **Circadian dysregulation** (wrong time of day for your chronotype)
- **Burnout** (depleted resources, nothing left)
- **Phenotype:** Fog & the Tide (stuck at low tide, no energy cycling)

3. Executive Function & Attention Difficulties

- **Acquired** (through stress, fatigue, overwhelm)
- **Heritable** (ADHD, autism)
- **Working memory overload** (CEO trying to hold too much)
- **Task initiation deficit** (Stabilizer offline)
- **Phenotype:** Stabilizer (can't start), CEO (stuck on wrong thing), Fog (can't sustain)

Key insight: Knowing which type you have determines which strategies will work.

16.3 The Brain Circuits of Procrastination

16.3.1 Prefrontal Cortex (The Executive Team)

Dorsolateral PFC (DLPFC):

- Working memory, cognitive control
- Response conflict, attention selection
- **Left DLPFC:** Approach motivation (Happy Little Kid: Chapter 1)
- **Right DLPFC:** Avoidance motivation (Grumpy Old Man: Chapter 2)

Ventromedial PFC:

- "Value" processing (what's important now?)
- Temporal discounting (immediate vs. delayed rewards)
- **Why we choose Netflix over work** (immediate gratification > delayed reward)

Anterior Cingulate Cortex (ACC):

- The CEO (Chapter 5)
- Holding things in mind, holding value, internal focus
- Response conflict, perseveration
- **Gets caught in guilt/resistance/avoidance cycle**

Inferior Frontal Gyrus (IFG):

- The Problem Child (Chapter 7)
- Response inhibition, brake system
- Stopping impulsive reactions
- Right IFG = defiant brake (oppositional when threat-sensitized)

Insula:

- Awareness of body, drive, wants, craving
- Interoception
- Just under IFG

16.3.2 Temporal Lobe (Memory and Emotion)

Parahippocampus / Hippocampus:

- Retrieval of experience
- Memory of past failures / successes
- Context for current task
- "Last time I tried this, it went badly" (Grumpy Old Man uses this)

Amygdala:

- Context with emotions

- Threat response to tasks
- Fear of failure
- **Task feels like threat** (limbic overreaction)

16.3.3 Basal Ganglia (Reward and Skill Learning)

Dopaminergic structures:

- Caudate, substantia nigra, nucleus accumbens
- Reward and stimulus seeking
- Pain, central discomfort
- Skill learning

When dysregulated:

- Trouble regulating frontal areas
- Can't override limbic system to initiate action
- Immediate rewards dominate (can't delay gratification)

ADHD connection:

- D2/D4 receptor differences
- Reduced dopamine signaling
- Immediate reward bias
- See Chapter 1 (Happy Little Kid) and Chapter 3 (Stabilizer)

16.3.4 The Procrastination Cascade

How it unfolds:

1. **Task appears** (work, project, obligation)
2. **Happy Little Kid says "Let's do this!"** (approach motivation, left frontal)
3. **Grumpy Old Man says "Don't!" (too much work for nothing)** (avoidance motivation, right frontal)
4. **CEO tries to reconcile** but gets stuck (ACC, frontal midline)
5. **Limbic system amplifies** (amygdala: "This is threatening!")
6. **Hippocampus retrieves** past failures ("Remember last time?")
7. **CEO perseverates** on unresolved conflict (approach vs. avoidance)
8. **Precentral areas struggle** to initiate (Stabilizer offline, no decision made)
9. **Guilt/resistance/avoidance cycle** builds and spins

Result: Procrastination. Not laziness; your brain's circuits are caught in unresolved approach-avoidance conflict.

16.3.5 The Compensation Cost: "Fine" Performance, Hidden Inefficiency

Here's something most people miss: **you can test fine on attention tasks while still having a bottleneck burning through your resources.**

Your overall performance might be average or above average. But look closer: you're muscling through with one component weak (vigilance, speed, carefulness). The effort required to maintain that "fine" performance? That's expensive.

You can feel the e-brake rubbing, so you're standing on the gas a little bit. It yields the sloppiness slightly, not enough to fail, but enough to drain you. Late in the day, stressed, tired, hungry, angry? That "good enough" performance collapses. The compensation stops working and the real deficit shows up.

This isn't "you're fine, stop complaining." This is "you're working harder than you should have to, and whatever you address as a bottleneck will free your resources." The productivity you think requires willpower? It's actually just friction from running compensatory patterns all day long.

16.3.6 Brittleness: When Fatigue and Stress Fight Each Other

Brittleness is the signature of fatigue and stress fighting each other.

You're tightening up (careful, careful, careful) while reactivity leaks through anyway, jumping the gun on tasks, snapping at people, making impulsive decisions you regret.

The pattern:

- You're trying to be careful and controlled
- But you're still reactive and impulsive
- Locked-up tension doesn't prevent mistakes: it creates them
- You're fighting yourself instead of flowing

Why this happens:

- Fatigue says: "Slow down, conserve energy, protect the system"
- Stress says: "Stay alert, threat incoming, be ready"
- Your brain simultaneously tightens up AND stays reactive
- You get the worst of both: tight AND impulsive

What brittleness feels like:

- On edge but exhausted
- Trying hard but making careless mistakes
- Snapping when you meant to be patient
- "I'm standing on the gas while the e-brake's on" (compensation metaphor from earlier)

- Locked-up muscles, shallow breathing, tight jaw: while still reactive

This is different from:

- **Relaxed impulsivity:** ADHD baseline, just reactive without tension
- **Calm sustained action:** Regulated state, flowing
- **Pure fatigue:** Just slow, foggy, heavy (no reactivity)

Brittleness in performance data:

- Low movement variability (holding still, tightening up)
- High impulsivity (jumping the gun, commission errors)
- Usually both present together
- "Went careful, careful, careful… and still jumped the gun 18 times"

How to address:

1. **Fix sleep first** (Chapter 13) - removes fatigue component
2. **Regulate stress** (Chapter 15) - removes threat sensitivity component
3. **Don't try to "just relax" or "be more careful"** - that's fighting it, makes it worse
4. **Neurofeedback:** Target both stress (right frontal, posterior cingulate) AND fatigue (C3, delta regulation) simultaneously
5. **Behavioral:** Reduce demands temporarily, build back slowly as resources restore

Brittleness is a sign you're over-extended. Not weak, not failing, over-extended. Your system is trying to perform through resource depletion. Honor that signal.

16.4 QEEG Patterns in Procrastination

Once you get your brain map, you can see which circuits are involved in YOUR procrastination.

16.4.1 Common Patterns

Anterior Cingulate (frontal midline):

- **Fast or slow-wave excess:** Lack of control or over-control (CEO dysregulated)
- **Calming rhythm excess:** Dread + procrastination (Grumpy Old Man + CEO stuck)
- **Slow waves:** Disinhibition, medial temporal involvement

Motor Cortex (left and right sensorimotor):

- **Left side:** Stabilizer (sustaining mode, narrow focus)

  - Low fast waves → can't sustain
- Excess slow waves → can't initiate (Frontal Slow: see Chapter 3)
- Sensorimotor rhythm patterns predict engagement capacity
- **Right side:** Supervisor (conflict supervision)
  - Over-inhibition → perfectionism paralysis
  - Under-inhibition → impulsivity

Posterior Cingulate (back midline):

- **Excess fast or slow activity:** Threat sensitivity (Lifeguard threat-sensitive)
- **Low resting rhythms:** Environmental scanning (distracted by everything)
- Hypervigilance prevents focus

Frontopolar region:

- **Approach motivation** (Happy Little Kid)
- Low activity → low motivation, can't engage

Right frontotemporal regions:

- **Avoidance, dread, resistance** (Grumpy Old Man)
- May impact insula
- High activity → task avoidance

Nucleus Accumbens (reward system):

- Dopamine dysregulation
- Immediate gratification bias
- Stimulus seeking (distractions more rewarding than work)

Your brain map shows which circuits are involved, then we can target them.

For QEEG options: See peakbraininstitute.com or andrewhillphd.com for current providers

---

16.5 Behavioral Strategies That Actually Work

Generic productivity advice ("just focus," "make a schedule," "use willpower") doesn't work for poet-brains. Here are strategies that work WITH your phenotypes.

16.5.1 Strategy 1: Getting Things Done (GTD) - Define Next Actions

David Allen's system, adapted for neurodivergent brains (Allen, 2001):

Core principles:

1. **Dump tasks** into project-based lists (get out of head, reduces working memory load)
2. **Keep to ONE set of lists in ONE place** (not scattered across apps, papers, memory)
3. **Make lists project-based** (not random)
4. **Put next action on top** (what's the immediate next step?)
5. **Put blockers below it** (what's preventing progress?)
6. **Put later stages below that** (future steps)
7. **Drop stuff in reliably** when it recurs in mind and at end of day

Why this works for poet-brains:

- **Reduces cognitive load** (CEO not holding everything in working memory)
- **Clarifies next action** (Stabilizer knows exactly what to do, reduces activation energy)
- **Identifies blockers** (addresses real obstacles, not vague "I should work on this")
- **One system** (not decision fatigue about where to put things)
- **Externalizes** (your brain's working memory is limited: use external system)

Visualization tools:

- **Outlines:** Hierarchical structure (main task → subtasks)
- **Mind mapping:** Brainstorm, then reorganize (great for Happy Little Kid, visual, non-linear)
- **Kanban boards:** Visual workflow (To Do → Doing → Done)
  - Can use columns for projects/contexts
  - Visual progress (satisfying for your approach system)
  - Limits work-in-progress (prevents overcommitment)

For Happy Little Kid (approach system): Mind mapping prevents shiny object syndrome (capture all ideas, then prioritize)

For Stabilizer: Next action clarity reduces activation energy (no ambiguity about what to do)

For CEO: Project-based lists reduce task-switching (grouped by context)

16.5.2 Strategy 2: Pomodoro Technique (Time Blocking and Sprinting)

The technique (Cirillo, 2006):

- **25 minutes work, 5 minutes break** (classic Pomodoro)
- Or **45 minutes work, 15 minutes break** (extended)

- Set timer, work until it rings, take break (no exceptions)
- No multitasking during work block

Why this works for poet-brains:

- **Scheduled procrastination** (break is coming: you can wait 25 minutes)
- **Sprint through** (not just "take first imperfect step": commit to full 25 min)
- **Task blocking** (less organizing what to do, more doing)
- **Shift and refresh** (break allows context switch, walk, reset)
- **External structure** (timer provides cue: Stabilizer responds to external cues)

Stack Pomodoros:

- Try to stack 2-5 Pomodoro blocks on one topic / task area
- Builds momentum (easier to continue than start)
- Reduces context-switching costs (CEO not constantly re-orienting)
- Hyperfocus becomes productive (sustained on one thing)

For Timekeeper: Pomodoro provides structure for racing thoughts (25 min container)

For Stabilizer: Timer provides external initiation cue (alarm = "start now")

For CEO: Task blocking reduces switching (stay with one thing for 2-5 Pomodoros)

For Happy Little Kid (approach system): Break provides novelty hit (prevents boredom during sustained work)

16.5.3 Strategy 3: Structured Procrastination

The technique:

1. Write out ALL the things you have to do (big list)
2. **Put the most scary item at the top** (the one you really don't want to do)
3. Add everything else below (emails, errands, small tasks, chores)
4. **Procrastinate the scary thing by doing the other things**

Why this works (paradoxically):

- Your house is clean, but you didn't do your taxes: okay, well, your house is clean!
- You chewed through 10-20 minute tasks that are less overwhelming
- Suddenly you have one or two things left on your list
- "Well, I can't make that hard call, I guess… because my house is clean, my laundry's done, I made some tea. Oh, okay."
- **The act of self-care and small wins builds up momentum**

- Eventually you just... do the thing

For Grumpy Old Man: Reduces dread (build wins before facing biggest effort)

For Stabilizer: Easier tasks activate the motor system (momentum builds, gets you in gear)

For Happy Little Kid: Variety of tasks satisfies engagement need

---

16.5.4 Strategy 4: Mindful Procrastination (The Three-Part Process)

This is meditation during the sensation of overwhelm, a way to work through resistance without fighting it.

Part 1: Notice Without Reacting

- Feel the dread, resistance, overwhelm when facing a task
- Note it: "Here's my procrastination. Here's my resistance. It's fine."
- Don't add secondary reaction (guilt, shame, "I should just do it")
- Just observe: "This is the feeling tone of resistance. This is what dread feels like."
- The act of noting lets you release the sensation (it shows up, you note it, it passes)

Part 2: Notice the Cost (The Accounting)

- As you sit with resistance, start noticing the *expenditure*
- "I've been thinking about this one thing 17,000 times today. Ow."
- Not guilting yourself: just accounting for the energy cost of avoidance
- Eventually you start to index the cost differently
- The dread of doing it becomes less than the cost of avoiding it

Part 3: Visualize Forward (Task Imagination)

- Take a breath, let the dread wash away briefly
- Visually imagine what the task looks like (not doing it: just seeing it)
- "What does taking out the trash look like? Brushing my teeth? Making that call?"
- Imagine it, then let it go again
- Within minutes (or after days of practice), you'll find yourself just getting up and doing it
- The urge to act builds naturally when you stop fighting the resistance

Why this works:

- Reduces internal conflict (not fighting resistance)
- Builds intrinsic motivation (moved vs. pushed)
- Trains your CEO to let go of perseveration

- Honors resistance (sometimes it's wisdom) while reducing its control

For CEO: Reduces perseveration on "I should be working" loops

For Grumpy Old Man: Noting practice reduces secondary dread about procrastination

For Stabilizer: Visualization + reduced resistance allows natural motor activation

---

16.5.5 Strategy 5: Strategic Social Accountability

The technique:

- **If people motivate you:** Get buddies, body doubling, deliver projects for others
- **Learn to say no:** Stress = feeling of being overextended
- **Un-commit / prune** (but act, don't react)
- **When you want to say yes, sit with it** for a bit (don't commit immediately)

Why this works:

- **External accountability** (Stabilizer responds to external cues better than internal)
- **Social motivation** (Happy Little Kid likes people, connection)
- **Reduces overcommitment** (prevents overwhelm that creates procrastination)
- **Strategic yes/no** (not reactive: protects resources)

Body doubling:

- Working alongside someone else (in person or virtual)
- Parallel work (not collaboration: just presence)
- Reduces activation energy (Stabilizer activates from social cue)
- Accountability (less likely to get distracted)

Delivering for others:

- External deadline (more motivating than internal)
- Social pressure (don't want to let people down)
- Immediate consequences (not abstract future)

For Stabilizer: External cues (people, deadlines) provide activation

For Happy Little Kid (approach system): Social element satisfies connection need

For Grumpy Old Man: Reduces overcommitment (less dread from being overextended)

16.6 ADHD-Specific Strategies

16.6.1 Activation Energy Hacks

The problem: Your Stabilizer (left motor/premotor) has high activation energy for tasks.

The hacks: These bypass the Stabilizer's activation barrier: the gap between deciding and doing. If you've ever stood at your desk knowing exactly what to do and still couldn't start, that's the gap these target.

1. Task Chaining (Momentum Building)

- Link tasks together (finish one → immediately start next)
- First task easy (low activation energy: brush teeth, make coffee)
- Each task creates momentum for next
- Don't stop between tasks (momentum is precious)

Example chain:

- Wake → bathroom → coffee → open laptop → check email → start work
- Each step easier than starting from zero

2. External Deadlines (Not Internal)

- Internal: "I should finish this by Friday" (weak)
- External: "Meeting with client Friday 10am" (strong)
- Public commitment (tell someone your deadline)
- Consequences (real, not abstract)

3. Dopamine Timing (Strategic Rewards)

- Small reward after task completion (not before)
- Immediate (not delayed: ADHD brains need immediate feedback)
- Varied (novelty maintains dopamine response)
- Examples: coffee after first task, walk after Pomodoro set, social media after work block

4. Environment Design (Reduce Friction)

- Make starting easy (materials ready, workspace clear)
- Make distractions hard (phone in other room, apps blocked)
- Visual cues (project materials visible = reminder)
- Dedicated workspace (context cue for "work mode")

16.6.2 Working with the Stabilizer

Understanding your Stabilizer (left precentral/postcentral):

- Handles task initiation, execution, follow-through

- When offline (Frontal Slow: excess theta, low beta): "I know what to do, can't make myself do it"
- Responds to: external cues, momentum, structure (not willpower)

Strategies:

- **External cues:** Alarms, timers, people, deadlines
- **Momentum:** Start with easiest task, build from there
- **Structure:** Pomodoro, time blocking, routines
- **Morning activation:** Consistent wake time, morning light, movement (see Chapter 13)

What doesn't work:

- "Just try harder" (Stabilizer doesn't respond to effort)
- "Use willpower" (willpower is limited resource)
- "Be more disciplined" (discipline requires Stabilizer to be online)

See Chapter 3 (Stabilizer) for full discussion of Frontal Slow phenotype and neurofeedback protocols.

16.6.3 CEO Training (Anterior Cingulate Flexibility)

The problem: CEO gets stuck on wrong thing, can't switch to important task.

The training:

- **Cognitive flexibility exercises** (switch between tasks deliberately)
- **Meditation** (open awareness: see Chapter 17)
- **Neurofeedback** (anterior cingulate flexibility training)
- **Pomodoro stacking** (sustained focus on one thing, then switch)

Project Inertia vs. Momentum Maintenance:

- **Project inertia:** Hard to start (Stabilizer offline)
- **Momentum maintenance:** Once started, easier to continue
- **Strategy:** Lower activation energy for starting, then ride momentum

Understanding task resistance:

- **Is it Grumpy Old Man dread?** (effort-based avoidance)
  - Solution: Address anxiety (Chapter 2, Chapter 14), structured procrastination
- **Is it Stabilizer offline?** (activation energy deficit)
  - Solution: External cues, task chaining, momentum building
- **Is it CEO stuck?** (perseverating on wrong thing)
  - Solution: Cognitive flexibility training, meditation, forced task-switching

See Chapter 5 (CEO) for full discussion of anterior cingulate and "stickiness."

16.7 Autism-Specific Strategies

16.7.1 Executive Function Scaffolding

The challenge: Internal organization difficult, need external structure.

The scaffolding:

1. Visual schedules:

- Time-blocked calendar (visual representation of day)
- Color-coded (work, personal, rest)
- Reduces decision fatigue (schedule decides, not you)

2. Checklists:

- Step-by-step for complex tasks
- Check off each step (satisfying, progress visible)
- Reduces working memory load (don't have to remember steps)

3. Routines:

- Same sequence every day (morning, work start, work end, evening)
- Automaticity (reduces cognitive load)
- Predictability (reduces anxiety)

4. Timers and alarms:

- External cues for transitions
- Prevents hyperfocus from derailing schedule
- Time blindness compensation

16.7.2 Sensory Environment Optimization

The principle: Productivity environment = sensory-friendly environment

For Princess & Pea (and many autistic brains):

Reduce sensory input:

- Quiet space (or noise-canceling headphones, white noise)
- Controlled lighting (not fluorescent, not too bright)
- Comfortable temperature (often cooler than average)
- Minimal visual clutter (clean workspace)

Optimize for focus:

- Dedicated workspace (context cue)

- Ergonomic setup (comfort allows sustained work)
- Sensory tools (fidgets, weighted lap pad, compression clothing)

Why this matters:

- Sensory overwhelm depletes resources
- Can't focus if the environment is an assault
- Not "high maintenance": sensory processing sensitivity
- Optimizing environment = optimizing productivity

See Chapter 8 (Princess & Pea) for full discussion of sensory processing sensitivity.

16.7.3 Interest-Based vs. Obligation-Based Motivation

The reality: Autistic brains (and many ADHD brains) struggle with obligation-based tasks.

Interest-based motivation:

- Task aligns with special interest or curiosity
- Intrinsic motivation (want to do it)
- Can hyperfocus for hours
- High quality work

Obligation-based motivation:

- Task is "should" or external demand
- Extrinsic motivation (have to do it)
- Struggle to initiate and sustain
- Depleting, exhausting

Strategies:

- **Find interest angle** in obligation tasks (curiosity, challenge, learning)
- **Pair with interest** (listen to favorite music while doing boring task)
- **Gamify** (turn obligation into challenge, track progress)
- **Restructure life** (if possible) around interests (see Chapter 19)

The limitation: Can't always avoid obligation tasks. But finding interest angle helps.

16.7.4 Honoring Hyperfocus (Not Interrupting Flow)

The gift: Autistic hyperfocus = sustained deep work (hours without break)

The challenge: Interruptions feel violent (CEO stuck in flow, can't switch)

Strategies:

- **Protect hyperfocus time** (block calendar, communicate boundaries)

- **Batch interruptions** (check email 2x day, not constantly)
- **Transition rituals** (when you must switch, 5 min wind-down, then switch)
- **Honor the flow** (if you're in it, ride it: don't force arbitrary breaks)

Caution: Hyperfocus can derail other priorities. Balance needed.

See Chapter 21 (Creative Flow) for full discussion of flow states.

16.8 Neurofeedback for Productivity

My approach: QEEG-guided neurofeedback addresses resource limits that create procrastination.

Timeline: Few months to see changes in basic resources (attention, stress, sleep, motivation, creativity, processing speed).

Note: Won't instantly make you productive, but removes obstacles.

16.8.1 Protocols by Phenotype

For Stabilizer (task initiation deficit):

- Theta suppression / beta enhancement (left frontal) wakes the "engine that won't start"
- SMR training builds sustained attention capacity
- See Chapter 18 for full theta/beta ratio protocols and left frontal activation

For Grumpy Old Man (effort-based avoidance):

- Right frontal alpha training calms catastrophizing, reduces frontotemporal avoidance patterns
- Amygdala regulation reduces threat response to tasks
- See Chapter 18 for protocols

For CEO (stuck on wrong thing):

- Anterior cingulate flexibility training reduces perseveration, improves task-switching
- See Chapter 18 for frontal midline protocols

For Lifeguard (threat sensitivity, distraction):

- Posterior cingulate calming reduces constant threat scanning
- DMN regulation for less distraction
- See Chapter 18 for protocols

For Happy Little Kid (can't finish projects):

- Left frontal training for sustained attention (not just initiation), impulse control (finishing before starting new)
- Reward pathway optimization for completion satisfaction
- See Chapter 18 for protocols

16.9 Nootropics and Supplements

My evidence-based recommendations:

Omega-3s (DHA and EPA):

- Brain function support, membrane health
- 1-2g daily (combined DHA+EPA)
- Safe, well-researched

Magnesium:

- Required for brain function, nerve firing
- Also supports sleep, stress response
- 200-350mg daily (glycinate or threonate; 350mg is the supplemental upper limit)
- Most people deficient

Citicoline / CDP-Choline:

- Mildly stimulating
- Increases processing speed
- May remyelinate damaged neurons
- 250-500mg daily
- Good for Fog, Stabilizer

L-Theanine (with caffeine):

- Softens caffeine's over-focus and anxiety
- Balances stimulation
- 200-350mg with coffee
- Good for Timekeeper, Grumpy Old Man

Caffeine:

- In moderation supports focus and task action
- Cutoff 2pm (see Chapter 13)
- Synergistic with L-theanine
- Temporary Stabilizer activation

Cautions:

- **Be careful with "smart drugs"** or research chemicals (unproven, potentially unsafe)

- **Many nootropics are hype** (not evidence-based)
- **If already performing well, may not need**
- **If strong ADHD or fatigue, supplement strategy may make sense**

Contrast with stimulant self-medication:

- Supplements support (don't force)
- No tolerance (unlike prescription stimulants, cocaine)
- Sustainable (not borrowing from tomorrow)
- See Chapter 14 for stimulant discussion

16.10 Sleep as Productivity Foundation

Critical principle: You can't out-hack poor sleep.

Your morning routine IS your productivity routine. The MVP protocol from Chapter 13, consistent wake time, morning light within 30 minutes, gentle movement, caffeine/stress-free first hour, early eating cutoff, does more for your productivity than any task management system.

Why sleep matters for productivity:

- **ADHD:** 20.5% reduction in slow-wave activity (Furrer et al., 2019) → more theta during day → worse executive function
- **Working memory:** Sleep deprivation impairs (CEO can't hold information)
- **Emotional regulation:** Poor sleep → amygdala hyperreactivity (Lifeguard more reactive, Grumpy Old Man louder)
- **Processing speed:** Fatigue slows Timekeeper (or makes Fog worse)
- **Task initiation:** Poor sleep keeps Stabilizer offline (can't start anything)

The vicious cycle:

- Poor sleep → can't focus → use stimulants → worse sleep → repeat

The solution:

- Optimize sleep first using Chapter 13's MVP protocol
- Then add productivity strategies (this chapter)
- Then consider neurofeedback (if resource limits persist)

See Chapter 13 for the complete morning routine protocol that sets up your entire day's productivity.

16.11 Why Stimulants Seemed to "Fix" Productivity

Many poet-brains have discovered that stimulants make productivity possible. **Why they work:** They artificially activate your Stabilizer (left frontal beta increase), suppress theta (wake up Frontal Slow pattern), increase dopamine (Happy Little Kid energized), and improve working memory (CEO can hold more). "Finally I can focus."

But they don't train circuits, they borrow from them. The activation you feel is stolen from tomorrow. Sleep architecture suffers (disrupting the foundation of executive function), tolerance builds (need escalating doses), dread amplifies (Grumpy Old Man and Timekeeper activated), and the crash leaves you more paralyzed than before.

The sustainable alternative:

- **Sleep optimization first** (Chapter 13's MVP: addresses root cause of theta excess)
- **Neurofeedback** (train Stabilizer to activate naturally: theta/beta protocols)
- **Behavioral strategies** (external cues, task chaining, environment design)
- **Nootropics** (support systems: citicoline, moderate caffeine, not force them)

See Chapter 14 for stimulant genetics (Frontal Slow, dopamine receptor variants), substance-phenotype patterns, and why chronic use makes ADHD worse long-term.

16.12 The Action Cadence: Unifying Framework

"Action Cadence" is what I call the rhythm of moving from paralysis to action. It integrates all the strategies above into one coherent approach:

The elements:

1. **Mindfulness**: Notice resistance, dread, overwhelm without reacting (noting practice)
2. **Motion**: Move your body (walking desk, stretch, run) to activate motor cortex and wake Stabilizer
3. **Inhibitory tone**: SMR training, stillness practice, learning when to brake vs. when to release
4. **Noticing urge to act vs. avoid**: Observing the push-pull between Happy Little Kid (approach) and Grumpy Old Man (avoid)
5. **Cost accounting**: Tracking energy expenditure of resistance ("I've thought about this 17,000 times, that's expensive")

6. **External structure**: GTD, Pomodoro, body doubling, deadlines (offload to systems)

The rhythm:

- Notice resistance (mindfulness)
- Note the cost (accounting)
- Move your body (activation)
- Visualize the task (forward-facing)
- Let natural urge arise (intrinsic motivation)
- Act when moved (not when pushed)

This is the cadence. Not forcing. Not fighting. Observing, accounting, moving, visualizing, allowing. The action emerges naturally when you stop battling resistance.

16.13 The Integration: Stacking Strategies

The most powerful approach combines multiple levels:

16.13.1 Foundation (Must Have):

1. **Sleep optimized** (Chapter 13, non-negotiable)
2. **Basic stress managed** (Chapter 15, HRV, breathwork)
3. **Nutrition adequate** (omega-3s, magnesium, protein, hydration)

16.13.2 Behavioral (Daily Practice):

4. **GTD system** (one place for all tasks, next actions clear)
5. **Pomodoro technique** (25 min work, 5 min break, stack 2-5)
6. **Morning routine** (consistent wake, light, movement, sets up day; habits take a median of 66 days to become automatic, range 18-254 days) (Lally et al., 2010)
7. **Environment optimized** (sensory-friendly, distraction-minimized)

16.13.3 Phenotype-Specific (Tailored):

8. **For Stabilizer:** External cues, task chaining, momentum
9. **For Grumpy Old Man:** Structured procrastination, dread management
10. **For CEO:** Task blocking, cognitive flexibility training
11. **For Happy Little Kid (approach system):** Mind mapping, variety, gamification
12. **For Princess & Pea:** Sensory optimization, interest-based motivation

16.13.4 Advanced (If Needed):

13. **Neurofeedback** (address resource limits, ADHD, anxiety, sleep)
14. **Nootropics** (support when appropriate, not first line)
15. **Meditation** (builds attention, reduces anxiety, Chapter 17)

Start with foundation and behavioral. Add phenotype-specific. Consider advanced if resource limits persist.

16.14 Using the Mastery Loop: Procrastination Example

Scenario: You've been avoiding an important email for 3 days. Guilt is building.

1. NOTICE: "My Grumpy Old Man is generating dread about the effort this will take. My Stabilizer won't initiate. My CEO is stuck in the approach-avoidance loop."

2. NORMALIZE: "Of course I'm avoiding this. My right frontal is generating threat predictions about how badly this could go. My left motor cortex needs external activation to start. This is circuits, not character."

3. REGULATE: Choose tools:

- Mindful procrastination (note the dread, visualize the task, wait for natural urge)
- Structured procrastination (put email at top of list, do 3 easier things first, build momentum)
- Body doubling (call a friend, work alongside them virtually)

4. REASSIGN: "For this task, I need Happy Little Kid forward (find what's interesting about this), Grumpy Old Man consulting (what's the real risk?), Stabilizer executing (movement first, then type)."

5. REFLECT: After sending email: "It wasn't as much effort as predicted. My Grumpy Old Man was wrong. I can do hard things. Next time, I'll notice the pattern earlier and use structured procrastination."

This is mastery in practice. Not perfection. Just noticing, normalizing, regulating, reassigning, reflecting. Over and over.

16.15 The Promise

Productivity isn't about willpower or discipline. (Those require resources you may not have.)

Productivity is about:

- Understanding your brain's circuits (which phenotypes are involved?)
- Working with your phenotypes (not against them)
- Building resources (sleep, attention, stress regulation)
- Using external systems (GTD, Pomodoro, environment, accountability)
- Training circuits (neurofeedback, meditation, behavioral practice)

You're not lazy. Your Stabilizer is offline, or your Grumpy Old Man is generating dread, or your CEO is stuck, or your resources are depleted.

These are fixable.

The productivity you've been borrowing from stimulants. I can help you build it into your baseline.

MYTH vs REALITY:

MYTH: "Procrastination is laziness."
REALITY: Procrastination is your brain's threat-detection system mislabeling a hard task as a physical danger. Your Lifeguard spikes, your CEO shuts down, and your Stabilizer looks for any excuse to move away from the discomfort. It's not a character flaw, it's a phenotype constellation doing exactly what it evolved to do. The fix isn't willpower; it's teaching your brain that the hard task won't kill you.

If you only do one thing from this chapter: Use Action Cadence, when you're stuck, ask "Am I avoiding something hard, or is this genuinely not the right time?" and act accordingly.

16.16 Key Takeaways

Productivity isn't about willpower or discipline, it's about understanding which circuits are bottlenecking you and building the resources and systems that work with your brain, not against it.

- **Four types of procrastination, four interventions:** Stabilizer (can't start) → reduce friction, body doubling. CEO (stuck) → external cueing, GTD. Grumpy Old Man (avoiding) → challenge futility predictions. Fog (no resources) → honor rest.
- **GTD = external CEO:** Capture everything, process regularly, organize by context, review weekly. Frees your CEO from holding everything.
- **Pomodoro = structure for weak Stabilizer:** 25-minute blocks help initiation, prevent burnout, match Fog capacity.
- **Environment design beats willpower:** Reduce friction for starting, increase friction for distractions. Infrastructure, not discipline.

- **Neurofeedback targets bottleneck:** Theta/beta ratio (Stabilizer), SMR (Supervisor), left frontal beta (activation), right frontal alpha (anxiety), frontal midline theta (CEO flexibility).

16.17 Reader Reflections

Take a moment to consider your own productivity patterns:

1. **Which type of procrastination is yours?** Can't start (Stabilizer)? Stuck on wrong thing (CEO)? Avoiding due to effort dread (Grumpy Old Man)? Too exhausted (Fog)? Identifying your specific bottleneck determines which intervention works.
2. **What external systems have you tried?** GTD? Pomodoro? Accountability partners? Can you trace success/failure to how well the system matched your phenotype? (GTD for CEO, Pomodoro for Stabilizer, accountability for weak activation)
3. **If you use stimulants for productivity, what are they actually doing?** Helping you start (Stabilizer)? Sustaining attention (Supervisor)? Reducing dread so you can begin (Grumpy Old Man)? What's the cost, rebound, crash, tolerance?
4. **What would sustainable productivity look like?** Starting tasks without crisis? Sustaining attention without stimulants? Completing things without burnout? What would that change in your work and life?

Ch 17: Meditation & Contemplative Practice

Meditation Parcellation: How We Focus Attention

KEY INSIGHT:

Meditation isn't one thing. Your Grumpy Old Man needs different training than your Stabilizer. Match the practice to the phenotype, or you're just sitting there suffering mindfully.

Here's how I think about meditation types: Not by tradition or lineage, but by **the quality and object of attention**.

The four core types:

1. Single Point Attention (Absorption)

- **What:** Focus on one object to develop absorption and concentration
- **Examples:** Breath at nostrils, mantra, candle flame
- **Builds:** Sustained attention, prefrontal cortex, absorption states
- **Tradition:** Samatha (concentration meditation)

2. Present Time Attention (Observation Without Reaction)

- **What:** Watch whatever arises in present moment without engaging or directing
- **Examples:** Breath rising and falling, thoughts passing, sounds coming and going
- **Builds:** Metacognition, cognitive flexibility, DMN regulation, "just watching"
- **Tradition:** Vipassana (insight meditation), choiceless awareness

3. Feeling Tone, Internal (Awareness of Emotion)

- **What:** Generate and sustain specific internal emotional states
- **Examples:** Loving-kindness (Metta), compassion, joy, equanimity
- **Builds:** Positive emotion, self-compassion, amygdala regulation
- **Tradition:** Metta, Brahma Viharas

4. Feeling Tone, External (Somatic Awareness)

- **What:** Notice external sensations and body experience
- **Examples:** Body scan, room temperature, pressure of sitting, physical sensations
- **Builds:** Interoception, mind-body connection, somatic awareness

- **Tradition:** Body scan meditation (MBSR), somatic practices

All other meditation practices (TM, MBSR, Vipassana, Zen, etc.) use combinations of these four attentional qualities. The tradition matters less than what you're training your attention to do.

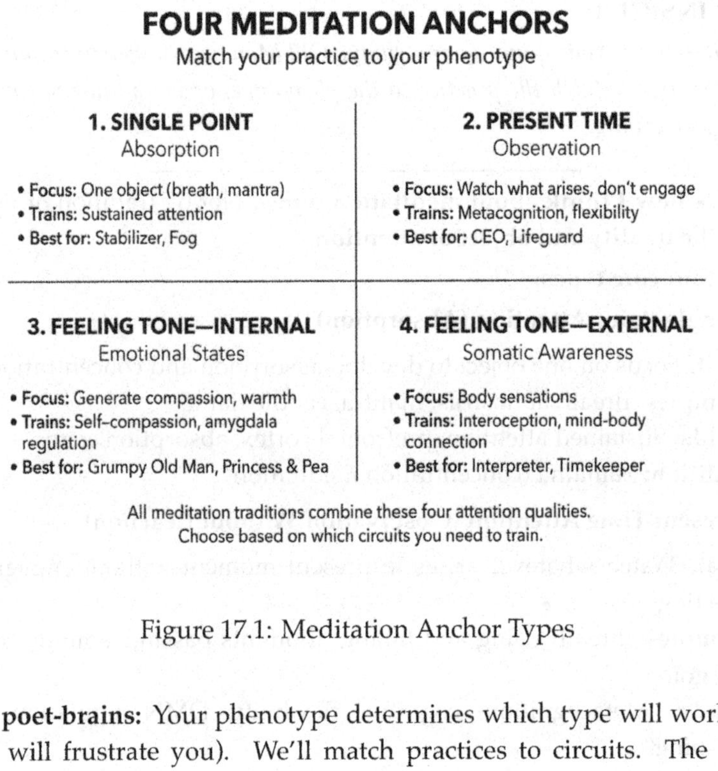

Figure 17.1: Meditation Anchor Types

For poet-brains: Your phenotype determines which type will work (and which will frustrate you). We'll match practices to circuits. The key is matching the attention quality to your circuit needs, if your Stabilizer needs strengthening (frontal slow-wave), single point attention builds sustained focus. If your CEO needs flexibility (stuck loops), present time observation trains letting go. If your Grumpy Old Man needs regulation (right frontal hyperactive, generating dread), feeling tone practices build self-compassion and reduce effort-avoidance. The tradition matters less than what you're training your attention to do.

Meditation is cadence training for attention and awareness: learning to slow, widen, or re-pace your internal stream.

Meditation as Biohacking

17.1 "Don't Just Do Something, Sit There!"

Mindfulness and meditation train your brain to function more efficiently, manage stress better, and maintain emotional balance. The old joke: "Don't just do something, sit there!" But for poet-brains, that's often the hardest thing, sitting with what is, without fixing, without doing.

What meditation trains: Neuroplasticity, stress reduction, emotional regulation, attention control. Meta-analyses confirm meditation programs reduce psychological stress and anxiety with moderate effect sizes, outperforming active control conditions (Goyal et al., 2014). Strong evidence for cortical thickness, reduced amygdala reactivity, strengthened prefrontal cortex. Regular practice also increases cortical GABA levels, supporting the calming effects yoga and meditation practitioners report (Streeter et al., 2010).

For poet-brains: Your CEO needs flexibility, Grumpy Old Man needs calming, Timekeeper needs slowing, Interpreter needs quieting, DMN needs regulation. Meditation trains all of these.

But here's the key: Meditation isn't one-size-fits-all. Your phenotype determines which practices will work (and which will frustrate you).

If meditation has been triggering for you before, that's not failure, that's your Lifeguard or Grumpy Old Man sounding the alarm. There are styles that work better for you. We'll match practices to phenotypes below.

A note on safety: Meditation is low-risk, not zero-risk. Extended silent retreats can destabilize people with active psychosis or acute trauma. Research documents a range of difficult experiences (heightened anxiety to depersonalization) particularly for those with trauma histories (Lindahl et al., 2017). Start short (5-10 minutes). If a practice consistently worsens symptoms, stop and try a different style. Meditation amplifies what's already there.

17.2 Before You Begin: Foundations First

Meditation works best on a foundation of decent sleep and managed stress. If you're chronically exhausted or in crisis mode, you'll fall asleep during practice or amplify anxiety. Address basics first (see Chapters 13-15 for sleep, stress, and anxiety regulation), then meditate. Otherwise you're trying to build on quicksand.

17.3 What Meditation Trains (The Circuits You Mapped)

Meditation trains the same circuits we've been discussing: prefrontal cortex (executive function), anterior cingulate (CEO flexibility), right frontal (Grumpy Old Man effort-dread), amygdala and posterior cingulate (Lifeguard threat reactivity), default mode network (Lifeguard rumination), which is hyperactive in anxiety and depression, and which meditation normalizes (Brewer et al., 2011). Eight weeks of practice measurably increases gray matter in hippocampus, posterior cingulate, and TPJ, and thickens cortical attention areas. Eight-week MBSR also reduces amygdala volume while increasing hippocampal volume, structural changes that correlate with reduced anxiety and improved emotional regulation. This isn't placebo. It's **neuroplasticity.** (Lazar et al., 2005; Hölzel et al., 2011)

For poet-brains specifically:

- CEO needs flexibility training → meditation practices letting go
- Grumpy Old Man needs calming → meditation reduces effort-dread reactivity
- Timekeeper needs slowing → meditation shifts beta to alpha
- Lifeguard needs present-focus → meditation reduces rumination
- Interpreter (Linguist) needs quieting → meditation accesses non-verbal awareness

But here's what matters: Your phenotype determines which practices work. Generic "just sit and breathe" fails for most poet-brains. You need matched practice to circuit.

17.4 Phenotype-Specific Meditation Practices

Your phenotype determines which meditation practices will work (and which will frustrate you). Here's your guide.

17.5 For Timekeeper: Shifting from Thoughts to Sensations

Your challenge: Your brain won't shut off. "Just breathe" doesn't work, too slow for fast brains. Racing thoughts hijack every meditation attempt.

17.5.1 Why "Just Breathe" Fails for You

The problem: Standard breath meditation assumes slow, steady processing. Your Timekeeper runs at 2x speed. Focusing on slow breathing feels like torture.

What happens: You try to breathe slowly → brain speeds up to compensate → more racing thoughts → frustration → quit.

17.5.2 Practices That Work for Timekeeper

1. Body Scan (Shifting from Cognitive to Somatic)

How:

- Lie down or sit comfortably
- Systematically focus on body parts (feet → legs → torso → arms → head)
- Notice sensations without judgment (tingling, warmth, pressure, nothing)
- When mind wanders to thoughts, return to body sensations
- 10-30 minutes

Why this works:

- Gives Timekeeper something to track (body parts, sensations)
- Shifts from thinking (fast) to sensing (slower)
- Uses your speed (scan quickly through body) without fighting it

2. Noting Practice (Labeling Without Engaging)

How:

- Sit comfortably, eyes closed or soft gaze
- Notice whatever arises (thoughts, sensations, emotions)
- Label it: "thinking," "planning," "worrying," "hearing," "feeling"
- Don't engage with content: just label and move on
- Fast labeling okay (matches your processing speed)

Why this works:

- Uses your speed (label quickly, move on)
- Creates space between thought and engagement
- Metacognition (observing thoughts, not being thoughts)
- Timekeeper gets to be fast (but not stuck in content)

3. Counting Breath (Giving Mind Something to Do)

How:

- Count each exhale: 1, 2, 3… up to 10, then start over
- When you lose count, start at 1
- Simple, but not easy (requires sustained attention)

Why this works:

- Gives Timekeeper a task (counting)
- Simple enough to sustain
- Notice when mind wanders (lose count)
- Builds attention without forcing slowness

4. Walking Meditation (Movement Helps Fast Processors)

How:

- Walk slowly, deliberately
- Notice each step (heel, ball, toe)
- Notice body sensations (movement, balance, breath)
- When mind wanders, return to walking sensations

Why this works:

- Movement matches processing speed better than stillness
- Gives Timekeeper changing input (not static)
- Easier to sustain than sitting still
- Can be done anywhere

17.5.3 Neurofeedback Support for Timekeeper

SMR training builds calm alertness (not racing, not drowsy) and reduces beta spindles. Prepares brain for meditation by training the "calm but ready" state.

Alpha training shifts from beta (thinking) to alpha (resting), especially at right posterior sites for calming racing minds.

Result: After 20-40 sessions, meditation becomes easier. Your brain learns to downregulate without substances. See Chapter 18 for full protocols.

17.6 For Fog: Building Sustained Attention

Your challenge: Drowsiness, difficulty sustaining attention, "spacing out" during meditation.

17.6.1 Working with Drowsiness

First, distinguish:

- **Drowsiness from sleep debt** (you need sleep, not meditation, go to bed)
- **Drowsiness from meditation depth** (deep relaxation, theta state, this is okay)
- **Drowsiness from avoidance** (mind checking out to avoid discomfort, address this)

If it's sleep debt: Address sleep first (Chapter 13). Meditation won't work if you're chronically fatigued.

17.6.2 Practices That Work for Fog

1. Concentration Meditation (Building Sustained Attention)

How:

- Focus on single object (breath, mantra, candle flame)
- When mind wanders or drifts, gently return

- Start with 5 minutes, build to 20-30 minutes
- Consistency matters more than duration

Why this works:

- Builds attention "muscle" (sustained focus)
- Trains Fog to stay online
- Strengthens prefrontal cortex
- Improves executive function

2. Eyes-Open Meditation (Prevents Drowsiness)

How:

- Sit comfortably, eyes open with soft gaze
- Focus on point in front of you (wall, floor, candle)
- Notice when eyes want to close (drowsiness signal)
- Gently keep eyes open, soft focus

Why this works:

- Eyes open prevents sleep
- Visual input keeps brain more alert
- Still meditative (soft gaze, not active looking)

3. Walking Meditation (Movement Prevents Sleepiness)

How:

- Walk slowly, deliberately (indoor or outdoor)
- Notice each step, body sensations
- If drowsiness arises, walk slightly faster
- Can be done with eyes open (prevents sleep)

Why this works:

- Movement keeps brain alert
- Changing input prevents drift
- Can modulate speed (faster if drowsy, slower if alert)

4. Shorter Sessions (Build Gradually)

How:

- Start with 5 minutes (sustainable)
- Gradually increase (add 1 minute per week)
- Multiple short sessions better than one long (if drowsiness is issue)

Why this works:

- Builds capacity without overwhelming
- Success breeds motivation
- Fog needs gradual building (not forcing)

17.6.3 Neurofeedback Support for Fog

Beta enhancement (if excess theta):

- Increases alertness, reduces drowsiness
- Theta suppression protocols
- Improves sustained attention

Alpha peak frequency training (if slowed alpha, COMT genotype):

- Speeds up processing
- Different from theta suppression (see Chapter 11)
- Improves cognitive tempo

Result: Meditation becomes possible. Your brain can sustain attention without drifting into fog.

17.7 For Princess & Pea: Self-Compassion for RSD

Your challenge: Emotional overwhelm, rejection sensitivity, harsh self-criticism. Sitting with your emotions feels unbearable.

17.7.1 Why Compassion Practices Are Essential

The problem: Princess & Pea feels everything intensely, including self-judgment.

Meditation without compassion:

- Amplifies self-criticism ("I'm doing this wrong")
- Increases emotional overwhelm (too much awareness, not enough kindness)
- Triggers RSD (perceiving "failure" at meditation)

Meditation with compassion:

- Softens harsh self-judgment
- Creates emotional safety
- Allows feeling without drowning
- Builds resilience to rejection sensitivity

17.7.2 Practices That Work for Princess & Pea

1. Loving-Kindness Meditation (Metta)

How:

- Sit comfortably, eyes closed
- Silently repeat phrases:
  - "May I be happy"

  - "May I be healthy"
  - "May I be safe"
  - "May I be at ease"
- Feel the intention (not just words)
- Extend to loved ones, neutral people, difficult people, all beings
- 10-20 minutes

Why this works:

- Counters harsh self-criticism (common with RSD)
- Increases positive emotions
- Reduces amygdala reactivity (less emotional hijacking)
- Softens emotional reactivity over time

Research: Reduces negative emotions, self-criticism; enhances social connection, empathy.

2. RAIN Practice (Structured Emotional Processing)

How:

- **R**ecognize: "I'm feeling ______"
- **A**llow: "It's okay to feel this"
- **I**nvestigate: "Where do I feel this in my body? What triggered it?"
- **N**urture: "What do I need right now? What would I say to a friend?"

Why this works:

- Provides structure for overwhelming emotions
- Validates experience (not "shouldn't feel this")
- Somatic awareness (body sensations, not just thoughts)
- Self-compassion (nurture step)

3. Compassion Practices (Self-Directed Kindness)

How:

- Place hand on heart
- Speak to yourself as you would to a friend
- "This is hard. I'm doing my best. I'm worthy of kindness."
- Notice resistance to self-compassion (common with RSD)
- Practice anyway

Why this works:

- RSD creates harsh self-judgment
- Compassion is antidote
- Physical touch (hand on heart) activates soothing system
- Builds self-compassion "muscle"

4. Sensory-Friendly Environment (Non-Negotiable)

How:

- Comfortable temperature (not too hot/cold)
- Quiet space (or white noise if needed)
- Comfortable seating (cushion, chair, whatever works)
- No scratchy clothing, uncomfortable positions
- Dim lighting (not harsh)

Why this works:

- Sensory overwhelm prevents meditation
- Princess needs environmental control
- Not "high maintenance": sensory processing sensitivity
- Comfort allows focus on practice (not discomfort)

17.7.3 Neurofeedback Support for Princess & Pea

Right TPJ regulation reduces emotional reactivity while maintaining empathy. Reduces RSD (rejection sensitivity dysphoria).

Sensory gating protocols filter intensity, allow meditation without sensory overload.

Alpha training provides calming without numbing, emotional regulation that preserves depth.

Result: You can feel deeply without drowning. Meditation becomes safe, not overwhelming. See Chapter 18 for protocols.

17.8 For CEO: Letting Go of Control

Your challenge: Your CEO wants to direct, control, prioritize every thought. "Open awareness" feels impossible, you keep trying to manage the meditation.

17.8.1 Why CEO Struggles with Meditation

The problem: CEO's job is to monitor, direct, prioritize. Meditation asks CEO to stop doing its job.

What happens:

- You sit to meditate → CEO starts directing ("focus on breath, not that thought, prioritize this sensation")
- You try "open awareness" → CEO tries to control what you're aware of
- You get stuck on "am I doing this right?" (CEO monitoring performance)
- Irritability when interrupted (CEO hates disruption)

17.8.2 Practices That Work for CEO

1. Open Awareness (Letting Thoughts Come and Go)

How:

- Sit comfortably, eyes closed or soft gaze
- Don't focus on anything specific
- Notice whatever arises (thoughts, sensations, sounds)
- Don't direct attention: let it move naturally
- When CEO tries to control, notice that too ("controlling, controlling")

Why this works:

- Trains CEO to relax control
- Cognitive flexibility (not stuck on one thing)
- Metacognition (noticing the controlling itself)

2. Choiceless Awareness (Not Picking What to Focus On)

How:

- Similar to open awareness
- Explicitly: "I'm not choosing what to notice"
- Whatever is loudest/most prominent gets attention
- CEO doesn't decide: awareness decides

Why this works:

- Directly challenges CEO's need to prioritize
- Builds trust in natural attention (not forced)
- Reduces "stickiness" (not locked onto one thing)

3. Noting Practice (Labeling Without Directing)

How:

- Notice whatever arises
- Label it: "thinking," "feeling," "hearing," "controlling"
- Don't engage: just label and move on
- Fast labeling okay (CEO likes activity)

Why this works:

- Gives CEO something to do (labeling)
- But not controlling content (just observing)
- Creates space between experience and reaction

4. Non-Directive Meditation (Allowing Mind to Wander)

How:

- Sit comfortably
- Allow mind to wander freely

- When you notice you're thinking, gently return to breath (or body, or nothing)
- Don't try to control where mind goes

Why this works:

- CEO learns it's okay to not direct
- Mind-wandering isn't "failure"
- Builds flexibility (letting go when stuck)

17.8.3 Neurofeedback Support for CEO

Anterior cingulate flexibility training:

- Reduces "stickiness"
- Improves task-switching
- Allows sustained attention when needed, flexibility when needed

Alpha-Theta (advanced):

- Deep relaxation (CEO offline)
- Creativity, insight
- Integration of unconscious material

Result: CEO learns to conduct (not micromanage). Meditation becomes spacious, not controlling.

17.9 For Interpreter (Linguist): Quieting the Narrator

Your challenge: You can't experience without narrating. Internal monologue never stops. "They talk too much", even to themselves.

Note: If your Interpreter runs in 24/7 narrator mode (the "Linguist" flavor of this phenotype) then this section is for you. This is about the constant verbal processing that can make meditation feel impossible.

17.9.1 Why Interpreter (Linguist) Struggles with Meditation

The problem: Your left language network externalizes (or internalizes) all processing verbally.

What happens:

- You sit to meditate → internal narrator starts: "I'm meditating now. Is this right? What should I focus on? This reminds me of..."
- You try to quiet mind → narrator describes the attempt: "I'm trying to quiet my mind. It's not working. Why is this so hard?"
- You can't know what you think until you narrate what you think

17.9.2 Practices That Work for Interpreter (Linguist)

1. Silent Retreats (Learning to Exist Without Narrating)

How:

- Attend silent meditation retreat (1 day to 10 days)
- No talking, reading, writing, eye contact
- Just sitting, walking, eating in silence
- Forces internal quiet (no external verbal input)

Why this works:

- Removes external language stimulation
- Left hemisphere quiets (no verbal processing needed)
- Right hemisphere activates (non-verbal awareness)
- Reveals how much you narrate (awareness is first step)

Caution: Start with 1-day retreat (not 10 days immediately). Can be intense for your Interpreter.

2. Non-Verbal Practices (Movement, Art, Music)

How:

- **Movement meditation:** Yoga, tai chi, qigong, walking
- **Art meditation:** Drawing, painting, sculpting (no words)
- **Music meditation:** Playing instrument, listening deeply (no analyzing)
- Focus on direct experience (not verbal description)

Why this works:

- Activates right hemisphere (non-verbal processing)
- Reduces left hemisphere dominance
- Direct experience (not mediated by language)
- Embodiment (not just thinking)

3. Body Scan (Shifting from Language to Sensation)

How:

- Systematically focus on body parts
- Notice sensations (not describe them verbally)
- When narrator starts ("this is tingling, that's tension"), notice and return to sensation
- Non-verbal awareness

Why this works:

- Somatic focus (body, not language)
- Interrupts narration habit
- Builds interoception (body awareness)

4. Mantra Meditation (Replacing Narration with Single Sound)

How:

- Choose simple mantra ("om," "peace," "one," or meaningless sound)
- Repeat silently
- When narrator starts complex thoughts, return to mantra
- Mantra is simple (not narrative)

Why this works:

- Gives language center something to do (mantra)
- But not complex narration (just one word / sound)
- Occupies Interpreter without feeding narration habit

17.9.3 Neurofeedback Support for Interpreter (Linguist)

Right hemisphere activation:

- Balances left language dominance
- Enhances non-verbal processing
- Interhemispheric integration

Reducing left frontal language hyperactivation:

- Quiets internal narrator
- Allows non-verbal experience

Result: You can experience life without constant narration. Meditation becomes direct, not mediated by language.

17.10 For Grumpy Old Man: Softening Effort-Dread

Your challenge: Catastrophizing, "what if" loops, anxiety during meditation. Sitting quietly amplifies future-threat prediction and resistance.

17.10.1 Practices That Work for Grumpy Old Man

1. Loving-Kindness Meditation (Self-Compassion)

How:

- Direct compassion toward self first (not others)
- "May I be safe. May I be peaceful. May I be free from suffering."
- Notice resistance ("I don't deserve this")
- Practice anyway

Why this works:

- Counters harsh self-judgment
- Softens catastrophizing

- Activates soothing system (not threat system)
- Reduces amygdala reactivity

2. Breath-Focused Meditation (Anchoring in Present)

How:

- Focus on breath (not controlling it, just noticing)
- When catastrophizing starts ("what if..."), return to breath
- Breath is present-moment anchor (not future threat)

Why this works:

- Interrupts rumination loops
- Anchors in present (not future catastrophes)
- Simple, accessible (breath always available)

3. Body Scan (Shifting from Thoughts to Sensations)

Why this works:

- Catastrophizing is cognitive (thoughts about future)
- Body scan is somatic (sensations in present)
- Shifts attention from threat simulation to body awareness

4. MBSR (Structured 8-Week Program)

What it is:

- Mindfulness-Based Stress Reduction (Jon Kabat-Zinn)
- 8 weeks, structured curriculum
- Combines sitting meditation, body scan, yoga
- Evidence-based for anxiety reduction

Why this works:

- Structure (CEO likes structure)
- Evidence-based (Grumpy Old Man trusts research)
- Gradual building (not overwhelming)
- Group support (not alone)

17.10.2 Neurofeedback Support for Grumpy Old Man

Right frontal alpha training calms anxiety, reduces catastrophizing, builds natural relaxation capacity.

Amygdala regulation reduces threat reactivity, improves emotional regulation.

Alpha-Theta (advanced) accesses deep relaxation states, processes trauma when applicable.

Result: Catastrophizing quiets. Meditation becomes calming, not anxiety-provoking. See Chapter 18 for protocols.

17.11 For Happy Little Kid (Approach System): Maintaining Interest

Your challenge: Meditation feels boring. Novelty wears off. Can't sustain practice. "I'll try this new technique!" (then abandon it).

17.11.1 Practices That Work for Happy Little Kid

1. Variety of Techniques (Satisfying Novelty-Seeking)

How:

- Rotate practices (breath focus Monday, body scan Tuesday, loving-kindness Wednesday, etc.)
- Explore different traditions (Zen, Vipassana, TM, MBSR)
- Try apps, teachers, styles
- Novelty within structure (same time daily, different technique)

Why this works:

- Satisfies novelty-seeking
- Prevents boredom
- Maintains interest
- Still builds meditation capacity (even with variety)

2. Walking Meditation (Movement, Changing Scenery)

Why this works:

- Movement satisfies restlessness
- Changing scenery provides novelty
- Can explore new routes (novelty)
- Easier to sustain than sitting still

3. Guided Meditations (External Structure, Variety)

Why this works:

- Teacher's voice provides structure
- Different teachers, styles provide novelty
- Apps offer hundreds of options (Headspace, Calm, Insight Timer)
- Less boring than silent sitting

4. Group Meditation (Social Element, Accountability)

Why this works:

- Social motivation (Happy Little Kid likes people, connection)
- Accountability (less likely to skip)
- Variety (different people, discussions)
- Community (connection)

5. Meditation Challenges (Gamification)

Why this works:

- Goals (30-day challenge, 100-day challenge)
- Dopamine from achievement
- Tracking progress (your approach system likes metrics)
- Completion satisfaction

17.11.2 Neurofeedback Support for Happy Little Kid

Left frontal training:

- Sustaining attention (not just initiating)
- Project completion capacity
- Impulse control (staying with practice)

Reward pathway optimization:

- Finding satisfaction in sustained practice
- Not just novelty dopamine

Result: You can sustain meditation practice. Novelty-seeking channeled into exploration of depth (not just breadth).

17.12 Neurofeedback-Enhanced Meditation

The synergy: Ancient wisdom meets modern technology.

17.12.1 Alpha-Theta Protocol (Deep States, Creativity, Integration)

What it is:

- Neurofeedback training to increase both alpha (resting/calming) and theta (deep relaxation) rhythms
- Promotes deep relaxation, meditation-like states
- Eyes closed, 20-30 minute sessions
- Often done lying down or reclining

Brain effects:

- Accesses deep meditative states faster
- Enhances creativity, insight
- Reduces anxiety, trauma symptoms
- Promotes integration of unconscious material
- Ego dissolution (similar to psychedelics, but controlled)

My protocol progression:

1. **Start with SMR** (regulate sleep and attention first)

2. **Move into Alpha-Theta** after sleep/executive function responding well
3. **Start with posterior midline** training approaches
4. **Evaluate bilateral posterior** approaches
5. **Determine which brain regions/combinations most impactful for your specific pattern**
6. **Combine Alpha-Theta and SMR in sequences**

Best for:

- Advanced meditators (already have attention control)
- Trauma processing (with clinical support)
- Creativity enhancement
- Deep relaxation states
- Lifeguard (trauma, threat sensitivity, also deep awareness and insight)

Cautions:

- Not for beginners (need attention control first: SMR foundation)
- Can surface unconscious material (need clinical support)
- Start slowly, allow time to adjust to new feedback loop
- Work with trained professional

Research evidence:

- Gruzelier (2009, 2014): Has shown, in small controlled studies, enhancement of aspects of creative performance and artistic expression with alpha/theta training
- Brandmeyer & Delorme (2013): Faster access to deep meditative states
- Garrison et al. (2013): Enhanced self-awareness, metacognition

---

17.12.2 SMR Protocol (Calm Alertness, Sleep, Attention)

What it is:

- Neurofeedback training to increase SMR (sensorimotor rhythm) at the sensorimotor cortex
- Promotes "calm but ready" state: like a cat watching birds on a windowsill
- Foundation protocol for meditation practitioners

Brain effects:

- Improves sleep quality and attention without tension
- Reduces anxiety, hyperarousal, beta spindles
- Prepares brain for meditation by training sustained calm alertness

Best for:

- Sleep issues, anxiety with hyperarousal, attention difficulties
- Foundation before advancing to Alpha-Theta training

Timeline: 20-40 sessions for lasting changes, often combined with meditation practice.

Research: Hoedlmoser et al. (2008) for sleep, Hammond (2005) for anxiety, Gruzelier (2014) for attention.

See Chapter 18 for detailed protocol, electrode placements, and session progressions.

17.12.3 Combining Neurofeedback and Meditation (Synergistic Effects)

My approach:

1. **Establish foundations** (sleep, stress, basic health, Chapter 13, Chapter 15)
2. **Begin meditation practice** (traditional techniques, build attention)
3. **Add neurofeedback** (SMR first, regulate sleep/attention)
4. **Integrate** (meditate during/after neurofeedback sessions)
5. **Advanced** (Alpha-Theta for deep states, creativity, trauma work)

Synergistic effects:

- **Faster access to deep states** (Brandmeyer & Delorme, 2013)
- **Improved sustained focus** (Van Lutterveld et al., 2017)
- **Enhanced self-awareness** (Garrison et al., 2013)
- **Accelerated personal growth** (state practice builds trait resources faster)

Why this works:

- Neurofeedback trains brain patterns that support meditation
- Meditation enhances neurofeedback effectiveness
- Each amplifies the other
- Faster progress than either alone

17.13 The Substance Parallel: Externally-Induced vs. Internally-Generated States

Many poet-brains have discovered that **cannabis and psychedelics can create meditative states.** This is true. These substances access real states (CEO quieting, ego dissolution, DMN shifts, enhanced pattern recognition) similar to what advanced meditators achieve.

Cannabis creates:

- Present-moment awareness (CEO stops task-switching)
- Introspection and creativity (DMN activation)
- Reduced catastrophizing and resistance (Grumpy Old Man quiets)
- Softened sensory overwhelm (Princess calms)

Psychedelics create:

- Cognitive flexibility (rigid patterns dissolve)
- Associative thinking and insight
- Ego dissolution (like advanced meditation states)
- New perspectives (DMN disruption)

These effects are real, not placebo. Substances can create states that meditators spend years learning to access.

17.13.1 But: Borrowed States vs. Built Capacity

The key difference: Substances give you the state. Meditation teaches you to generate it.

Externally-induced (substances):

- Temporary (hours, then return to baseline)
- Tolerance builds (need more for same effect)
- Dependence develops (need substance to access state)
- Don't build capacity (borrowed, not trained)

Internally-generated (meditation):

- Sustainable (skill doesn't fade)
- Gets easier with practice (no tolerance)
- Voluntary access (no substance needed)
- Builds lasting capacity (repeated practice strengthens trait resources over time)

17.13.2 What Meditation Builds That Substances Can't

Voluntary access on demand: You can enter calm, presence, or insight states in any context (work meetings, difficult conversations, challenges) without needing a substance.

Skill that transfers: The attention, flexibility, and regulation you build in meditation practice transfers to daily life. It's not just "meditation time", it becomes how your brain operates.

Structural brain changes: Gray matter increases, cortical thickening, lasting personality shifts (more compassion, less reactivity). Not temporary chemical states, durable structural change.

The parallel paths:

- Cannabis quiets CEO → Meditation trains CEO flexibility
- Psychedelics dissolve patterns → Meditation builds cognitive flexibility

- Substances create presence → Meditation builds capacity for presence
- Substances are borrowed access → Meditation is owned skill

See Chapter 14 for substance patterns, why borrowed states fail long-term, and neurofeedback as precision alternative.

17.14 Meditation for Addiction Recovery: Surfing Cravings

If you're in recovery or reducing substance use, meditation becomes a practical tool for the moment craving hits.

17.14.1 The Three Essential Anchors

Feeling Tone, External (Body Scan for Urge Surfing):

- **What:** Notice somatic sensations of craving itself
- **Where:** Chest, jaw, stomach: wherever you feel it physically
- **Practice:** Watch sensations change without reacting
- Cravings peak and pass in 20-30 minutes whether you use or not
- You're riding the wave, not being swept under

Present Time Attention (SOBER for Impulse Control):

- **What:** Anchor in present moment without engaging with urge
- **Practice:** Watch breath, thoughts, sensations arise and pass
- Creates pause between urge and action
- Space where prefrontal cortex can engage instead of amygdala
- Observing without reacting is the practice

Feeling Tone, Internal (Compassion for Shame):

- **What:** Generate internal state of compassion toward self
- **Practice:** Cultivate warmth, kindness, acceptance (especially when struggling)
- Shame drives use; self-compassion (internal feeling tone) breaks the cycle
- "This is hard. I'm struggling. I deserve kindness."

17.14.2 Why This Works

You're training the same circuits neurofeedback targets:

- **Prefrontal cortex** strengthens (executive control: pause between urge and action)
- **Amygdala** calms (emotional regulation: less hijacking)

- **Insula** enhances (interoception: notice cravings as sensations, not commands)
- **New pathways** form (urge → observe, not urge → use)

The integration: Neurofeedback trains baseline regulation. Meditation gives you a tool for the crisis moment. Sleep optimization (Chapter 13) repairs what substances damaged. Together: complete recovery.

See Chapter 14 for Mindfulness-Based Relapse Prevention (MBRP) research, evidence, and how meditation integrates with neurofeedback for addiction.

17.15 Practical Implementation: Starting Your Practice

My Basic Meditation Practice (20 Minutes)

Setup:

- Morning, after sun salutations, before coffee
- Sit upright, comfortably balanced, eyes closed
- Use timer app (Insight Timer): 3 bells at start, 1 bell at 5 min, 3 bells at end

Minutes 1-5: Single Point Awareness (Samatha)

- Focus on breath sensation at upper lip (air crossing as you breathe)
- When mind wanders (it will), gently return to that spot
- This is the practice: noticing distraction, returning to breath

Minutes 6-20: Present Time Awareness (Vipassana)

- Shift to breath rising/falling in belly and body
- "When breathing in, know you are breathing in"
- When mind wanders, return to breath sensation
- Optional: Note feeling-tone (comfortable, anxious, calm) or thought-type (planning, remembering), then return

The key: Noticing and redirecting IS the practice (not "having blank mind")

Consistency beats duration: Daily 5 minutes > weekly 60 minutes

For variety: Try noting/labeling (acknowledges distraction briefly, returns to breath)

17.15.1 Choosing Practice for Your Phenotype:

- **Grumpy Old Man** → Loving-kindness, breath-focused, body scan
- **CEO** → Open awareness, noting, non-directive
- **Happy Little Kid** → Variety, walking, guided, group practice
- **Lifeguard** → Body scan, grounding, present-moment
- **Princess & Pea** → Compassion, RAIN, sensory-friendly environment
- **Interpreter** → Silent practice, non-verbal, body scan
- **Timekeeper (racing)** → Slowing practices, body scan, counting
- **Fog** → Concentration, eyes-open, walking, shorter sessions

---

17.16 Resources

Standard resources (apps, books, MBSR programs) are widely available, Insight Timer is free with thousands of guided practices, *Altered Traits* by Goleman & Davidson covers the neuroscience, local MBSR programs offer 8-week structured training.

For EEG-informed meditation:

Clinics offering neurofeedback-enhanced meditation use QEEG assessment to identify your phenotypes, then create protocols targeting your specific circuits (SMR for calm focus, Alpha-Theta for deep states). Some offer free weekly mindfulness groups (in-person and online) plus personalized meditation protocols.

Contact & current options:
peakbraininstitute.com | andrewhillphd.com

17.17 The Promise

Meditation isn't about emptying your mind. (Impossible for poet-brains.)

Meditation is about changing your relationship to thoughts.

Your CEO learns to let go (not control every thought).
Your Grumpy Old Man learns to soften (not generate futility predictions for every scenario).
Your Timekeeper learns to slow (not race constantly).
Your Interpreter learns to be (not narrate constantly).
Your Princess learns to feel (without drowning).

The presence, calm, and insight you've been trying to access with cannabis or psychedelics, meditation builds the capacity to access them voluntarily, sustainably, without borrowing from tomorrow.

You can train your brain to access these states on demand. No substances required.

If you only do one thing from this chapter: Pick *one* meditation style that matches your phenotype (see the guide above), do 5 minutes a day for 30 days, and ignore everything else.

17.18 Key Takeaways

Meditation is not about emptying your mind, it's about training your relationship with your phenotypes. Different practices train different circuits using four attention qualities: Single Point, Present Time, Feeling Tone Internal, Feeling Tone External.

- **Four attention qualities:** Single Point (absorption), Present Time (observation without reaction), Feeling Tone Internal (emotional states like compassion), Feeling Tone External (somatic awareness). All meditation uses combinations of these.
- **Phenotype-specific matching:** Grumpy Old Man → loving-kindness. CEO → Present Time (letting go). Lifeguard → body scan. Princess & Pea → self-compassion. Stabilizer → Single Point.
- **Foundation first:** Meditation works best on decent sleep and managed stress, don't try to meditate your way out of sleep deprivation.
- **Neurofeedback-enhanced meditation:** Alpha-theta accelerates deep states. SMR builds attention platform. Neurofeedback trains baseline, meditation gives moment-to-moment tools.
- **Start small:** 5-10 minutes daily beats 60 minutes weekly. Consistency matters more than duration.

17.19 Reader Reflections

Take a moment to consider your own meditation practice (or potential practice):

1. **Which phenotype-specific practice matches your current struggle?** Feeling Tone, Internal (loving-kindness for Grumpy Old Man dread, compassion for Princess & Pea RSD)? Present Time (open awareness for CEO stickiness)? Feeling Tone, External (body scan for Lifeguard threat sensitivity)? Single Point (absorption training for Stabilizer)?
2. **What's been your experience with meditation (if you've tried)?** Did it help or make things worse? Can you trace the outcome to whether the practice type (Single Point, Present Time, Feeling Tone) matched your phenotype needs?

3. **What's your biggest obstacle to starting or sustaining practice?** Falling asleep (Fog/Stabilizer issue)? Amplifying anxiety (wrong practice for Grumpy Old Man)? Boredom (Happy Little Kid needs engagement)? Can't focus (weak Supervisor/Stabilizer)? How could you address that specific phenotype obstacle?
4. **What would 30 days of consistent practice look like?** 5-10 minutes every morning? Body scan when anxious? What's small enough to actually do, specific enough to track? Consistency beats duration.

Ch 18: Neurofeedback: Individualized Training

Soothe the Tortured, Sharpen the Gifted

If you've done the work in Chapters 13–17 (sleep, stress regulation, productivity, meditation), you've already been training your circuits. Neurofeedback is the precision accelerator. It is not the prerequisite.

I've been doing this for decades. Mapping brains, training brains, watching people transform their nervous systems one session at a time. I've run hundreds of thousands of neurofeedback sessions in clinical settings. I've watched anxious, scattered, tortured poet-brains learn to regulate themselves, not through willpower, not through substances, but through practice.

And here's what I know: **neurofeedback isn't magic. It's practice.**

You're teaching your brain new rhythms, new patterns, new ways of being. The calm you've been trying to steal with alcohol? We can train your right frontal cortex to generate it. The focus you've been borrowing from stimulants? We can strengthen your Supervisor. The quiet you could never find? We can teach your CEO to let go.

Neurofeedback is how you train lasting changes in underlying rhythms instead of borrowing new ones from chemicals.

An honest note on limitations: Neurofeedback requires 20-40+ sessions, typically costs $100-200 per session, and most insurance doesn't cover it. Not everyone can afford it. Not everyone has access to a QEEG-trained provider. The research base is growing but uneven: strong evidence for ADHD and epilepsy, promising for anxiety and insomnia, still limited for some other conditions. Some practitioners use outdated or one-size-fits-all protocols without QEEG guidance, which wastes time and money. If you pursue neurofeedback, find a provider who does quantitative EEG assessment first, uses individualized protocols, and adjusts based on your response. If cost or access is a barrier, every other tool in Part II still works. Neurofeedback accelerates the process, but sleep, stress regulation, meditation, and behavioral strategies build real change on their own.

18.1 A Story: Sterman's Cats and the Discovery of SMR

Before we dive into protocols, let me tell you how neurofeedback was discovered. It's a story about cats, chicken broth, and rocket fuel.

The year: 1967. The scientist: Dr. Barry Sterman.

Dr. Sterman was testing the dangers of rocket fuel (methylhydrazine) to establish safety parameters for astronauts. Being the 1960s, animal research was more widespread, and he exposed a group of cats to the toxin.

One subset of cats proved seizure resistant. They shrugged off the impacts of the toxin while other cats had seizures.

Why?

It turned out this group had participated in a much more pleasant experiment several months earlier. They'd been rewarded (with a squirt of chicken broth) whenever they made a certain brain wave that cats naturally produce.

This brain wave: SMR (Sensorimotor Rhythm), a specific frequency band in the brain.

What SMR does:

- Lets you sit still while staying alert
- Supports both sleep quality and focused learning
- Provides seizure resistance through increased inhibitory tone
- Builds voluntary control over automatic systems
- Creates the brain's natural "idle gear"

The metaphor: Cats use SMR to sit perfectly still on the windowsill watching birds, calm, focused, ready to act but not acting.

The clinical insight: Being able to make SMR robustly makes brains seizure resistant. And it helps with ADHD (sitting still while focusing = literally opposite of ADHD).

This accidental discovery launched the field of neurofeedback.

Citation: Sterman, M. B., & Fairchild, M. D. (1967). Subconvulsive effects of 1,1 dimethylhydrazine on locomotor performance on the cat. *Defense Technical Information Center*. https://doi.org/10.21236/AD0664549

Why this matters for you:

- SMR is foundational protocol (sleep, attention, calm focus)
- Neurofeedback has 50+ years of research: well-established for ADHD and anxiety, with growing evidence across other conditions
- The same training that made cats seizure-resistant helps poet-brains regulate

---

18.2 What Is Neurofeedback?

Neurofeedback is training your brain to self-regulate through real-time feedback on brain wave activity.

The process:

- Sensors on your scalp detect your brain's electrical activity
- Computer analyzes activity in real-time
- Feedback provided via video game or music (plays smoothly when you produce desired patterns, pauses when you don't)
- Your brain learns through operant conditioning (unconscious learning, you don't have to "try")
- 20-40 sessions, 2-4 times/week, changes build through neuroplasticity

Not "zapping": You're receiving information about your brain state, not electrical stimulation. Your brain learns to self-regulate based on feedback.

18.3 A Client Story: Sarah (Anxiety → Calm)

Composite, like every case in this book. The pattern is one I have seen many times; the person is not one person.

Sarah, 34, entrepreneur. Came in after "trying everything", therapy, SSRIs, benzos, alcohol. Waking at 3am catastrophizing about her business. Couldn't function without wine at night. Convinced nothing would help.

Her brain map: Right frontal hyperactivation (Grumpy Old Man dominant), posterior cingulate elevated (Lifeguard stuck ON), LVF pattern (GABAA genetics, family history of alcoholism confirmed).

Protocol: Right frontal calming, posterior midline regulation. Pair with MBRP (Ch 14), sleep (Ch 13), loving-kindness meditation (Ch 17). 40 sessions over 5 months.

What changed: "I didn't know I could wake up without dread. The catastrophizing voice is still there, but it's not screaming anymore. I can hear it, evaluate it, and let it go. Wine is optional now, not necessary. I didn't think this was possible."

QEEG after: Right frontal activity normalized (less catastrophizing), frontal asymmetry more balanced (Happy Little Kid came online), sleep spindles up. Her Grumpy Old Man learned to stand down. Her Lifeguard learned present moment is safe.

18.4 What QEEG-Guided Neurofeedback Looks Like in Practice

18.4.1 Training Toward Your Goals, Not Population Averages

Core principle: The best neurofeedback doesn't train you to be average. It trains you toward YOUR goals.

What this means:

- QEEG shows what's unusual for you (compared to population)
- But unusual isn't always "bad" (might be your gifts)
- Your brain patterns are hints about how your resources function
- Train toward YOUR goals (not population norms)

Example:

- High beta might be problem (anxiety, racing thoughts: Timekeeper)
- OR high beta might be gift (fast processing, quick thinking)
- Context matters (what are your goals? what's causing problems?)

The approach with individualized, QEEG-guided protocols:

1. **QEEG-guided** (start with brain map, understand unique patterns)
2. **Goal-oriented** (what do YOU want to change?)
3. **Individualized protocols** (tailored to phenotype, not one-size-fits-all)
4. **Iterative** (adjust based on feedback, re-assess every 20-25 sessions)
5. **Gentle, gradual** (1-4 channel training, changes build over time)
6. **Integrated** (mindfulness coaching, lifestyle support, team collaboration)

What to look for in a provider:

Good signs:

- Starts with QEEG assessment (brain map before training)
- Asks about YOUR goals, not just symptoms
- Individualized protocols based on your brain patterns
- Adjusts protocols based on your feedback
- Integrates with lifestyle, therapy, other supports

Red flags:

- Automated protocol selection (computer chooses for you without clinical input)
- One-size-fits-all approach (everyone gets same training)
- Z-score training as primary method (training "to" databases in real-time, pushes you toward average)
- Promises fast results ("cured in 10 sessions")
- Dismisses side effects ("push through it")

18.5 From Brain Map to Protocol: How It Works

The assessment combines three sources:

1. QEEG Brain Mapping. Sensors record your brain's electrical activity. You get visual maps showing patterns and comparison to population norms.

2. Behavioral Testing. Performance tests measure attention, impulsivity, consistency.

3. Clinical Context. Your symptoms, history, goals, what's worked or hasn't.

From data to protocols:
We map your brain patterns to your phenotype constellation. Your phenotypes help predict which protocols may work best. Protocols are iterative, we adjust based on your response.

18.6 What to Expect: The Neurofeedback Journey

What a session looks like: 5 minutes setup, 20-30 minutes training (you watch feedback while your brain learns), 5 minutes wrap-up. Your job? Pay attention to the feedback. Your brain does the learning unconsciously.

The typical arc (20-40 sessions over 3-6 months):

Early sessions (1-10): Your brain is learning what gets rewarded. Effects are subtle: gentle calming, focusing, or activation that lasts a few hours. Sleep often improves first (within 2-4 sessions). Tell your provider what you notice. If something feels wrong (too sleepy, too wired, sleep disrupted), speak up immediately. Protocols can be adjusted.

Building phase (10-30): Changes become more consistent. You notice shifts in daily life, less reactive, better focus, improved sleep. Many people describe it as **"someone cleaned the windshield"**: the world feels clearer, brighter, higher-contrast. Information lands without fight. You're working less hard to think. Mid-course re-assessment (QEEG + behavioral tests) shows objective progress and guides protocol adjustments.

Integration (30-40+): Trait regulation becomes baseline. Changes often continue after training ends (neuroplasticity momentum). Your traits have range now, not stuck. Maintenance sessions (monthly or quarterly) if desired, or graduate.

18.6.1 What Progress Actually Looks Like

Progress isn't "pattern disappears." It's "pattern still there, but doesn't take over as quickly."

You'll know it's working when you're in a situation that used to wreck you, and you're fine. Same setting, different response. You might think, "Wait, how did I live with all that stress all the time?" The recognition comes retrospectively, not in the moment.

The brittleness softens: Reactivity drops. Tension releases into flexible resilience. Obsessive mode still exists, but you can work with it instead of being controlled by it. You have range of motion, engage the pattern when useful, release it when not. Not sedation, not elimination: regulation.

18.6.2 Individual Variation: Some Brains Are "Stubborn"

Not everyone responds at the same rate. **Some people are "stubborn at responding"**, slower to show changes on QEEG even when noticing subjective improvements. This is individual variation, not treatment failure.

If maps aren't changing but you're noticing differences:

- Trust your experience
- Maps may lag behind subjective improvements
- Keep training for now, but revisit the protocol if maps and experience still diverge after 20+ sessions. The map often catches up; if it does not, that is information worth acting on, not failure
- Mid-course protocol adjustments can help

Don't judge only by maps:

- Your lived experience matters more than map changes
- Especially with kids: "long-tail effects" continue unfolding for weeks or months after training stops
- Retrospective clarity: "It was crystal clear looking back, even though we weren't sure in real time"
- Developing brains have neuroplasticity momentum: changes continue after training ends

This is common and normal. Some brains need 40+ sessions to show map changes that others show in 20. Some people feel changes immediately that don't show on maps until months later. Keep going.

Timeline: Notice changes by 20 sessions. Lasting changes by 40 sessions. Deep transformation for complex issues (addiction, trauma, severe patterns) may take 60+ sessions.

18.7 Side Effects: What's Normal, What's Not

Normal (desired): Gentle calming, focusing, or activation that lasts a few hours after session. These are good signs, your brain is responding to training.

Unwanted (adjust protocol): Too sleepy, too wired, sleep disrupted, mood worsened, headaches. These mean the protocol needs adjustment, wrong direction, too much, or wrong sites.

What to do: Tell your provider immediately. Don't "push through." Think of it like working out with wrong form. Effects wear off within a day or two if you stop reinforcing them. Finding the right protocol is part of the process. Gentle, gradual, iterative, not forcing.

18.8 The Foundation: Three Models Working Together

Neurofeedback protocols combine three levels:

1. Arousal (too fast vs. too slow): Under-aroused (Stabilizer, Fog) → wake up. Over-aroused (Grumpy, Lifeguard, Timekeeper) → calm down.

2. Laterality (left approach vs. right withdrawal): Left activation = approach/joy. Right activation = withdrawal/anxiety.

3. Phenotypes (which specific circuit): Target the 12 phenotypes from Part I. Not just "calm the brain" but "reduce the Grumpy Old Man's effort-dread" or "wake the Stabilizer's motor engagement."

Integration example: Anxiety + Depression = Over-aroused + right > left asymmetry + Grumpy hyperactive + Happy Little Kid offline → train right frontal calming AND left frontal activation.

18.8.1 How Phenotypes Map to Protocols

Your phenotypes help predict which protocols may work best (Arns et al., 2008; Johnstone et al., 2005). Four core patterns have strongest treatment prediction:

1. **Frontal Slow** (Stabilizer), predicts stimulant response, reduce slow waves
2. **Low Voltage Fast** (Grumpy Old Man), predicts GABAergic response, calming training
3. **Beta Spindles** (Timekeeper, Grumpy), predicts anxiety, SMR to calm racing
4. **Slowed Alpha** (Fog), predicts stimulant nonresponse, speed up rhythm

---

18.9 How to Read This Chapter

Quick overview? Read through "What to Expect", you'll understand the process and timeline.

Considering neurofeedback? Read everything through "Protocols by Phenotype", you'll see how it maps to your brain.

Clinician or super-nerd? Read it all, this chapter includes protocol details. For technical implementation, consult a QEEG-trained practitioner.

You can't read this chapter "wrong." Take what serves you.

18.10 Protocols by Phenotype: What We Train

For lay readers: The descriptions below show how neurofeedback targets specific circuits. The key insight: precision, not generic "brain training." Your phenotype determines your protocol.

For clinicians/practitioners: The descriptions below show which brain regions and patterns are targeted for each phenotype. For complete technical implementation details, consult BCIA certification materials or QEEG training courses.

Here's what neurofeedback looks like for each of the twelve phenotypes. These are starting points, your specific protocol will be individualized based on your QEEG, goals, and response.

If several of these sound like you, that's normal. Most people have 3-5 active phenotypes. The brain map and your goals determine which we train first, in what order, and how protocols layer together over time.

18.10.1 Happy Little Kid (Left DLPFC) - Activating Approach

When to train: Depression, anhedonia, lack of motivation, can't engage with life

What we train: Left frontal activation, the approach motivation circuit

What this does: Strengthens your brain's natural capacity for engagement, increases positive affect, builds the ability to feel motivated and interested in life

Timeline: 20-40 sessions. Early changes: easier mornings, things feel more interesting. Consolidation: sustained motivation without needing constant external intensity.

18.10.2 Grumpy Old Man (Right DLPFC) - Reducing Effort-Dread

When to train: Anxiety, catastrophizing, RSD, can't turn off worry

What we train: Right frontal calming, the circuit that generates relaxation and reduces threat assessment

What this does: Builds natural calm your brain can access on demand, reduces constant threat assessment, softens catastrophizing while preserving your protective wisdom

Timeline: 30-40 sessions (anxiety patterns take longer to retrain). Early changes: less reactive to triggers, better sleep. Consolidation: baseline sense of calm, reduced need for substances to manage anxiety.

18.10.3 Problem Child (Right IFG) - Strengthening the Brake

When to train: Anger without brakes, oppositionality, impulsive aggression

What we train: Right frontal inhibition circuits, the brake system that stops reactions, plus the underlying threat circuits fueling the intensity

What this does: Strengthens your brain's ability to pause before reacting, regulates anger intensity, maintains healthy assertiveness without explosive episodes

Timeline: 40-60 sessions (this is complex training, addressing both the brake system and the underlying threat activation takes time)

18.10.4 CEO (Anterior Cingulate) - Training Flexibility

When to train: Stuck on wrong thing, can't let go, OCD-like loops, inflexibility

What we train: Frontal midline flexibility, the circuit that decides what to focus on and when to let go

What this does: Builds your brain's ability to shift attention when needed, reduces getting stuck in mental loops, maintains focus when appropriate without perseverating when it's time to move on

Timeline: 30-40 sessions. Early changes: easier switching between tasks, less rumination. Consolidation: can genuinely let go of unresolved conflicts without obsessing.

18.10.5 Lifeguard (Posterior Cingulate) - Calming the Scanner

When to train: Hypervigilance, rumination, PTSD, can't stop scanning for threats

What we train: Posterior midline regulation, the circuit constantly monitoring your environment and internal state for potential threats

What this does: Reduces constant environmental scanning, softens rumination loops, maintains healthy awareness without exhausting hypervigilance

Timeline: 40-60 sessions (trauma-related patterns require more time to retrain)

18.10.6 Princess & Pea (Right TPJ) - Regulating the Gain

When to train: RSD, sensory overwhelm, emotional flooding, processing everything at volume 11

What we train: Right temporal-parietal regulation, the circuit that sets the gain on sensory and emotional input

What this does: Regulates how intensely you experience input from the world, maintains your deep empathy without overwhelming flood, reduces rejection sensitivity intensity

Timeline: 30-40 sessions

18.10.7 Stabilizer (Sensorimotor Cortex) - Waking the Engine

When to train: Task initiation paralysis, can't start tasks, Frontal Slow pattern

What we train: Left motor planning regions, the circuit that initiates action and sustains engagement. Also sensorimotor rhythm training for attention and sleep.

What this does: Builds your brain's natural activation capacity, improves ability to start tasks, enhances sleep architecture as a foundation

Timeline: 40-60 sessions. Early changes: easier mornings, can actually start tasks. Consolidation: sustainable activation without needing stimulants.

18.10.8 Supervisor (Low Beta/SMR) - Calibrating the Brake

When to train: Impulsivity (too weak) or perfectionism (too strong), can't balance quality control

What we train: Right sensorimotor region, the circuit that provides inhibitory control and quality checking. Training differs if your Supervisor is too weak (impulsive) or too strong (perfectionist paralysis).

What this does: Builds balanced inhibition capacity, maintains healthy quality control without perfectionist paralysis

Timeline: 30-40 sessions

18.10.9 Timekeeper (Alpha Frequency) - Calibrating Processing Speed

When to train: Racing thoughts/anxiety (too fast) OR cognitive slowing/laggy processing (too slow)

What we train: For racing: Calming rhythms in posterior or frontal midline regions, plus sensorimotor rhythm for calm alertness. For sluggish: Training to speed up your brain's natural rhythm (if you have the genetic variant, see Chapter 12, Field Guide).

What this builds: Processing speed that matches context, fast when you need to think quickly, slow when you're resting, optimal tempo for your specific brain

Timeline: 40-60 sessions (your brain's natural tempo can shift gradually with sustained training, typically 0.5-1 Hz change in IAF, measurable in QEEG)

Critical distinction: Motor activation issues (Stabilizer, responds to stimulants) vs. processing speed variants (Timekeeper, doesn't respond to stimulants, may get more anxious). Different phenotypes, different brain patterns, different training approaches. QEEG distinguishes which. This is why some "ADHD" doesn't respond to stimulants. It's actually a processing speed variant, not a motor activation issue.

18.10.10 The Fog (Low Energy State) - Context-Dependent Approach

When to train: Chronic brain fog, post-viral cognitive slowing, everything-takes-more-effort state

What we train (depends on root cause):

- **Type 1 (Motor activation issue):** Left motor planning regions, treat as Stabilizer offline
- **Type 2 (Processing speed variant):** Train to speed up your brain's natural rhythm, treat as Timekeeper sluggish
- **Chronic fog:** Network connectivity training (varies by what your QEEG shows), plus approaches that increase frontal blood flow and metabolism

What this builds: Depends on type, motor activation (Type 1), processing speed (Type 2), or network integration (chronic fog)

Timeline: 40-60+ sessions. Fog often requires concurrent root cause work (sleep disorders, inflammation, hormones, viral recovery).

The wisdom: Some fog is protective rest (honor it, Chapter 12). Chronic fog that doesn't respond to rest needs investigation and intervention. Brain mapping distinguishes protective rest from dysfunctional patterns.

18.10.11 Interpreter & Bard - Often Train Indirectly

Language (Interpreter) and prosody (Bard) issues often improve through other phenotype training:

- CEO training (reduces verbal loops, sticky narration)
- Lifeguard training (calms rumination that drives constant processing)
- Princess & Pea training (right hemisphere social-sensory includes Bard prosody processing)

Specific language protocols exist but are specialized (left temporal networks for Interpreter, right temporal networks for Bard). Most clients see language and prosody improvements through phenotype-targeted training that addresses underlying dysregulation. If direct language training is needed, consult a QEEG-trained practitioner for individualized approach.

18.11 SMR Training: The Foundation Protocol

18.11.1 What SMR Does (Revisiting Sterman's Discovery)

Remember the cats? They were rewarded for making sensorimotor rhythm, and became seizure-resistant.

What SMR creates:

- **"Calm but ready" state** (like a cat watching birds on a windowsill, perfectly still, perfectly focused)
- **Inhibitory tone** (voluntary inhibition, controlling automatic resources)
- **Sleep spindles** (the brain's natural consolidation rhythm during sleep)
- **Attention without tension** (sitting still while focusing, opposite of ADHD)

18.11.2 SMR for Multiple Complaints

For Sleep (Chapter 13):

- Enhances sleep spindles: the brain's natural consolidation rhythm during stage 2 sleep (Lambert-Beaudet et al., 2021)
- Improves sleep-wake transition (calm alertness → restful sleep)
- Reduces racing brain activity that disrupts sleep
- "Can't turn brain off" pattern, SMR trains the off switch
- Typically 20-30 sessions, often practiced before bed

For Anxiety with Hyperarousal (Chapters 14, 15):

- Beta spindles (spindling excessive fast activity) = GABAergic dysregulation
- Clinical signature: "I can't turn my brain off" (anxiety, over-arousal)
- SMR calms beta spindles without substances (alcohol, benzos, cannabis)
- Builds inhibitory control that reduces reliance on GABAergic substances
- Alternative to borrowed calm from alcohol/benzos

For Cannabis Dependence (Chapter 14):

- Builds calm focus without cannabis; reduces anxiety in substance-dependent patients (Sokhadze et al., 2008)
- Reduces CEO mental stickiness (anterior cingulate flexibility)

- Repairs sleep architecture (often disrupted by chronic cannabis use)
- Restores natural ability to downregulate without external help
- 40-60 sessions for complete cannabis recovery

For ADHD/Stabilizer (Chapters 14, 16):

- Builds sustained attention capacity (sitting still while focusing)
- Complements theta/beta ratio training (address under-arousal PLUS build inhibitory control)
- Repairs sleep architecture damaged by chronic stimulant use
- Critical for stimulant recovery (sleep restoration + attention building)

For Meditation Prep (Chapter 17):

- Prepares brain for meditation by training "calm but ready"
- Makes it easier to sustain meditation practice (attention without tension)
- Reduces restlessness and distractibility during sitting practice
- Foundation before advancing to alpha-theta deep states

If you've ever felt like your brain won't stop buzzing at bedtime, or your body can't settle even when you're exhausted, SMR training targets that exact pattern.

18.11.3 SMR Training Approach

Where training happens:

- Sensorimotor cortex: the strip across the top of your brain that handles both sensing and moving
- Right side focuses more on inhibitory control (Supervisor)
- Left side focuses more on motor initiation and sustained attention (Stabilizer)
- Midline for bilateral regulation

What we're training:

- The sensorimotor rhythm: your brain's "calm but ready" state
- Like training a cat to sit perfectly still on a windowsill watching birds

Session structure:

- 30-50 minutes, 2-4 times per week
- Regular practice builds lasting capacity

Timeline: 20-40 sessions for stable changes

Why it's foundational: SMR is often the first training protocol because it establishes basic regulation capacity. Once your brain can access this "calm but ready" state reliably, you can advance to more specialized training if needed.

18.12 Alpha Training: Calming Over-Arousal

18.12.1 When Alpha Training is Essential

For Anxiety (Grumpy Old Man, Timekeeper):

- Right frontal calming training reduces threat assessment
- Reduces catastrophizing, rumination, worry loops
- Builds natural relaxation capacity (not borrowed from substances)
- 30-40 sessions for anxiety (takes longer than attention training)

For Benzodiazepine Withdrawal (Chapter 14):

- Critical support during medical taper
- Right frontal training teaches brain to generate calm naturally
- Reduces rebound anxiety (withdrawal symptom)
- Must be concurrent with medical supervision (benzo withdrawal dangerous)
- Replaces borrowed calm from benzos with trained capacity

For Racing Thoughts (Timekeeper, Sleep Issues):

- Right posterior calming training for racing minds
- Shifts from thinking/racing mode to resting/calm mode
- Especially effective for sleep when racing thoughts prevent sleep onset
- Can train before bed or during day (effects generalize)

For Meditation Support (Chapter 17):

- Helps Timekeeper shift from thinking to sensing
- Reduces rumination and catastrophizing during meditation
- Makes meditation feel calming (not anxiety-provoking)

If meditation has always made you more anxious, not less, your alpha is probably suppressed. This fixes the foundation.

18.12.2 Alpha Training Approach

Where training happens:

- Right frontal regions for threat assessment and worry
- Right posterior regions for calming racing visual thoughts
- Both hemispheres for general calming when needed

What we're training:

- Alpha rhythms: your brain's natural relaxation frequency
- Teaches your nervous system how to downshift from thinking mode to resting mode
- Builds calm you can access voluntarily

Session structure:

- 30-50 minutes per session
- Regular practice is key to building lasting capacity

Timeline for different goals:

- Anxiety patterns: 30-40 sessions
- Sleep support: 20-30 sessions
- Benzo taper support: Training runs concurrent with medical taper (weeks to months)

18.13 Theta/Beta Ratio: The Core ADHD Protocol

18.13.1 Why This Is Well-Studied for ADHD

The pattern (Frontal Slow):

- Excess slow-wave activity (theta and delta rhythms) in frontal regions
- Reduced fast-wave activity (beta rhythms)
- Elevated slow-to-fast wave ratio
- **Strongest predictor of stimulant response** in ADHD research
- Stable across time (not a transient state)

If stimulants work for you but you want off them, this protocol trains the same circuit they're compensating for.

What theta/beta training does:

- Suppresses theta (reduces slow-wave activity)
- Enhances beta (increases fast-wave activity)
- **Effect sizes comparable to methylphenidate in some studies** (Arns et al., 2009), with sustained improvements at 6-month follow-up (van Doren et al., 2019), though results are heterogeneous across studies
- Wakes the "engine that won't start" (Stabilizer)
- Builds lasting capacity (not borrowed activation)

18.13.2 Theta/Beta for Stimulant Dependence (Chapter 14)

The problem stimulants were solving:

- Stabilizer offline (can't initiate tasks)
- Frontal Slow pattern (excess theta, low beta)
- "I can finally focus" with stimulants

The neurofeedback solution:

- **Normalizes the same ratio** that predicts stimulant response

- Wakes Stabilizer naturally (left frontal beta enhancement, theta suppression)
- **No tolerance** (doesn't stop working like stimulants do)
- **No withdrawal** (no crash, no rebound lethargy)
- **Builds durable capacity**: most clients maintain gains long-term; some benefit from occasional tune-ups

Timeline: 40-60 sessions + 6-18 months for full dopamine system recovery

Critical addition: Sleep architecture repair (SMR training) concurrent with theta/beta ratio work, because stimulants can disrupt sleep, which worsens ADHD in a vicious cycle

18.13.3 Theta/Beta for Productivity (Chapter 16)

For task initiation paralysis:

- Can't start tasks despite knowing what to do
- Procrastination despite consequences
- "Activation energy deficit" not willpower problem

The training:

- Left motor planning region activation training
- Often combined with SMR for sustained attention
- Behavioral strategies concurrent (external cues, task chaining)

Result: Sustainable activation without stimulants, can initiate tasks naturally

18.13.4 Theta/Beta Training Approach

Where training happens:

- Left motor planning regions: where the Stabilizer lives
- Sometimes bilateral training for broader regulation

What we're training:

- Reducing slow-wave dominance while building fast-wave capacity
- Teaching the "engine that won't start" to engage naturally
- This is the pattern most predictive of stimulant response, we're training what stimulants temporarily provide

Session structure:

- 30-50 minutes, 2-4 times per week
- Consistency is critical for building lasting capacity

Timeline for different goals:

- ADHD symptoms: 40 sessions minimum

- Stimulant dependence recovery: 60+ sessions recommended
- Sleep architecture repair: Concurrent SMR training

Progress tracking: Re-assessment every 20-25 sessions shows objective brain changes

---

18.14 Client Story: Jason (ADHD, Activation Without Pills)

Composite, like every case in this book. Any medication change here happened with his prescriber, and that is the only way it should happen.

Jason, 42, creative professional. ADHD diagnosed at 25. Adderall 40mg daily for 15 years. "It worked, until it didn't." Sleep wrecked: 3-4 hours a night, couldn't fall asleep, couldn't wake up. Anxiety through the roof. Couldn't start work without pills, crashed hard when they wore off. Tolerance trap. Needed more, got less.

His brain map: Classic Frontal Slow pattern, excessive slow-wave activity in left motor planning regions (Stabilizer offline). Low sensorimotor rhythm capacity. Mildly slowed dominant rhythm (mild processing speed issue, but ADHD pattern dominant).

Protocol: Left motor planning activation training (wake the Stabilizer), SMR for sleep (bilateral sensorimotor training), integrated sleep optimization (consistent wake time, morning light). Concurrent stimulant taper coordinated with prescriber, held dose stable first 2 months, began gradual reduction month 3 as sleep and task initiation improved. 50 sessions over 6 months.

What changed: "I can start work without panic or pills. Morning routine actually works now. I wake up and my body just… moves. Sleep improved first (month 2), then task initiation got easier (month 3-4). Stimulants down to 10mg as-needed, not 40mg mandatory. Some days I don't take them at all. I didn't think I'd ever be off the rollercoaster."

QEEG after: Slow-to-fast wave ratio normalized. Sensorimotor rhythm capacity up in left motor regions. Sleep spindles up (deeper stage 2 sleep, more deep slow-wave sleep). His Stabilizer learned to engage. His motor cortex found its own gas pedal.

18.15 Alpha-Theta: Deep States and Trauma Processing

18.15.1 The Advanced Protocol (After SMR Foundation)

What alpha-theta does:

- Accesses deep relaxation states (hypnagogic: between wake and sleep)
- Enhances creativity, insight, integration
- Processes trauma, unconscious material
- Similar to meditation deep states or psychedelic experiences
- BUT: Internally generated, voluntary, sustainable

When to use:

- After SMR foundation established (need attention control first)
- For trauma (Lifeguard threat sensitivity, PTSD)
- For substance patterns (Peniston protocol, 80% abstinence rates)
- For creativity (artists, musicians, writers)
- For meditation deepening (advanced practitioners)

18.15.2 Alpha-Theta for Substance Use (Peniston Protocol)

The classic application (Chapter 14):

- Developed for alcoholism and PTSD in veterans
- Sustained abstinence rates significantly above control groups (Peniston & Kulkosky, 1989; Scott et al., 2005)
- Processes underlying anxiety, trauma that drives use
- Ego dissolution (similar to psychedelic therapy but controlled)

Protocol structure:

1. Temperature biofeedback (5-10 sessions, relaxation foundation)
2. Alpha training (5-10 sessions, learning to relax)
3. Alpha-theta training (20-30 sessions, deep states)

Why it works for addiction:

- Accesses deep relaxation (what alcohol provided)
- Processes unconscious triggers (trauma, anxiety)
- Reduces stress reactivity (amygdala regulation)
- Ego dissolution (breaks rigid patterns)

Best for: Grumpy Old Man + alcohol, Lifeguard + trauma/substances, Princess & Pea + emotional overwhelm

Clinical observation: I've run Peniston protocol with dozens of clients. My outcomes are consistent with the high abstinence rates reported in early trials. Watched brains that couldn't generate calm without alcohol learn to drop into deep alpha-theta states. Watched CEO obsessions release during sessions. Watched Grumpy Old Man effort-dread soften. Watched Lifeguard threat sensitivity finally stand down. This isn't borrowed calm from substances, it's trained capacity your brain builds and keeps.

18.15.3 Alpha-Theta for Meditation (Chapter 17)

Synergistic effects:

- Faster access to deep meditative states
- Enhanced creativity and insight
- Accelerated personal growth
- Meditation practice + alpha-theta = amplification

Research:

- Brandmeyer & Delorme (2013): Faster access to deep states
- Gruzelier (2009): Enhanced creativity, artistic performance (small controlled studies, promising but sample sizes were modest; replications are ongoing)
- Garrison et al. (2013): Enhanced self-awareness, metacognition

Timeline: 20-30 alpha-theta sessions after SMR foundation

18.15.4 Alpha-Theta Training Approach

Where training happens:

- Posterior regions of the brain
- Sometimes midline sites

What we're training:

- Deep relaxation states: the hypnagogic zone between waking and sleeping
- Access to states similar to deep meditation or certain psychedelic experiences
- But self-generated, voluntary, and sustainable

Session structure:

- 20-30 minutes, eyes closed, lying down or reclining
- You're learning to access very deep rest states on command

Important considerations:

- This is advanced training: not appropriate for beginners
- Requires foundation of attention control first (SMR training typically comes before this)
- Can bring up deep material that needs clinical support to process
- Must work with trained professional

Integration: Often combined with visualization practices, and can support trauma processing work when clinically appropriate

---

18.15.5 Interpreter, Bard, Timekeeper - Specialized Protocols

These phenotypes often train as part of other patterns:

- Interpreter issues often improve with CEO/Lifeguard training
- Bard regulation through Princess & Pea protocols
- Timekeeper (alpha frequency training for slowed alpha, beta regulation for racing)

18.16 Neurofeedback Protocols by Phenotype: Quick Reference

Here's a complete summary of training approaches for all 12 phenotypes:

Phenotype	Target	What We Train
Happy Little Kid	Left DLPFC	Increase left frontal activation, reduce frontal asymmetry; alpha asymmetry training shows lasting mood improvements at 1-5 year follow-up (Baehr et al., 2001)
Grumpy Old Man	Right DLPFC	Calm right frontal hyperactivation, reduce catastrophizing
Stabilizer	Left sensorimotor	Build SMR (idle gear), reduce theta/beta ratio
CEO	Frontal midline	Reduce stuck loops (theta or beta), improve flexibility
Supervisor	Right sensorimotor	Calibrate brake (strengthen if weak, soften if rigid)
Lifeguard	Posterior cingulate	Calm environmental scanning, reduce rumination
Problem Child	Right IFG	Strengthen inhibitory brake, regulate threat response
Princess & Pea	Right TPJ	Regulate high-gain processing, reduce flooding
Bard	Right posterior temporal	Improve prosody processing, reduce flooding
Interpreter	Left posterior temporal	Enhance word retrieval, support language processing
Timekeeper	Alpha peak frequency	Train optimal processing speed (context-dependent)
The Fog	Multiple sites	Address underlying cause (sleep, processing speed, etc.)

Note: These are general guidelines. Actual protocols are individualized based on QEEG assessment, symptom profile, and treatment goals. For complete technical details, see the QEEG Field Guide (Hill & Lomeli, forthcoming).

18.17 The Promise

You can train your brain.

This isn't theory. This is what I do. Every day. With clients who come in tortured and leave with tools.

It takes 40 sessions, not 40 minutes. The capacity you build tends to be durable.

No drug-like tolerance or withdrawal. No borrowing from tomorrow.

MYTH vs REALITY:

MYTH: "Neurofeedback is just biofeedback / placebo / unproven." **REALITY:** EEG biofeedback broadly has thousands of peer-reviewed publications spanning 50+ years. The FDA has granted 510(k) clearance for EEG biofeedback devices as relaxation tools (Class II medical devices), though this is device clearance, not efficacy endorsement for specific conditions. Multiple RCTs and meta-analyses indicate clinically meaningful effects for ADHD, anxiety, and peak performance, though results are heterogeneous and still debated (Arns et al., 2009; Duric et al., 2012; Gruzelier, 2014). It's not fringe, it's just not yet mainstream. The confusion comes from: (1) wide variability in practitioner skill, (2) no standardized protocols (yet), and (3) the fact that it's slow and expensive compared to medication. But if you're stuck after trying everything else, it's often the first thing that actually moves the needle. Not for everyone, not instantly, but it can work when other approaches haven't.

About "just biofeedback": Neurofeedback IS biofeedback, specifically, EEG biofeedback (brain wave training). It's one type within a family of physiological feedback training methods. Understanding the relationship helps clarify why we sometimes use temperature biofeedback before alpha-theta training, or combine HRV training with neurofeedback protocols.

OPTIONAL: Why the Research Looks Mixed

For the methodologically curious.

Clinically, neurofeedback is individualized: QEEG, phenotype matching, iterative protocol adjustments. Most RCT studies do the opposite, single fixed protocols for everyone in a diagnostic category, no phenotype matching, short training durations (12-20 sessions when 30-40 are needed), small

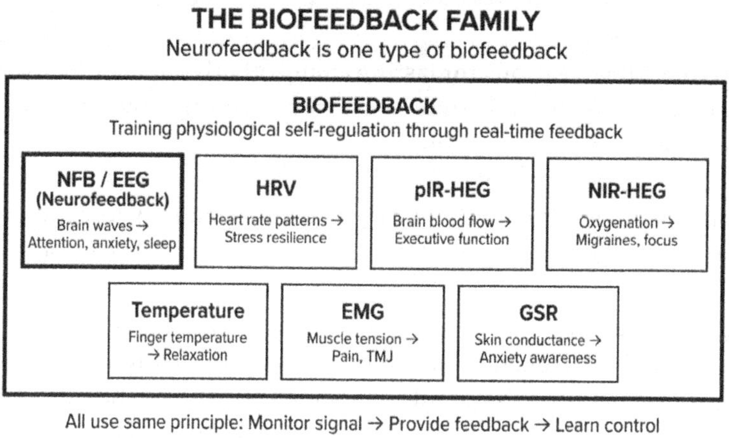

Figure 18.1: Biofeedback Family

samples, and heterogeneous groups that wash out individual effects. It's like testing "medication for ADHD" by giving everyone the same dose regardless of presentation.

Bottom line: The evidence base underestimates clinical efficacy because it tests neurofeedback the wrong way. Individualized, phenotype-matched protocols produce stronger outcomes. The research reflects methodological constraints, not treatment limits.

If you only do one thing from this chapter: If you're genuinely stuck after trying sleep, substances cleanup, HRV, and meditation, get a QEEG. It will tell you what your brain is actually doing, not what you think it's doing.

18.18 Key Takeaways

Neurofeedback isn't magic, it's practice. You're teaching your brain new rhythms through operant conditioning.

- **Operant conditioning for brain waves:** EEG sensors measure in real time; a computer rewards desired patterns; your brain learns to generate those patterns voluntarily. Non-invasive, no "zapping," just feedback and learning.
- **What you can train:** Calm (right frontal alpha), focus (theta/beta ratio for ADHD), activation (left frontal beta), cognitive flexibility (frontal midline

theta), deep states (alpha-theta), sleep (SMR). Each phenotype has specific protocols.

- **Timeline: 20-40 sessions for lasting change:** Early shifts in 5-10 sessions, consolidation by 20, measurable phenotype change by 40+. Building neural pathways takes repetition.
- **Evidence base:** Multiple RCTs and meta-analyses confirm clinically meaningful effects for ADHD, substance use, and anxiety/depression (Arns et al., 2009; Duric et al., 2012; Gruzelier, 2014). 50+ years of research. Not New Age.
- **QEEG-guided approach:** Target your phenotypes (1-4 channels), iterative protocol adjustments, integrated with sleep/meditation/lifestyle.
- **Alternative to borrowing:** Builds the calm/focus/activation you've been renting from substances, no drug-like tolerance or withdrawal. Durable capacity.

18.19 Reader Reflections

Take a moment to consider neurofeedback for your brain:

1. **Which phenotype causes you the most suffering?** Grumpy Old Man dread? Stabilizer paralysis? CEO perseveration? Happy Little Kid offline? Princess & Pea overwhelm? Identifying your primary bottleneck determines which protocol to start with.
2. **What would it mean to build regulation internally instead of borrowing it?** To own your calm and focus cadence rather than renting it? No tolerance, no rebound, capacity you own.
3. **Are you willing to commit to 40 sessions?** Neurofeedback builds over 20 weeks (2x/week). Can you invest 5 months to build durable capacity?
4. **What's your next step?** Get QEEG assessment? Research local practitioners? Or start with foundations first (Ch 13 sleep, Ch 17 meditation) then add neurofeedback?

You have the tools now. Sleep, HRV, meditation, neurofeedback, productivity systems. Part II gave you the intervention toolkit. Part III shows you how to build a life around it. Time to integrate.

Part III
Living Gifted

Overview: Integration, Mastery, Conducting

Mastery Loop Step: REFLECT + Full Integration

You've learned your phenotypes (Part I).
You've learned the tools (Part II).
Now it's time to **integrate**, to build a life around your brain, not against it.

This section is about **mastery**. Not "fixing" yourself. Not becoming neurotypical. Not suppressing your gifts to reduce your torture. Not pathology, configuration.

Mastery is learning to conduct the orchestra you were born with.

Conducting is mostly about cadence: who plays when, how loud, and for how long.

What you're learning: Step 5 of the Poet-Brain Mastery Loop, how to **REFLECT** on your patterns and integrate the full practice into daily life, relationships, creative work, and self-mastery.

Navigate Part III by what you need:

- **Redesigning your life, work, environment?** Chapter 19 (Building Your Life).
- **Struggling with relationships, RSD, social exhaustion?** Chapter 20 (Social Navigation).
- **Want to access creative flow without substances?** Chapter 21 (Creative Flow).
- **Ready for the full mastery practice and action plan?** Chapter 22 (Self-Mastery), this is where everything integrates.

Stop fixing yourself. Start designing. Parts I and II gave you the map and the tools. Part III is where you learn to navigate: designing life around your hardware, not against it. Take what resonates. Leave what doesn't. Build your own conductor's score.

Who Gets Missed: Late Diagnosis, Gender, Hormones, and Masking

The phenotype model doesn't care about demographics. Circuits are circuits. But the world around those circuits varies enormously, and that shapes who gets identified, who gets help, and who spends decades compensating without knowing why.

Late-diagnosed adults are the majority of this book's audience. If you're reading this at 35, 45, 55 and thinking *this explains everything*, you're not alone. Late diagnosis is the norm for intelligent, compensating brains. You built workarounds sophisticated enough to fool every screener, teacher, and clinician. The cost: decades of effort that felt inexplicably harder than it should have, plus the grief of "why didn't anyone catch this?" That grief is real. Sit with it. Then use the map.

Gender matters for phenotype expression. Women and people socialized female are disproportionately late-diagnosed because their phenotypes present differently. The hyperactive ADHD boy gets flagged in second grade. The inattentive girl with a rich inner world, high anxiety, and perfect grades gets flagged never. Autistic women mask more effectively (and at higher personal cost) than autistic men. The Princess & the Pea and Lifeguard phenotypes often read as "anxiety" in women and get medicated rather than mapped. If you're a woman who's been treated for anxiety or depression for years without resolution, consider whether the underlying pattern is sensory, social, or attentional.

Hormonal transitions amplify phenotypes. Puberty, pregnancy, postpartum, perimenopause, menopause. Estrogen modulates serotonin, dopamine, and GABA. When estrogen drops (luteal phase, perimenopause), every phenotype gets louder. The Grumpy Old Man generates more dread. The Timekeeper races. The Princess & the Pea's gain increases. If your phenotypes seem to cycle monthly or worsened dramatically at a hormonal transition point, that is usually your existing circuitry losing a buffer it relied on. Hormonal context changes the volume, not the instrument. **But:** if symptoms are genuinely new to you, especially postpartum, or include mania or psychosis, get assessed. Amplification of a known pattern is different from the emergence of something you have never experienced.

Cultural masking adds another layer. Neurodivergent people in marginalized communities often mask not just their neurodivergence but their cultural identity. The cognitive load of maintaining multiple masks simultaneously is enormous. If you're Black, Latinx, Indigenous, queer, immigrant, or otherwise navigating spaces not built for you, your phenotype expression is filtered through additional survival strategies. The Lifeguard runs hotter in environments with real external threat. The Princess & the Pea's social radar calibrates to actual danger, not just perceived. Your masking is adaptive and costly. The tools in this section work regardless of context, but the cost of implementation varies. Honor that.

The bottom line: Your circuits don't care about your demographics. But your path to recognition, diagnosis, and tools was shaped by them. Everything in this book applies to you.

Managing Multiple Phenotypes at Once

Most poet-brains don't have one loud phenotype. They have three or four playing over each other like a symphony tuning up before a show. This is normal. This is expected. And if this is your lived experience, nothing is wrong with you, you're simply running a high-bandwidth, high-gain brain with overlapping circuits.

Here's the good news:

You don't need to "fix" everything at once. You only need to know which phenotype to work with first.

There's a natural order to calming or activating the brain that makes everything else easier. Think of it as triage for your inner orchestra, who gets your attention first, who can wait, and who only sounds chaotic because someone else is out of tune.

1. Start With the Stabilizer (or Fog)

When your motor engagement system is offline, nothing works.

Executive function, mood, attention, everything rides on whether your Stabilizer can get your body into motion.

If you're frozen, overwhelmed, or unable to start, don't jump straight to anxiety tools, productivity hacks, or emotional insight.

Wake the motor system first.

This can be tiny:

- stand up
- walk for two minutes
- cold splash
- light exposure
- one Pomodoro block
- SMR or midline frontal training if you're doing neurofeedback

When the Stabilizer comes online, the rest of your phenotypes become easier to read and regulate.

2. Next Regulate the Mood Axis (Happy Kid + Grumpy Old Man)

Once you're moving, check your left–right frontal balance.

Are you stuck in withdrawal-mode?

Is the Grumpy Old Man narrating doom?

Is the Happy Little Kid nowhere to be found?

If the Stabilizer is running but your mood axis is tilted, you'll misinterpret everything as danger or failure. This is where:

- sunlight
- activation rituals
- HRV breathing
- left-frontal activation practices
- right-frontal calming
- compassion meditation

...do most of the heavy lifting.

Balancing the approach/withdrawal system brings your interpretations back into proportion.

3. Quiet the Threat Circuits (Lifeguard + Grumpy + Princess)

If your body is moving and your mood axis is balanced but you still feel flooded, avoidant, jumpy, or oversensitive, check the gain of your threat circuits.

When Lifeguard is hypervigilant or Princess & Pea is reading every flicker of emotion as danger, your brain can't trust its own interpretations.

This is where tools like:

- slow exhale HRV
- body-scan meditation
- sensory gating strategies
- reducing stimulus load
- right-frontal calming
- SMR training

...turn the internal volume down.

4. Then Address Executive Function (CEO + Supervisor + Problem Child)

Trying to fix executive function before the earlier layers is a recipe for self-blame.

Executive function is not the captain, it's the last subsystem to come online when the rest of the brain is regulated.

When the body is moving, the mood axis is balanced, and the threat circuits are calm, the CEO becomes clear and decisive instead of punitive. The

Supervisor stops catastrophizing. The Problem Child stops slamming the brakes.

This is the moment for:

- productivity tools
- task batching
- Pomodoros
- planning
- switching rules
- prioritization

Only now do they work as intended.

5. Sensory & Language Phenotypes Smooth Out Last

Interpreter, Bard, and Speaker often flare when the rest of the system is stressed. They're downstream of mood, threat, and pacing. When you regulate earlier circuits, overinterpretation drops, social nuance clears, and language flow returns. You don't usually need to "fix" your sensitivity. Just turn down the global gain.

6. The Quick-Start Hierarchy

When everything hits at once: body and pacing first (Stabilizer/Fog/Timekeeper), then mood axis (Happy Little Kid/Grumpy Old Man), then threat circuits (Lifeguard/Princess & Pea), then executive control (CEO/Supervisor/Problem Child), then sensory-language processing (Interpreter/Bard). All six systems from Part I, in triage order. This solves 80% of "my whole brain is screaming" days.

You don't have to fix everything at once. Start with the phenotype that's loudest. The others will quiet as the foundation improves.

When one phenotype settles, you'll notice three others soften automatically. Everything feels tangled, but everything is connected.

Let's build a life worthy of your exquisite, complex brain.

Ch 19: Building Your Life Around Your Phenotype

Stop Fixing Yourself. Start Designing.

You've spent years trying to fix yourself. Trying to be more organized. More social. More motivated. More calm. More neurotypical.

How's that working?

The world is designed for neurotypical brains. Average sensitivity. Average processing speed. Average approach-avoid balance. Average everything.

You're running different hardware. When you try to force yourself into a neurotypical mold, you end up exhausted, burned out, and miserable.

The mold is wrong.

This chapter is about designing a life that fits your phenotypes, not forcing your phenotypes to fit a life designed for someone else's brain.

The shift:

- From: "How do I fix myself to fit this life?"
- To: "How do I design this life to fit my brain?"

The domains:

- Work (environment, deadlines, collaboration)
- Relationships (communication, RSD, sensory needs)
- Parenting (if applicable - poet-brains raising poet-brains)
- Creativity (harnessing your gifts)
- Energy management (knowing when to push, when to rest)

Let's build a life that works.

19.1 The Foundation: Oscillation Is Life

Before we get into work, relationships, and creativity, we need to talk about rhythm.

Your brain is not a computer in a steady "on" state. It's an ecosystem of oscillations: electrical rhythms, hormonal pulses, temperature cycles, shifting attentional modes, social engagement systems that open and close like flowers over the course of a day.

Life design is about honoring those oscillations as cadences: predictable patterns you can build around instead of random chaos you're always fighting.

When we talk about "regulation" in this book (of mood, attention, arousal, pain, social safety, sensory input) **what we're really talking about is rhythmic regulation.**

You've met your phenotypes. You know their tempos and thresholds, how fast they spin up, how slowly they wind down, how easily they get knocked off balance.

As we covered in Chapter 13 (Sleep), circadian rhythm is your master conductor. Morning light, consistent wake time, and syncing to the Earth's photoperiod create the foundation for everything. When that big rhythm is off, everything that sits on top of it gets noisy, your Happy Little Kid gets fragmented, your Lifeguard threat-sensitive, your Princess & Pea sensitivity dials up, your Fog arrives more often.

For life design, the key insight: Morning is your master lever. The time when you have most control, before other people's chaos starts. The cleanest slate for behavior, tiny habits here cascade all day. It's also the easiest place to build identity: "I am someone who..." is simple to enforce when you're not yet exhausted.

Think of morning as where your internal regulatory domains take their marching orders. The first 60-90 minutes of your day are like programming a sequencer that will run in the background for the next 16 hours.

You don't need an Instagram-worthy routine. You need:

- Light that tells your clock what time it is
- Movement that tells your body you're alive and expected to use the hardware today
- A tiny bit of intentionality about what kind of brain you're bringing online

Your morning is not a test of willpower. It's a piece of infrastructure.

You're not trying to prove you're disciplined. You're building a small, repeatable pattern that keeps your circadian rhythm roughly in phase with the planet's, protects your regulatory domains from unnecessary chaos, and gives your phenotypes a stable stage to perform on.

19.1.1 Harm Reduction Through Snobbery

Let's talk about snobbery.

You've probably noticed: I'm not very interested in purity culture. I don't think the goal is to become a clean, sober, monk-like organism that never does anything messy, fun, or ill-advised.

I am very interested in harm reduction through snobbery.

Snobbery here means: **if you're going to mess with your brain, raise your standards. Be picky. Be difficult. Be high-maintenance on purpose.**

In circadian terms, that looks like:

Being snobby about light:

- Real daylight before screens, whenever possible
- "If the sun is up, I prefer photons from a star, not a rectangle"

Being snobby about late-night screen use:

- If you're going to doom-scroll, do it with warm, dimmed screens
- Not a blinding blue blast aligned perfectly with your melatonin curve

Being snobby about when you take stimulants or sedatives:

- Caffeine earlier and less, or not every day
- Alcohol as a deliberate event, not nightly anesthesia protocol

Being snobby about bedtime violations:

- You can absolutely stay up late for a concert or a date
- You just don't do it randomly every night "because Netflix asked you nicely"

The goal is not never to break rhythm. The goal is to make your rhythm worth defending most of the time.

When you adopt a bit of snobbery, your internal conversation shifts from:

"I should probably stop doing this, it's bad for me."

to:

"My brain is high-end gear. This thing isn't good enough for it on a Tuesday."

That framing is especially useful for the gifted, tortured brain that rebels against rules but respects quality. You're not denying yourself; you're curating your inputs.

19.1.2 Phenotype-Specific Morning Anchors

The detailed how (timing light, food, caffeine, exercise, wind-down) is in Chapter 13 (Sleep). Here's why different phenotypes treat morning as their main life-design lever:

The Happy Little Kid:

- Why: Morning is when approach drive is high; unstructured it turns into chaos
- Morning focus: Simple first-hour script (light, movement, planning) that channels energy before distractions invade

The Grumpy Old Man:

- Why: Morning sets perceived threat level of whole day
- Morning focus: Gentle, predictable routine that signals safety (same light, same breakfast, same route)

The Lifeguard:

- Why: Morning routine tells hypervigilant system "we can tolerate stress on purpose"
- Morning focus: Predictable + tiny controllable challenge (cold rinse, short workout)

The Princess & Pea:

- Why: Sensory load at wake-up sets tone for reactivity
- Morning focus: Soft, gradual stimulation (light first, then sound, then tasks; no jarring alarms)

The Stabilizer:

- Why: Low arousal and slow boot-up make whole day feel behind schedule
- Morning focus: Chunked activation (light → warm-up movement → small winnable task before anything cognitively heavy)

The Fog:

- Why: Chronic low energy needs rhythm to distinguish protective rest from dysfunction
- Morning focus: Consistent wake time even when foggy (anchor the rhythm, honor the rest)

You don't need a complicated spreadsheet of habit stacks. You need a tiny menu of non-negotiable anchors that align your brain's rhythms with daylight and with your life demands.

19.1.3 Why This Belongs in Life Design (Not Just Sleep)

Circadian alignment isn't just about "getting better sleep." It's about:

- Giving your internal circuits a shared tempo
- Making your regulatory tools from Part II actually usable
- Reducing background noise so real problems are easier to see
- Making it easier to be a decent friend, partner, parent, colleague

- Creating daily structure where your particular weirdness becomes asset, not liability

Without rhythm, your phenotypes are each running on their own clock. Once you give them a shared beat through circadian alignment, the same quirky circuits can suddenly work together instead of against each other.

For deeper protocols, see Chapter 13 (Sleep). But understand them through this lens: not as self-improvement tasks, but as ways of increasing the quality of oscillation across your entire brain.

19.2 Work: Designing Your Environment

Your work environment can either support your phenotypes or fight them. Here's how to design for your specific configuration.

19.2.1 If Your Stabilizer Is Offline (Task Initiation Struggles)

What tends to go wrong:

- Can't start tasks, even when you want to
- Mornings are impossible
- Procrastination that feels like paralysis
- Need external pressure to activate

Design constraints that fit:

- **Morning work blocks** (when activation is highest - don't waste it on email)
- **External accountability** (body doubling, coworking spaces, check-ins with a colleague)
- **Task chunking** (break projects into starts small enough to begin)
- **Movement breaks** (re-activate Stabilizer when it slips out of gear)
- **No afternoon meetings** (protect your activated state for deep work)

2-week experiment:

- Wake 6am, morning light + exercise, start most important task by 8am
- Track: How many days did you start without massive resistance?

19.2.2 If Your Supervisor Is Weak (Impulsivity, Can't Sustain)

What tends to go wrong:

- Distracted constantly (golden retriever chasing shiny objects)
- Start projects, don't finish
- Can't sustain attention on boring tasks
- Meetings derail your whole day

Design constraints that fit:

- **Distraction-free environment** (no notifications, close door, headphones)
- **Single-tasking** (finish current before starting next - external rule)
- **Longer focus blocks** (50-90 min Pomodoro, not 25 - you need time to get into gear)
- **External structure** (deadlines with consequences, daily stand-ups)
- **Finish-one-first rule** (written, visible, enforced)

2-week experiment:

- One project at a time, distraction-free environment, 90-min blocks
- Track: How many projects did you finish vs. start?

19.2.3 If Your CEO Gets Stuck (Obsessive, Can't Switch)

What tends to go wrong:

- Get locked onto wrong priority
- Interruptions feel like violence
- Can't let go of minor issues
- Perfectionism on unimportant details

Design constraints that fit:

- **Protected focus blocks** (no interruptions for 2-3 hours)
- **Forced switching** (timer goes off, you switch - external cue)
- **Priority system** (CEO needs help deciding - use external framework like Eisenhower matrix)
- **"Good enough" deadlines** (time's up = you're done, prevents endless refinement)
- **Solo work** (can't tolerate constant interruptions)

2-week experiment:

- 3-hour uninterrupted blocks, timer forces task switch every 90 min
- Track: Did forced switching reduce stuckness?

19.2.4 If Your Princess & Pea Is Dominant (Sensory Sensitivity)

What tends to go wrong:

- Open offices are torture
- Fluorescent lights, background noise overwhelming
- Social exhaustion from constant interaction
- Need recovery time no one understands

Design constraints that fit:

- **Sensory-optimized space** (quiet, dim, comfortable, temperature-controlled)

- **Remote work** (if possible - control your environment)
- **Noise-canceling headphones** (non-negotiable)
- **Small teams or solo work** (not open office chaos)
- **Recovery time built in** (after meetings, after social interaction)
- **Async communication** (email/Slack over constant meetings)

2-week experiment:

- Optimize your workspace (lighting, sound, comfort), limit meetings to 2/day max
- Track: Energy levels, sensory overwhelm incidents

19.2.5 If Your Timekeeper Is Racing (Fast Processing, Burnout Risk)

What tends to go wrong:

- Work too fast, burn out
- Can't downshift at end of day
- Racing thoughts interfere with sleep
- Chronic stress from constant high-speed

Design constraints that fit:

- **Hard stop times** (end work at 6pm, no exceptions)
- **Pacing strategies** (intentionally slow down, take breaks)
- **Calm environment** (reduce stimulation at work)
- **Evening wind-down ritual** (transition from work to rest)
- **No work email after hours** (protect your downshift time)

2-week experiment:

- Hard stop at 6pm, 30-min wind-down routine, no screens after 8pm
- Track: Sleep quality, racing thoughts at night

19.2.6 If Your Fog Is Chronic (Low Energy, Cognitive Slowing)

What tends to go wrong:

- Afternoon crashes
- Can't maintain 9-5 schedule
- Need more recovery time than job allows
- Forced productivity when brain needs rest

Design constraints that fit:

- **Honor your rhythm** (if you're slow mornings, don't force morning productivity)
- **Flexible schedule** (if possible - work when you're actually functional)
- **Shorter work blocks** (4-6 hours of focused work, not 8-10)
- **Recovery time** (built into schedule, not "I'll rest when I'm done")

- **Address underlying causes** (sleep disorders, post-viral, hormones - see Chapter 13)

2-week experiment:

- Work 10am-4pm (if flexible), prioritize sleep/recovery, track energy patterns
- Track: Productive hours, fog severity

19.3 Relationships: Phenotype Compatibility

Your phenotypes affect how you relate. Understanding this prevents years of "what's wrong with me?" in relationships.

19.3.1 Princess & Pea + RSD in Relationships

What tends to go wrong:

- Partner's tone shift → you're convinced they're leaving
- Mild criticism → feels like annihilation
- Constantly checking "are we okay?"
- Emotional exhaustion from amplification

Design constraints that fit:

- **Direct communication** (ask "are you upset?" instead of assuming)
- **Repair rituals** (after RSD-driven overreaction)
- **Sensory needs communicated** (not assumed partner will know)
- **Recovery time** (alone time to discharge absorbed emotions)
- **Partner education** (explain RSD, it's real, it's neurobiological)

2-week experiment:

- When you feel rejected, pause and ask directly before spiraling
- Track: How often was it RSD vs. actual rejection?

19.3.2 Stabilizer Offline + Partner Expectations

What tends to go wrong:

- Partner expects you to initiate (dates, chores, plans)
- You can't, they resent you
- "Why do I have to do everything?"
- You feel shame, they feel burdened

Design constraints that fit:

- **External structure** (shared calendar, automated reminders)
- **Partner as accountability** (not nagging - collaboration)
- **Task division** (you do what you CAN initiate, they do what you can't)
- **Explain your Stabilizer** (it's not laziness, it's offline motor cortex)

19.3.3 Verbal Processor + Internal Processor

(In phenotype terms: Interpreter-dominant brains process by talking, externalizing thought through language. Internal processors think before speaking. Neither is wrong; the mismatch creates friction.)

What tends to go wrong:

- You talk to think, they think you're dominating conversation
- They process internally, you think they're withholding
- Communication mismatch creates resentment

Design constraints that fit:

- **"Let me think out loud"** (signal when you're processing, not lecturing)
- **Processing time** (give internal processor time before expecting response)
- **Turn-taking** (you talk, then stop, then they talk)
- **Journaling** (external processing that doesn't require partner's attention)

19.4 Communication: Translation Between Worlds

You're navigating between neurodivergent and neurotypical communication styles. Here's the translation guide.

19.4.1 When You're Interpreter-Dominant (Literal Language)

What tends to go wrong:

- Miss sarcasm, take things literally
- Don't catch hints
- Need direct communication, get frustrated with indirect

Translation strategies:

- **Ask for clarity** ("Are you being sarcastic or serious?")
- **Request directness** ("Can you tell me directly what you need?")
- **Explain your processing** ("I'm literal - indirect doesn't land for me")

19.4.2 When You're Bard-Dominant (Prosody-Focused)

What tends to go wrong:

- Hear threat in neutral tones
- Over-read prosody
- Assume hostility where none exists

Translation strategies:

- **Check interpretations** ("Did you mean that sarcastically?")
- **Distinguish RSD from reality** (pause, assess, verify)
- **Explain your sensitivity** ("I pick up tone shifts - sometimes I misread")

19.5 Parenting: Poet-Brains Raising Poet-Brains

If you're neurodivergent and raising neurodivergent kids, you're teaching regulation you're still learning.

19.5.1 The Intergenerational Pattern

What you'll see:

- Your kids have your phenotypes (genetics)
- Their struggles mirror yours
- You recognize their torture (you lived it)
- You want to spare them what you endured

The opportunity:

- You understand them (neurotypical parents often don't)
- You can give them the map early (you didn't have it)
- You can teach tools (neurofeedback, sleep, self-compassion)
- You can normalize their experience ("Of course you feel this way. Here's why.")

The challenge:

- You're still learning to regulate your own circuits
- Your dysregulation triggers theirs (and vice versa)
- You can't give what you don't have (yet)

19.5.2 Phenotype-Aware Parenting

Stabilizer offline kid:

- External structure (routines, visual schedules)
- Morning activation (light, movement before school)
- Don't shame for "laziness" (it's offline motor cortex)

Supervisor weak kid:

- Distraction-free homework space
- One task at a time (finish before starting next)
- External deadlines (not relying on internal brake)

Princess & Pea kid:

- Sensory-optimized environment (quiet, comfortable)
- Validate their sensitivity (it's real, not dramatic)
- Teach boundaries early (protect your nervous system)

CEO stuck kid:

- Help with transitions (advance warning, timers)
- Forced switching (prevent obsessive loops)

- Normalize rigidity (it's anterior cingulate, not stubbornness)

19.6 Creativity: Harnessing Your Gifts

Your phenotypes are creative superpowers, when you know how to use them.

19.6.1 Pattern Recognition (Associative Mind)

The gift:

- You see connections others miss
- Metaphors emerge automatically
- Innovation comes from unexpected synthesis

How to harness:

- **Capture systems** (notes, voice memos when patterns emerge)
- **Multiple projects in rotation** (satisfy pattern-hungry mind without chaos)
- **Integration time** (let patterns percolate, don't force)

19.6.2 Sensitivity as Creative Fuel

The gift (Princess & Pea):

- Depth of experience others can't access
- Emotional territory for art, writing, music
- Living in high definition

How to harness:

- **Protect your sensitivity** (don't numb it with substances)
- **Channel into output** (art, writing, music as expression)
- **Sensory optimization** (create when environment supports, not fights)

19.6.3 Speed as Creative Advantage

The gift (Timekeeper racing):

- Rapid synthesis, quick wit
- High-bandwidth processing
- Improvisation, thinking on feet

How to harness:

- **Capture quickly** (ideas move fast, record them)
- **Brainstorm sessions** (use speed for idea generation)
- **Slow for refinement** (speed for creation, slow for editing)

19.7 Energy Cadence: When to Push, When to Rest

The principle: Your phenotypes have rhythms. Work with them, not against them. You don't need perfect energy; you need a readable cadence.

Push when:

- Happy Little Kid is engaged (ride the enthusiasm)
- Stabilizer is activated (morning, after exercise)
- Supervisor is balanced (quality work without perfectionism)
- Timekeeper is optimal (not too fast, not too slow)

Rest when:

- Happy Little Kid goes offline (don't force engagement)
- Fog arrives (honor the protection)
- Timekeeper is racing (downshift before burnout)
- Princess & Pea is overwhelmed (recovery time is necessary)

The wisdom: You can't be "on" all the time. Your brain has cycles. Design life that honors them.

19.8 Key Takeaways

Stop trying to fix yourself to fit a neurotypical life. Start designing a life that fits your brain, work with your phenotypes, not against them.

- **Oscillation is life:** Your brain is an ecosystem of rhythms (circadian, ultradian, hormonal), not a computer in a steady "on" state. When the big rhythm (circadian) is off, everything that sits on it gets noisy. Morning light + consistent wake time = foundation.
- **Harm reduction through snobbery:** If you're going to mess with your brain, raise your standards, real daylight over screens, quality substances over daily anesthesia, deliberate violations over random chaos.
- **Work design matches phenotype:** Stabilizer needs morning blocks. Supervisor needs distraction-free environment. CEO needs protected focus blocks. Princess & Pea needs sensory optimization. Timekeeper needs hard stop times. Fog needs flexible schedule.
- **Relationships require translation:** Explain your phenotypes to people who matter. Princess & Pea needs direct communication. Stabilizer needs external structure, not shame. Verbal processor + internal processor need turn-taking agreements.
- **Energy management:** Push when circuits are engaged. Rest when they need it. Design around real cadences (real mornings, real fog windows, real social limits) not fantasies.

19.9 Reader Reflections

1. **What aspects of your current life are designed for a neurotypical brain, not yours?** Work schedule? Social commitments? Living space? Where are you forcing yourself into a mold that doesn't fit your phenotype configuration?
2. **How's your circadian rhythm?** Consistent wake time? Morning light? Can you trace mood / energy / sleep issues to circadian misalignment?
3. **Which phenotype-specific work design could you implement this week?** One constraint that matches your top phenotype.
4. **If you're in a relationship, where's the phenotype mismatch?** How could you translate between worlds instead of resenting differences?

Ch 20: Social Navigation for Sensitive Brains

When 'Hey' Feels Like a Firing Squad

If your brain is wired for big feelings, big pattern-recognition, and big sensory input, the social world is rarely "neutral."

A casual "hey, can we talk later?" can feel like a firing squad. A loud restaurant can feel like an assault. A group chat can feel like you're being graded in real time by an invisible jury.

For many gifted, tortured brains, the core problem is not "I'm bad at people." It's that your nervous system is running social encounters on hard mode:

- Rejection sensitivity dialed up to 11
- Sensory channels taking in way more data than usual
- A history of being "too much" or "too weird," so you learned to mask

In earlier chapters, you met some of the main characters in this story:

- The Princess & Pea, who feels social slights and micro-signals with painful intensity (Chapter 8)
- The Lifeguard, constantly scanning the room for danger, real or imagined (Chapter 6)
- The Happy Little Kid, jumping into conversations impulsively, then obsessing over what they said afterward
- The Fog, who spaces out or shuts down when social input exceeds capacity

This chapter is about giving those characters a fighting chance in the social world. We're going to:

- Take rejection sensitivity seriously (because it is real)
- Unpack the costs and uses of masking
- Build boundaries that work for porous, highly empathic nervous systems
- Design social environments and strategies that respect sensory and social differences

Social design is about social cadence: how often you interact, how long you stay in, and how much buffer you need afterward.

The goal is not to turn you into a "normal" social animal. The goal is to build a social life that fits your actual brain, instead of constantly punishing it.

20.1 RSD: When Rejection Feels Like a Physical Blow

Rejection Sensitive Dysphoria (RSD) isn't drama, and it isn't you being weak. It's what happens when your threat-detection and emotional amplification systems are very tightly coupled.

For some phenotypes (especially our Princess & Pea plus some ADHD and autistic presentations) social threat doesn't land as "mild discomfort." It lands like:

- A full-body shame flush
- Immediate catastrophic predictions ("I've ruined everything")
- Urges to disappear, apologize excessively, or pre-emptively blow up the relationship

RSD does two main things:

1. Amplifies real rejection
A cold comment or an actual distancing from someone important will hit harder and take longer to process.

2. Generates false alarms
Neutral or ambiguous situations get interpreted as definite rejection: a delayed text, a brief tone shift, someone being quiet because they're tired.

Your job is not to talk yourself out of feelings. Your job is to separate signal from noise and handle both more gently.

20.1.1 Is This Rejection or an RSD Spike?

Here's a simple three-step check when your social alarm slams to red:

1. Body check
"Do my sensations feel like a sudden wave?"

Heart racing, stomach dropping, heat in the face, urge to flee = likely an RSD wave.

2. Evidence check
"What exact data do I have?"

Words they said, behaviors you saw, what actually happened, not imagined motives.

3. Pattern check
"Have I had this reaction before in similar situations that turned out fine?"

If yes, you might be running an old script in a new context.

You don't need to be certain it's not rejection. You just need enough doubt about your first interpretation to try a different move.

20.1.2 Ask, Don't Mind-Read (Basic Scripts)

RSD trains you to mind-read in the worst possible way: assume you know what people think, and assume it's bad.

One powerful counter-move is explicit clarification, even if it feels awkward. For example:

- "Hey, I noticed you were quiet earlier when I brought that up. Did I say something that landed badly?"
- "My brain is telling me I messed this up and you're annoyed. Is that what's happening, or is something else going on?"
- "When you said 'we should talk later,' my anxiety spiked. Is this about something serious, or just logistics?"

The key ingredients:

- Name your reaction as yours ("my brain is telling me…")
- Ask an open, non-accusatory question
- Actually listen to the answer, even if your inner critic is heckling

Sometimes you will discover, yes, they are upset. That's information. More often, you'll discover they're stressed, tired, distracted, or worried about something entirely different.

You're not doing this to get reassurance on demand; you're doing it to update your model of reality, which is how RSD gradually loses some of its power.

20.1.3 Self-Soothing When You're Triggered

Clarifying with others is not always possible in the moment. You still need internal tools.

Some quick moves when you're in a rejection spiral:

Name the state
"This is an RSD wave. It feels like dying, but it is a nervous system event."

Ground the body

- Cold water on the face or hands
- Pressing your feet firmly into the floor, noticing pressure and temperature
- 4–6 slow exhales with long out-breaths

Time box the story
Give yourself 5–10 minutes to write down the catastrophic story in full detail. Then step away and do something else for a while before deciding what it "means."

Self-soothing doesn't make RSD vanish. It makes it survivable without self-sabotage, less "I text them 28 times apologizing," more "I wait, then check in if needed."

20.2 Authenticity vs. Masking: Costly Costumes

"Masking" is the set of things you do to appear more socially acceptable or "normal":

- Suppressing stims or fidgets
- Forcing eye contact
- Copying tone, slang, or body language
- Hiding your real interests, needs, or distress
- Laughing things off when you're actually hurt or overwhelmed

For many autistic and ADHD folks, masking starts early and becomes second nature. It keeps you from being bullied, excluded, or punished. It also costs a lot.

20.2.1 The Costs of Long-Term Masking

Chronic, heavy masking is associated with:

- Exhaustion and burnout
- Depersonalization ("I don't know who I am when I'm not performing")
- Depression and anxiety
- Delayed or missed diagnosis ("you seem fine")
- Relationships built on a false version of you

Masking "works" in the short term because it reduces overt conflict and makes you easier to be around, for everyone except you.

But let's not throw it out entirely. Complete, unfiltered authenticity in every context is also not realistic or safe.

20.2.2 Strategic Authenticity (Choosing Contexts)

Instead of all-or-nothing, think in terms of strategic authenticity:

- Some contexts are high mask by necessity: job interviews, medical appointments, certain family gatherings
- Some contexts can be low mask or no mask: close friends, ND-friendly communities, online spaces, specific relationships built on mutual weirdness

You have a right to environments where you don't have to constantly pretend. You also have a choice about where to invest your limited masking energy.

A useful exercise:

- Make three columns: High Mask, Medium Mask, Low Mask

- List common contexts (work, specific friends, family groups, online spaces)
- Then ask: "Is there one place I can move from High to Medium, or Medium to Low, over the next few months?"

That might look like:

- Telling a work friend you're autistic or ADHD after trust is built
- Stimming more openly around people who have already shown kindness
- Letting one friend see your meltdown instead of hiding every time

Each small move of authenticity frees bandwidth and reduces the pressure cooker effect that leads to blowups or collapses.

20.2.3 Finding Your People

One of the biggest upgrades you can give a sensitive nervous system is better company.

Signs of ND-friendly people / communities:

- They accept "no" without punishment
- They're curious about differences instead of threatened by them
- They're willing to adjust environment (lights, sound, timing) without making you feel like a burden
- They don't demand constant performance for access to connection

Where they often cluster:

- Interest-based communities (hobbies, fandoms, maker spaces, open-source projects)
- Neurodivergent and mental health spaces (with the caveat that not all are healthy)
- Creative and technical subcultures
- Online groups where text-based, asynchronous communication is normal

Social navigation gets dramatically easier when the base expectation is "we are all a bit weird here" instead of "blend in or be out."

20.3 Boundaries for Porous Nervous Systems

Highly sensitive, empathic, stimulus-reactive brains are porous: other people's moods, needs, and chaos seep in fast and deep.

Without boundaries, you become:

- The default therapist friend
- The colleague who always picks up slack

- The person who stays at the party two hours past safe capacity because someone might feel abandoned

Boundaries are not just "saying no." They're design decisions about:

- Where your time goes
- What environments you allow
- Which emotional states you take responsibility for (hint: only yours)

20.3.1 Social Energy Is a Finite Budget

Think of your social capacity as a daily or weekly budget. For some phenotypes:

- The Happy Little Kid feels rich in the moment and overspends, then crashes
- The Lifeguard spends most of the budget on scanning for danger
- The Princess & Pea gets hit with hidden "fees" (unanticipated slights, noise, microaggressions)
- The Fog may not notice the budget is gone until the system shuts down

You don't have to quantify it perfectly. Just acknowledge: **"Every social thing costs something, even if I love the people."**

Practical moves:

- Plan buffer time after big social events
- Avoid stacking high-cost events back-to-back
- Treat recovery (alone time, sensory rest) as a scheduled part of social life, not a failure

20.3.2 Saying No (Especially When You Want to Please Everyone)

People-pleasing is often a trauma-informed optimization: you learned that keeping others happy is safer.

Boundaries for people-pleasers need scripts that feel doable, not confrontational. For example:

- "I really want to, but I don't have the bandwidth this week."
- "That sounds fun and my brain is already at capacity, can we pick a shorter/earlier/quieter version?"
- "I'm going to head out in a bit so I don't hit the wall."

You can also pre-declare limits:

- "I can hang until 9, then I have to bail to be functional tomorrow."
- "I can do one big social thing this weekend, want it to be this?"

Enforcing these boundaries will feel selfish at first. It's not. It's the only way to avoid the pattern where you say yes until you secretly resent everyone and then disappear.

20.3.3 Protecting Your Sensory Environment

Boundaries are also about sense data, not just people.

Common upgrades:

- Headphones or earplugs in loud places
- Choosing seating that gives you a wall behind you and a view of exits (Lifeguard-friendly)
- Negotiating for different venues ("coffee shop instead of bar," "walk instead of crowded restaurant")
- Taking planned sensory breaks at events (stepping outside, bathroom reset, quiet corner scroll)

You are not being high-maintenance when you ask for these things. You're doing basic plumbing work on your nervous system.

20.4 Sensory-Social Differences: Why Parties Are Exhausting

Neurotypical social spaces are often designed with assumptions like:

- Background noise is fun
- More people = more energy
- Overlapping conversations are stimulating, not threatening
- Eye contact, quick banter, and small talk are default settings

For a lot of ND phenotypes, those assumptions are inverted.

20.4.1 What a Party Looks Like Under the Hood

At a typical party, your nervous system may be juggling:

Auditory overload

Music, clinking, multiple conversations, sudden laughter spikes

Visual overload

Movement everywhere, flashing lights, many faces and micro-expressions

Social decoding

Interpreting tone, sarcasm, subtext, body language

Threat monitoring (hello Lifeguard)

Is anyone upset? Am I in the way? Did I say something wrong?

Self-monitoring (Princess & Pea + RSD)

How am I coming across? Did they just flinch? Should I rephrase that?

No wonder you're wrecked after two hours.

Nothing is wrong with you for finding this hard. The setup is mismatched to your regulatory domains: arousal, sensory processing, and social engagement are all being hammered at once.

20.4.2 One-on-One vs. Group Dynamics

Many sensitive brains do far better in:

- One-on-one conversations
- Small groups with clear structure (game nights, D&D, book clubs, co-working)
- Asynchronous text or voice messages

Group dynamics often demand:

- Rapid context switching
- Split attention across multiple speakers
- Higher tolerance for ambiguity and interruption

When possible, steer your social life toward formats where your nervous system can succeed:

- Invite a friend for a walk or coffee instead of meeting them at a huge party
- Join small, structured groups instead of open, drop-in social events
- Use online spaces where you can read, pause, and respond in your own time

You're not antisocial for preferring different formats. You're engineering social environments compatible with your brain's IO ports.

20.4.3 Making Parties Less Terrible (If You Want to Go)

Sometimes you want to go anyway: for friends, family, networking, or just curiosity. A few hacks:

Have a role
Being the person who brings snacks, DJs, or helps set up/clean gives you structure and natural conversation starters.

Anchor person
Identify one person you can retreat to when you're untethered. Agree ahead of time that you'll check in with each other.

Arrival and exit plan
Decide how long you'll stay, and how you'll leave. "Irish goodbye" is a perfectly valid strategy if formal goodbyes are draining.

Scheduled sensory breaks
Plan to step outside every 30–45 minutes. Don't wait until you're fried.

Think of it like visiting a high-altitude city: you can absolutely go, but maybe you bring oxygen and don't try to sprint stairs.

20.5 Case Snapshots: Sensitive Brains in the Wild

20.5.1 Case 1: The Slack Spiral (Princess & Pea + Happy Little Kid)

Jordan, 31, works in a remote team. They post an idea in a group channel. Their manager reacts with a neutral "Let's think on this" and no emoji.

Jordan's nervous system:

- Interprets "Let's think on this" as "terrible idea, I'm disappointed"
- RSD wave hits: heat, nausea, replaying every message they've sent for months
- They start typing an apology DM, then delete it, then send three follow-up messages clarifying what they "really meant"

We teach Jordan to:

- Pause and run the three checks (body, evidence, pattern)
- DM their manager later with a script: "Hey, my brain sometimes misreads tone. When you said 'let's think on this,' did you mean 'bad idea' or 'needs refinement' or just 'I'm busy'?"
- Use a self-soothing protocol before sending follow-ups

Outcome:

Half the time, the manager meant "interesting, I'm just slammed." The other half, they actually had feedback, which Jordan could then hear without drowning in shame.

20.5.2 Case 2: The Holiday Hangover (Lifeguard + Princess & Pea)

Amira, 27, spends three days with extended family. Loud house, political debates, kids screaming, constant criticism flying around.

By day two:

- Sleep is wrecked
- Hypervigilance is maxed: any raised voice = threat
- They interpret every comment about their job or life as a referendum on their worth
- After the trip, they're flattened for a week

We don't tell Amira to "just be less sensitive." We:

- Plan sensory exits (walks, errands, hiding in a quiet room) into each day
- Practice pre-scripted boundaries, like "I'm not discussing work this trip" or "Let's change the subject"
- Arrange post-visit recovery days as a non-negotiable, not a luxury

With those in place, Amira still finds holidays hard, but they're no longer multi-week nervous system injuries.

20.6 Putting It Together: Designing a Social Life That Fits

Social navigation for sensitive brains is not about learning the rules and following them better. It's about honest mapping and deliberate design:

- Knowing that RSD and hypervigilance distort your perception, but don't invalidate it
- Accepting that masking has both uses and real costs
- Treating social energy as finite and worth budgeting
- Recognizing that your sensory profile is not negotiable, but your environment often is
- Choosing formats, people, and contexts that let your nervous system show up as a partner, not an enemy

Your social regulatory domain doesn't exist in isolation. It's entangled with:

- Arousal and sleep (see Chapter 13)
- Mood and threat sensitivity (Lifeguard, Grumpy Old Man)
- Cognitive bandwidth (Fog days vs hyperfocus days)
- Pain and physical state (when your body hurts, everyone is more annoying)

So expect variability over time:

- There will be seasons where you're more extroverted and seasons where you're a cave goblin
- There will be weeks where you can handle loud events and weeks where even phone calls feel like too much
- Life phases: health changes, caregiving, big projects, will shift your capacities

The point is not to stabilize yourself into one fixed social identity. The point is to stay in conversation with your nervous system, adjust expectations, and build relationships where that conversation is allowed.

If there's a single takeaway from this chapter, let it be this:

You are not "too sensitive for this world." You are sensitive in a world that often runs on default settings. You are allowed (more than allowed, required) to change the settings wherever you can.

20.7 Using the Mastery Loop: RSD Trigger Example

Scenario: Friend's text reply was short and felt cold. Your brain says: "They hate me. I ruined everything."

1. NOTICE: "My Princess & Pea is amplifying social pain. My Grumpy Old Man is generating dread about handling this. My body has that full-flush RSD feeling."

2. NORMALIZE: "Of course I'm interpreting this as rejection. My right TPJ processes social cues with higher gain. My right frontal is threat-biased. This is my Princess & Pea doing what she does. Not reality, amplification."

3. REGULATE: Choose tools:

- Body check (pause, breathe, notice the wave)
- Evidence check (what actually happened? Short text. That's it.)
- Ask for clarity ("Hey, your text felt brief: everything okay?" or wait 2 hours and see)

4. REASSIGN: "I'm not leading with Princess & Pea catastrophizing. I'm bringing Happy Little Kid curiosity forward: 'Maybe they're just busy. I'll reach out tomorrow if still concerned.' "

5. REFLECT: Next day, friend responds warmly: "Sorry, was in a meeting!" Pattern confirmed: **My Princess & Pea generates false alarms. When I pause and check evidence, the catastrophe rarely happens.** This is how RSD loses power, one data point at a time.

This is how you navigate the social world. Not by eliminating sensitivity (impossible, and you'd lose your gifts). By noticing patterns, normalizing responses, regulating reactivity, choosing who leads, and learning from data.

20.8 Key Takeaways

For sensitive, pattern-detecting, high-gain brains, the social world runs on hard mode. The goal is not to become "normal", it's to build a social life that fits your actual nervous system.

- **RSD is real circuit configuration:** Right frontal (Grumpy Old Man "too much effort to handle this") + right TPJ (Princess & Pea amplification of social pain) = rejection lands like full-body shame flush with overwhelming sense of "can't deal with this." Not drama, not "too sensitive", measurable hyperactivation. Your CEO may be involved here too, if it verges into a relationship or breakup-focused OCD.
- **Three-step RSD check:** Body check (is this a wave?), evidence check (what actually happened?), pattern check (have I felt this before in situations that turned out fine?). Separate signal from amplified noise.
- **Ask, don't mind-read:** Explicit clarification ("My brain is telling me I messed up, is that happening?") updates your model of reality, weakens RSD over time by providing actual data instead of catastrophic assumptions.

- **Strategic authenticity, not universal:** High mask when necessary (job interviews), low/no mask when safe (close friends, ND communities). Chronic heavy masking = exhaustion, depersonalization, depression. Complete authenticity everywhere also isn't safe. Choose contexts strategically.
- **Social energy is finite:** Every social interaction costs something (even if you love the people). Plan buffer time, avoid stacking high-cost events, treat recovery as scheduled necessity not failure. Sensory-social load is real, parties = auditory overload + social decoding + threat monitoring + self-monitoring simultaneously.

20.9 Reader Reflections

Take a moment to consider your own social navigation:

1. **How does RSD show up for you?** "Can we talk later?" = firing squad? Delayed text = they hate you? Neutral tone = rejection? Can you identify your specific RSD amplification patterns and trace them to right frontal + right TPJ hyperactivation?
2. **What does masking cost you versus protect you from?** Exhaustion and depersonalization (costs)? Necessary safety in certain contexts (protection)? Where are you high-masking out of necessity versus habit? Where could you move to medium or low mask?
3. **What's your social energy budget?** How many social events per week before depletion? What drains most (parties = sensory overload, work meetings = masking, family = history)? What recharges (solitude, specific people)?
4. **What weekly social cadence actually works for you?** How many nights out, how many zero-people days?
5. **What would a social life designed for your nervous system look like?** More one-on-ones? Text over phone? Sensory-friendly venues? Advance notice for changes? What's one change you could make this month that honors your actual nervous system?

Ch 21: Creative Flow States

When the Noise Stops, and The Magic Happens

You don't need me to tell you what flow feels like.

You've been there:

- The clock vanishes
- Your inner critic finally shuts up for a blessed hour
- Ideas actually line up instead of stampeding you
- You look up and there's a thing in the world that didn't exist before

For gifted, tortured brains, flow isn't just pleasant. It's one of the only states where all your extra wiring feels like an advantage instead of a liability. The noise stops. The magic happens.

Flow feels like your creative cadence finally locking in: everything firing in time instead of tripping over itself.

This chapter is about what flow actually is, what your brain is doing in those moments, and how to build more deliberate pathways into that state using meditation, neurofeedback (especially alpha-theta and SMR), and some smart bottleneck management around anxiety, attention, and self-sabotage.

21.1 What Flow Actually Is

Psychologist Mihaly Csikszentmihalyi (whose name is, frankly, also a flow challenge) described flow as a state where:

- Challenge and skill are well matched
- Attention is fully absorbed
- Time distortion is common
- Self-consciousness fades
- The activity is rewarding in and of itself

Notice what's not in that list: "effortless" or "relaxed." Flow can be calm, but it can also feel intense, demanding, even a little edgy. What's constant is that your resources are fully recruited and well organized. Your circuits are aligned and working toward the same goal for a change.

Under the hood, a few things are happening:

- Your prefrontal cortex dials down some of its self-monitoring and second-guessing functions
- Large-scale networks toggle between internally focused (default mode) and externally / task focused (task-positive) modes in a more flexible way
- Neurochemical systems: especially dopamine, norepinephrine, and endocannabinoids, shift toward a sweet spot: alert, motivated, not overwhelmed
- Brain rhythms move into patterns that support stable attention and creative association, including changes in alpha, theta, and sometimes SMR ranges

Flow is not one exact brain state so much as a family of organized states where your cognitive, emotional, and motor systems are coherently aimed at the same target.

21.2 The Brain in Flow: A Quick Tour

Let's keep the neuroscience tight but real.

21.2.1 Prefrontal Quieting

In flow, parts of the prefrontal cortex involved in self-critique and time tracking turn down a bit. This is often called *transient hypofrontality*, "temporarily less frontal activity."

What that feels like:

- Less intrusive self-talk ("this sucks, you suck")
- Less awareness of time passing
- Less rumination about past and future

You're not lobotomized; the PFC is still online for planning and sequencing. It's just not running an endless commentary on your performance.

For the Princess & Pea, that means less RSD chatter.
For the Lifeguard, less catastrophic simulation.
For the Happy Little Kid, fewer impulsive detours driven by novelty every four seconds.

21.2.2 Network Toggling: DMN and Task-Positive Networks

Two big networks matter here:

- **Default Mode Network (DMN)** – associated with mind-wandering, autobiographical thinking, self-referential processing, and creative association

- **Task-Positive Network (TPN)** – associated with focused, externally oriented tasks

In normal life, these tend to anti-correlate: when one is up, the other is down.

In flow, you often see more fluid toggling and better coordination:

- DMN contributes insight, imagery, and unexpected associations
- TPN keeps you tethered to the actual task and external constraints

Flow is not "TPN only" laser focus. It's collaboration between internal and external modes. That's why flow is so fertile for creativity: you're not just grinding; you're also recombining.

21.2.3 Neurochemistry: Dopamine, Norepinephrine, Endocannabinoids

In flow, you typically land in a zone of high but not excessive dopamine and norepinephrine:

- **Dopamine:** motivation, reward prediction, pattern recognition, "this is interesting, keep going"
- **Norepinephrine:** alertness, signal-to-noise tuning, "pay attention to this, not that"

Too little of those? You're bored, foggy.
Too much? You're anxious, jittery, scattered.

Flow is the Goldilocks band.

There's also evidence for endocannabinoid involvement, your brain's own internal cannabinoid system. These molecules can contribute to:

- Pain reduction
- Enhanced pattern recognition
- A sense of smooth "connectedness" in thought and movement

That's one reason some people mistakenly chase creative flow with external cannabis: they're trying to pharmacologically replicate an internal state that the brain can generate on its own.

21.2.4 Oscillations: Alpha, Theta, SMR and Creativity

All of this plays out on top of rhythmic brain activity, your EEG bands.

Three brainwave ranges matter a lot for creativity and flow:

Alpha (resting/calming rhythms)
Often associated with relaxed alertness, idling, and inhibition of irrelevant inputs. In creative tasks, slightly increased alpha over some regions can be linked to allowing internal associations to surface while keeping noise down.

Theta (deep relaxation/drowsiness rhythms)
Linked to drowsiness, hypnagogic imagery, and memory processes. In certain contexts, especially frontal midline theta, it's associated with sustained internal focus and working memory. Alpha-theta states, particularly eyes-closed and deeply relaxed, have been shown to support creative insight, emotional processing, and access to non-linear, associative material.

SMR (Sensorimotor Rhythm, calm focus state) Associated with a state of calm, inhibited motor activity and stable attention. Training SMR is classically associated with less impulsivity, better sleep architecture, and more consistent focus, the "cat on windowsill" state.

Alpha-theta neurofeedback trains you to drop into a deeply relaxed, internally focused, semi-dreamy but aware state. That "edge of sleep" place is often where surprising connections and imagery bubble up. Prime soil for creativity.

When you train SMR, you're building a stable, calm attentional platform: less fidget, less micro-startle, fewer jumps in and out of tasks. That's prime soil for sitting your butt in the chair and actually working the craft.

Put simply:

- **Alpha-theta helps you open the doors to new material**
- **SMR helps you sit with it long enough to make something real**

21.3 Creativity as Generativity (Why Practice Beats Genius)

There's a romantic myth that creativity is a lightning strike. You're either a natural or you're not, and the best ideas happen when you're young and wildly inspired.

The data are not on the myth's side.

Across multiple fields (art, science, music, writing) a few patterns show up:

- People who produce a lot of work tend to have more high-impact pieces. Quantity predicts quality because each attempt is a lottery ticket with accumulated skill behind it
- "Career age" (how long you've been seriously practicing a craft) often matters more than chronological age for peak work
- Many creators have multiple peaks across life, especially if they keep experimenting with new problems, methods, or mediums

Creativity, in other words, is generativity: The willingness to keep making things, and the nervous system capacity to tolerate the uncertainty, boredom, and self-doubt that come with long practice.

From a brain perspective, that means:

- Repeatedly engaging networks for idea generation (DMN, associative cortex)
- Repeatedly engaging networks for selection, editing, and execution (PFC, TPN, motor systems)
- Repeatedly moving between exploration (open, divergent thinking) and exploitation (focused, convergent refinement)

Flow states are wonderful, but they're not the whole story. Flow helps you:

- Bridge the gap between "intention" and "action"
- Spend enough time in the zone where practice actually rewires circuits
- Experience creating as rewarding enough that you want to come back

Long-term, what matters most is not how often you get struck by divine inspiration, but how often you can enter usable flow and return to the work.

21.4 The Creative Phenotype (Gifted, Tortured, Wired for Flow)

Some brains are especially primed for creativity:

- High baseline associative thinking
- Strong pattern recognition
- Big emotional range
- Sensory sensitivity
- Tendency toward obsessive focus or runaway distraction

In other words: a lot of the phenotypes in this book.

The flip side is that these same traits bring bottlenecks:

- Anxiety that spikes right when you try to start
- Perfectionism that kills ideas in the cradle
- Boredom with routine that prevents practice from compounding
- Cycles of all-night sprints and total collapse

The creative phenotype isn't "has better ideas." It's "has more volatile ingredients and higher gain on the system."

Flow work, especially with tools like meditation and neurofeedback, is how you install governors and channels so that volatility becomes fuel instead of arson.

21.5 "They See Poetry Everywhere": Associative Flow

Poet-brains cannot experience life directly. They immediately:

- **Narrativize** (Left Language Network: "That's just like life!")
- **Metaphorize** (Right Posterior: Finding patterns in shoelaces)
- **Meta-process** (CEO: "What does this mean?")

This is constant flow:

- Associative thinking = creativity engine (DMN active)
- Pattern-detection = innovation source (seeing connections others miss)
- Metaphorical thinking = artistic depth (everything is symbol, meaning, poetry)

The torture: You can't turn it off. Constant meaning-making. Overthinking. Paralysis by analysis.

The gift: This is where art comes from. Where innovation emerges. Where paradigm shifts happen.

Channeling the gift:

- Creative work (writing, art, music, design)
- Problem-solving (seeing solutions others miss)
- Innovation (connecting disparate ideas)
- Teaching (making complex ideas accessible through metaphor)

Your curse is your gift, when you learn to conduct it.

21.6 Flow States for Neurodivergent Brains

21.6.1 ADHD and Flow (Hyperfocus)

The gift:

- Hyperfocus IS flow (when conditions right)
- Can sustain for hours (when engaged)
- High-quality output (deep work)
- Loses track of time (complete absorption)

The challenge:

- Initiating flow (Stabilizer offline: hard to start)
- Sustaining on boring tasks (need novelty, challenge, interest)
- Interruptions break flow (hard to re-enter)
- Hyperfocus on wrong thing (CEO stuck)

Accessing flow:

- Clear goals (structure for ADHD brain)

- Immediate feedback (maintains engagement)
- High interest (intrinsic motivation)
- External deadline (activates urgency)
- Eliminate distractions (protect flow once entered)

21.6.2 Autism and Flow (Deep Focus)

The gift:

- Deep focus on special interests = sustained flow
- Can maintain for hours/days (exceptional endurance)
- Mastery-level work (depth of expertise)
- Predictable flow (same conditions = same state)

The challenge:

- Interruptions feel violent (CEO stuck, can't switch)
- Obligation tasks don't trigger flow (need interest-based)
- Sensory overwhelm breaks flow (Princess overload)
- Social demands interrupt (need protected time)

Accessing flow:

- Predictability (structure, routine)
- Special interests (intrinsic motivation)
- Protected time (no interruptions)
- Sensory-optimized environment (comfortable, controlled)

21.6.3 HSP and Flow (Optimal Stimulation)

The gift:

- Depth of processing (rich, layered work)
- Sensory richness (when not overwhelming)
- Emotional depth (art, writing, empathy-based work)

The challenge:

- Sensory overload breaks flow (too much input)
- Emotional overwhelm (RSD, criticism sensitivity)
- Need optimal stimulation (not too much, not too little)

Accessing flow:

- Sensory-friendly environment (controlled input)
- Emotional safety (low self-consciousness)
- Optimal challenge (engaging but not overwhelming)

21.6.4 Creative Brains and Flow (Constant Potential)

The gift:

- Associative thinking always available (DMN active)
- Pattern-detection on overdrive (see connections constantly)
- "They see poetry everywhere" (constant meaning-making)
- Creativity engine never turns off

The challenge:

- TOO MUCH flow (can't turn off pattern-detection)
- Overthinking (constant analysis)
- Can't just be (always meaning-making)

Channeling it:

- Creative work (gives outlet for constant associations)
- Scheduled creative time (container for overflow)
- Meditation (changing relationship to constant flow: see Chapter 17)
- Neurofeedback (DMN regulation: see Chapter 18)

21.7 Flow vs. Substances

Many poet-brains have discovered that substances create flow-like states:

Cannabis:

- Activates DMN (associative thinking, creativity)
- Quiets CEO (less self-monitoring)
- Reduces self-consciousness (ego quiets)
- Time distortion (similar to flow)

Psychedelics:

- Enhance associative thinking (pattern-detection on steroids)
- Ego dissolution (transient hypofrontality, like flow)
- Creative insights (DMN disruption → new perspectives)
- Enhanced connectivity (brain networks integrate)

These are real effects. Substances can create states similar to flow.

But:

- **Externally-induced** (drug creates state, not you)
- **Temporary** (hours, then baseline)
- **Don't build capacity** (borrowed, not trained)
- **Tolerance** (need more for same effect)
- **Dependence** (using substance to access creativity)

True flow:

- **Internally-generated** (you create conditions, enter state voluntarily)
- **Sustainable** (skill builds with practice)
- **No tolerance** (gets easier, not harder)
- **Independence** (access anytime, no substance needed)

See Chapter 14 for full discussion of substance-creativity myth.

21.8 Accessing Flow (Practical Strategies)

21.8.1 Environmental Design

- Minimize distractions (phone off, apps blocked, door closed)
- Optimize sensory input (comfortable, not overwhelming)
- Dedicated creative space (context cue for flow)
- Time protection (block calendar, communicate boundaries)

21.8.2 Skill Development

- Build capacity for challenge (practice, training, learning)
- Gradual difficulty increase (don't jump to expert)
- Mastery mindset (growth, not fixed)

21.8.3 Neurofeedback for Flow

- **Alpha-Theta training** (deep states, creativity, insight)
- **SMR training** (calm alertness, sustained focus)
- **DMN regulation** (associative thinking without rumination)
- See Chapter 18 for protocols

21.8.4 Meditation for Flow

- **Open awareness** (CEO quiets, allows flow)
- **Noting practice** (metacognition, observing without engaging)
- **Body scan** (embodiment, reduces self-consciousness)
- See Chapter 17 for practices

21.9 Phenotype-Specific Flow Recipes

The ADHD/autism/HSP framing above is useful, but your phenotype profile is more precise. Here's how to match your flow strategy to the circuits that block or enable it:

Happy Little Kid (approach system offline): Novelty on rails. Your flow killer is boredom, you need high variety *inside* strict containers. Set a tight time box (45 minutes), change the sub-task every 15, and keep the dopamine hits coming through novelty within structure. Playlists, environment changes, alternating creative modes (write, sketch, outline) all help. The container prevents drift; the variety keeps Happy Little Kid engaged.

Grumpy Old Man (effort-dread): Low-stakes warm-ups. Your flow killer is the appraisal that it's not worth the effort before you've even started. Begin with something so easy it doesn't trigger dread, freewriting, doodling, arranging materials. Once you're five minutes in, the effort appraisal often recalibrates. Don't aim for quality. Aim for movement.

Stabilizer (can't start): Frictionless starts. Your flow killer is the activation gap between deciding and doing. Remove every obstacle between intention and action: open the document the night before, have tools ready, use a physical ritual (stand up, walk to desk, sit down, start). Don't think, begin. The Stabilizer wakes up through movement, not motivation.

Supervisor (perfectionism): Separate creation from evaluation. Your flow killer is quality control firing during generation. Give yourself explicit permission to produce garbage. First draft = no Supervisor allowed. Set a "revision session" later so the Supervisor knows it will get its turn. If perfectionism still blocks you, set a timer and commit to output quantity, not quality.

Lifeguard (threat-scanning): Safety rituals first. Your flow killer is the feeling that the environment isn't secure. Build a predictable warm-up: same time, same place, same sequence. Check that your physical space feels safe. Close the door. Limit exposure windows (90 minutes, then break). Once the Lifeguard confirms "safe," it can relax enough for flow to emerge.

Fog & the Tide (low energy): Ride your tide. Your flow killer is forcing creativity when your brain is at low tide. Track your energy cycles for a week, when do you feel clearest? Schedule creative work there. Keep the friction absurdly low for foggy periods: voice memos instead of writing, outlines instead of prose. Don't fight the Fog. Work around it.

CEO (stuck in loops): Break the loop with external input. Your flow killer is perseveration, grinding on one problem without progress. Switch tasks deliberately (CEO needs help releasing). Talk to someone. Walk. Change rooms. Use a noting practice ("stuck, stuck, stuck") to observe the loop without feeding it. The CEO unsticks through interruption, not force.

Princess & the Pea (sensory overwhelm): Optimize the sensory environment ruthlessly. Your flow killer is too much input. Noise-canceling headphones. Controlled lighting. Comfortable temperature. No scratchy clothing. Remove visual clutter. Your Princess processes everything at high gain, reduce the input so your creative signal isn't drowned by sensory noise.

21.10 When Your Brain Takes a Seat Behind Your Face

Paul Simon actually wrote two companion songs called "Think Too Much" ((a) and (b)) and together they map the whole problem. In (b), he described the left side of the brain dominating the right, while the right side labors through the long and speechless night. That's the Stabilizer and Supervisor jammed, left GO and right STOP fighting each other, unable to negotiate. In (a), he asked about something different: whether you've ever experienced a period of grace, a moment when your brain just takes a seat and lets you be.

That's the flip side. The period of grace is what happens when they negotiate well. The Supervisor becomes poised rather than reactive. You're balanced between thoughts instead of drowning in them. The brake works, the engine runs, and neither one is stuck.

That's flow. That's what you're after.

Not constant. Not permanent. But reliable enough that you can access it when you need it, when you sit down to create, when you need to solve a hard problem, when you want to feel fully alive instead of constantly managing twelve circuits simultaneously.

For poet-brains, that period of grace is both easier and harder to access than for neurotypical brains:

Easier because:

- Your associative networks (DMN) are already hyperactive: connections happen automatically
- Your pattern-detection is on overdrive: you see relationships others miss
- Your depth of processing creates richness most people can't access
- Your hyperfocus (ADHD) or deep focus (autism) IS flow when conditions are right

Harder because:

- Your CEO won't stop monitoring and second-guessing
- Your Grumpy Old Man predicts everything will be wasted effort
- Your Timekeeper races too fast to settle into sustainable rhythm
- Your Princess amplifies every micro-signal into potential rejection
- Your Lifeguard scans for threats even when you're safe

The work is teaching your circuits to collaborate instead of compete. When Happy Little Kid engages, Stabilizer initiates, CEO facilitates without perseverating, and the rest of the orchestra supports instead of sabotages, that's when grace arrives.

The period of grace isn't something you force. It's what emerges when you've trained your phenotypes well enough that they know how to play together.

21.11 The Promise

Your poet-brain is built for flow.

Your associative thinking (DMN), your pattern-detection (right posterior), your depth of processing (when Fog is gift, not curse), your hyperfocus (ADHD), your deep focus (autism), these are flow states waiting to be conducted.

The challenge: Learning to access flow voluntarily, channel it productively, and sustain it without substances.

The tools: Environmental design, skill development, neurofeedback, meditation, understanding your phenotypes.

Your curse is your gift. Time to channel it.

21.12 Key Takeaways

Creativity is not a lightning strike, it's an emergent property of a brain with enough rhythmic stability, reliable creative cadences, and regulatory capacity to spend time in flow, repeatedly, over years.

- **Short version: flow is your orchestra playing one song instead of twelve radios on different stations.** Your prefrontal cortex shuts up, your networks toggle smoothly, dopamine hits the sweet spot. You're alert but not anxious, absorbed but not forcing it.
- **Creativity as generativity:** Quantity predicts quality: each attempt is a lottery ticket with accumulated skill. Career age (time practicing) matters more than chronological age. Practice compounds when nervous system can tolerate uncertainty and return to work repeatedly.
- **Creative phenotypes = volatile ingredients:** High associative thinking, strong pattern recognition, big emotional range, sensory sensitivity, tendency toward obsessive focus or runaway distraction. Higher gain = more creative potential but also more dysregulation risk.
- **Phenotype-specific flow recipes:** Happy Little Kid needs novelty on rails (strict containers, high variety inside). Lifeguard needs safety rituals first (predictable warm-up, limited exposure). Fog needs frictionless starts (ultra-low friction, external scaffolding). Match recipe to phenotype.

- **Substances create pseudo-flow:** Alter same systems that support flow (dopamine, prefrontal quieting) but erode baseline through tolerance, rebound, sleep disruption. More attempts at accessing flow states, less actual completed work that compounds over time.

21.13 Reader Reflections

Take a moment to consider your own creative flow:

1. **When have you experienced real flow?** Clock vanished, inner critic shut up, ideas lined up instead of stampeding? What were the conditions (time, environment, activation level) that allowed flow? Can you identify your flow prerequisites?
2. **Do you recognize your creative phenotype's bottlenecks?** Anxiety spiking when you start (Grumpy Old Man)? Perfectionism killing ideas in cradle (overactive Supervisor)? Boredom preventing practice (Happy Little Kid needs novelty)? All-night sprints then collapse (Stabilizer / Fog)?
3. **Which phenotype-specific flow recipe matches your needs?** Happy Little Kid (novelty on rails)? Lifeguard (safety rituals first)? Fog (frictionless starts)? What's one element you could implement this week?
4. **What would "more days where it's slightly easier to begin, slightly easier to stay, and slightly more rewarding to return" look like?** Not transcendent states every day, just more usable flow, more often. What would a sustainable creative cadence look like over a year? What would that change in your creative output?

Ch 22: Self-Mastery: Conducting Your Orchestra

You're Not Broken. You Were Under-Instructed.

You're not broken. You're an exquisite, complex instrument in a world designed for simple tools. Mastery isn't fixing yourself, it's learning the controls you should have received at birth.

Most of those controls are about cadence: when to let a circuit lead, when to quiet it, and how quickly you can move from one to the other.

Remember the Introduction? "The trouble with poets is they talk too much."

But the real trouble wasn't that you're broken. The real trouble is **nobody gave you the controls.**

You've spent years (maybe decades) trying to regulate yourself with whatever worked:

- Alcohol to quiet the Grumpy Old Man's dread
- Stimulants to wake the Stabilizer's engine
- Cannabis to calm the CEO's sticky attention
- Intensity and drama to activate the Happy Little Kid when it went offline
- Perfectionism to satisfy the Supervisor's quality control
- Isolation to protect the Princess & the Pea from overwhelm

You were trying to regulate circuits that neuroscience barely understands and psychiatry often medicalizes without offering real solutions. You were under-regulated. Not broken. No one gave you the instruction manual.

Now you have the map. You know your phenotypes. You understand why you feel what you feel, why you struggle with what you struggle with, and why you've been trying to regulate yourself the way you have.

Now you have the tools. Sleep optimization. Neurofeedback protocols. Meditation practices. Behavioral strategies. Substance understanding. Anxiety regulation. Productivity systems matched to your circuits.

Now comes mastery. Learning to conduct the orchestra you were born with.

22.1 The Orchestra: Your Twelve Instruments

You've met all twelve phenotypes and the six systems they organize into (Part I). Here's the master map, your conductor's score:

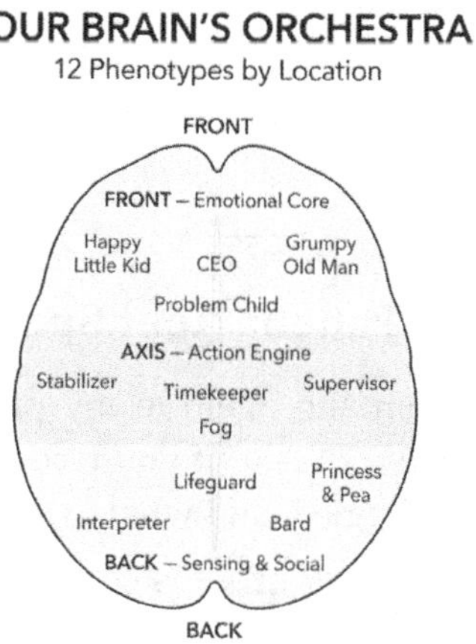

Figure 22.1: Orchestra Map

Your job as conductor: Learn which system needs regulation (Motivation/Executive/Emotional Regulation/Orienting/Language/Processing) and which specific phenotype to address. When you NOTICE a struggle, ask: "Which instrument is this? Which system?" Then use the Mastery Loop (Notice → Normalize → Regulate → Reassign → Reflect) with precision. All have gifts. Choosing consciously instead of reactively is mastery.

Composite, like every case in this book. The pattern is one I have seen many times; the person is not one person.

Marcus came in full catastrophe: kicked out of his grad program for missing deadlines, girlfriend had left, living on a friend's couch, convinced he was broken beyond repair. His brain map showed the classic "tortured poet" pattern, all five phenotypes screaming: Stabilizer offline (excess slow waves in left motor cortex, couldn't start tasks), Grumpy Old Man loud (right frontal racing activity, generating overwhelming dread about every task), CEO stuck (frontal midline excess, OCD-like loops), Lifeguard threat-sensitive (posterior cingulate elevated, constant scanning), Princess & Pea overwhelmed (right temporal-parietal overactive, RSD). "Smartest guy in most rooms," I told him, "but miserable because every circuit is cramping up at once."

Sixty sessions later, motor activation normalized, right frontal calmed, cingulates released. A year later: back in his program, back with his girlfriend, working full-time. "I didn't think this was possible," he said. His brain map showed the shift: measurable improvement across all five phenotypes. His tortured poet is still there, still sensitive, still intense, still gifted. But the circuits aren't cramping up anymore. Same essence, better regulation. The phenotypes shifted.

Marcus had what I call **the Gifted Poet Pattern.** Let me show you what that means.

22.2 The Gifted Poet Pattern: Your Specific Constellation

There's a pattern I see again and again in my practice. If you're reading this book, you probably have it. And if you recognize yourself here, you'll understand why you've struggled, and what to do about it.

22.2.1 The Pattern: Five Phenotypes in Constellation

1. Weak Stabilizer (left frontal)

- Low beta, excess theta or alpha
- Can't start tasks, can't sustain attention
- Activation energy deficit
- Hard to stay engaged when awake

2. Weak Supervisor (right frontal)

- Similar pattern on right side
- Impulse control struggles (subtle or obvious)
- Over-inhibition or under-inhibition

3. Hyperactive CEO (anterior cingulate)

- Fast or slow waves in excess (usually alpha or theta)
- Micromanaging, perseverative, obsessive
- Can't let go, can't switch easily
- "Think of this, think of this, hey think of this"

4. Hyperactive Lifeguard (posterior cingulate)

- Fast waves, excess activation
- Threat-sensitive, hypervigilant, ruminating
- "Heads up, heads up, heads up"
- Anxiety, worry, can't relax

5. Princess & Pea Overwhelmed (right TPJ)

- Slow waves, high-gain processing

- Sensory flooding, social intensity
- Can't ignore anything: every texture, sound, expression gets in

22.2.2 Why This Constellation Happens

You're built fast. High processing speed. High intelligence. Ferrari brain.

But you're running on resource depletion. Poor sleep. Chronic stress. Fatigue. Fog.

So your Stabilizer and Supervisor (the circuits that should activate and regulate) are offline or weak. They can't keep you in gear. They can't keep you asleep at night.

Your brain compensates. CEO micromanages to keep you on task. Lifeguard hyperscans to keep you safe. Princess & Pea processes everything to make sure nothing's missed.

These are gifts being used as compensation. And when you use a gift through fatigue, it cramps.

- CEO's steel trap mind can't unstick
- Lifeguard's vigilance becomes anxiety
- Princess & Pea's sensitivity becomes overwhelm

You look like: ADHD + OCD + anxiety + sensory processing disorder + high sensitivity + giftedness, all at once.

You are: A high-performing brain driving with the e-brake on, standing on the gas to compensate, and cramping up from the effort.

22.2.3 The Intervention Hierarchy for This Pattern

Step 1: Sleep (non-negotiable)

- Fix the foundation first (Chapter 13)
- Left frontal beta needs deep sleep to recover
- MVP protocol, circadian anchoring, no shortcuts
- This is primary: everything else is secondary

Step 2: Left frontal beta training (Stabilizer activation)

- Theta/beta ratio protocol (Chapter 18)
- Wake up the engine that won't start
- Brings Stabilizer back online
- Sleep improves (same circuit), attention improves

Step 3: Watch CEO and Lifeguard relax (secondary release)

- Don't directly target yet: watch them respond
- As Stabilizer comes online, CEO stops micromanaging
- As sleep deepens, Lifeguard stops hyperscanning

- "You can relax, CEO. The Stabilizer's back on the job."

Step 4: If needed, target CEO/Lifeguard directly

- Anterior cingulate flexibility training (Chapter 5)
- Posterior cingulate calming (Chapter 6)
- But often they release on their own once primary issue resolves

Step 5: Address Princess & Pea (sensory overwhelm)

- Right TPJ regulation (Chapter 8)
- Sensory environment optimization
- Usually less urgent once fatigue resolves

22.2.4 The Test: Is This Your Pattern?

Ask yourself:

1. Do you have high intelligence but low productivity? (Fast brain, weak activation)
2. Do you struggle to start tasks AND struggle to sleep? (Stabilizer dual function)
3. Do you get obsessive or ruminative when you're tired? (CEO/Lifeguard compensation)
4. Does the world feel too intense, sounds, textures, emotions, social cues? (Princess & Pea high-gain)
5. Do stimulants help short-term but make things worse long-term? (Borrowing from tomorrow)

If yes to 3+, you likely have the Gifted Poet Pattern.

22.2.5 Your Giftedness Is Not the Problem

The Gifted Poet Pattern is my name for a constellation I see repeatedly in practice, not an established diagnosis. It describes a high-performing brain under resource constraint, compensating brilliantly, and cramping up from the effort.

Your CEO's micromanaging? That's giftedness. If you could use it when you decided, it's a superpower, steel trap mind, deep focus, relentless pursuit of understanding.

Your Lifeguard's hypervigilance? That's giftedness. If regulated, it's awareness, attunement, ability to read context and threat with extraordinary nuance.

Your Princess & Pea's sensitivity? That's giftedness. High-gain processing, catching what others miss, feeling deeply, connecting authentically.

The problem is not the gifts. It's the cramping.

When you can't regulate, when you can't choose to engage or disengage, when you're always on, when it's controlling you instead of you controlling it, that's when gifts become torture.

Mastery is: Unclench the resource. Full range of motion. You decide when to use the steel trap, when to scan for threats, when to process everything deeply.

Not sedating the gifts. Regulating them.

Same essence. Better control. The tortured poet becomes the gifted poet who can rest.

22.3 The Mastery Loop: Notice → Normalize → Regulate → Reassign → Reflect

Here's the framework for conducting your orchestra. This is what mastery looks like in practice.

The Five-Step Mastery Loop:

Run it often enough, and this loop becomes your default cadence for handling trouble: see, understand, adjust, reassign, learn.

1. **NOTICE**: Name which phenotype is leading
2. **NORMALIZE**: This is hardware, not character flaw
3. **REGULATE**: Match tool to phenotype
4. **REASSIGN**: Engage with new state
5. **REFLECT**: Track what worked

22.3.1 Step 1: NOTICE - Name Which Phenotype Is Leading

The practice: When you're struggling, pause and ask: "Which phenotype is driving this?"

Examples:

- Can't start working → Stabilizer offline
- Catastrophizing about meeting → Grumpy Old Man loud
- Snapped at partner → Problem Child (brake failure under fatigue)
- Can't let go of a slight → CEO stuck
- Overwhelmed at party → Princess & Pea + Lifeguard (sensory/social overload)
- Racing thoughts at 3am → Timekeeper won't slow down
- Everything feels heavy → Fog (low-energy state)

The skill: Recognizing the pattern. Not "I'm broken" but "my Stabilizer is offline" or "my Grumpy Old Man is generating dread."

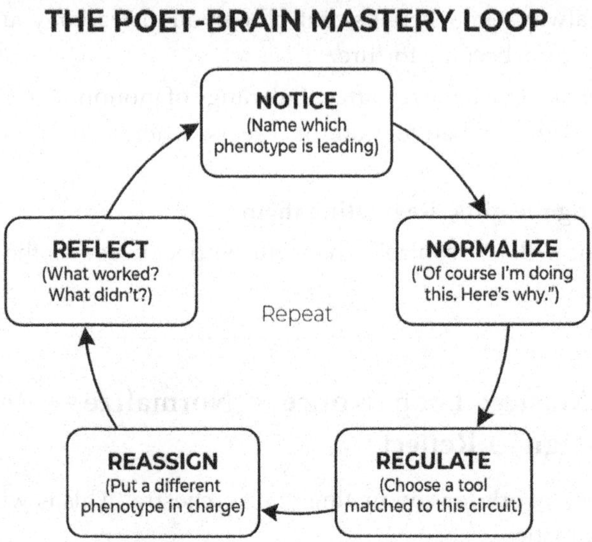

Figure 22.2: Mastery Loop

Why this matters: You can't regulate what you can't name. Noticing which phenotype is active is the first step to choosing a response instead of reacting automatically.

Quick check-in:

- What am I feeling? (emotion)
- What am I doing (or not doing)? (behavior)
- Which phenotype does this match? (pattern recognition)

22.3.2 Step 2: NORMALIZE - "Of Course. Here's Why."

The practice: Once you've named the phenotype, normalize it. This isn't pathology, it's your brain doing what it's wired to do.

Examples:

- "Of course my Stabilizer is offline. I didn't sleep well. Frontal Slow gets worse with poor sleep." (Chapter 3)
- "Of course my Grumpy Old Man is generating dread. I have LVF pattern and genetic predisposition to effort-avoidance." (Chapter 2)
- "Of course my Problem Child came out. I'm exhausted and my brake system fails under fatigue." (Chapter 7)

- "Of course my Princess & the Pea is overwhelmed. I'm processing social information with higher gain." (Chapter 8)
- "Of course my CEO is stuck. I have frontal midline theta dysregulation and this is a loop." (Chapter 5)

The skill: Self-compassion through neuroscience. Not "what's wrong with me?" but "here's exactly which circuit is doing what, and here's why."

Why this matters: Shame makes everything worse. Normalization creates space for regulation. When you understand why your brain is doing what it's doing, you can respond skillfully instead of spiraling.

The reframe:

- From: "I'm broken, I'm failing, what's wrong with me?"
- To: "My ______ is ______, which makes sense because ______. Here's what I can do about it."

22.3.3 Step 3: REGULATE - Choose a Tool from Part II

The practice: Once you've noticed and normalized, choose an intervention matched to the phenotype.

Quick reference guide: Find the phenotype that's loudest right now. Grab the matched tool. You don't need to read the whole list, just your circuit.

If Stabilizer is offline (can't start):

- Movement first, motivation second (Chapter 3)
- External structure (body doubling, deadlines)
- Morning light + exercise (activate naturally)
- SMR neurofeedback (if chronic)

If Grumpy Old Man is generating dread (effort-overwhelm):

- Right frontal alpha training (Chapter 2)
- HRV biofeedback (Chapter 15)
- Breathing (physiological sigh, box breathing)
- Challenge catastrophic thoughts (CBT)

If Problem Child brake is failing (anger, oppositionality):

- Sleep first (non-negotiable) (Chapter 7)
- Pause before reacting (three breaths)
- Right IFG training (strengthen brake)
- Give yourself agency (choices within boundaries)

If CEO is stuck (loops, can't let go):

- Noting practice (label without engaging) (Chapter 5)
- External cueing (timer, stand up, pattern-break)
- NAC (if appropriate - glutamate modulation)

- Open awareness meditation (train letting go)

If Lifeguard is hypervigilant (scanning, ruminating):

- Grounding (present moment, present safety) (Chapter 6)
- PCC alpha training (calm environmental scanner)
- Body scan meditation (shift from thoughts to sensations)
- Trauma-informed work (if PTSD)

If Princess & Pea is overwhelmed (RSD, sensory):

- Sensory environment optimization (reduce load) (Chapter 8)
- Right TPJ regulation (turn down gain)
- Loving-kindness meditation (self-compassion for RSD)
- Boundaries (protect your nervous system)

If Supervisor is dysregulated (impulsivity or perfectionism):

- SMR training in right sensorimotor region (cat on windowsill state) (Chapter 4)
- Stillness practice (if weak - train inhibition)
- "Good enough" practice (if strong - release brake)
- Balance training (know when to apply, when to release)

If Timekeeper is racing (anxiety, can't slow down):

- SMR training (calm alertness) (Chapter 11)
- Body scan (shift from thoughts to sensations)
- Sleep optimization (racing Timekeepers need deep sleep)
- Beta spindle reduction (if present)

If Fog is chronic (brain fog, cognitive slowing):

- Sleep first (foundation) (Chapter 12)
- Address underlying causes (viral, sleep disorders, hormones)
- Alpha frequency training (if slowed alpha)
- Honor natural rhythm (if protective fog)

The skill: Matching intervention to phenotype. Not generic advice, precision tools for specific circuits.

Why this matters: You've tried to regulate before. But you were using blunt instruments (substances) for delicate circuitry. Now you have precision tools matched to your specific dysregulation.

22.3.4 Step 4: REASSIGN - Put a Different Phenotype in the Lead

The practice: Context-dependent leadership. Choose which phenotype leads based on what the situation requires.

Examples: Pick the scenario closest to yours. Notice which phenotypes lead and which consult, that's the conducting.

Exploring new opportunity:

- Bring Happy Little Kid forward (engagement, enthusiasm)
- Let Grumpy Old Man consult (risk assessment)
- CEO decides (given context, which voice wins?)
- Stabilizer executes (get into gear)

High-risk decision:

- Bring Grumpy Old Man forward (effort-cost assessment, critical thinking)
- Lifeguard assesses (actual threat present?)
- Let Happy Little Kid consult (what's the opportunity?)
- CEO decides (balance risk and opportunity)
- Supervisor applies brake (don't act impulsively)

Creative work:

- Let CEO rest (don't direct, don't control)
- Bring Happy Little Kid online (engagement, joy)
- Let Supervisor be weak (don't quality-control too early)
- Timekeeper sets pace (fast for brainstorming, slow for refinement)

Social situation with RSD risk:

- Princess & Pea monitors (social nuance)
- Bard decodes (prosody, tone)
- Lifeguard checks (is this actual threat or RSD amplification?)
- Grumpy Old Man assesses (is handling this worth the effort?)
- CEO decides response (given data, what's skillful?)

Recovery time:

- Honor the low Tide (rest, deep processing, let the ebb do its work)
- Happy Little Kid rests (don't force engagement)
- Stabilizer idles (no productivity demands)
- Supervisor releases (no quality control on rest)

The skill: Conscious leadership assignment. Not "my anxiety is in control" but "I'm choosing to let my Grumpy Old Man assess this risk, then I'll decide."

Why this matters: You're not at the mercy of whichever phenotype is loudest. You're the conductor. You choose which instrument leads based on what the music requires.

22.3.5 Step 5: REFLECT - What Worked, What Didn't

The practice: After using the model, reflect. Did it work? What would you do differently?

Questions to ask:

- Did I correctly identify which phenotype was active?
- Was my regulation strategy effective?
- Did reassigning leadership help?
- What would I do differently next time?
- What did I learn about my orchestra?

Keep a phenotype journal:

- Date, situation, phenotype identified, strategy used, outcome
- Over time, you'll see patterns
- You'll learn which strategies work for your specific configuration
- You'll get faster at noticing and regulating

The skill: Learning from experience. Your orchestra is unique. What works for someone else's configuration might not work for yours. Reflection helps you refine your conducting.

Why this matters: Mastery isn't perfection. It's getting better at noticing, regulating, and choosing. Reflection is how you improve.

22.4 Traits, Regulation, and States: Three Layers of Change

Here's the wisdom from mapping 25,000 brains: **Your brain CAN change. But you need to understand three different layers, and they change on different timescales.**

When people first hear about their phenotypes, they sometimes worry: "Does this mean I'm stuck this way forever?"

No. But to understand what changes and how, you need to distinguish traits from regulation from states.

22.4.1 Traits: Your Resources (Stable, Measurable, Slowly Changeable)

Traits are your circuit resources, the baseline patterns we measure on QEEG:

- Focus capacity (your baseline ability to concentrate)
- Processing speed (your brain's clock speed)
- Sensitivity level (your baseline responsiveness)
- Threat sensitivity (how reactive your avoidance system runs)
- Motor initiation capacity (how easily your Stabilizer engages)

Here's what makes traits different from states: I can see your traits on a brain map regardless of how you're feeling in the moment. You might walk in calm or anxious, rested or exhausted, your trait markers are still there.

Frontal slow pattern. Right frontal asymmetry. Slowed alpha peak. These are structural features of your circuits, not reflections of your current mood.

Traits are stable but not frozen. With sustained training (neurofeedback, meditation, sleep optimization, HRV biofeedback) traits shift slowly at a deep level. This is the real change. Not a temporary state shift, but your resources themselves getting stronger, more resilient, more flexible.

The evidence:

- Neurofeedback: Measurable phenotype shifts typically emerge over 20-40 sessions, with continued improvement through 40+ (varies widely by phenotype, protocol match, and adherence; published RCTs report effect sizes ~0.8 for some indications) (Arns et al., 2009; Duric et al., 2012)
- Meditation: Measurable changes in prefrontal thickness, amygdala reactivity
- Sleep optimization: Improved frontal activation, better regulation
- HRV training: Increased heart rate variability, better stress resilience

Marcus's story (a composite, like every case in this book): Across a long course of training, his trait markers moved on the map, and they moved across several phenotypes rather than one. His circuits aren't cramping up anymore. Same person, stronger resources. What convinced me was the timescale: this was slow change over months, which is what trait change looks like when it is real rather than a good week.

22.4.2 Regulation: How Your Traits Tend to Operate (The Tendency)

Regulation is the flexibility of your traits, how stuck or how fluid they are in practice:

- Can you engage your focus capacity *when you choose*, or is it stuck on or stuck off?
- Can your sensitivity dial up for intimacy and dial down for crowds, or is it always at 11?
- Does your threat assessment system flex appropriately to context, or does it cramp up regardless?

Regulation is the tendency. Two people can have the same trait resources (same sensitivity, same processing speed) but different regulation. One can modulate, turn it up for creative work, turn it down for a noisy restaurant. The other is stuck at one setting. Same resources, different flexibility.

Training primarily targets regulation first. Neurofeedback, meditation, behavioral practice, these teach your circuits to operate across a wider range instead of being stuck. And over time, as regulation improves, the trait resources themselves shift. The circuits get stronger, more resilient, more efficient. That's the deep change.

22.4.3 States: How You Feel Right Now (Rides on Top)

States = how you're feeling and performing in this moment:

- Currently focused or dispersed
- Currently anxious or calm
- Currently activated or flat

States change quickly. Calm in the morning, anxious by afternoon, calm again by evening. A good night's sleep, a bad phone call, a meditation session, states shift in minutes to hours.

Here's the key: You **can't directly control states through willpower**. "Just be calm" doesn't work. States are outcomes, not levers. They ride on top of your trait strength and regulation. Better traits + better regulation = more flexible, more resilient states. You still have bad days. But the bad days are less bad, and you recover faster.

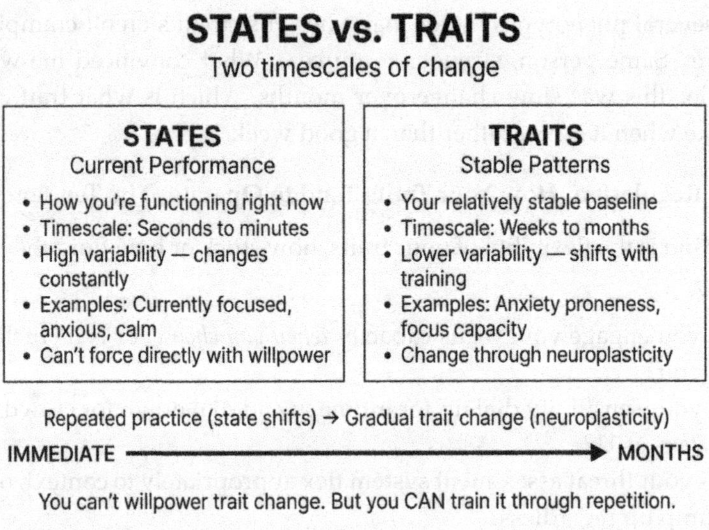

Figure 22.3: Traits, Regulation, and States

22.4.4 How This Maps to Your Phenotypes

Your **phenotypes are trait resources**, stable circuit patterns measurable on QEEG:

- Frontal slow (Stabilizer): motor initiation capacity
- Right frontal activity (Grumpy Old Man): threat sensitivity resource
- Midline patterns (CEO): cognitive flexibility resource
- Posterior vigilance (Lifeguard): environmental scanning resource
- Alpha frequency (Timekeeper): processing speed resource

These are visible on your brain map regardless of your current state. Walk in calm or panicking. I still see the trait markers.

Training shifts regulation first, then traits follow. As you train, your regulation improves, your circuits become less stuck, more flexible. Over weeks and months, the trait resources themselves shift. That's what QEEG before/after shows. Not elimination of who you are, deeper, stronger, more resilient resources.

Marcus is still a sensitive, intense, gifted poet-brain. But his resources are stronger. His regulation is more flexible. His states are more manageable. Same essence, better equipped.

22.4.5 The Practical Wisdom

For immediate relief (state shifts):

- Use the tools when you need them
- HRV when anxious (calms within minutes)
- Morning light when foggy (activates within hours)
- Behavioral strategies when stuck (shifts immediately)
- This is useful: but it's managing states, not changing resources

For lasting change (trait shifts):

- Consistency over intensity
- Repeated practice builds neuroplasticity
- 20-40 sessions for most neurofeedback protocols
- Weeks to months for trait consolidation
- This is deep training: your resources themselves getting stronger

Both matter:

- States: Immediate relief when you need it
- Traits: Baseline improvement so you need less coping
- Regulation: The bridge: better regulation means states recover faster AND traits shift over time

The mistake: Trying to willpower a state change ("just focus!" "just relax!") or believing traits can't change ("I'll always be this way, it's genetic").

The truth: States can't be forced, but they ride on trainable traits. Traits are stable, but they shift with sustained practice. The slow change is the real change.

The reframe:

- From: "I'm stuck with these traits" → To: "My resources can strengthen with sustained training"
- From: "Just be calm" (forcing states) → To: "Train the traits that produce calm" (build the resource)
- From: "Quick fix" (state relief) → To: "Train for months" (trait improvement)

Self-mastery: Not perfection. Not elimination of your nature. Strengthening your resources, improving your regulation, so your states take care of themselves more often. Your essence, with range.

22.5 Building the Brain You'll Have 5 Years From Now

Here's one of the most powerful frameworks I teach: **Everything you're doing today is building the brain you'll have 5 years from now.**

Your brain isn't static. It's constantly adapting, reorganizing, strengthening some connections while pruning others. This process (neuroplasticity) never stops. The question isn't whether your brain will change. The question is: **What are you training it to become?**

22.5.1 The Lifecourse Perspective: Your Brain Across Decades

Your brain at 25 isn't your brain at 45 isn't your brain at 65. Different life stages bring different challenges, different resources, different regulatory demands. And critically: **different capacities for adaptation.**

The neuroscience is clear: Your brain remains plastic throughout life. You can strengthen circuits, build new connections, shift baselines. But the nature of that plasticity changes:

Young adulthood (20s-30s):

- High plasticity, rapid adaptation
- Building career, relationships, identity
- Risk: Establishing dysregulated patterns that become entrenched
- Opportunity: Training regulation skills that compound over decades

Midlife (40s-50s):

- Hormonal transitions (perimenopause, andropause) affect circuits
- Accumulated stress or accumulated mastery
- Risk: "I'm too old to change" becomes self-fulfilling
- Opportunity: Wisdom + tools = most effective regulation period

Later life (60s+):

- Continued plasticity (slower but real)
- Use it or lose it becomes more pronounced
- Risk: Cognitive decline if circuits aren't challenged
- Opportunity: Deep practice consolidates into mastery

The critical insight: Today's dysregulation becomes tomorrow's baseline. Today's regulation practice becomes tomorrow's ease.

22.5.2 What You're Training Right Now

If you're using alcohol nightly to calm your Grumpy Old Man:

- You're training dependence on external regulation
- 5 years: Tolerance, worse anxiety, damaged sleep architecture
- Your brain adapts to expect alcohol: becomes MORE anxious without it

If you're practicing HRV biofeedback + neurofeedback:

- You're training internal regulation capacity
- 5 years: Lower baseline anxiety, better stress resilience, sustainable calm
- Your brain learns to generate calm: becomes LESS anxious naturally

If you're chronically sleep-deprived:

- You're training your Stabilizer to stay offline, your CEO to micromanage, your Lifeguard to hypervigilate
- 5 years: Entrenched ADHD patterns, harder to reverse
- Your brain adapts to fatigue as baseline: dysregulation becomes "normal"

If you're consistently sleeping 7-9 hours:

- You're training optimal circuit function every night
- 5 years: Stronger attention, better mood regulation, resilient phenotypes
- Your brain consolidates regulation during sleep: baseline keeps improving

If you're avoiding all challenge (hiding from your triggers):

- You're training avoidance, narrowing your window of tolerance
- 5 years: More fragile, smaller life, increased sensitivity
- Your brain prunes unused capacity: you lose range

If you're practicing graduated exposure + regulation tools:

- You're training resilience, expanding your window of tolerance
- 5 years: Wider range, bigger life, maintained sensitivity without overwhelm
- Your brain builds capacity: you gain range while keeping gifts

22.5.3 The Compounding Effect

Here's what makes this powerful: Small, consistent changes compound exponentially.

One meditation session: Temporary state calm (minutes)
100 meditation sessions: Measurable trait shift (baseline anxiety decreases)
1000 meditation sessions over 5 years: Fundamentally different nervous system (you're not the same person)

One night of good sleep: Better mood tomorrow
100 nights of consistent sleep: Improved phenotype baselines
1825 nights over 5 years: You've rebuilt your circuits

The math:

- 20 minutes of HRV training daily = 121 hours per year = 605 hours over 5 years
- 40 neurofeedback sessions = equivalent to thousands of hours of unguided practice
- Consistent sleep optimization = ~10,000 hours of optimized consolidation over 5 years

This is building, not borrowing. You're training capacity that accumulates.

22.5.4 The 5-Year Question

Ask yourself:

Where will my circuits be in 5 years if I continue my current patterns?

- Current sleep pattern → where does that lead?
- Current substance use → what baseline am I training?
- Current stress level → what's that building?
- Current regulation practice (or lack thereof) → who am I becoming?

And then ask:

Where do I want my circuits to be in 5 years?

- What kind of baseline anxiety / focus / energy / sensitivity do I want?
- What range of states do I want access to?
- What kind of resilience do I want to have built?
- What version of my poet-brain do I want to be conducting?

The gap between those two answers is your work.

22.5.5 Agency in the Lifecourse

The gift of this framework: You're not passive. Your brain's trajectory isn't predetermined.

Yes, there are constraints:

- Genetics set initial parameters
- Trauma and early experience shape development
- Aging affects plasticity speed
- Life circumstances create real limitations

But within those constraints, you have profound agency. The tools in this book (sleep, neurofeedback, meditation, HRV, behavioral strategies) these WORK because your brain remains plastic. You can shift baselines. You can build new patterns. You can train different regulation.

5 years from now, you'll have a different brain. The question is: **Will it be the one you trained intentionally, or the one that formed by default?** The person reading this book five years from now will score differently on the self-assessment. That is the point.

This is what self-mastery means: Taking responsibility for the brain you're building. Not through shame ("I should have started earlier") but through agency ("I'm starting now, and 5 years from now I'll be grateful I did").

Everything you do today is practice. Every regulation tool you use is training. Every night of good sleep is consolidation. Every moment of conscious phenotype leadership is building the conductor you're becoming.

You're not managing symptoms. You're building capacity. You're not coping with your brain. You're training it.

5 years. Start now.

22.6 Try the Poet-Brain Mastery Loop: A Recent Struggle

NOTICE: Pick a moment from this week when you struggled. Name which phenotype was leading. ("My Stabilizer was offline and I couldn't start the project" or "My Grumpy Old Man was generating dread about the presentation.")

NORMALIZE: "Of course this happened, here's exactly which circuit was doing what, and here's why." (Not "what's wrong with me?" but "this is what this phenotype does when dysregulated.")

REGULATE: Choose one tool from Part II you could have used. (Morning light for Stabilizer? HRV breathing for Grumpy? Noting meditation for stuck CEO? What matches this phenotype?)

REASSIGN: Who should have been leading instead? (Maybe Happy Little Kid should lead exploration, with Grumpy Old Man consulting on risks, and CEO deciding, not Grumpy screaming alone.)

REFLECT: What would you do differently next time? What did you learn about your orchestra's patterns? (This is how mastery builds, learning from each iteration.)

Practice this loop daily for 30 days. You'll get faster, more skillful, more confident. The art of conducting.

22.7 The Internal Board Meeting: A Guided Exercise

Scenario: New job opportunity. Exciting but risky. Four phenotypes are active.

NOTICE: Happy Little Kid is excited ("This could be amazing!"). Grumpy Old Man is generating dread ("Too much effort, probably won't work"). CEO is stuck between them. Stabilizer is worried about execution ("Can I actually start?"). You've named the players. No one is wrong. They're all giving you data.

NORMALIZE: Of course Happy Little Kid lights up at opportunity. Of course Grumpy Old Man flags risk. Of course CEO is stuck between competing goals. Of course Stabilizer worries about follow-through. Every voice is doing its job.

REGULATE: Happy Little Kid: check whether this is genuine interest or just novelty-chasing. Grumpy Old Man: assess real effort-to-payoff, not futility fantasies. CEO: set a decision deadline (one week, then commit). Stabilizer: break execution into small starts.

REASSIGN: This is about opportunity and growth. Happy Little Kid leads. Grumpy Old Man consults on risk. CEO decides with data from both. Stabilizer executes in small steps. You're conducting, not being conducted.

REFLECT (one month later): Happy Little Kid's engagement kept you going. Grumpy's realistic assessment reduced dread. CEO's deadline prevented endless rumination. Stabilizer's chunking made starting possible. Next time: use the model earlier. Trust Happy Little Kid more. Give Grumpy a specific job instead of free-range futility.

This is the practice. Notice, normalize, regulate, reassign, reflect. You get faster at it. More skillful. More confident. The art of conducting.

22.8 A Different Constellation: Priya

Marcus had the classic Gifted Poet Pattern: five phenotypes cramping at once, all driven by resource depletion. But not every poet-brain looks like Marcus.

Composite, like every case here. The pattern recurs; the person is not one person.

Priya was a 41-year-old UX designer, diagnosed ADHD at 38 after her daughter's evaluation. Her brain map told a different story: Timekeeper racing (excess beta, fast alpha, couldn't slow down), Bard overactive (over-reading threat in every conversation, misinterpreting neutral tone as hostile), Princess & the Pea flooded (sensory overload in open offices, couldn't filter background noise from signal). Her Stabilizer and CEO were fine. Her problem wasn't activation. It was speed, social processing, and sensory overwhelm.

For three decades she'd compensated: caffeine to push through the afternoon Tide, alcohol to quiet social noise after work, rigid routines to reduce unpredictability. She'd built a successful career by designing environments she could control. Then perimenopause amplified everything. The Timekeeper raced into insomnia. The Bard heard hostility in every Slack message. The Princess & the Pea that made her brilliant at UX now made open-plan offices unbearable.

Her loop looked different from Marcus's. **Notice:** "My Timekeeper is racing and my Bard is reading threat in a neutral email." **Normalize:** "Of course. Late diagnosis means 30 years of compensating without knowing why. Perimenopause amplifies beta activity. This isn't getting worse, it's getting louder." **Regulate:** SMR training to slow the Timekeeper. Loving-kindness meditation to soften the Bard's threat interpretation. Sensory environment redesign for Princess & the Pea (noise-canceling headphones, work-from-home days). **Reassign:** Let Princess & the Pea lead during design work (that sensitivity is the job). Let Bard consult, not lead, during email. **Reflect:** The alcohol was quieting all three at once, which is why it worked so well and cost so much.

Forty sessions later, her Timekeeper found a sustainable tempo. Her Bard still reads social nuance, but with range instead of threat-lock. Her Princess & the Pea still catches what others miss, but she can turn the gain down when she needs to. Same gifts. Less torture. Different constellation, same principle: conduct, don't sedate.

22.9 Your Next Steps

This Week:

1. **Identify your dominant phenotypes** (review Part I, note your top 3-5)
2. **Start sleep optimization** (Chapter 13: morning light within 30 minutes of waking, consistent wake time)

3. **Begin HRV practice** (Chapter 15: 5 minutes daily)

This Month:

1. **Implement one intervention** matched to your dominant phenotype:
   - Stabilizer offline? Behavioral activation + morning routine
   - Grumpy Old Man loud? HRV biofeedback + right frontal calming
   - CEO stuck? Noting practice + external cueing
   - Princess & Pea overwhelmed? Sensory optimization + loving-kindness
   - Timekeeper racing? SMR training + sleep optimization
2. **Track changes** in sleep quality, mood, focus, RSD frequency
3. **Consider QEEG** for phenotype-specific protocol (see Resources for providers)

This Year:

1. **Neurofeedback training** (20-40 sessions if appropriate)
2. **Build sustainable practices** through consistency (6-12 months)
3. **Find your people** (fellow poet-brains, online or in person)

Resources:

- **The book's home:** giftedandtortured.com
- **The author:** andrewhillphd.com (articles, YouTube @DrHill, podcast)
- **The clinic:** peakbraininstitute.com (QEEG brain mapping, neurofeedback, locations)
- **The technical companion:** *The QEEG Field Guide* (Hill & Lomeli, forthcoming)

22.10 Key Takeaways

You're not broken. You were under-instructed. Now you have the manual.

- **The Mastery Loop:** Notice (name the phenotype), Normalize (circuit, not flaw), Regulate (match tool to phenotype), Reassign (choose who leads), Reflect (learn from pattern). Not perfection. Getting better at conducting.
- **Repetition trains phenotypes.** Every session, every practice, every consistent morning shifts your baseline. You're training three levels: traits (months), regulation (weeks), states (immediate). Consistency beats intensity.
- **Traits, regulation, states.** Traits = circuit resources (measurable, plastic, trainable). Regulation = flexibility of those traits (stuck vs. full range of motion). States = moment-to-moment experience (ride on top of the other two). All three are trainable. Honor your essence, embrace plasticity.

- **Conducting, not eliminating.** You don't silence instruments. You choose which leads based on context. Happy Little Kid for exploration. Grumpy Old Man for risk assessment. CEO for prioritization. Context-dependent leadership. These are levers, not labels, and levers move.

22.11 Reader Reflections

1. **Which phenotypes did you recognize most strongly?** Can you name your dominant three and how they interact?
2. **Try the Mastery Loop on a recent struggle.** Walk through all five steps for one specific moment.
3. **Where have you been trying to force a state change instead of training the underlying resource?** What would shift if you trained the trait instead?
4. **What's one tool from Part II you'll commit to for 30 days?** Pick one. Start.

22.12 The Final Beat

The trouble with poets is they talk too much. But maybe the real trouble is **no one gave them a map.**

You have the map now. You know your phenotypes. You understand your circuits. You can see yourself in these patterns, not as pathology, but as configuration.

You have the tools now. Targeted interventions matched to your specific dysregulation. Not substances that borrow from tomorrow, but training that builds capacity you keep.

You have the model now. Notice, normalize, regulate, reassign, reflect. The practice of mastery. The art of conducting.

You'll still be a poet. You'll still think too much, feel too much, see poetry everywhere. But you'll be a poet who knows how to conduct.

In "Think Too Much (a)," Paul Simon asked whether you've ever experienced a period of grace, when your brain just takes a seat and lets you be.

That's the opposite of the other version, where the left side of the brain dominates the right, and the right side labors through the long and speechless night. Same album, same brain, different states. "Thinking too much" is the Stabilizer and Supervisor locked in combat: left GO and right STOP unable to negotiate, the approach system revving while the brake grinds. The period of grace is what happens when they find their rhythm. The Supervisor becomes poised instead of reactive. You're balanced between thoughts rather than drowning in them.

You've felt it. Maybe not for long. Maybe not reliably. But you've felt it. The CEO lets go. The Grumpy Old Man quiets. The Lifeguard stops scanning. The Stabilizer moves and the Supervisor watches without clenching. Your twelve circuits play the same piece without you white-knuckling the conductor's stand.

That's not the goal. The goal is conducting well, noticing, normalizing, regulating, reassigning, reflecting. Learning which instrument leads in which moment. Building the skill through repetition until the orchestra knows the piece.

The period of grace is what happens when you've practiced enough.

Maybe you think too much. Or maybe you think exactly as much as you're built to think, and now you know how to conduct it.

Not perfectly, not endlessly, but in cadences you choose, more and more of the time.

Good job. Be weird. Time to play your music.

Before You Go: Your Field Kit

You found yourself somewhere in these pages. Here is the part you can carry.

There is a free **Poet-Brain Field Kit** that goes with the book:

- All twelve phenotypes on printable **reference cards**
- The **where-to-start** essentials: morning light, sleep, and how to find a QEEG-guided provider
- Reader updates as new tools go live

It is free. First name and email, nothing else.

Scan with your phone's camera

or visit **peakbrainpress.com/gifted-bonus**

Glossary of Terms & Acronyms

Brain Regions & Networks

ACC (Anterior Cingulate Cortex): Frontal midline structure that monitors conflict and switches attention. Home of the CEO phenotype.

Amygdala: Deep brain structure that processes threat and emotional significance. Connected to Lifeguard (threat detection) and Princess & Pea (emotional amplification).

Broca's Area: Left frontal region responsible for speech production (the "Speaker"). Connected to Wernicke's area via the arcuate fasciculus.

DLPFC (Dorsolateral Prefrontal Cortex): Left DLPFC drives approach motivation (Happy Little Kid). Right DLPFC drives avoidance and effort assessment (Grumpy Old Man).

DMN (Default Mode Network): Brain network active during rest, mind-wandering, and self-reflection. Includes the posterior cingulate (Lifeguard), medial prefrontal cortex, and angular gyrus.

IFG (Inferior Frontal Gyrus): Key node for response inhibition and braking. Right IFG is central to the Problem Child phenotype, the circuit that slams the emergency brake when threat or frustration is detected.

PCC (Posterior Cingulate Cortex): Hub of the Default Mode Network. Home of the Lifeguard phenotype, environmental scanning, contextual awareness, and rumination.

Precentral Cortex / SMA (Supplementary Motor Area): Motor regions involved in movement initiation and inhibition. Home of the Stabilizer (left) and Supervisor (right) phenotypes.

TPJ (Temporoparietal Junction): Left TPJ processes language and meaning (Interpreter). Right TPJ processes social cues, sensory information, and self-other boundaries (Princess & the Pea and Bard).

Wernicke's Area: Left posterior temporal region responsible for language comprehension and generation. Home of the Interpreter phenotype.

Measurement & Methods

EEG (Electroencephalography): Recording of electrical brain activity from sensors on the scalp.

fMRI (Functional Magnetic Resonance Imaging): Brain imaging that measures blood flow to infer neural activity. Higher spatial precision than EEG; lower temporal resolution.

QEEG (Quantitative EEG): Statistical analysis of EEG data, comparing an individual's brain activity patterns to normative databases. The "brain map" referenced throughout this book.

Brain Rhythms

Alpha (8-12 Hz): Idling/resting rhythm. Healthy alpha indicates calm alertness. Excess alpha in posterior regions can indicate disengagement; deficit can indicate anxiety.

Beta (13-30 Hz): Active processing rhythm. Moderate beta supports focus; excess beta creates racing thoughts, anxiety, and the "can't turn off" feeling.

Delta (0.5-4 Hz): Deep sleep rhythm. Excess delta during waking hours contributes to brain fog.

SMR (Sensorimotor Rhythm, 12-15 Hz): Low beta rhythm over motor cortex associated with calm, still alertness, the Stabilizer's "idle gear." Key target in neurofeedback training.

Theta (4-8 Hz): Slow rhythm associated with drowsiness, mind-wandering, and cognitive overwhelm. Excess frontal theta is a common ADHD marker.

Theta/Beta Ratio: Ratio of slow (theta) to fast (beta) activity, often elevated in ADHD. A primary neurofeedback training target.

Neuroscience Concepts

BAS (Behavioral Activation System): Approach motivation circuit in left frontal cortex. Drives engagement, exploration, positive affect. The Happy Little Kid's engine.

BIS (Behavioral Inhibition System): Avoidance motivation circuit in right frontal cortex. Drives withdrawal, effort conservation, threat assessment. The Grumpy Old Man's engine.

Frontal Asymmetry: The relative balance of left (approach) vs. right (avoidance) frontal activation. Left-dominant = more engaged; right-dominant = more withdrawn.

HRV (Heart Rate Variability): Beat-to-beat variation in heart rate. Higher HRV indicates better autonomic flexibility and stress resilience. Trainable through biofeedback and breathwork.

IAF / PAF (Individual/Peak Alpha Frequency): The speed of your brain's dominant alpha rhythm. Faster = quicker processing (Timekeeper running hot). Slower = brain fog, cognitive sluggishness.

LVF (Low Voltage Fast): EEG pattern characterized by low-amplitude, fast activity. Linked to GABAA receptor genes and family history of alcoholism. Genetically predisposed to find alcohol calming.

Neuroplasticity: The brain's ability to reorganize and form new connections through experience and training. The mechanism behind neurofeedback, meditation, and behavioral change.

RSD (Rejection Sensitivity Dysphoria): Intense emotional pain from perceived rejection or criticism. Clinical concept (Dodson), widely recognized in ADHD community, not yet a formal DSM diagnosis. Associated with right TPJ hyperactivation.

Genetics

COMT (Catechol-O-Methyltransferase): Enzyme that breaks down dopamine and norepinephrine. Genetic variants (Val / Met) affect prefrontal dopamine levels and stress resilience.

GABAA Receptor Genes: Genetic variants affecting the brain's primary inhibitory neurotransmitter system. Associated with LVF pattern and predisposition to find alcohol and benzodiazepines calming.

The Twelve Phenotypes (Quick Reference)

#	Name	Location	Core Function
1	Happy Little Kid	Left DLPFC	Approach motivation, joy, engagement
2	Grumpy Old Man	Right DLPFC	Effort assessment, avoidance, withdrawal
3	Stabilizer	Left sensorimotor	Motor initiation, task engagement, "go"
4	Supervisor	Right sensorimotor	Impulse control, quality monitoring, "stop"
5	CEO	Anterior cingulate	Task switching, conflict resolution, flexibility
6	Lifeguard	Posterior cingulate	Environmental scanning, threat detection, rumination

#	Name	Location	Core Function
7	Problem Child	Right IFG / fronto-basal ganglia	Reactive opposition, emotional braking
8	Princess & the Pea	Right TPJ	Social sensitivity, sensory processing, RSD
9	Interpreter	Left TPJ / Wernicke's	Language comprehension, word-finding, verbal processing
10	Bard	Right posterior temporal	Prosody, tone-of-voice, sarcasm detection
11	Timekeeper	Global alpha frequency	Processing speed, time perception, cognitive tempo
12	The Fog & the Tide	Distributed	Processing efficiency, energy management, inflammation

---

Methods & Interventions

Alpha-Theta Training: Advanced neurofeedback protocol accessing deep relaxation states. Used for trauma processing, creativity enhancement, and substance use recovery (Peniston Protocol).

MBRP (Mindfulness-Based Relapse Prevention): Evidence-based program combining mindfulness meditation with relapse prevention strategies for substance use.

Neurofeedback (EEG Biofeedback): Non-invasive brain training using real-time EEG feedback. The brain learns to generate desired patterns through operant conditioning. Typically 20-40+ sessions.

Peniston Protocol: Alpha-theta neurofeedback protocol developed for alcoholism and PTSD. Involves temperature biofeedback foundation followed by deep-state alpha-theta training. Early trials reported 70-80% abstinence rates; later replication varies by population and protocol.

The Mastery Loop: Five-step self-regulation method: Notice (identify which phenotype) → Normalize (it's a circuit, not a flaw) → Regulate (use tools) → Reassign (choose who leads) → Reflect (learn from pattern).

Resources

---

giftedandtortured.com

Home of this book. Updates, errata, community, and additional content as it develops.

peakbrainpress.com

All books from Peak Brain Press, including companion workbooks, audiobook editions, and forthcoming titles.

andrewhillphd.com

Articles, guides, and podcast covering sleep, meditation, substances, QEEG, and neurodivergent brain optimization. YouTube: @DrHill.

peakbraininstitute.com

QEEG brain mapping, neurofeedback training, and clinical services. Locations in Los Angeles, Orange County, New York, St. Louis, West Palm Beach, London, and Stockholm. 100% remote services available, including remote QEEGs. Provider referral network for those outside service areas.

Also by Andrew Hill

Half a Second More: The Meditation Guide for Brains That Won't Sit Still

If Chapter 17 resonated, this book goes deeper. Phenotype-matched meditation protocols, the neuroscience of why "just breathe" fails for fast brains, and a 30-day program designed for people who have tried meditation and quit. Available at peakbrainpress.com.

For Practitioners & Technical Readers

The QEEG Field Guide (Hill & Lomeli, forthcoming)

Complete practitioner manual covering QEEG methodology and interpretation, genetic factors shaping phenotypes, medication selection based on EEG patterns, and neurofeedback protocols for all 12 phenotypes. For practitioners who want to implement the Poet-Brain Phenotype Model clinically.

References Cited

Russell, J. A. (2018). Fifty years of advances in neuroendocrinology. *Brain and Neuroscience Advances, 2*. https://doi.org/10.1177/2398212818812014

Abi-Jaoude, E., et al. (2022). The neural correlates of tic inhibition. *Clinical Neurophysiology Practice, 7*, 54-64.

Ashton, C. H. (2002). *Benzodiazepines: How They Work and How to Withdraw* (The Ashton Manual). Newcastle University. Retrieved from https://www.benzo.org.uk/manual/

AbouAsally, M., et al. (2025). Neurofeedback for long COVID brain fog: A secondary analysis. *Applied Psychophysiology and Biofeedback, 50*(1), 45-58.

Acevedo, B. P., Aron, E. N., Aron, A., Sangster, M. D., Collins, N., & Brown, L. L. (2014). The highly sensitive brain: An fMRI study of sensory processing sensitivity. *Brain and Behavior, 4*(4), 580-594.

Achal, S., et al. (2016). Individual differences in adult reading are associated with left temporo-parietal to dorsal striatal functional connectivity. *Cerebral Cortex, 26*(10), 4069-4081.

Adamaszek, M., et al. (2010). Evidence of neurotoxicity of ecstasy: Sustained effects on electroencephalographic activity in polydrug users. *PLOS ONE, 5*(11), e14097.

Afrash, S., Saemi, E., Gong, A., & Doustan, M. (2023). Neurofeedback training and motor learning: The enhanced sensorimotor rhythm protocol is better or the suppressed alpha or the suppressed mu? *BMC Sports Science, Medicine & Rehabilitation, 15*(1), 93. https://doi.org/10.1186/s13102-023-00706-3

Akimoto, Y., et al. (2013). Irony comprehension: Social conceptual knowledge and emotional response. *Neuropsychologia, 51*(8), 1560-1569.

Allen, D. (2001). *Getting Things Done: The Art of Stress-Free Productivity*. Penguin Books.

Anton, R. F., et al. (2006). Combined pharmacotherapies and behavioral interventions for alcohol dependence: The COMBINE study. *JAMA, 295*(17), 2003-2017.

Arioli, M., et al. (2024). Peak alpha frequency is linked to visual temporal attention in 10-month-old infants. *Developmental Science, 27*(2), e13445.

Arns, M., Gunkelman, J., Breteler, M., & Spronk, D. (2008). EEG phenotypes predict treatment outcome to stimulants in children with ADHD. *Journal of Integrative Neuroscience, 7*(3), 421-438. https://doi.org/10.1142/s0219635208001897

Arns, M., de Ridder, S., Strehl, U., Breteler, M., & Coenen, A. (2009). Efficacy of neurofeedback treatment in ADHD: The effects on inattention, impulsivity and hyperactivity: A meta-analysis. *Clinical EEG and Neuroscience, 40*(3), 180-189. https://doi.org/10.1177/155005940904000311

Aron, A. R., Fletcher, P. C., Bullmore, E. T., Sahakian, B. J., & Robbins, T. W. (2003). Stop-signal inhibition disrupted by damage to right inferior frontal gyrus in humans. *Nature Neuroscience, 6*(2), 115-116. https://doi.org/10.1038/nn1003

Aron, A. R., Robbins, T. W., & Poldrack, R. A. (2004). Inhibition and the right inferior frontal cortex. *Trends in Cognitive Sciences, 8*(4), 170-177. https://doi.org/10.1016/j.tics.2004.02.010

Aron, E. N., & Aron, A. (1997). Sensory-processing sensitivity and its relation to introversion and emotionality. *Journal of Personality and Social Psychology, 73*(2), 345-368.

Aron, E. N., Aron, A., & Jagiellowicz, J. (2012). Sensory processing sensitivity: A review in the light of the evolution of biological responsivity. *Personality and Social Psychology Review, 16*(3), 262–282. https://doi.org/10.1177/1088868311434213

Auksztulewicz, R., Friston, K. J., & Nobre, A. C. (2017). Task relevance modulates the behavioural and neural effects of sensory predictions. *PLOS Biology, 15*(12), e2003143. https://doi.org/10.1371/journal.pbio.2003143

Aylett, E., Small, N., & Bower, P. (2018). Exercise in the treatment of clinical anxiety in general practice: A systematic review and meta-analysis. *BMC Health Services Research, 18*(1), 559.

Bardi, L., Gheza, D., & Brass, M. (2017). TPJ-M1 interaction in the control of shared representations: New insights from tDCS and TMS combined. *NeuroImage, 146*, 734-740. https://doi.org/10.1016/j.neuroimage.2016.10.050

Barone, D. A., et al. (2024). Neurophysiological signatures of mild traumatic brain injury. *Journal of Clinical Neurophysiology, 41*(2), 156-165.

Bühler, J., Weber, S., Loukas, S., Walther, S., & Aybek, S. (2024). Non-invasive neuromodulation of the right temporoparietal junction using theta-burst stimulation in functional neurological disorder. *BMJ Neurology Open, 6*(1), e000525. https://doi.org/10.1136/bmjno-2023-000525

Blanke, O., & Arzy, S. (2005). The out-of-body experience: Disturbed self-processing at the temporo-parietal junction. *The Neuroscientist, 11*(1), 16-24. https://doi.org/10.1177/1073858404270885

Bateman, J. R., et al. (2019). Aprosodia and prosoplegia: Lesion data and theoretical implications. *Neurocase, 25*(3-4), 144-154.

Beaman, C. P., & Williams, T. I. (2010). Earworms ("stuck song syndrome"): Towards a natural history of intrusive thoughts. *British Journal of Psychology, 101*(4), 637-653. https://doi.org/10.1348/000712609X479636

Begum-Ali, J., Goodwin, A., Mason, L., Pasco, G., Charman, T., Johnson, M. H., & Jones, E. J. H. (2022). Altered theta-beta ratio in infancy associates with family history of ADHD and later ADHD-relevant temperamental traits. *Journal of Child Psychology and Psychiatry, 63*(9), 1057-1067. https://doi.org/10.1111/jcpp.13563

Benis, D., et al. (2023). EEG abnormalities in a patient with long COVID and brain fog. *Clinical EEG and Neuroscience, 54*(3), 312-315.

Bloch, M. H., et al. (2013). N-Acetylcysteine in the treatment of pediatric trichotillomania. *Journal of the American Academy of Child & Adolescent Psychiatry, 52*(3), 231-240.

Bluschke, A., Broschwitz, F., Kohl, S., Roessner, V., & Beste, C. (2016). The neuronal mechanisms underlying improvement of impulsivity in ADHD. *Scientific Reports, 6*, 31178. https://doi.org/10.1038/srep31178

Bodenmann, S., et al. (2009). The functional Val158Met polymorphism of COMT predicts interindividual differences in brain alpha oscillations. *Journal of Neuroscience, 29*(35), 10855-10862.

Bolton, T. A. W., Wotruba, D., Buechler, R., Theodoridou, A., Michels, L., Kollias, S., Rössler, W., Heekeren, K., & Van De Ville, D. (2020). Triple network model dynamically revisited: Lower salience network state switching in pre-psychosis. *Frontiers in Physiology, 11*, 66. https://doi.org/10.3389/fphys.2020.00066

Bonnelle, V., Leech, R., Kinnunen, K. M., Ham, T. E., Beckmann, C. F., De Boissezon, X., Greenwood, R. J., & Sharp, D. J. (2011). Default mode network connectivity predicts sustained attention deficits after traumatic brain injury. *Journal of Neuroscience, 31*(38), 13442-13451. https://doi.org/10.1523/JNEUROSCI.1163-11.2011

Botvinick, M. M., Huffstetler, S., & McGuire, J. T. (2009). Effort discounting in human nucleus accumbens. *Cognitive, Affective, & Behavioral Neuroscience, 9*(1), 16-27. https://doi.org/10.3758/CABN.9.1.16

Botta, A., Lagravinese, G., Bove, M., Pelosin, E., Bonassi, G., Avenanti, A., & Avanzino, L. (2022). Sensorimotor inhibition during emotional processing. *Scientific Reports, 12*(1), 6998. https://doi.org/10.1038/s41598-022-10981-8

Bouny, P., Arsac, L. M., Pratviel, Y., Boffet, A., Touré Cuq, E., & Deschodt-Arsac, V. (2022). A single session of SMR-neurofeedback training improves selective attention emerging from a dynamic structuring of brain-heart interplay. *Brain Sciences, 12*(6), 794. https://doi.org/10.3390/brainsci12060794

Bower, J. E., Ganz, P. A., Irwin, M. R., Kwan, L., Breen, E. C., & Cole, S. W. (2011). Inflammation and behavioral symptoms after breast cancer treatment: Do fatigue, depression, and sleep disturbance share a common underlying mechanism? *Journal of Clinical Oncology, 29*(26), 3517-3522.

Bowen, S., Witkiewitz, K., Clifasefi, S. L., Grow, J., Chawla, N., Hsu, S. H., ... & Larimer, M. E. (2014). Relative efficacy of mindfulness-based relapse prevention, standard relapse prevention, and treatment as usual for substance use disorders: A randomized clinical trial. *JAMA Psychiatry, 71*(5), 547-556.

Baehr, E., Rosenfeld, J. P., & Baehr, R. (2001). Clinical use of an alpha asymmetry neurofeedback protocol in the treatment of mood disorders: Follow-up study one to five years post therapy. *Clinical Electroencephalography, 32*(1), 10-13.

Balban, M. Y., Neri, E., Kogon, M. M., Weed, L., Nouriani, B., Jo, B., Holl, G., Zeitzer, J. M., Spiegel, D., & Huberman, A. D. (2023). Brief structured respiration practices enhance mood and reduce physiological arousal. *Cell Reports Medicine, 4*(1), 100895. https://doi.org/10.1016/j.xcrm.2022.100895

Brandmeyer, T., & Delorme, A. (2013). Meditation and neurofeedback. *Frontiers in Psychology, 4*, 688.

Brewer, J. A., Worhunsky, P. D., Gray, J. R., Tang, Y. Y., Weber, J., & Kober, H. (2011). Meditation experience is associated with differences in default mode network activity and connectivity. *PNAS, 108*(50), 20254-20259. https://doi.org/10.1073/pnas.1112029108

Buckner, R. L., Andrews-Hanna, J. R., & Schacter, D. L. (2008). The brain's default network: Anatomy, function, and relevance to disease. *Annals of the New York Academy of Sciences, 1124*, 1-38.

Buhle, J. T., et al. (2014). Cognitive reappraisal of emotion: A meta-analysis of human neuroimaging studies. *Cerebral Cortex, 24*(11), 2981-2990.

Buijze, G. A., Sierevelt, I. N., van der Heijden, B. C., Dijkgraaf, M. G., & Frings-Dresen, M. H. (2016). The effect of cold showering on health and work: A randomized controlled trial. *PLoS ONE, 11*(9), e0161749.

Bzdok, D., et al. (2016). Left inferior parietal lobe engagement in social cognition and language. *Neuroscience & Biobehavioral Reviews, 68*, 319-334.

Buzzell, G. A., Beatty, P. J., Paquette, N. A., Roberts, D. M., & McDonald, C. G. (2017). Error-induced blindness: Error detection leads to impaired sensory processing and lower accuracy at short response-stimulus intervals. *The Journal of Neuroscience, 37*(11), 2895-2903. https://doi.org/10.1523/jneurosci.1202-16.2017

Cai, W., Chen, T., Szegletes, L., Supekar, K., & Menon, V. (2018). Aberrant time-varying cross-network interactions in children with ADHD and the triple network model. *Biological Psychiatry: Cognitive Neuroscience and Neuroimaging, 3*(3), 263-273. https://doi.org/10.1016/j.bpsc.2017.10.005

Causse, M., Chua, Z., Peysakhovich, V., Del Campo, N., & Matton, N. (2016). Anticipation of a mentally effortful task recruits dorsolateral prefrontal cortex: An fNIRS validation study. *Frontiers in Human Neuroscience, 10*, 146.

Cavanagh, J. F., & Frank, M. J. (2014). Frontal theta as a mechanism for cognitive control. *Trends in Cognitive Sciences, 18*(8), 414-421.

Cavanagh, J. F., & Shackman, A. J. (2015). Frontal midline theta reflects anxiety and cognitive control. *International Journal of Psychophysiology, 98*(2), 279-288.

Ceballos, N. A., Bauer, L. O., & Houston, R. J. (2009). Recent advances in electrophysiological research on addiction. *Current Drug Abuse Reviews, 2*(3), 227-242.

Chabot, R. J., Merkin, H., Wood, L. M., Davenport, T. L., & Serfontein, G. (1999). Behavioral and electrophysiologic predictors of treatment response to stimulants in children with attention-deficit/hyperactivity disorder. *Journal of Child Neurology, 14*(6), 343–351. https://doi.org/10.1177/088307389901400601

Chand, G. B., Wu, J., Hajjar, I., & Qiu, D. (2017). Interactions of the salience network and its subsystems with the default-mode and central-executive networks in normal aging and mild cognitive impairment. *Brain Connectivity, 7*(7), 401-412. https://doi.org/10.1089/brain.2017.0509

Chang, S. E., & Guenther, F. H. (2020). Involvement of the cortico-basal ganglia-thalamocortical loop in developmental stuttering. *Frontiers in Psychology, 11*, 3389.

Chang, S. E., Zhu, D. C., Choo, A. L., & Angstadt, M. (2015). White matter neuroanatomical differences in young children who stutter. *Brain, 138*(Pt 3), 694-711.

Cieslak, M., Ingham, R. J., Ingham, J. C., & Grafton, S. T. (2015). Anomalous white matter morphology in adults who stutter. *Journal of Speech, Language, and Hearing Research, 58*(2), 268-277. https://doi.org/10.1044/2015_JSLHR-S-14-0193

Cirillo, F. (2006). *The Pomodoro Technique*. FC Garage.

Clark, C. R., et al. (2004). Spontaneous alpha peak frequency predicts working memory performance across the age span. *International Journal of Psychophysiology, 53*(1), 1-10.

Clarke, A. R., Barry, R. J., McCarthy, R., & Selikowitz, M. (2001). EEG-defined subtypes of children with attention-deficit/hyperactivity disorder. *Clinical Neurophysiology, 112*(11), 2098-2105. https://doi.org/10.1016/S1388-2457(01)00668-X

Clarke, A. R., Barry, R. J., Dupuy, F. E., Heckel, L. D., McCarthy, R., Selikowitz, M., & Johnstone, S. J. (2011). Behavioural differences between EEG-defined subgroups of children with attention-deficit/hyperactivity disorder. *Clinical Neurophysiology, 122*(7), 1333-1341. https://doi.org/10.1016/j.clinph.2010.12.038

Coan, J. A., & Allen, J. J. (2004). Frontal EEG asymmetry as a moderator and mediator of emotion. *Biological Psychology, 67*(1-2), 7-50.

Cooke, D. F., Taylor, C. S., Moore, T., & Graziano, M. S. (2003). Complex movements evoked by microstimulation of the ventral intraparietal area. *PNAS, 100*(10), 6163-6168. https://doi.org/10.1073/pnas.1031751100

Corcoran, A. W., et al. (2018). Toward a reliable, automated method of individual alpha frequency (IAF) quantification. *Psychophysiology, 55*(7), e13064.

Coutin-Churchman, P., et al. (2006). Clinical correlates of quantitative EEG alterations in alcoholic patients. *Clinical Neurophysiology, 117*(4), 740-751.

Cunningham, J. W., et al. (2023). Relationship between acute glucose variability and cognitive impairment in type 2 diabetes: A meta-analysis. *PLOS ONE, 18*(8), e0289782.

D'Rozario, A. L., et al. (2022). CPAP therapy increases slow wave sleep and improves daytime function in obstructive sleep apnea. *Journal of Clinical Sleep Medicine, 18*(3), 769-779.

Dambacher, F., Sack, A. T., Lobbestael, J., Arntz, A., Brugman, S., & Schuhmann, T. (2014). The role of right prefrontal and medial cortex in response inhibition: Interfering with action restraint and action cancellation using transcranial magnetic brain stimulation. *Journal of Cognitive Neuroscience, 26*(8), 1775–1784. https://doi.org/10.1162/jocn_a_00595 https://doi.org/10.1162/jocn_a_00803

Davidson, R. J. (1992). Anterior cerebral asymmetry and the nature of emotion. *Brain and Cognition, 20*(1), 125-151.

Davidson, R. J., & Fox, N. A. (1989). Frontal brain asymmetry predicts infants' response to maternal separation. *Journal of Abnormal Psychology, 98*(2), 127-131.

Decker, M. J., et al. (2009). Electroencephalographic correlates of Chronic Fatigue Syndrome. *Behavioral and Brain Functions, 5*, 43.

DeWall, C. N., et al. (2010). Acetaminophen reduces social pain: Behavioral and neural evidence. *Psychological Science, 21*(7), 931-941.

Davidson, R. J. (1998). Affective style and affective disorders: Perspectives from affective neuroscience. *Cognition & Emotion, 12*(3), 307-330.

Diekelmann, S., & Born, J. (2010). The memory function of sleep. *Nature Reviews Neuroscience, 11*(2), 114-126. https://doi.org/10.1038/nrn2762

Dimidjian, S., Barrera, M., Martell, C., Muñoz, R. F., & Lewinsohn, P. M. (2011). The origins and current status of behavioral activation treatments for depression. *Annual Review of Clinical Psychology, 7*, 1-38.

Dodell-Feder, D., Koster-Hale, J., Bedny, M., & Saxe, R. (2011). fMRI item analysis in a theory of mind task. *NeuroImage, 55*(2), 705-712.

Drewes, J., et al. (2022). Resting-state alpha peak frequency and within-trial changes in alpha peak frequency both predict visual dual-pulse segregation performance. *Cerebral Cortex, 32*(24), 5455-5466.

Drummond, S. P. A., Brown, G. G., Stricker, J. L., Buxton, R. B., Wong, E. C., & Gillin, J. C. (1999). Sleep deprivation-induced reduction in cortical functional response to serial subtraction. *NeuroReport, 10*(18), 3745-3748. https://doi.org/10.1097/00001756-199912160-00004

Dunkley, B. T., et al. (2015). Low-frequency connectivity is associated with mild traumatic brain injury. *NeuroImage: Clinical, 7*, 611-621.

Duffy, J. F., & Czeisler, C. A. (2009). Effect of light on human circadian physiology. *Sleep Medicine Clinics*, 4(2), 165-177. https://doi.org/10.1016/j.jsmc.2009.01.004

Duric, N. S., Assmus, J., Gundersen, D., & Elgen, I. B. (2012). Neurofeedback for ADHD: A randomized and controlled clinical trial. *BMC Psychiatry, 12*, 107. https://doi.org/10.1186/1471-244X-12-107

Eghdami, S., et al. (2024). The safety and efficacy of N-acetylcysteine as an augmentation in the treatment of OCD in adults. *Journal of Affective Disorders.*

Ehlers, C. L., & Criado, J. R. (2007). Event-related oscillations in alcoholism research. *Alcohol Research & Health, 31*(1), 76-80.

Edenberg, H. J., Dick, D. M., Xuei, X., et al. (2004). Variations in GABRA2, encoding the alpha 2 subunit of the GABA(A) receptor, are associated with alcohol dependence and with brain oscillations. *American Journal of Human Genetics, 74*(4), 705-714. https://doi.org/10.1086/383283

Eisenberger, N. I., Lieberman, M. D., & Williams, K. D. (2003). Does rejection hurt? An fMRI study of social exclusion. *Science, 302*(5643), 290-292.

Eisma, J., et al. (2021). Frontal midline theta differentiates separate cognitive control strategies. *Scientific Reports, 11*, 14510.

El-Mekkawy, M., et al. (2022). QEEG biomarkers for sleepiness and non-restorative sleep. *Clinical Neurophysiology, 133*, 86-95.

Enoch, M. A., White, K. V., Harris, C. R., Rohrbaugh, J. W., & Goldman, D. (2002). The relationship between two intermediate phenotypes for alcoholism: Low voltage alpha EEG and low P300 ERP amplitude. *Journal of Studies on Alcohol, 63*(5), 509-517.

Eschmann, K. C. J., et al. (2018). Topographical differences of frontal-midline theta activity. *Developmental Cognitive Neuroscience, 30*, 87-98.

Espay, A. J., Aybek, S., Carson, A., Edwards, M. J., Goldstein, L. H., Hallett, M., LaFaver, K., LaFrance, W. C., Lang, A. E., Nicholson, T., et al. (2018). Current concepts in diagnosis and treatment of functional neurological disorders. *JAMA Neurology, 75*(9), 1132. https://doi.org/10.1001/jamaneurol.2018.1264

Fernandez-Mendoza, J., et al. (2016). Insomnia is associated with cortical hyperarousal as early as adolescence. *Sleep, 39*(5), 1029-1036.

Filik, R., et al. (2019). What is the difference between irony and sarcasm? An fMRI study. *Cortex, 115*, 112-122.

Finley, A. J., et al. (2024). Resting EEG periodic and aperiodic components predict cognitive decline over 10 years. *Neurobiology of Aging, 135*, 17-28.

Finley, W. W., Smith, H. A., & Etherton, M. D. (1975). Reduction of seizures and normalization of the EEG in a severe epileptic following sensorimotor biofeedback training: Preliminary study. *Biological Psychology, 2*(3), 189-203. https://doi.org/10.1016/0301-0511(75)90019-8

Flisiak-Antonijczuk, H., Adamowska, S., Chładzińska-Kiejna, S., Kalinowski, R., & Adamowski, T. (2014). Neurofeedback in the treatment of patients diagnosed with ADHD: A review of research. *Pediatria i Medycyna Rodzinna, 10*(1), 91-96. https://doi.org/10.15557/pimr.2014.0014

Forss, N., & Jousmäki, V. (1998). Sensorimotor integration in human primary and secondary somatosensory cortex. *Brain Research, 781*(1-2), 259-267. https://doi.org/10.1016/S0006-8993(97)01240-7

Freschl, J., et al. (2022). The development of peak alpha frequency from infancy to adolescence and its role in visual temporal processing: A meta-analysis. *Developmental Cognitive Neuroscience, 57*, 101146.

Fultz, N. E., Bonmassar, G., Setsompop, K., Stickgold, R. A., Rosen, B. R., Polimeni, J. R., & Lewis, L. D. (2019). Coupled electrophysiological, hemodynamic, and cerebrospinal fluid oscillations in human sleep. *Science, 366*(6465), 628-631.

Furrer, M., Jaramillo, V., Brandeis, D., Roth, C., Breu, J., Plessen, K. J., Walitza, S., Drechsler, R., & Huber, R. (2019). Sleep EEG slow-wave activity in medicated and unmedicated children and adolescents with ADHD. *Translational Psychiatry, 9*(1), 324. https://doi.org/10.1038/s41398-019-0659-3

Gaber, T. A. Z. K. (2024). Quantitative EEG in COVID-19 cognitive dysfunction. *Clinical EEG and Neuroscience, 55*(1), 89-97.

Gallo, S., Paracampo, R., Müller-Pinzler, L., Severo, M. C., Blömer, L., Fernandes-Henriques, C., … & Gazzola, V. (2018). The causal role of the somatosensory cortex in prosocial behaviour. *eLife, 7*, e32740.

Gangemi, A., et al. (2024). Long-term cortical activity changes in COVID-19 patients with anosmia and cognitive fog. *Brain Research, 1825*, 148701.

Geng, J. J., & Vossel, S. (2013). Re-evaluating the role of TPJ in attentional control: Contextual updating? *Neuroscience & Biobehavioral Reviews, 37*(10), 2608-2620. https://doi.org/10.1016/j.neubiorev.2013.08.010

Garrison, K. A., et al. (2013). Effortless awareness: Using real time neurofeedback to investigate correlates of posterior cingulate cortex activity in meditators' self-report. *Frontiers in Human Neuroscience, 7*, 440.

Gold, R., & Faust, M. (2010). Semantic integration during metaphor comprehension in Asperger syndrome. *Brain and Language, 113*(3), 124–134. https://doi.org/10.1016/j.bandl.2010.03.002

Goldin, P. R., & Gross, J. J. (2010). Effects of MBSR on emotion regulation in social anxiety disorder. *Emotion, 10*(1), 83-91.

Gong, A., Nan, W., Yin, E., Jiang, C., & Fu, Y. (2020). Efficacy, trainability, and neuroplasticity of SMR vs. alpha rhythm shooting performance neurofeedback training. *Frontiers in Human Neuroscience, 14*, 94. https://doi.org/10.3389/fnhum.2020.00094

Goyal, M., et al. (2014). Meditation programs for psychological stress and well-being: A systematic review and meta-analysis. *JAMA Internal Medicine, 174*(3), 357-368.

Grant, J. E., et al. (2016). N-Acetylcysteine in the treatment of excoriation (skin-picking) disorder. *JAMA Psychiatry, 73*(5), 490-496.

Gray, J. A. (1982). The neuropsychology of anxiety: An enquiry into the functions of the septo-hippocampal system. *Oxford University Press.*

Froeliger, B., Garland, E. L., & McClernon, F. J. (2012). Yoga meditation practitioners exhibit greater gray matter volume and fewer reported cognitive failures: Results of a preliminary voxel-based morphometric analysis. *Evidence-Based Complementary and Alternative Medicine*, 2012, 821307. https://doi.org/10.1155/2012/821307

Marsland, A. L., Gianaros, P. J., Kuan, D. C., Sheu, L. K., Krajina, K., & Manuck, S. B. (2015). Brain morphology links systemic inflammation to cognitive function in midlife adults. *Brain, Behavior, and Immunity, 48*, 195-204. https://doi.org/10.1016/j.bbi.2015.03.015

Gruzelier, J. (2009). A theory of alpha/theta neurofeedback, creative performance enhancement, long-distance functional connectivity and psychological integration. *Cognitive Processing, 10*(Suppl. 1), 101–109. https://doi.org/10.1007/s10339-008-0248-5

Gruzelier, J. H. (2014). EEG-neurofeedback for optimising performance. *Neuroscience & Biobehavioral Reviews, 44*, 124-141.

Gu, D., et al. (2023). Sleep EEG biomarkers predict cognitive deficits in obstructive sleep apnea. *Sleep Medicine, 102*, 45-53.

Hammond, D. C. (2005). Neurofeedback with anxiety and affective disorders. *Child and Adolescent Psychiatric Clinics of North America, 14*(1), 105-123.

Haggard, P. (2017). Sense of agency in the human brain. *Nature Reviews Neuroscience, 18*(4), 196-207. https://doi.org/10.1038/nrn.2017.14

Harel, Y., et al. (2025). EEG-based prediction of cognitive performance during sleep deprivation. *Sleep, 48*(1), zsae234.

Hartikainen, K. M. (2021). Emotion-attention interaction in the right hemisphere. *Brain Sciences, 11*(7), 1006.

Helfrich, R. F., Fiebelkorn, I. C., Szczepanski, S. M., Lin, J. J., Parvizi, J., Knight, R. T., & Kastner, S. (2018). Neural mechanisms of sustained attention are rhythmic. *Neuron, 99*(4), 854-865.e5. https://doi.org/10.1016/j.neuron.2018.07.032

Hernandez, L. M., et al. (2015). Neural signatures of autism spectrum disorders: Insights into brain network dynamics. *Neuropsychopharmacology, 40*(1), 171-189.

Herning, R. I., Better, W., & Cadet, J. L. (2008). EEG of chronic marijuana users during abstinence. *Clinical Neurophysiology, 119*(2), 321-331.

Hertrich, I., Dietrich, S., & Ackermann, H. (2020). The margins of the language network in the brain. *Frontiers in Communication, 5*, 519955.

Heyer, D. B., et al. (2021). Verbal and general IQ associate with supragranular layer thickness and cell properties of the left temporal cortex. *Cerebral Cortex, 31*(12), 5343-5357.

Hill, A. R. (2012). *Measuring & Modulating Hemispheric Attention* [Doctoral dissertation, University of California, Los Angeles]. eScholarship. https://escholarship.org/uc/item/55c35139

Hoedlmoser, K., Pecherstorfer, T., Gruber, G., Anderer, P., Doppelmayr, M., Klimesch, W., & Schabus, M. (2008). Instrumental conditioning of human sensorimotor rhythm (12-15 Hz) and its impact on sleep. *Sleep, 31*(10), 1401-1408. https://doi.org/10.5665/sleep/31.10.1401

Hölzel, B. K., et al. (2011). Mindfulness practice leads to increases in regional brain gray matter density. *Psychiatry Research: Neuroimaging, 191*(1), 36-43.

Howarth, A., et al. (2024). EEG power spectral density differences in OSA with and without excessive daytime sleepiness. *Sleep, 47*(2), zsad289.

Huang, H., Li, R., & Zhang, J. (2023). A review of visual sustained attention: Neural mechanisms and computational models. *PeerJ, 11*, e15351. https://doi.org/10.7717/peerj.15351

Park, B., Fareri, D., Delgado, M., & Young, L. (2021). The role of right temporoparietal junction in processing social prediction error across relationship contexts. *Social Cognitive and Affective Neuroscience, 16*(8), 772-781. https://doi.org/10.1093/scan/nsaa072

Johnstone, J., Gunkelman, J., & Lunt, J. (2005). Clinical database development: Characterization of EEG phenotypes. *Clinical EEG and Neuroscience, 36*(2), 99-107. https://doi.org/10.1177/155005940503600209

Jurado-Barba, R., et al. (2020). Neuropsychophysiology of alcohol dependence. *Frontiers in Psychiatry, 11*, 600.

Kaiser, R. H., et al. (2015). Depressive rumination, the default-mode network, and the dark matter of clinical neuroscience. *Biological Psychiatry, 78*(4), 224-230.

Kalechstein, A. D., et al. (2009). Quantitative EEG abnormalities are associated with memory impairment in recently abstinent methamphetamine-dependent individuals. *The Journal of Neuropsychiatry and Clinical Neurosciences, 21*(3), 254-258.

Kang, W., Hernández, S. P., Rahman, M. S., Voigt, K., & Malvaso, A. (2022). Inhibitory control development: A network neuroscience perspective. *Frontiers in Psychology, 13,* 651547. https://doi.org/10.3389/fpsyg.2022.651547

Karimi-Rouzbahani, H., Woolgar, A., & Rich, A. N. (2021). Neural signatures of vigilance decrements predict behavioural errors before they occur. *eLife, 10,* e60563. https://doi.org/10.7554/eLife.60563

Kashetsky, N., et al. (2023). Efficacy of N-acetylcysteine in trichotillomania, skin-picking disorder and onychophagia. *Journal of the European Academy of Dermatology and Venereology, 37*(1), e73-e76.

Kawohl, W., et al. (2009). Functional magnetic resonance imaging of tics and tic suppression in Gilles de la Tourette syndrome. *Journal of Psychiatric Research, 43*(6), 595-604.

Hughes, G. (2018). The role of the temporoparietal junction in implicit and explicit sense of agency. *Neuropsychologia, 113,* 1-5. https://doi.org/10.1016/j.neuropsychologia.2018.03.020

Koob, G. F., & Volkow, N. D. (2016). Neurobiology of addiction: A neurocircuitry analysis. *Lancet Psychiatry, 3*(8), 760-773.

Krall, S. C., Rottschy, C., Oberwelland, E., Bzdok, D., Fox, P. T., Eickhoff, S. B., Fink, G. R., & Konrad, K. (2015). The role of the right temporoparietal junction in attention and social interaction as revealed by ALE meta-analysis. *Brain Structure and Function, 220*(2), 587-604. https://doi.org/10.1007/s00429-014-0803-z

Kopčanová, M., et al. (2024). Resting-state EEG signatures of Alzheimer's disease are driven by periodic but not aperiodic changes. *Neurobiology of Disease, 190,* 106380.

Kopańska, M., et al. (2022). Changes in EEG recordings in COVID-19 patients as a basis for more accurate QEEG diagnostics and EEG neurofeedback therapy. *Journal of Clinical Medicine, 11*(9), 2622.

Kok, B. E., & Fredrickson, B. L. (2010). Upward spirals of the heart: Autonomic flexibility, as indexed by vagal tone, reciprocally and prospectively predicts positive emotions and social connectedness. *Biological Psychology, 85*(3), 432-436. https://doi.org/10.1016/j.biopsycho.2010.09.005

Kopřivová, J., et al. (2013). Prediction of treatment response and the effect of independent component neurofeedback in OCD. *Neuropsychobiology, 67*(4), 210-223.

Kox, M., van Eijk, L. T., Zwaag, J., van den Wildenberg, J., Sweep, F. C., van der Hoeven, J. G., & Pickkers, P. (2014). Voluntary activation of the sympathetic nervous system and attenuation of the innate immune response in humans. *PNAS, 111*(20), 7379-7384. https://doi.org/10.1073/pnas.1322174111

Krause, D. L., et al. (2016). Prediction of treatment outcome in patients with OCD. *Frontiers in Psychology, 6,* 1993.

Krone, L. B., Yamagata, T., Blanco-Duque, C., Guillaumin, M. C. C., Kahn, M. C., van der Vinne, V., McKillop, L. E., Tam, S. K. E., Peirson, S. N., Akerman, C. J., Hoerder-Suabedissen, A., Molnár, Z., & Vyazovskiy, V. V. (2021). A role for the cortex in sleep-wake regulation. *Nature Neuroscience, 24*(9), 1210-1215. https://doi.org/10.1038/s41593-021-00894-6

Kropf, E., Syan, S. K., Minuzzi, L., & Frey, B. N. (2019). From anatomy to function: The role of the somatosensory cortex in emotional regulation. *Brazilian Journal of Psychiatry, 41*(3), 261-269. https://doi.org/10.1590/1516-4446-2018-0183

Lambert-Beaudet, F., Journault, A. A., Rudziavic Provençal, A., Bastien, C. H., & Godbout, R. (2021). Neurofeedback for insomnia: Current state of research. *World Journal of Psychiatry, 11*(10), 897-914. https://doi.org/10.5498/wjp.v11.i10.897

Lally, P., van Jaarsveld, C. H. M., Potts, H. W. W., & Wardle, J. (2010). How are habits formed: Modelling habit formation in the real world. *European Journal of Social Psychology, 40*(6), 998-1009. https://doi.org/10.1002/ejsp.674

Lazar, S. W., et al. (2005). Meditation experience is associated with increased cortical thickness. *NeuroReport, 16*(17), 1893-1897.

Lee, M. H., et al. (2012). Quantitative EEG changes after CPAP treatment in obstructive sleep apnea. *Sleep Medicine, 13*(9), 1141-1147.

Leech, R., & Sharp, D. J. (2014). The role of the posterior cingulate cortex in cognition and disease. *Brain, 137*(Pt 1), 12-32. https://doi.org/10.1093/brain/awt162

Leipold, S., et al. (2022). Neural decoding of emotional prosody in voice-sensitive cortex predicts emotion recognition. *Cerebral Cortex, 32*(16), 3492-3507.

Lehrer, P. M., & Gevirtz, R. (2014). Heart rate variability biofeedback: How and why does it work? *Frontiers in Psychology, 5*, 756. https://doi.org/10.3389/fpsyg.2014.00756

Li, W., Howard, M. O., Garland, E. L., McGovern, P., & Lazar, M. (2017). Mindfulness treatment for substance misuse: A systematic review and meta-analysis. *Journal of Substance Abuse Treatment, 75*, 62-96.

Lindahl, J. R., Fisher, N. E., Cooper, D. J., Rosen, R. K., & Britton, W. B. (2017). The varieties of contemplative experience: A mixed-methods study of meditation-related challenges in Western Buddhists. *PLOS ONE, 12*(5), e0176239. https://doi.org/10.1371/journal.pone.0176239

Lin, C., Huang, C., Tsai, Y., Chueh, T., Hung, C., Chang, Y., & Hung, T. (2021). Resting theta/beta ratios mediate the relationship between motor competence and inhibition in children with attention deficit/hyperactivity disorder. *Frontiers in Psychology, 12*, 649154. https://doi.org/10.3389/fpsyg.2021.649154

Liu, J., Zhu, Y., Sun, H., Ristaniemi, T., & Cong, F. (2020). Sustaining attention for a prolonged duration affects dynamic organizations of frequency-specific functional connectivity. *Brain Topography, 33*(6), 677-692. https://doi.org/10.1007/s10548-020-00795-0

Liu, S., Hao, X., Liu, X., He, Y., Zhang, L., An, X., & Ming, D. (2022). Sensorimotor rhythm neurofeedback training relieves anxiety in healthy people. *Cognitive Neurodynamics, 16*(3), 531-544. https://doi.org/10.1007/s11571-021-09732-8

Lizio, R., et al. (2011). Electroencephalographic rhythms in Alzheimer's disease. *International Journal of Alzheimer's Disease, 2011*, 927573.

Loayza, F. R., Obeso, I., Redondo, R. G., Villagra, F., Luis, E., Obeso, J. A., Jahanshahi, M., & Pastor, M. A. (2022). The motor inhibitory network in patients with asymmetrical Parkinson's disease: An fMRI study. *Brain Imaging and Behavior, 16*(3), 1349-1361. https://doi.org/10.1007/s11682-021-00587-5

Long, Y., et al. (2021). Associations between sleep duration, sleep quality and EEG delta power. *Annals of Translational Medicine, 9*(8), 673.

Loo, S. K., & Makeig, S. (2012). Clinical utility of EEG in attention-deficit/hyperactivity disorder: A research update. *Neurotherapeutics, 9*(3), 569-587. https://doi.org/10.1007/s13311-012-0131-z

López-Caneda, E., et al. (2017). The brain of binge drinkers at rest: Alterations in theta and beta oscillations. *Frontiers in Behavioral Neuroscience, 11*, 168.

López-Sanz, D., et al. (2016). Alpha band disruption in the AD-continuum starts in the subjective cognitive decline stage. *Brain, 139*(12), 3095-3108.

López-Sanz, D., et al. (2020). Magnetoencephalography applied to the study of Alzheimer's disease. *Progress in Molecular Biology and Translational Science, 165*, 25-61.

Lusicic, A., et al. (2018). Transcranial magnetic stimulation in the treatment of OCD. *CNS Neuroscience & Therapeutics, 24*(4), 292-300.

Mander, B. A., Winer, J. R., & Walker, M. P. (2017). Sleep and human aging. *Neuron, 94*(1), 19-36.

Maier, S. J., Szalkowski, A., Kamber, L., Bader, S., Berner, F., Becker, G., ... & Philipsen, A. (2024). Lateral prefrontal cortex emotional processing in adult ADHD: An fMRI study. *Psychological Medicine, 54*(3), 521-531.

Manganotti, P., et al. (2025). Quantitative EEG findings in post-COVID-19 brain fog. *Brain Sciences, 15*(1), 89.

Mashal, N., & Kasirer, A. (2011). Thinking maps enhance metaphoric competence in children with autism and learning disabilities. *Research in Developmental Disabilities, 32*(6), 2045–2054. https://doi.org/10.1016/j.ridd.2011.08.012

Massimini, M., et al. (2024). Sleep-like cortical dynamics during wakefulness after brain injury. *Brain, 147*(3), 892-905.

Masten, C. L., Eisenberger, N. I., Borofsky, L. A., Pfeifer, J. H., McNealy, K., Mazziotta, J. C., & Dapretto, M. (2009). Neural correlates of social exclusion during adolescence. *Social Cognitive and Affective Neuroscience, 4*(2), 143-157.

Matthys, W., Vanderschuren, L. J., & Schutter, D. J. (2013). The neurobiology of oppositional defiant disorder and conduct disorder. *Development and Psychopathology, 25*(1), 193-207. https://doi.org/10.1017/S0954579412000272

Ni, Z., Gunraj, C., Nelson, A. J., Yeh, I., Castillo, G., Hoque, T., & Chen, R. (2009). Two phases of interhemispheric inhibition between motor related cortical areas and the primary motor cortex in human. *Cerebral Cortex, 19*(7), 1654-1665. https://doi.org/10.1093/cercor/bhn201

McMackin, R., Dukic, S., Costello, E., Pinto-Grau, M., Fasano, A., Buxo, T., Heverin, M., Reilly, R., Muthuraman, M., Pender, N., Hardiman, O., & Nasseroleslami, B. (2020). Localization of brain networks engaged by the sustained attention to response task provides quantitative markers of executive impairment in amyotrophic lateral sclerosis. *Cerebral Cortex, 30*(9), 4834-4846. https://doi.org/10.1093/cercor/bhaa076

Meghdadi, A. H., et al. (2021). Resting state EEG biomarkers of cognitive decline associated with Alzheimer's disease and mild cognitive impairment. *PLOS ONE, 16*(2), e0244180.

Menary, K., et al. (2013). Associations between cortical thickness and general intelligence in children, adolescents and young adults. *Intelligence, 41*(5), 597-606.

Menon, V. (2011). Large-scale brain networks and psychopathology: A unifying triple network model. *Trends in Cognitive Sciences, 15*(10), 483-506. https://doi.org/10.1016/j.tics.2011.08.003

Menon, V. (2023). 20 years of the default mode network: A review and synthesis. *Neuron, 111*(16), 2469-2487. https://doi.org/10.1016/j.neuron.2023.04.023

Menon, V., & Uddin, L. Q. (2010). Saliency, switching, attention and control: A network model of insula function. *Brain Structure and Function, 214*(5-6), 655-667. https://doi.org/10.1007/s00429-010-0262-0

Mesulam, M. M., et al. (2019). Word comprehension in temporal cortex and Wernicke area: A PPA perspective. *Neurology, 92*(6), 244-253.

Mohammadi, M. R., Khaleghi, A., Nasrabadi, A. M., Rafieivand, S., Begol, M., & Zarafshan, H. (2015). EEG classification of ADHD and normal children. *Biomedical Engineering Letters, 6*(2), 66-73. https://doi.org/10.1007/s13534-016-0218-2

Moreau, Q., Chamberland, V., Moses, L., Milanova, G., & Dumas, G. (2025). Online HD-tRNS over the right temporoparietal junction modulates social inference but not motor coordination. *eNeuro, 12*(10), ENEURO.0155-25.2025. https://doi.org/10.1523/ENEURO.0155-25.2025

Nicholson, A. A., et al. (2018). Intrinsic connectivity network dynamics in PTSD during amygdala downregulation using real-time fMRI neurofeedback. *Human Brain Mapping, 39*(11), 4552-4566.

Nicolson, R., & Castellanos, F. X. (2000). Reconsidering the association between attention-deficit hyperactivity disorder and dopamine. *American Journal of Psychiatry, 157*(7), 1057-1058.

Noldy, N. E., et al. (1994). Quantitative EEG changes in cocaine withdrawal: Evidence for long-term CNS effects. *Neuropsychobiology, 30*(4), 189-196.

Noordermeer, S. D. S., Luman, M., & Oosterlaan, J. (2016). A systematic review and meta-analysis of neuroimaging in oppositional defiant disorder (ODD) and conduct disorder (CD) taking attention-deficit hyperactivity disorder (ADHD) into account. *Neuropsychology Review, 26*(1), 44-72. https://doi.org/10.1007/s11065-015-9315-8

Nosková, E., et al. (2019). Augmentation therapy of N-acetylcysteine for OCD: A meta-analysis. *European Neuropsychopharmacology, 29*(10), 1193-1205.

Nwakamma, C., et al. (2024). Parameterized resting-state EEG in mild traumatic brain injury. *Brain Injury, 38*(3), 234-245.

Obert, A., et al. (2016). Processing of ironic language: An fMRI study. *Cortex, 82*, 212-222.

Ociepka, M., et al. (2022). High individual alpha frequency brains run fast, but it does not necessarily make them smart. *Intelligence, 92*, 101644.

Ochsner, K. N., & Gross, J. J. (2005). The cognitive control of emotion. *Trends in Cognitive Sciences, 9*(5), 242-249.

Ohayon, M. M., Carskadon, M. A., Guilleminault, C., & Vitiello, M. V. (2004). Meta-analysis of quantitative sleep parameters from childhood to old age in healthy individuals: Developing normative sleep values across the human lifespan. *Sleep, 27*(7), 1255-1273. https://doi.org/10.1093/sleep/27.7.1255

Oken, B. S., Salinsky, M. C., & Elsas, S. M. (2006). Vigilance, alertness, or sustained attention: Physiological basis and measurement. *Clinical Neurophysiology, 117*(9), 1885-1901. https://doi.org/10.1016/j.clinph.2006.01.017

Ortelli, P., et al. (2023). Fatigue and EEG alterations in post-COVID syndrome. *Clinical Neurophysiology, 144*, 137-145.

Pan, N., Long, Y., Qin, K., et al. (2026). Mapping ADHD heterogeneity and biotypes by topological deviations in morphometric similarity networks. *JAMA Psychiatry*. Published online February 25, 2026. https://doi.org/10.1001/jamapsychiatry.2026.0001

Park, J., et al. (2024). The effect of age on the intrinsic functional brain network. *Neuroscience Letters, 815*, 137502.

Paulesu, E., Frith, C. D., & Frackowiak, R. S. J. (1993). The neural correlates of the verbal component of working memory. *Nature, 362*(6418), 342-345. https://doi.org/10.1038/362342a0

Patel, S., et al. (2018). Right hemisphere regions critical for expression of emotional prosody. *Frontiers in Neurology, 9*, 224.

Peniston, E. G., & Kulkosky, P. J. (1989). Alpha-theta brainwave training and beta-endorphin levels in alcoholics. *Alcoholism: Clinical and Experimental Research, 13*(2), 271-279.

Peniston, E. G., & Kulkosky, P. J. (1990). Alcoholic personality and alpha-theta brainwave training. *Medical Psychotherapy, 3*, 37-55.

Peniston, E. G., & Kulkosky, P. J. (1991). Alpha-theta EEG biofeedback training in alcoholism and post-traumatic stress disorders. *International Journal of Psychosomatics, 38*(1-4), 46-52.

Peterson, B. S., et al. (1998). A functional magnetic resonance imaging study of tic suppression in Tourette syndrome. *Archives of General Psychiatry, 55*(4), 326-333.

Piai, V., Rommers, J., & Knight, R. T. (2018). Lesion evidence for a critical role of left posterior but not frontal areas in alpha-beta power decreases during context-driven word production. *European Journal of Neuroscience, 48*(7), 2622-2629. https://doi.org/10.1111/ejn.13695

Pichon, S., Rieger, S. W., & Vuilleumier, P. (2013). Persistent affective biases in human amygdala response following implicit priming with negative emotion concepts. *NeuroImage, 62*(3), 1610-1621.

Porges, S. W. (2011). *The Polyvagal Theory: Neurophysiological Foundations of Emotions, Attachment, Communication, and Self-Regulation*. W. W. Norton & Company.

Posthuma, D., et al. (2001). Are smarter brains running faster? Heritability of alpha peak frequency, IQ, and their interrelation. *Behavior Genetics, 31*(6), 567-579.

Puschmann, S., Steinkamp, S., Gillich, I., Mirkovic, B., Debener, S., Thiel, C. M., & Goebel, R. (2017). The right temporoparietal junction supports speech tracking during selective listening: Evidence from concurrent EEG-fMRI. *Journal of Neuroscience, 37*(47), 11505-11516. https://doi.org/10.1523/JNEUROSCI.1007-17.2017

Puttaert, D., et al. (2021). Decreased alpha peak frequency is linked to episodic memory impairment in pathological aging. *Frontiers in Aging Neuroscience, 13*, 711375.

Quesque, F., & Brass, M. (2019). The role of the temporoparietal junction in self-other distinction. *Brain Topography, 32*(6), 943-955. https://doi.org/10.1007/s10548-019-00737-5

Raichle, M. E. (2015). The brain's default mode network. *Annual Review of Neuroscience, 38*, 433-447.

Raju, B., & Tadi, P. (2022). Somatosensory Cortex. *StatPearls*. PMID: 32310375.

Ramanathan, D. S., Gulati, T., & Ganguly, K. (2015). Sleep-dependent reactivation of ensembles in motor cortex promotes skill consolidation. *PLOS Biology, 13*(9), e1002263. https://doi.org/10.1371/journal.pbio.1002263

Ramsay, I. S., et al. (2021). Individual alpha peak frequency is slower in schizophrenia and related to deficits in visual perception and cognition. *Scientific Reports, 11*, 17852.

Rangaswamy, M., et al. (2002). Beta power in the EEG of alcoholics. *Biological Psychiatry, 52*(8), 831-842.

Rathee, S., et al. (2020). Peak alpha frequency in relation to cognitive performance. *Journal of Neuroscience Research, 98*(9), 1681-1691.

Razafimandimby, A., et al. (2009). Neural networks of emotional discourse comprehension. *NeuroImage, 47*, S173.

Redcay, E. (2008). The superior temporal sulcus performs a common function for social and speech perception. *Neuroscience & Biobehavioral Reviews, 33*(1), 31-41.

Ribeiro, T. F., Carriello, M. A., de Paula, E. P., Garcia, A. C., da Rocha, G. L., & Teive, H. A. G. (2023). Clinical applications of neurofeedback based on sensorimotor rhythm: A systematic review and meta-analysis. *Frontiers in Neuroscience, 17*, 1195066. https://doi.org/10.3389/fnins.2023.1195066

Rizzolatti, G., & Craighero, L. (2004). The mirror-neuron system. *Annual Review of Neuroscience, 27*, 169-192. https://doi.org/10.1146/annurev.neuro.27.070203.144230

Ross, E. D. (1993). Nonverbal aspects of language. *Neurologic Clinics, 11*(1), 9-23.

Ross, E. D., & Monnot, M. (2023). Affective prosody and its disorders. *Handbook of Clinical Neurology, 185*, 195-212.

Rubia, K., Halari, R., Smith, A. B., Mohammad, M., Scott, S., & Brammer, M. J. (2009). Shared and disorder-specific prefrontal abnormalities in boys with pure attention-deficit/hyperactivity disorder compared to boys with pure CD during interference inhibition and attention allocation. *Journal of Child Psychology and Psychiatry, 50*(6), 669-678. https://doi.org/10.1111/j.1469-7610.2008.02022.x

Saad, J. F., Kohn, M. R., Clarke, S., Lagopoulos, J., & Hermens, D. F. (2018). Is the theta/beta ratio for ADHD inherently flawed? *Journal of Attention Disorders, 22*(9), 815-826. https://doi.org/10.1177/1087054715578270

Safar, K., et al. (2021). Increased functional connectivity and dysregulated slow waves following mild traumatic brain injury in youth. *Journal of Neurotrauma, 38*(19), 2722-2732.

Santiesteban, I., Banissy, M. J., Catmur, C., & Bird, G. (2012). Enhancing social ability by stimulating right temporoparietal junction. *Current Biology, 22*(23), 2274-2277. https://doi.org/10.1016/j.cub.2012.10.018

Santiesteban, I., Banissy, M. J., Catmur, C., & Bird, G. (2015). Using tDCS to explore the role of the right temporo-parietal junction in theory of mind and cognitive empathy. *Frontiers in Psychology, 6*, 230.

Saxe, R., & Kanwisher, N. (2003). People thinking about thinking people: The role of the temporo-parietal junction in "theory of mind." *NeuroImage, 19*(4), 1835-1842.

Schwiedrzik, C. M., Zarco, W., Everling, S., Wimmer, K., Freiwald, W. A., & Fox, A. S. (2015). Face patch resting state networks link face processing to social cognition. *PLOS Biology, 13*(9), e1002245. https://doi.org/10.1371/journal.pbio.1002245

Silani, G., Lamm, C., Ruff, C. C., & Singer, T. (2013). Right supramarginal gyrus is crucial to overcome emotional egocentricity bias in social judgments. *Journal of Neuroscience, 33*(39), 15466-15476. https://doi.org/10.1523/JNEUROSCI.1488-13.2013

Schaum, M., Pinzuti, E., Sebastian, A., Lieb, K., Fries, P., Mobascher, A., Jung, P., Wibral, M., & Tüscher, O. (2021). Right inferior frontal gyrus implements motor inhibitory control via beta-band oscillations in humans. *eLife, 10*, e61679. https://doi.org/10.7554/eLife.61679

Schurz, M., Radua, J., Aichhorn, M., Richlan, F., & Perner, J. (2014). Fractionating theory of mind: A meta-analysis of functional brain imaging studies. *Neuroscience & Biobehavioral Reviews, 42*, 9-34.

Scott, W. C., & Kaiser, D. (1998). Augmenting chemical dependency treatment with neurofeedback training. *Journal of Neurotherapy, 3*(1), 66.

Scott, W. C., Kaiser, D., Othmer, S., & Sideroff, S. I. (2005). Effects of an EEG biofeedback protocol on a mixed substance abusing population. *American Journal of Drug and Alcohol Abuse, 31*(3), 455-469. https://doi.org/10.1081/ADA-200056807

Steel, P. (2007). The nature of procrastination: A meta-analytic and theoretical review of quintessential self-regulatory failure. *Psychological Bulletin, 133*(1), 65-94. https://doi.org/10.1037/0033-2909.133.1.65

Streeter, C. C., Whitfield, T. H., Owen, L., Rein, T., Karri, S. K., Yakhkind, A., ... & Jensen, J. E. (2010). Effects of yoga versus walking on mood, anxiety, and brain GABA levels. *Journal of Alternative and Complementary Medicine, 16*(11), 1145-1152. https://doi.org/10.1089/acm.2010.0007

Seeley, W. W. (2019). The salience network: A neural system for perceiving and responding to homeostatic demands. *Journal of Neuroscience, 39*(50), 9878-9882. https://doi.org/10.1523/JNEUROSCI.1138-17.2019

Seeley, W. W., Menon, V., Schatzberg, A. F., Keller, J., Glover, G. H., Kenna, H., Reiss, A. L., & Greicius, M. D. (2007). Dissociable intrinsic connectivity networks for salience processing and executive control. *Journal of Neuroscience, 27*(9), 2349-2356. https://doi.org/10.1523/JNEUROSCI.5587-06.2007

Selosse, G., et al. (2025). Neural correlates of emotional vocalizations. *Social Cognitive and Affective Neuroscience, 20*(1), nsae089.

Shafto, M. A., et al. (2007). On the tip-of-the-tongue: Neural correlates of increased word-finding failures in normal aging. *Journal of Cognitive Neuroscience, 19*(12), 2060-2070.

Shaw, P., Stringaris, A., Nigg, J., & Leibenluft, E. (2014). Emotion dysregulation in attention-deficit/hyperactivity disorder. *American Journal of Psychiatry, 171*(3), 276-293. https://doi.org/10.1176/appi.ajp.2013.13070966

Shibata, M., et al. (2014). Integration of cognitive and affective networks in humor comprehension. *Neuropsychologia, 65*, 137-145.

Shibata, M., Worbe, Y., Bhatt, V., et al. (2015). Dorsal anterior cingulate cortex modulates supplementary motor area in voluntary motor control. *Frontiers in Human Neuroscience, 9*, 330.

Shufman, E., et al. (1996). EEG spectral analysis of heroin addicts: Comparison of current addicts, abstinent addicts, and normal controls. *Israel Journal of Psychiatry and Related Sciences, 33*(3), 196-206.

Silva-Passadouro, B., et al. (2024). Systematic review of qEEG in fibromyalgia, ME/CFS and long COVID. *Clinical Neurophysiology, 158*, 178-191.

Sinclair, J. D. (2001). Evidence about the use of naltrexone and for different ways of using it in the treatment of alcoholism. *Alcohol and Alcoholism, 36*(1), 2-10.

Skeide, M. A., et al. (2015). Genetic dyslexia risk variant is associated with neural differences in phonological processing in children. *Developmental Cognitive Neuroscience, 13*, 1-10.

Slater, J., Joober, R., Koborsy, B. L., Mitchell, S., Sahlas, E., & Palmer, C. (2022). Can electroencephalography (EEG) identify ADHD subtypes? A systematic review. *Neuroscience & Biobehavioral Reviews, 139*, 104752. https://doi.org/10.1016/j.neubiorev.2022.104752

Sokhadze, T. M., et al. (2008). EEG biofeedback as treatment for substance use disorders. *Applied Psychophysiology and Biofeedback, 33*(1), 1-28.

Sridharan, D., Levitin, D. J., & Menon, V. (2008). A critical role for the right fronto-insular cortex in switching between central-executive and default-mode networks. *PNAS, 105*(34), 12569-12574. https://doi.org/10.1073/pnas.0800005105

Steel, P. D., & Ferrari, J. (2013). Sex, education and procrastination: An epidemiological study of procrastinators' characteristics from a global sample. *European Journal of Personality, 27*(1), 51-58.

Sterman, M. B., & Fairchild, M. D. (1967). Subconvulsive effects of 1,1-dimethylhydrazine on locomotor performance on the cat. *Defense Technical Information Center.* https://doi.org/10.21236/AD0664549

Stickgold, R. (2005). Sleep-dependent memory consolidation. *Nature, 437*(7063), 1272-1278. https://doi.org/10.1038/nature04286

Stinnett, T. J. (2023). Neuroanatomy, Broca Area. *StatPearls*. PMID: 30252352.

Swick, D., & Turken, A. U. (2002). Dissociation between conflict detection and error monitoring in the human anterior cingulate cortex. *PNAS, 99*(25), 16354-16359.

Tanabe, S., et al. (2020). Cohort-based EEG analysis in Alzheimer's disease using transfer entropy. *Clinical Neurophysiology, 131*(9), 2195-2201.

Takeuchi, D., Hirabayashi, T., Tamura, K., & Miyashita, Y. (2011). Reversal of interlaminar signal between sensory and memory processing in monkey temporal cortex. *Science, 331*(6023), 1443-1447. https://doi.org/10.1126/science.1199967

Tang, Y. Y., Hölzel, B. K., & Posner, M. I. (2015). The neuroscience of mindfulness meditation. *Nature Reviews Neuroscience, 16*(4), 213-225. https://doi.org/10.1038/nrn3916

Tang, Y. Y., et al. (2007). Short-term meditation training improves attention and self-regulation. *PNAS, 104*(43), 17152-17156.

Tang, Y. Y., et al. (2011). Short-term meditation induces white matter changes in the anterior cingulate. *PNAS, 108*(35), 15649-15652.

Tarapore, P. E., et al. (2013). Magnetoencephalographic imaging of resting-state functional connectivity predicts postsurgical neurological outcome. *Neurosurgery, 73*(4), 569-577.

Tarasi, L., et al. (2024). Individual alpha frequency contributes to the precision of human visual processing. *Journal of Neuroscience, 44*(15), e1318232024.

Tarun, A., Wainstein-Andriano, D., Sterpenich, V., Bayer, L., Perogamvros, L., Solms, M., Axmacher, N., Schwartz, S., & Van De Ville, D. (2021). NREM sleep stages specifically alter dynamical integration of large-scale brain networks. *iScience, 24*(1), 101923. https://doi.org/10.1016/j.isci.2020.101923

Tesink, C. M. J. Y., Buitelaar, J. K., Petersson, K. M., van der Gaag, R. J., Kan, C. C., Tendolkar, I., & Hagoort, P. (2009). Neural correlates of pragmatic language comprehension in autism spectrum disorders. *Brain, 132*(7), 1941–1952. https://doi.org/10.1093/brain/awp103

Thayer, J. F., & Lane, R. D. (2000). A model of neurovisceral integration in emotion regulation and dysregulation. *Journal of Affective Disorders, 61*(3), 201-216.

Thibodeau, R., Jorgensen, R. S., & Kim, S. (2006). Depression, anxiety, and resting frontal EEG asymmetry: A meta-analytic review. *Journal of Abnormal Psychology, 115*(4), 715-729.

Thome, J., Terpou, B. A., McKinnon, M. C., & Lanius, R. A. (2020). The neural correlates of trauma-related autobiographical memory in posttraumatic stress disorder: A meta-analysis. *Depression and Anxiety, 37*(4), 321-345. https://doi.org/10.1002/da.22977

Töllner, T., et al. (2017). Two independent frontal midline theta oscillations during conflict detection and adaptation. *Journal of Neuroscience, 37*(9), 2504-2515.

Tsakiris, M., Costantini, M., & Haggard, P. (2008). The role of the right temporo-parietal junction in maintaining a coherent sense of one's body. *Neuropsychologia, 46*(12), 3014-3018. https://doi.org/10.1016/j.neuropsychologia.2008.06.004

Tsuchimoto, S., Shibusawa, S., Mizuguchi, N., Kato, K., Ebata, H., Liu, M., Hanakawa, T., & Ushiba, J. (2017). Resting-state fluctuations of EEG sensorimotor rhythm reflect BOLD activities in the pericentral areas: A simultaneous EEG-fMRI study. *Frontiers in Human Neuroscience, 11*, 356. https://doi.org/10.3389/fnhum.2017.00356

Turk-Browne, N. B., Norman-Haignere, S. V., & McCarthy, G. (2010). Face-specific resting functional connectivity between the fusiform gyrus and posterior superior temporal sulcus. *Frontiers in Human Neuroscience, 4*, 176. https://doi.org/10.3389/fnhum.2010.00176

Uddin, L. Q. (2015). Salience processing and insular cortical function and dysfunction. *Nature Reviews Neuroscience, 16*(1), 55-61. https://doi.org/10.1038/nrn3857

Uddin, L. Q., Supekar, K., Lynch, C. J., Khouzam, A., Phillips, J., Feinstein, C., Ryali, S., & Menon, V. (2013). Salience network-based classification and prediction of symptom severity in children with autism. *JAMA Psychiatry, 70*(8), 869-879. https://doi.org/10.1001/jamapsychiatry.2013.104

van der Vinne, N., Vollebregt, M. A., van Putten, M. J., & Arns, M. (2017). Frontal alpha asymmetry as a diagnostic marker in depression: Fact or fiction? *NeuroImage: Clinical, 16*, 79-87.

Van Lutterveld, R., et al. (2017). Meditation is associated with increased brain network integration. *NeuroImage, 158*, 18-25.

van Veen, V., & Carter, C. S. (2002). The anterior cingulate cortex as a conflict monitor: fMRI and ERP studies. *Physiology & Behavior, 77*(4-5), 477-482.

Vassena, E., Deraeve, J., & Alexander, W. H. (2020). Causal role of lateral prefrontal cortex in mental effort and fatigue. *PNAS, 117*(29), 16888-16896.

Vassolo, N., et al. (2025). Neural correlates of sarcasm comprehension in typical development. *Developmental Science, 28*(1), e13456.

van Doren, J., Arns, M., Heinrich, H., Vollebregt, M. A., Strehl, U., & Loo, S. K. (2019). Sustained effects of neurofeedback in ADHD: A systematic review and meta-analysis. *European Child & Adolescent Psychiatry, 28*(3), 293-305. https://doi.org/10.1007/s00787-018-1121-4

Volkow, N. D., Wang, G. J., Kollins, S. H., Wigal, T. L., Newcorn, J. H., Telang, F., ... & Swanson, J. M. (2009). Evaluating dopamine reward pathway in ADHD: Clinical implications. *JAMA, 302*(10), 1084-1091. https://doi.org/10.1001/jama.2009.1308

Volkow, N. D., et al. (2010). Motivation deficit in ADHD is associated with dysfunction of the dopamine reward pathway. *Molecular Psychiatry, 15*(11). https://doi.org/10.1038/mp.2010.97

Wang, Z., Fei, X., Liu, X., Wang, Y., Hu, Y., Peng, W., Wang, Y.-W., Zhang, S., Xu, M., et al. (2022). REM sleep is associated with distinct global cortical dynamics and controlled by occipital cortex. *Nature Communications, 13*, 6896. https://doi.org/10.1038/s41467-022-34720-9

Wilking, M., Ndiaye, M., Mukhtar, H., & Ahmad, N. (2013). Circadian rhythm connections to oxidative stress: Implications for human health. *Antioxidants & Redox Signaling, 19*(2), 192-208. https://doi.org/10.1089/ars.2012.4889

Watanabe, A. T., et al. (2006). Developmental changes in the neural basis of interpreting communicative intent. *Social Cognitive and Affective Neuroscience, 1*(2), 107-121.

Wei, H. T., Kulzhabayeva, D., Erceg, L., Kates Rose, M., Spencer, K. A., Robin, J., Bialystok, E., & Meltzer, J. A. (2024). Cognitive components of aging-related increase in word-finding difficulty. *Aging, Neuropsychology, and Cognition, 31*(6), 987-1019. https://doi.org/10.1080/13825585.2024.2315774

Whitfield-Gabrieli, S., & Ford, J. M. (2012). Default mode network activity and connectivity in psychopathology. *Annual Review of Clinical Psychology, 8*, 49-76. https://doi.org/10.1146/annurev-clinpsy-032511-143049

Winterer, G., et al. (1998). Quantitative EEG predicts relapse in patients with chronic alcoholism. *Psychiatry Research, 78*(1-2), 101-113.

Witkiewitz, K., Bowen, S., Douglas, H., & Hsu, S. H. (2013). Mindfulness-based relapse prevention for substance craving. *Addictive Behaviors, 38*(2), 1563-1571.

Woltering, S., Jung, J., Liu, Z., & Tannock, R. (2012). Resting state EEG oscillatory power differences in ADHD college students. *Behavioral and Brain Functions, 8*, 60. https://doi.org/10.1186/1744-9081-8-60

Womelsdorf, T., et al. (2010). Theta-activity in the anterior cingulate cortex predicts task rules and their adjustments after errors. *PNAS, 107*(11), 5248-5253.

Wright, K. P., Jr., McHill, A. W., Birks, B. R., Griffin, B. R., Rusterholz, T., & Chinoy, E. D. (2013). Entrainment of the human circadian clock to the natural light-dark cycle. *Current Biology, 23*(16), 1554-1558. https://doi.org/10.1016/j.cub.2013.06.039

Walker, M. P., & van der Helm, E. (2009). Overnight therapy? The role of sleep in emotional brain processing. *Psychological Bulletin, 135*(5), 731-748. https://doi.org/10.1037/a0016570

Walker, M. P. (2017). *Why We Sleep: Unlocking the Power of Sleep and Dreams*. Scribner.

Wu, J., et al. (2025). Widespread connectivity changes with cognitive fatigue in healthy adults. *Cortex, 172*, 45-58.

Yano, J. M., Yu, K., Donaldson, G. P., Shastri, G. G., Ann, P., Ma, L., ... & Hsiao, E. Y. (2015). Indigenous bacteria from the gut microbiota regulate host serotonin biosynthesis. *Cell, 161*(2), 264-276. https://doi.org/10.1016/j.cell.2015.02.047

Yan, X., et al. (2023). Diabetes and cognitive function: An evidence-based current perspective. *World Journal of Diabetes, 14*(2), 114-132.

Yeung, N., & Cohen, J. D. (2006). The neural basis of error detection: Conflict monitoring and the error-related negativity. *Psychological Review, 113*(4), 931-959.

Zaboski, B. A., et al. (2021). Electroencephalographic correlates and predictors of treatment response in OCD. *Clinical EEG and Neuroscience, 52*(6), 403-417.

Zaccaro, A., Piarulli, A., Laurino, M., Garbella, E., Menicucci, D., Neri, B., & Gemignani, A. (2018). How breath-control can change your life: A systematic review on psycho-physiological correlates of slow breathing. *Frontiers in Human Neuroscience, 12*, 353.

Zapparoli, L., et al. (2024). Mapping Gilles de la Tourette syndrome through the lens of distress and relief. *Translational Psychiatry, 14*, 44.

Zhang, D., et al. (2018). Speech prosodies of different emotional categories activate different brain regions in adult cortex. *Scientific Reports, 8*, 16125.

Zhang, H., et al. (2023). Targeting sleep EEG in alcohol use disorder. *Sleep Medicine Reviews, 68*, 101751.

Zhao, W., et al. (2025). Peak alpha frequency as an objective biomarker for cognitive decline in isolated REM sleep behavior disorder. *Annals of Neurology, 97*(1), 123-135.

Zhou, H. X., et al. (2019). Rumination and the default mode network: Meta-analysis of brain imaging studies and implications for depression. *NeuroImage, 206*, 116287.

About the Author

Andrew Hill, PhD is a cognitive neuroscientist and founder of Peak Brain Institute in Los Angeles. Over 25 years he has reviewed more than 25,000 brain maps, working with overwhelmed entrepreneurs, burnt-out creatives, professional athletes, and people who were simply told their brains were "too much." He is a co-author of *The QEEG Field Guide* (Hill & Lomeli, forthcoming).

He lives in Los Angeles with too many screens, not enough sleep, and a brain that still thinks too much.

Connect

peakbraininstitute.com clinic and brain mapping

peakbrainpress.com books and learning materials

giftedandtortured.com companion site for this book

Also from Peak Brain Press

Half a Second More

The Meditation Guide for Brains That Won't Sit Still

Phenotype-matched meditation for fast brains.

peakbrainpress.com

One Last Thing

If the book gave you a mirror, take the free **Poet-Brain Field Kit** with you: all twelve phenotypes on printable cards, plus where to start.

Scan with your phone's camera
or visit **peakbrainpress.com/gifted-bonus**

States become traits with repetition.

Made in the USA
Monee, IL
13 September 2026

62981866R00243